PAINTINGS AND LIFESTYLES OF JAMMU REGION

PAINTINGS AND LIFESTYLES OF JAMMU REGION

(From 17th to 19th Century A.D.)

(In Two Volumes)

(Volume–1)

Raj Kumar

Publications

KALPAZ PUBLICATIONS

DELHI-110052

Paintings and Lifestyles of Jammu Region

Rs. 1450 (Set)

ISBN: 81-7835-441-1 (Set)
ISBN: 81-7835-577-9 (Vol. 1)

Published in 2006 in India by
Kalpaz Publications
C-30, Satyawati Nagar, Delhi-110052
E-mail : Kalpaz@hotmail.com

Laser Typesetting at : Master Computers, Delhi
Printed at : Salasar Imaging System, Delhi

Contents

Foreword

Indian painters, artists, architects and writers made a tremendous contribution to the flourishment of art, architecture and literature during the medieval period. Their works depict the nature of socio-economic life of the given period. One of the dominant recent trends of historiography is to use paintings as a source for the study of social history in the different parts of the world. Jammu is one of those regions of India which produced several leading painters from 17th to 19th centuries. These painters worked comprehensively to explore different aspects of the lifestyles of Jammu region. Their paintings depict major trends of the socio-economic development of the region.

Only few scholars have attempted to study these paintings and their works mainly concentrate on aesthetic aspects of the paintings. Dr. Raj Kumar has used these paintings as a source of the history of Jammu region. It is important to mention here that Jammu region is very poor in terms of the availability of the contemporary literary sources of the history. Therefore, to write the social history of the region one has to utilise the materials provided by non-literary sources. The paintings of Jammu region, studied by Dr. Raj Kumar, shows that painters were well versed with the standard of living and fashions of the period.

The present work of Dr. Raj Kumar exposes the history of the dresses, ornaments and hairstyles of Jammu as depicted in the paintings of the region. His study discloses some important and rare facts regarding the contribution of the Dogra rulers (Raja Kirpal Pal to Pratap Singh) to the flourishment of art and crafts. More importantly it entails a detailed account of the different features of the fashions existed in the Jammu region. He has pinpointed that people of the region were not only influenced by the physical environment of the region for the use of dresses, ornaments and making of different hairstyles, but they also believed in cultural exchange with other parts of India. His work can be utilized to study the processes of the cultural synthesis in the region.

Dr. Raj Kumar's study widens the scope of social and economic history of Jammu region. In his endeavour he attempts to preserve and propagate the significance of the heritage of Jammu region. The young as well as senior scholar will be benefited from the present work in terms of research and teaching of the history of Jammu region.

9th Sept. 2005

Prof. Jigar Mohammed
Department of History.
University of Jammu.
Jammu.

Preface

The history of Jammu Pahari paintings a specific meaning which in 1678 A.D., was introduced by Raja Kirpal Pal, who inherited the small state of Basohli, situated in the North-Western range of the Himalaya's. These paintings formulated a new genre that came into existence in the Indian paintings and the 'primitive' or parent styled of it was called 'Basohli school of paintings'. It stands for decorative traditional style of painting in the hills and reflects its political of Jasrota, Mankot, Chamba, Nurpur, Bilaspur, Kulu and Mandi. The paintings were patronized by its local chiefs, who were mostly Rajputs. Rajputs princess claim to be the descendents of Rama's son Kasu, who came from Ayodhya.

The theme selected by the painters in the Jammu paintings have been carefully examined in this study in order to highlight various themes of their social life. Study reveals that Jammu painters have derived most of the themes from the Sanskrit texts known as *Ramayana*, *Mahabharata*, *Rassamanjari*, *Gita Govinda*, *Bhagwata Purana*, *Ragas*, *Raginis*, etc. At the same time achievements, hobbies, living creatures, political and social cultural activities etc. of the rulers and of the society have also been aptly painted by them.

Thus, the works of the Jammu painters (known as Devidasa, Pandit Seu, Nainsukh, Manak, Hari Chand, Jagat Ram commonly known as Chunnia, Channu, Ruldoo, Aziz, etc.) played a vital role in highlighting the Dogra art and culture from 17th to 19th centuries. Meanwhile, whatever techniques and methods were developed in the new style of paintings, they learnt it and then applied them in the Jammu paintings.

The paintings display variety of dresses known as *Kurta* or *Kameez*, *pagri*, *topi*, *jama*, *dhoti*, *kaccha*, *paejama*, *kamarband*, etc.

The dresses were used by Dogra males. The Dogra women have been displayed with the dresses of *choli*, *kurta*, *peswaj*, *dupatta*, *ghaghra*, *salwar*, *paejama*, etc. Besides, the covers of the naked body, the analytical study of the paintings disclose that ornaments were also used for the decoration of the body and also as a defence against evil spirits by both the sexes. Males used to wear *kalagi*, necklace, armlets, bracelets, finger-rings, etc. and female adorn themselves with more ornaments in comparison to males. This in its ultimate sense also reflected the economic condition of a person and of the areas. They also decorated their bodies with *tikka*, *bindi*, *shinghar patti*, nose rings, necklaces, armlets, bracelets, anklets, etc. as a sign of *suhag*. The ornaments were made of gold, silver, gilt, etc. with inset of precious stones. Study also shows that the people of Jammu region had exciting and skilful knowledge about the different hairstyles of the period.

Moreover, colour scheme of the paintings displayed rich and barren periods of the area in terms of quality of colours. The influence of the Rajputana, Mughals and Sikh's ateliers were clearly shown in the paintings regarding the selection of colours. Though the colours depict the identity of the areas, its physical features, sentiments and emotions. Intermixing of colours has also been experimented by the Jammu painters both on wall and paper according to their interest in the beauty of nature.

The Jammu painters were inspired by the natural scenery of the hills. They illustrated hills, flowering trees, animals, birds, surrounding landscape, and etc. They painted the natural treasure of art, i.e., 'nature' in an appropriate manner.

In the paintings of that period, the purpose of the painting was noble one. It also was considered as an auspicious item in homes during the ceremonial functions, like marriages and etc. That is why it has been portrayed in household, in palaces, in temples and other public buildings according to appropriate themes as required there for different purpose.

To compile this Doctorate of Philosophy thesis. I profoundly express my deep gratitude to Prof. Jigar Mohammed, Head, Department of History, University of Jammu with whose help and guidance. I was able to complete this research project. I would also like to express my sincere thanks to the 'Teachers' of the Department of History, University of Jammu for their help.

I am greatly indebted to the Director of Archives and Dogra Art Museum of Jammu, for providing me permission to take some photographs of the paintings which helped me a lot. I am also thankful to the librarian and all staff members of the art gallery, who extended their support to me during me research work. I am also thankful to the librarian and staff members of the Archaeological Department Survey of India (Jammu) for their co-operation during the collection of data for this study.

Thanks are also extended to the librarian and staff members of the Archives and Archaeological Department of Patiala. I am also grateful to the staff members of the History Department of Patiala and its central library for their assistance.

Thanks are also due to the National Museum of Delhi. I also take this opportunity to place on record my deep sense of gratitude to the librarian and staff members of the Archives and Archaeological Department of India (Delhi) and the Jahawarlal Nehru University, Delhi for their help and co-operation.

Lastly, I am also thankful to the Dr. Aftab Ahmed Khan, Department of Political Science, Government Amar Singh College, Srinagar for his co-operation during my research work.

I am also highly grateful to my mother (Smt. Amrita Devi), who morally encouraged me time and again to complete this job. I am also thankful to my wife, who served me at the time of my study.

Raj Kumar

List of Illustrations

List of Plates

Chapter 2 Dresses

Fig. 2 D.A.G. Jammu. Acc. No. 10/57, Kharaq Singh; 19th Century A.D. Jammu

Fig. 3 D.A.G. Jammu. Acc. No. 11/58, Sher Singh; 19th Century A.D. Jammu.

Fig. 4 D.A.G. Jammu. Acc. No. 12/59, Noo Nihal Singh; 19th Century A.D. Jammu.

Plate XIII. Fig. 1 D.A.G. Jammu. Acc. No. 13/60, Maharaja Gulab Singh; 19th Century A.D. Jammu.

Fig. 2 D.A.G. Jammu. Acc. No. 240/6287, Raja Jagat Singh; 19th Century A.D. Jammu.

Fig. 3 D.A.G. Jammu. Acc. No. 232/279, Prem Lila; 19th Century A.D. Jammu.

Fig. 4 D.A.G. Jammu. Acc. No. 118, Khwaja Khizar; 19th Century A.D. Jammu.

Plate XIV. Fig. 1 D.A.G. Jammu. Acc. No. 21, Ranbir Singh; 19th Century A.D. Jammu.

Fig. 2 D.A.G. Jammu. Acc. No. 21, Pratap Singh; 19th Century A.D. Jammu.

Fig. 3 D.A.G. Jammu. Acc. No. 21, Amar Singh; 19th Century A.D. Jammu.

Fig. 4 D.A.G. Jammu. Acc. No. 21, Ram Singh; 19th Century A.D. Jammu.

Plate XV. Fig. 1 D.A.G. Jammu. Acc. No. 211/258, Raga Madhur; 19th Century A.D. Jammu.

Fig. 2 D.A.G. Jammu. Acc. No. 548, Male and two Female; 19th Century A.D. Jammu.

Fig. 3 D.A.G. Jammu. Acc. No. 241, Durga; 19th Century A.D. Jammu.

Plate XVI. Fig. 1 D.A.G. Jammu. Acc. No. 138, Shiva Parvati; Early 20th Century A.D. Jammu.

Fig. 2 D.A.G. Jammu. Acc. No. 532, Rama and Panchyat; Artist Hari Chand; 19th Century A.D. Jammu.

Fig. 3 D.A.G. Jammu. Acc. No. 115/162, Kaliya Damon; 19th Century A.D. Jammu.

	Fig. 3	A shirt of an attendant.
	Fig. 4	Ranbir Singh on a Royal Throne with an attendant.
Plate XXII.	Fig. 1	D.A.G. Jammu. Acc. No. 144/223; Invasion of the Monkey; 18th Century A.D. Jammu.
	Fig. 2	D.A.G. Jammu. Acc. No. 176/223; *Daksh-Yajan* (Birbh-ddra-usinatting) in; Hwan Kund; 19th Century A.D. Jammu.
	Fig. 3	D.A.G. Jammu. Acc. No. 254/301; *Bharat Milap*; 19th Century A.D. Jammu.
Plate XXIII.	Fig. 1	D.A.G. Jammu. Acc. No. 22/53 *Ragini Devagiri Hindol*; 19th Century A.D. Jammu.
	Fig. 2	D.A.G. Jammu. Acc. No. 288/275; A Lady Near the Spring, Early 20th Century A.D. Jammu.
	Fig. 3	D.A.G. Jammu. Acc. No. 154; Peter Lakhni Nayika; 19th Century A.D. Jammu.
	Fig. 4	D.A.G. Jammu. Acc. No. 32/79; *Ragini Dowhari of Hindola*, 18th Century A.D. Jammu.
Plate XXIV.	Fig. 1	D.A.G. Jammu. Acc. No. 105/152 *Sati-Parikshan*; 18th Century A.D. Jammu.
	Fig. 2	D.A.G. Jammu. Acc. No. 209/256; Rama and other Avatars; 19th Century A.D. Jammu.
	Fig. 3	D.A.G. Jammu. Acc. No. 99; Krishna and Radha in a love scene; 19th Century A.D. Jammu.
Plate XXV.	Fig. 1	D.A.G. Jammu. Acc. No. 85/256; Sanjay-Relating the Mahabharata to Daritrashtra; 19th Century A.D. Jammu.
	Fig. 2	D.A.G. Jammu. Door Panel; Representative of Lord Shiva.
	Fig. 3	Sadhu Blessing to Gulab Singh and his Troops; Wall-Painting; Sui-Simbli Temple.

	Fig. 3	Rama and Lakshman Return to Aoudhy received by Hanuman; Wall-Painting of Purmandal Temple.
Plate XXXII.	Fig. 1	A Sadhu, Mediating, carrying a Kambala on the left shoulder; Wall-Painting of Purmandal Temple.
	Fig. 2	Krishna and Two Ladies Carrying Vessels on Head. Wall-Painting of Purmandal Temple.
	Fig. 3	A Toy-seller with two children. Wall-Painting of Purmandal Temple.
Plate XXXIII.	Fig. 1	Suchet Singh proceeding in a War Procession, Wall-Painting of Ramnagar Palace.
	Fig. 2	Darbar scene of Maharaja Suchet Singh; Wall-Painting of Ramnagar Palace.
	Fig. 3	Suchet Singh celebrating his victory; Wall-Painting of Ramnagar Palace.
Plate XXXIV.	Fig. 1	Ragini; Wall-Painting of Ramnagar Palace.
	Fig. 2	Representative of Lord Shiva; Wall-Painting; Ramnagar Palace.
	Fig. 3	Battle scene of Mahabharata; Wall-Painting; Ramnagar Palace.
Plate XXXV.	Fig. 1	Raja Suchet Singh as a soldier's in a uniform; Wall-Painting Ramnagar Palace.
	Fig. 2	A culture scene in the Darbar Hall of Raja Suchet Singh. Wall-Painting; Ramnagar Palace.
	Fig. 3	A war preparatory scene of Raja Suchet Singh; Wall-Painting; Ramnagar Palace.
Plate XXXVI.	Fig. 1	Fighting scene of Mahabharata Epic, Wall-Painting; Ramnagar Palace.
	Fig. 2	A war Scene of Mahabharata; Wall-Painting of Ramnagar Palace.
	Fig. 3	'The Battle Scene of Krishna and Rukamni' Wall-Painting of Ramnagar Palce.

	Fig. 2	Vishnu and Laxmi, Saiva Math, Mansar; Wall-Painting.
Plate XXXXVII.	Fig. 1	Rama bathing prior to his anointment, Saiva Math. Mansar, Wall-Painting.
	Fig. 2	A Nayika, Saiva Math. Mansar Wall-Painting.
	Fig. 3	A Nayak, Saiva Math. Mansar, Wall-Painting.
Plate XXXXVIII.	Fig. 1	D.A.G. Jammu. Acc. No. 22/69. Reclining, A woman in Yellow Dress; 18th century A.D. Jammu; Artist Channu.
	Fig. 2	D.A.G. Jammu Acc. No. 23/70; A Woman with Sitar; 19th century A.D. Jammu.
	Fig. 3	Darbar scene of Maharaja Gulab Singh; Door Panel D.A.G. Jammu.
Plate XXXXIX.	Fig. 1-to-Fig. 13	Male's shoes
Plate XXXXX.	Fig. 1-to-Fig. 5	Female's shoes.

Abbreviations

The following list of the standard Abbreviations are used:

Acc.	Accession
A.W.I.	Art of World, India Five Thousand Years of Indian Art.
A.B.R.	Antiquities of Basohli and Ramnagar.
A.I.	The Art of India.
A.C.H.P.	Art and Cultural Heritage of Patiala.
A.A.I.	Art and Archaeology of India.
A.C.I.P.	Arts and Crafts of India and Pakistan.
A.N.	The Akbarnama.
B.P. M.	The Bhagwata Painting from Mankot.
B.M.G.S.	Biography of Maharaja Gulab Singh.
B.P.	Basohli Painting.
B.P. R.	Basohli Painting of the Rasamanjari.
C.I.P.	Centres of India Painting.
C.F.S.	Colour, form and Space.
C.H.K.K.	A Cultural History of Kashmir and Kishtwar.
C.D.M.C.	Colour Decoration in Mughal Court.

C.P. I.	Court Painting of India.
C.V.	Chitrasutra of the Vishnudharmottara.
C.H.H.	The Cultural Heritage of the Himalayan.
C.T.O.C.A.	Colour Theory for Oil Colour and Acrylics.
C.T.C.C.A.M.I.	Costumes, Textiles, Cosmetics and Coiffures in Ancient and Medieval India.
D.A.G.J.	Dogra Art Gallery Jammu.
D.L.G.	Dogri Lok Geet.
D.O.A.I.	Dresses and Ornaments in Ancient India.
D.W.P.J.K.	Dogra Wall Painting in Jammu and Kashmir.
E.I.A.	Encyclopaedia of Indian Art.
E.E.K.	Economy of Early Kashmir.
Fig.	Figure
G.H.	Geology of Himalayan.
G.N.	Gulab-nama.
G.S.	The Grihya-Sutra.
G.P.	Guler Painting.
G.P.	Garhwal Painting.
G.S.	Gulab Singh.
H.I.	Handicrafts in India.
H.C.H.G.	History and Culture of Himalayan Gujjars
H.I.P.	A History of Indian Painting; Manuscript; Mughal and Decani Tradition.

H.I.P.	A history of India Painting; The Mural Tradition.
H.I.P.	A History of Indian Painting; Pahari Tradition.
H.I.P.	A History of Indian Painting; Rajasthani *Tradition.*
H.C.	History of Costume.
H.I.I.A.	History of Indian and Indonesian Art.
H.C.H.S.	History and Culture of the Himalayan States.
H.I.D.	A History of Indian Dress.
H.P.H.S.	History of the Punjab Hill States.
H.S.	History of Srinagar.
H.I.U.B.	History of Indian Under Babar.
H.P.J.K.B.	Himalayan Principalities in Jammu, Kashmir and Bhadarwha.
I.M.A.	India and Modern Art.
I.H.C.D.	Introduction to the History and Culture of Dogras.
I.I.A.	Introduction to Indian Art.
I.M.P.	Indian Miniature Painting.
I.C.	Indian Costumes.
I.M.M.C.	Indian Miniatures of the Mughal Court.
I.H.	Indian Hairstyles.
I.P.	Indian Painting.
I.J.O.D.D.	Indian Jewellery, Ornaments and Decorative Designs.
I.D.	Indian Dresses.
J.W.P.	Jammu Wall Painting.
J.R.P.	Jammu Regamala Painting.

J.K.T.	The Jammu and Kashmir Territories.
J.S.P.	Jammu Shrines and Pilgrimages.
J.L.M.	A Journey to Lake Mansarovar.
K.V.	Kashmir Valley.
K.V.P.	Kangra Valley Painting.
K.P.G.G.	Kangra Painting of Gita Govind.
K.P.B.S.S.	Kangra Painting of the Bihari Sat Sai.
L.M.	Later Mughal.
L	Ladakh.
L.D.R.J.	Lahore Darbar and Rani Jindan.
M.R.D.R.F.J.K.	Maharaja Ranjit Dev and the Rise and Fall of Jammu Kingdom.
M.I.P.	Medieval Indian Painting.
M.F.F.I.A.	Masterpieces of Female Form Indian Art.
M.M.I.	Miniatures of Musical Inspiration.
Mm.	Museum.
N.B.I.	North Barriers of India.
P.S.	Painting of the Sikhs.
P.P.S.P.	Pahari Paintings and Sikh Portraits.
P.W.H.C.	Position of Women in Hindu Civilization.
P.M.	Punjab Murals.
P.P.	Punjab Paintings.

P.I.C.A.A.	A Pageant of Indian Culture, Art and Archaeology.
P.P.	Puri Painting.
P.N.W.F.P.K.	The Punjab North-West Frontier Provinces and Kashmir.
P.H.K.	Political History of Kashmir.
P.U.S.	Punjab Under the Sultans.
P.F.A.	Pahari Folk Art.
P.R.	Pahari Ragamala.
P.F.F.P.I.	Pahari Folklore and Folklore Painters of India.
Pb.	Punjab.
P.A.I.	The Painter of Ancient India.
P.A.C.	Punjab Art and Culture.
R.P.	Rajput Painting.
R.D.	Rajdarshani.
R.L.	The Religion of Love.
R.A.	Royal Arts.
R.T.	Rajatarangini.
R.P.B.	The Ragamala Painting from Basohli.
Ref.	Reference.
S.E.H.K.	Social Economic History of Kashmir.
S.I.A.	The Study of Indian Art.
S.H.J.R.	A Short History of Jammu Raj.
S.C.	Sketching in Colour.
S.G.I.	The Story of Great Invention.
S.E.H.P.	The Social and Economic History of Punjab.
S.E.I.P.	Studies in Early Indian Painting.
Tr.	Translation.

T.I.P.	Technique of Indian Painting.
T.C.O.W.H.	Textiles, Costumes and Ornaments of the Western Himalayas.
T.K.P.	Travels in Kashmir and the Punjab.
T.H.P.H.P.	Travels in Himalayan Provinces of Hindustan and the Punjab.
T.H.W.P.	Trans-Himalayan Wall Painting.
T.A.P.I.	Treasures of Asia Painting of India.
T.J.	The Tuzuk-I-Jahangiri.
T.K.	Travels in Kashmir.
U.C.I.	The Use of Colour in Interiors.
W.M.P.	The World Miniatures Paintings.
W.P.W.H.	Wall Paintings of the Western Himalayas.
Y.C.	Yuan-Chawang.

Introduction

The Jammu paintings, are the repository of elegant dresses and ornaments that played a very important role in shaping the mind set and the physical beauty of Dogra cultural life. Dogra tradition with references to its costumes and ornaments is found at different occasions, a unique entity with unique shape. Infact the history of the costume and ornament goes back to the ancient period. With the advancement of the civilization, love for materialism influenced man's way of thinking and the basic needs i.e., food, clothing and shelter, were subjected to tremendous changes so as to make it more useful and attractive. From the various accounts of the writers, it appears that as the food to sustain the life, clothing devices were discovered by the civilized man both for reasons of hygienic and austhetics. In the long run, man began to feel that his dress determined his status in the society and man's dress began to indicates his occupation, nationality and his sex. The colour and style of the dress of an individual were also regarded as the bases for determining his ideas and temperament.

The paintings from the seventeenth to nineteenth centuries reveal the use of jackets, tunic, waistband, *pagri*, coats and trousers of various kind. Though their use is confirmed by the sources of the early times, and the paintings display the popularity of these dress and their common use. All these seems to have been influenced (as evident from various paintings) by the Mughal-Rajasthani dress. The use of articles of clothing increased in that period, and have been divided on the bases of their regional languages. The division in the only source of the great demarcating line between them. The etymologies of most of the paintings dealing with the costumes and textiles are obscure, but in resemblance they draw a better picture of special life of the people than the Dogri prose and poetry.

From the paintings of that period, one witnesses that dresses and ornaments were the most important aspect of the socio-cultural life of the people. The earliest evidences of its existence are found in the Basohli miniature paintings. As we take up the example of a Basohli ruler.[1] He is seated on a cushion, and is supported by a beautiful pillow. The portrait also reflects on the domestic life of the areas, as the ruler is depicted with smoking *hookah* and his two attendances, one has been depicted as a *chuari-bearer* and another has been shown listening his message seated in his front. So far his moustache style is concerned, it appears outrightly that this style in Dogra style (Fig. 1).

The costumes from the very beginning have played a very important role in expressing the advancement of the material-culture of the human race. The paintings, also reflect material culture of the past tradition of the *Dogra* society and fashioned various clothes according to the requirement of the seasons. As we take up the example of reclining *nayika*,[2] she wears a yellow dress made of cotton or linen cloth. It shows that after the winter, i.e., in the spring season, colourful cloth were used in the region. Besides, it also indicates that *nayika* keeps a hand-fan in her hand, reason obviously makes clear that she is feeling little bit hotness (Fig. 1).

It is also believed when we examine the picture of *Baramasa* '*sawan* is the month of lovers'[3] that a work of a painter or an artist is both imitative and imaginative. These twin set of elements in reality and supplied of mind show another physical feature of the area that during the month of *sawan*, raining season in the areas of Jammu was observed and sky has been shown covered by the clouds in a thrilling manner and mango fruit of the season have been ripened entirely. Peacock and *koyal* have been shown getting enjoy of the moment. The musician women have been shown wearing *dupattas*, *choli* and *ghaghra* made of cotton cloth of different colour. Whereas the Radha has been shown as a royal lady wearing a costly and superior dress than the musicians. Krishna has also been shown wearing a silken *kameez* of orange colour (Fig. 2).

Sexual attraction is probably as old as cell life. The portraits of the *Rasamanjari*[4] demonstrated that dresses and ornaments besides the cosmetics have played an important role for the sexual attraction. It also reveals the domestic life of the areas. A night scene of a *nayaka* and *nayika* that both have been laid down on bed, *nayaka* has slept and *nayika* is looking very eagerly towards the *nayaka*. She has ornamented herself with the precious ornaments to her naked body, and wrapped a transparent *dupatta*. So far her cups are concerned, they have been displaced naked. It appears that she is awaiting for sexual intercourse. Whereas her life partner i.e., *nayaka* is shown with attractive clothes with a beautiful *kaccha*, a Mughalian style of turban and ornaments (Fig. 1).

From the paintings of the period, it also appears that Dogra society was a religious society. It is witnessed from the portrait of Lord Krishna[5] that they were used to decorate their gods and Goddess with precious ornaments of various kinds i.e., *mukuta*, necklaces, ear rings, bracelets, finger-rings, etc. (Figs. 1, 2, 3).

The socio-cultural history of the Dogra life has been superbly depicted in the paintings of Jammu. The art schools exposed the living styles of the Dogras even the local tradition, for example, marriage ceremonial hours scrutinized with great mastery. A scene of the wall-paintings of Ramnagar Palace,[6] most of the women figured have been shown in sad mood at the time of send-off to the bride along with bridegroom. They wore *peswaj*, and *dupattas* of different colours (Fig. 3). Besides the socio-cultural life of the areas, the portrait of the Diversion of the *Jamuna*[7] displayed that the occupation of the people of the Jammu, was mostly agriculture as shown from the picture of Sudama, who is drawing the *hal*. It was the man-stay of their economy and livelihood. The expression of the portrait also indicates that the people of the areas had to felt that the irrigation system should be improved for the betterment of the economic life.[8] The cows (animals) are also shown happy due to that system, more quantity of the grass would be grown up in the areas. Portrait also shows that Dogra society was a rural society, they were used to rearer animals (Fig. 1).

There is a another illustration of *Bhagawat Purana*[8] who displayed the physical characteristics of the areas particularly during summer i.e., in the month of June. Almost all the *kandi* areas of the Jammu was plunged into fire due to the prickly sunlight. Portrait also shows that sometimes natural calamities or draught gripped the region and people were used to lead unhappy life due to the lack of animal grass and hardly sustaining themselves (Fig. 2).

Paintings also demonstrated another characteristic of the Dogra society that *sati* system was prevalent among the royal class in the 18th century. As evident from *sati-parikashan*[9] that number of Pandits, who have been shown organizing this procession (Fig. 1). But this act was condemned by the Dogra society as a criminal act against the women, and gradually, in the 19th century, it was stopped as witnesses from the picture of Rani Bandrali[10] (the widow of Maharaja Ranbir Singh) (Fig. 3).

Dance and music have also been a vital part of Dogra society who celebrated the festive occasion like marriage, festivals, etc. There is a beautiful example pertaining to this cultural activity as shown in a *darbar* scene of Maharaja Suchet Singh.[11] He has been displayed on a handsome stage smoking the *hookah* along with his security guards and *darbaris*. They have been depicted getting entertainment of the music along with a dance party (Fig. 2).

Besides the dance and music, Dogra society had another source of entertainment i.e., hunting, catching, etc. This element of their character, can be found from the picture of Maharaja Suchet Singh on horse back.[12] He has also been depicted proceeding on hunting and a beautiful dog showed running along with him (Fig. 1).

Paintings demonstrated that Dogra society was divided into different classes. It is visible from their dresses and ornaments. The picture of *Sati-Parikashan*[13] shows that Brahmin was an educated class, they used to perform every ritual and rite of the society. They have been displayed wearing *dhoti* and a scarf as their traditional dress. Their hairstyle has shown in the shape of Sadhu (Fig. 1). Whereas the warrior class or the ruling class i.e., Rajput,[14] they have been painted with a uniform proceeding on a military procession with arms and ammunition and their General displayed wearing an elegant dress made from the superior kind of cloth. Their hairstyle is shown very aggressive (Fig. 1). Other classes i.e., musician and servants of the ruler, they are shown wearing inferior quality of clothes and ornaments.

The history of dress and ornament is as old as the history of the human. The paintings of the period reveal the index of the human culture. Ornament indicates the refined taste of both the sexes and deep love for ornamentation which had been conditioned by the prevalent customs and beliefs, material means and aesthetic vision. Paintings also display for that ornament and jewellery was natural, an aid to beauty. Love for beauty and adornment is inherent in nature and man alike. Nature adorns its creations to work its rules. Spiritual ideas of beauty have always been interlinked with the physical and formal ideas in history. The love of the jewellery becomes inherent in mankind and the adornment of form becomes important for the beautification of the spirit. Paintings also reveal that Dogra society was close to the law of nature, both the male and the female used to deck their body with various kinds of ornaments i.e., nose-rings, ear-rings, necklaces, bracelets, armlets, etc. All these ornament also go back to the primitive history of the Dogra. It also shows that most of the Dogra ornaments and jewellery have taken their inspiration for the natural objects and show the Mughal and Rajasthani influence.

So far as the characteristic of the Basohli figures of both the man and the women are concerned, they have been liberally covered with ornaments and jewellery, and even the demons showed wearing necklaces. The crowns of gods and the necklaces, bracelets and ear-rings of women are decorated displayed bettle-wings cut into diamond shaped pieces which greatly heighten the decorative effect of the painting.[15] Study further exposes that Dogra professionals like *sunar* or *sunarai* who prepared fine specimens of the ornaments. These ornaments are known as *chakk*, *nam*, *karan-phul*, *jhumaka*, *kundalas*, *arsi*, etc. which were popular among the elite class of the Dogra society. Besides, the pearls were also used. Whereas some portraits also demonstrate that poor strata of the society was a contented lot.

The Dogra ruling class i.e., Rajput[16] have been shown wearing an elegant *kalangi* at the auspicious and festive occasion on the turban. Besides the beautiful *kalangi*, they also were shown wearing precious kind of ornaments made of gold and precious-stones like necklaces, rings, bracelets, armlets etc. to accumulate the energy (power) of a divinity.

The Jammu paintings and the literature of the period also shed light that men-folk and women-folk famous for their beauty and ingenuity of hairstyles. It forms some concept of the Dogra hairstyles and coiffures. The Dogra paintings elaborate details of the hairstyle popular among Dogra people. They also elaborate the profession and status of individual. For example, the ruling class of the Dogra i.e., Rajput has been shown in aggressive hairstyle. Their figures having long a flowing moustaches trimmed beard in Mughal style. The paintings of the 19th century demonstrated upward moustaches and loose beard of Sikh style. The Brahmins (Pandits) have been shown having long hair combed back and long beard. They have been identified as the follower of Hinduism. So far the women hairstyle is concerned, they have been mostly painted with covered *dupatta*.

The work of the painter of the Jammu region displayed a variety of themes. The core theme of these paintings is men and women, who were the important objects of the paintings. The human figures were associated with the portraits, of hills, trees, birds, valleys, fruits, rivers, buildings and the lakes which generally was the part of the background and add a spatial dimension. The Sanskrit texts like the *Ramayana*, *Mahabharata, Bhagawat Purana, Gita-Govinda, Rasamanjari, Bihari Sat Sai* were popularly painted by the Jammu painter and its themes were religious, sociatial and cultural in nature.

The use of colour in Jammu painting is not naturalistic. The main purpose is to express the emotions and aesthetic pleasure of the Dogra society. The most dominant colours of these paintings are bright, red, green, sky, yellow, orange, chocolate, etc. and they came in tones. A deep conception about the nature of the various colours, with their interest in the beauty of nature and the Jammu painters have given special attention in colour.

Study also exposes that the art of wall-paintings and miniature paintings had been commonly practiced from the seventeenth to nineteenth centuries. In Jammu region it was common to use them as a tradition in the decoration of temples, palaces, houses and shrines. It became a popular embellishment in that period as a popular education. It appears that 'tempra' techniques were adopted in the Jammu wall-painting. The wall as well as the miniature paintings were coated on a dry surface and colours used in a binding material was soluble in water along with gum emulsion or yolk of the egg. There is another remarkable feature in the drawing known as linear and lyrical.

The term 'fashion' is as old as time as new as tomorrow, is one of the most powerful force in our lives. It influences, what we wear, the way we talk, the food we eat, the way we live, how and where we travel, what we look at, what we listen to. It is also what makes us sometimes wear more clothes than we may actually need and sometimes less than is needed to protect us from the cold or sun. With reference to Jammu painting each period has its own fashion display that the mode of wearing of the Dugger dress were as much alive to the extravagant of the fashion as in any other parts in India. The intensity with which changes in fashion were followed by the Jammu people every-where at all levels of society is the evidence of its social significance.

With the establishment of the British rule in India from 1800 A.D. to 1947 A.D., there occurred a great changed in the material cultural of India. However, the Indian renaissance gave new modes of costumes infact a touch of refinement and grace hither to unknown. Fashions are not static. There is always a movement which has a certain direction. If there is only absolute constant pertaining to fashion, it cannot develop. Thus, it is the fact, that it is always changing as evident from the paintings of the period, sometimes rapidly, sometimes slowly, but it is never static or dormant. This element of change from Rajasthani to Mughal, Mughal to Sikh and Sikh to British is recognized in the definition of fashion. Our imperative to understand that fashions are always in harmony with their era. The directions in which fashion are moving are called fashion trends, it also have been preserved by the painter in the paintings. For example, as we observe, that Indian people gave up the old articles of clothing and heavy ornaments now the people are shedding the traditional values and wearing bush-shirts, pants, coats and ties, etc. The ornaments now, they put are light weight and simple. Some have gone to the extant of wearing hippy dresses, keeping hippy-cut hairstyles and moustaches.

The purpose of the dress is not only to cover the naked body, but it also supplements beauty and outlook of the wearer as paintings demonstrate. Similarly, the ornaments also add the beauty and the outlook of the person. Therefore, the economic factors are also important and responsible for both the dresses and ornament, the have-nots were shown wearing simple clothes made of cheap material and the rich person are shown wearing dresses and ornaments of very decorative nature and made of costly material. A person who wears ordinary clothes reflects that his financial condition is not of good standards. Natural resources of the areas are equally important and responsible for the dresses and ornaments. Therefore, in the place, where cotton fabric was produced in plenty, the people used to wear various material for clothing. Similarly, in the place, where gold and silver are more available, people put ornaments of gold and silver. If pearls, semi-precious stones and gems were more available, people put to use gems and pearls more in that areas. So the clothes and ornaments consciousness gave birth to various fashions. The contemporary ideas of different fashions and life-styles popular among the people is the result of the development of human civilization.

Notes and References

1. Plate 1; Portrait of Raja Kirpal Pal; Basohli; circa (1690-93) Punjab. Museum; Patiala. Here after refered as Pb-Mon. Patiala. *Note:* Smoking *hookah* was a popular feature not among the males but also to the females of the Dogra society. 'A *rani* smoking a *hookah*'; Ramnagar Palace; Suchet Singh's bedroom. See Chapter 2, Plate XXX, Fig. 1.

2. Plate XXXXVIII; D.A.G.J.; Acc. No. 22/69. 'Reclining, A woman in Yellow Dress,' 19th century A.D. Artist; Channu, Jammu. See Chapter 2.

3. Plate III; 'Sawan is the month of lovers, Illustration to the *Baramasa*, Basohli; Early 18th century A.D. See Chapter 2.

4. Plate VII; 'The Dilemma of the Heroine'; Illustration to the *Rasamanjari*; Basohli; circa (1695 A.D.); D.A.G. Jammu. See Chapter 2.

5. Plate IX; 'The Ecstray of love'; Illustration to the *Gita Govinda*; Basohli; (1730 A.D.); Pb. Mm. Patiala.

6. Plate XXXVII; 'A marriage scene; Ramnagar Palace; Wall-Painting. See Chapter 2.

7. Plate IV; 'The Diversion of the Jamuna'; Illustration to the *Bhagawata Purana*; Basohli; circa 1730 A.D.; Pb. Mm. Patiala. See Chapter 2.

8. Plate V; 'Krishna Swallows the Forest fire'; Illustration to the *Bhagawata Purana*; Tira-Sujanpur, Early 18th century A.D. See Chapter 2.

9. Plate XXIV; D.A.G.J.; Acc. No. 105/152; *Sati-Parikashan* Jammu School 18th century A.D. See Chapter 2.

10. Plate XXVII; Portrait of Rani Bandrali; Purani Mandi Temple, Jammu. See Chapter 2.

11. Plate XXXV; Portrait of Maharaja Suchet Singh along with, guards and *Darbaris* and a musician party; Ramnagar Palace. See Chapter 2.

12. Plate XXXVIII; 'A Hunting scene of Maharaja Suchet Singh, Ramnagar Palace. See Chapter 2.

13. Plate XXIV; D.A.G.J.; Acc. No. 105/152; *Sati-Parikashan* Jammu School; 18th century. See Chapter 2.

14. Plate XXXII; Portrait of Suchet Singh; In a war procession Ramnagar Palace. See Chapter 2.

15. M.S. Randhawa; Basohli Painting; First edition 1959, reprint, Feb. 1981; p. 30. Hereafter the title of this book referred as B.P.

16. *Note :* Farishta's statement appears to be founded on authorities, lost to us, but trustworthy, and to be handled by him in a critical spirit. For example, he is quite sound in his account of the origin of Rajputs. As he says the *Brahman* and *Kshatriya* existed from time immemorial, but the Rajputs are only known since the beginning of the *Kaliyuga.* They attained power after Vikramajit's demise, something more than 1600 years ago (when he wrote) and he derives their origin from the children of *rajas* by female slaves, the sons of Raja Suraj being the first to bear the title of Rajput. The history of Raja Suraj is closely connected by him with that of Persia. He makes Krishna, elected king by the people of Behar, contemporary with Tahmorasp of Persia. Krishna's eldest son Maharaja (see figure) succeeded him and divided the people of India into tribes and castes (H.A. Rose; *A Glossary of the Tribes and Castes* of the Punjab and North-West Frontier Province. Punjab: 1883, 1970, 1990; Vol. 1, pp. 20-21). *Note :* Term *Rajas* which is composed of three English words, Ra + ja + s, 'Ra' means 'way' or thought, 'Ja' means living *mana*, 'S' stands for stainthood, i.e., '*Nam*' or '*Kalma*' or '*Sabad*'; but Brahman misinterpreted the term and exploited the Kshatriya from the original duty of the man, to study Vedas, to serve humanity, etc.

1

Painter, Theme and Area

Painter

This history of art and culture of the Jammu region goes back to the ancient period. However, from the 17th century to onwards there was a tremendous progress in the field of art and culture in that areas. These art and cultural traditions were carried by the hereditary artists from one generation to another in those days either for Dogra court or for general royalty. It shows that there was a great influence of the Rajputana, Mughals, Sikhs and the European in art connoisseurs in the portrayal of Jammu, it is true, that it has been instrumental in providing the new lease of life in this field of painting, but with this many changes have taken place in the format, dresses, ornaments, hairstyles and in the style of paintings itself. Thus, the Jammu painters seem to have acclimatized themselves according to the need of the hour with expert *kalam* or brushes. This intelligent guesswork of the earliest Pahari miniatures painting attributed to Basohli, are illustrations to *Rasamanjari*, or a 'Bouquet of Delight' written in Sanskrit in the fifteenth century A.D. Its theme is of *nayikas* and *nayakas*, heroes and heroines, lovers and the beloved. They have been classified according to the experience of the age alongwith the physical, mental and emotional characteristics. It also displays the social conditions of the people of all classes and of the strata of society i.e., from upper-class to lower-class, rulers, generals, courtiers, middle-classes including moneylender and shopkeepers, artisans, peasants and the landless workers. Most of the paintings were painted by a well-known painter Devidasa for Raja Kirpal Pal of Basohli (1678-1695 A.D.). He was a great scholar and patron of art and literature. His style painting include two females attendances also:[1] One shown carrying a sword in downward manner on the right shoulder and waving *chouri* with left hand and another shown sitting in his front for the service of *hookah*. In this picture new style was characterized by liberal use of (*mula-rangas*) primary colours—red, blue and yellow as new facial formula. It indicates from the noses of both the sexes that they have long nose stylised as the symbol of the Aryan race, eyes like lotus petal, eyebrows well-dressed as the modern man do short from the width and receding foreheads. The dresses of both the sexes also display Mughal's fashion influence. Raja Kirpal Pal is shown wearing a long *kurta* made of superior kind of cotton cloth, *pagri* of white colour in backward slopping and a tight-*paejama* of red and black colour of vertical lining design. The female attendances which have been displayed to his service wear well-fitted *paejamas* of vertical lining design. Who wears blue and blackish strips and another is wearing white and red strip. Over the *paejama*, they wear white transparent *peswaj* decorated by stitching *gota* or tape on the borders of *mung* colour with blackish shade and scarf's of lac red and *munga* colour with blackish shade having golden embroidery around the circumferences worn by them. Their dress also shows the Mughal influence. The ornaments worn by both of these female attendances are similar. They wear *tikka* of dice shape having white pearls strings dangling on the forehead. A string of white pearls of the *tikka* is also attached with the ear-ornament. They wear light and refine type of ear-ornaments made of white pearls and gold dices. The necklaces of these women also made of white pearls, strand strings of black having gold pendants. The *chura* also made of gold metal decorated with white pearls attaching round the both sides of the borders. The same kind of armlets, an ornamental fillet has been decorated by sticking white pearls on its borders. Anklets are displayed made out of silver or gilt kind of metal. In the picture Raja Kirpal Pal displayed wearing a necklace made of red and black pearls of a single row. The ornaments and jewellery which have been worn by both the sexes display (Mewar) Rajputana's fashion influences. The hairstyle of Raja Kirpal Pal also shed light the reflection of the Rajputana (Mewar) having long flowing moustaches like the wing of a bird and long stem, shaven beard and head has been covered by the turban. The female attendances having long hair falling on waist covered by the *dupattas* as it was the fashion of the Northern Indian women. The background of the picture has been filled up with warm yellow colour (flame), evoking the bright sunlight, high in horizontal ground of pinkish and *munga* colours. The piece of the triangular dresses which had been used for sitting by the Kirpal Pal shows having bright orange colour background and brocade design, is stylised similar to those of the painting of Rajputana (Mewar) (Fig. 1). In this earlier works,[2] the red borders were commonly used as a new style for the decoration of the picture (Figs. 1 and 2). In the picture 'on the way to the tryst',[3] illustration to *Rasamanjari* it bears plantation of artificial trees, dark green background, dresses of two ladies which have been displayed with *choli, sari* over the *ghaghras*, and loose long hairstyle, *dhoti* of Indian tradition worn by Krishna. Architectural feature of the buildings display the Rajputana's (Mewar) fashion influence (Fig. 1). It appears that most of the Rajput Pahari painters in connection with the sister art, such as poetry and the drama, and many of the other pictures of this school depict subject borrowed from the Indian classical writings, particularly figures of ideal types, for instance, the *nayikas* or hero-lovers, were designed by the Pahari artist of the seventeenth and eighteenth centuries. This denote that this art had its romantic aspects also. In the most of the examples, however, the 'lover and the beloved' take the form of Krishna and Radha respectively. Romance pass and religion being symbolized in the person of these popular divinities.[4] Such a brilliant phase of all these paintings activity was ceased at Basohli by Dhiraj Pal[5] (1720-25 A.D.), when he became the ruler of Basohli. He wears a white long leaf printed *kurta* made of superior kind of cotton cloth, backward pressed turban tied by a yellow piece of cloth and a short towel hanged over the shoulders of red and white lining design. He has been displayed reciting some *mantras* of his religion and three horizontal lining of the ashes kind have been drawn on the forehead as the symbol of the Shivaite faith. His facial features line drawing display same as mentioned above. His smoke colour moustaches are shown long and flowing in manners, shaven head and beard. Dress shows Mughal in fashion. Hairstyle shows Rajputana fashion influence the horizontal marks on the forehead displays that he was the follower of Hinduism and stunch follower of Lord Shiva (Fig. 2).

After the death of Raja Dhiraj Pal, Medini Pal[6] ascended the throne of Basohli (1725-36 A.D.). He was also a great scholar lover and a patron of art and literature. He continued the past practice of Basohli tradition. He has been similarly painted in the same style by the Jammu painter as Raja Kirpal Pal. Though he has been painted with two male-attendances in place of two female. The male attendances of Raja Medini Pal displayed wearing a *kurta*, tight-*paejama*, scarf and a *pagri* slopping backward of Mughal style in different colours. Raja Medini Pal has been displayed wearing a same style of dress as of Raja Kirpal Pal. The difference between the two only appears from the ornaments and costume jewellery. Here, Raja Medini Pal wears golden locket of white studded stones having emerald hanging pendant, gold bracelets and finger rings. The two male attendances wear silver ornaments. The only comparison between the two rulers i.e., Raja Kirpal Pal and Medini Pal, is that economic condition of the Medini

Pal, appear more stronger than the Kirpal Pal, as is evident from the paintings of the courtiers in general.

Ornaments show Rajputana fashion influence. The hairstyle of Raja Medini Pal displays the same fashion as of the Raja Kirpal Pal. The Mughalian hairstyle can be trace out from the picture of Medini Pal's male attendance. One is shown carrying a sword and another is shown waving a *chouri*. He has shortened trimmed beard and short downward moustaches and his head has been shown covered with the turban (Fig. 1). The compositional elements of both the Rajputana and the Mughal assimilation of the early Basohli painting have also the same effects as Mankot paintings while depicting the picture of 'the birth of Krishna'[7] illustration to the *Bhagawata Purana* (Fig. 2). The themes of early Basohli paintings were also extended in other regions like Tira Sujanpur displaying the pictures of Krishna 'swallows the forest fire',[8] Krishna bringing the *parijata* from Indra's heaven,[9] and Krishna lifting the mountain Govardhana,[10] etc. (All illustrations to the *Bhagawata Purana*, Figs. 2, 3 and 4).

Jit Pal (1736-1757 A.D. son of Medini Pal of Basohli) reigned for 21 years i.e., middle of the eighteenth century. During his rule, the Basohli state became satellite of Jammu and was controlled by the Jammu ruler Dhruv Dev (1703-1735 A.D.). After the death of Aurangzeb in 1707, dynastic quarrels and the panic of Delhi and the disturbances in plains of India were well exploited by Nadir Shah who sack the capital in 1739. This was followed by an abrupt change in the general style of expression with Mughal influence in a new style of hill painting. It was replaced by the new type of expression with Mughal influence. This new style which was created by a family artist exist in the Chandigarh Museum and Lahore Museum which puzzles to art critics. The head of this family was Pandit Seu who had two sons, Nainsukh and Manak (Manaku). Manak had only one son Khushala by name. Nainsukh had four sons, Nikka, Kama, Gandhu and Ranjah. This family has been traced out to Guler. Very likely Seu with his two sons, Manak (Manaku) and Nainsukh was working at Delhi or Lahore.[11] Now with the general panic and feeling of the insecurity in the plains the widow of the last Governor of Lahore Mir Mannu, brought with her painters, artisans and courtiers and settled along with them in Jammu. They followed an ancient route of lower Hills from Nahan, Bilaspur, Siba, Guler, Nurpur, Basohli and Jammu. All were treated generously by Ranjit Dev (1735-1781). The artisans who stayed in Jammu played an important role in development of paintings of Basohli *Gita-Govinda* series of 1730, painted in parts by Manaku, one of the sons of Seu, was already milder in expression, with squatter, more placid figures, than the earlier *Rasamanjari* illustrations.[12]

Ranjit Dev son of Dhurv Dev (1735-1781 A.D.) was a man of character and had real administrative talent. But after the marriage of his daughter to Raja Amrit Pal of Basohli (1757-1763 A.D.) Basohli State to a large extent came under the control of Raja Ranjit Dev and Basohli school of painting was extincted. Manak migrated Guler. Ranjit Dev set up a small atelier at *Samadhian* in Jammu for the future school of miniature painting near the bank of Tawi. A cluster of temples constructed since ages. This change brought a new style of paintings under Ranjit Dev. The most important documents of this period are two portraits, one in the central Museum, Lahore, and another in the N.D. Mehta's collection of Ranjit Dev's youngest brother, Balwant Singh, painted by the artists Nainsukh of Jasrota and Vajan Shah respectively. They show the prince listening to a party of musicians and have been dated 1748. There pictures bear unmistakable traces of a Mughal trained hand of the period of Muhammad Shah. The drawing is light and delicate and naturalistic in intention. The general tones are cool and airy. The planning of the pictures depends on the receding planes of Mughal composition. It is difficult to imagine a more complete rejection of the Basohli style.[13]

In the collection of *Gita Govinda* series of Painting of Basohli, it has been rightly described to have been painted by one Manaka, a devotee of Vishnu at the behest of Raja Ranjit Dev in the first quarter (1730) of the 18th century A.D.[14] It appears from the art of painting that painter in India was almost like a *yogi* in his art. In fact, for painting or preparing sculptural from of deities, he had to reverently muse and visualize their *dhyanaslokas*, sit in a holy attitude of peace facing east and produce the picture with great devotion.[15] The portrait of Raja Gansar Dev[16] which intact the name of a well-known painter i.e., Nainsukh who worked at Jammu in the 18th century. Raja Balwant Singh gave him a *jagir* at Saruinsar lake town surrounded by the scenic beauty of the dense *jungle*. About the economic condition of the artist, in the *Kathasaritasagar*, it has been mentioned that a painter enjoyed ten villages as a gift from the king. The *chitrakara*, along with sculptors, jewellers, goldsmiths, wood-carvers, metal-craftsmen and others had an allocation of seats in the assembly of poets and scholars convened in the royal court as described by Raja Sekhara in his *Kavyamimamsa*.[17]

Besides the Balwant Singh's[18] portrait, there are some beautiful painting of the women who reveal the development of new style in the art and culture which were painted by the Jammu painters. They got trained hand during Muhammad Shah show of Mughal influence. The new style of development, for example, we can trace out in the picture of 'Reclining, a woman in yellow dress' has been painted by artist Channu.[19] The facial features of the picture display the pattern of the Basohli art. Moreover, the picture of the women has light and delicate lining drawing, psychological insight, mastery of depth in application of colours in naturalistic intention. The colours which have been painted in the picture are cool and bright. It shows that great development in the style of art and culture were taking place in composition with Mughals influences in Jammu region. She wears yellow *peswaj* of Iranian origin which has been decorated with the geometrical pattern of art from the borders itself and *dupatta* of pointed designed in the lining drawing. But in the early Basohli painting of the Kirpal Pal (1678-1695 A.D.), the most of the figures of the women have been painted with transparent *peswaj*. The ornaments which have been worn by the said lady also display the new style of development in the field of art in amalgamation with Mughal influence in the indigenous ornaments also. She wears heavy gold ornament on the forehead known as *tikka* having the crescent pattern of design. As such, effect is also indicated from the other ornaments. The sign of the indigenous jewellery, can be traced out from the necklaces of the lady. She wears necklace made of pearls and diamond-shaped pieces cut from the big precious stones of such types shows the early elements of the Basohli painting. Hairstyle displayed as usually adopted by the northern women's parted from the middle plaited or loose in style covered by the *dupatta*. The background of the picture has been portrayed with the Indian (*Krsna*) blue which shows some political problems in the ruling dynasty at the end of the Ranjit Dev's reign (1735-1781) (Fig. 1). This art of painting was also extended to Mankot, Ramnagar, Jasrota and Poonch, etc. The painters like Nikka, Kama, Gandhu and Ranjha sons of Nainsukh, were also well-known painters who lived at Basohli.[20] Nikka migrated to Chamba and there with his sons Harkhu and Chhajju developed Chamba paintings. Ranjha worked at Basohli, and his sons, Gur Shai and Sukhdayal, worked at Guler.[21] The new style which appears at Jammu by 1748 in this way was extended at Guler in the reign of Govardhan Chand (1745 to 1773).

After Ranjit Dev, the Jammu State became completely tributary to the Sikhs and literary accounts of the writers, elaborated that *Pahari* painters of the hill states migrated to Punjab in search of new patrons. They took their *Pahari* style with themselves, its delicate-line, flowing movements, architectural details, ladies beauty, nature's bounties which were not available in the Punjab plains. The following list identifies a family of major *Pahari* painters in Punjab plains who worked at Jammu as well as in the other Hill States:

Ghuman

Purkhu					Phattu
Ruldu	Chandu	Ramkrishan	Ramdayal		Garbhu
Ranjhu					
Kirpa	Bali	Bihari	Bhagat	Gulatu	Madhu (issueless)
Mangat Ram		Chuni Lal			

(Based on R.P. N. Singh's book).[22]

Apart from the R.P.N. Singh's book genealogy table, we furnish another genealogical table of the *Pahari* painters which has been given by Dr. B.N. Goswamy in his latest book on *Pahari* painters discussed below:

Datta
Bharthu
Hasnu
Seu

Manaku	Nainsukh				
Fattu	Khushala	Kama	Gandhu	Nikka	Ranjha
Milak	Hazari	Sikhnu	Lala	Sukhia	Sultanu
Madho	Mashi Ram	Bahadur	Harbhaj	Udmi	Arjan
	Gurdas	Chetu	Surjan		
	Harku	Gokal	Chajju	Garsahai	Sukhdayal
	Devi	Dhanajaya			
	Datta				
	Ramdayal	Damodar			
	Lachman	Shivsaran			
	Das				
	Chandu Lal				
	Attra	Saudagar	Javahar		
	Mahesu	Kanahaiya			

(Based on Dr. B.N. Goswamy's Painter's at Sikh court).[23]

Kashmiri contribution for the development of art in the paintings of Jammu region cannot be ignored. It is said that a famous set of *Ramayana* drawings from the hills has a colophon and when interpreted reveals that the drawings were done in Basohli in 1816 by the artist Ranjha, while another assertion is that they were rendered by a Kashmiri artist named Sudarsana.[24]

However, the beguilement of the early style was deteriorated in a sentimental mannerism in Jammu since the 16th of March 1846. Form 1846 onwards new style of development in the art and culture started. Maharaja Gulab Singh's portrait of war procession[25] (1846-1857) displays Sikh influence. The first example of the influence can be trace from his dress. He wears a forward slopping type of Sikh style of turban having multi-colours which reflects new style in the art and culture. The *kurta* which he and his Generals like Suchet Singh, etc. wear in this picture reaching below the knees having skirts type of heavy pleats in Sikh style and a *paejama* of Dogra tradition shows compositional character of both the Jammu and Punjabi region. Their upwards moustaches and the flowing beards also display Sikh influence. So far as the ornaments of the period are concerned, it shows the new development in the new style of art in traditional characteristics made of pearls, emerald beads studded in gold in composition with Mughal influences. Moreover, the ornaments and jewellery display the economic condition of the individual and the general public of the Jammu and Kashmir State. It shows that the economy of the areas became more strong in comparison with the early history of the area. The format of making the facial feature of the persons demonstrates early influences. In this portrait new style of development has been characterized by using the bright basic colours (primary colours) i.e., red, blue, yellow, black and white which are mentioned in the ancient literature of India (Fig. 1).

M.S. Randhawa and Krishna Chaitanya narrates that a picture has recently been searched out by the Punjab Museum now at Patiala, it contains the name of three painters of Jammu, viz., Arjan, Ruldu and Kanchanu. Kanchanu is described as a servant of Maharaja of Jammu (Fig. 7). The style of the turban of these painters indicate that they were possibly working under Maharaja Ranbir Singh of Jammu and Kashmir State (1887-1885 A.D.). A considerable volume of painting mainly portraiture was done during the reign of Ranbir Singh.[26] Besides the above-mentioned painters, the painter known as Aziz[27] also worked for Ranbir Singh (1857-1885 A.D.) at Jammu. He painted a picture of a deity known by the titled *Panchvaktas* as man like Ranbir Singh has been shown as appearing for worship of it. The new development in the style of art and culture effected by the Sikh influences is visible in this picture (Fig. 4). The compositional characteristics of amalgamation with Mughals, Sikhs and local lasted up to the period of Partap Singh (1885-1897) as is evident from his picture 'Prince Partap Singh on Horse Back'[28] (Fig. 1). In the same period i.e., in the closing of the 19th century, there was a great change in the development of new style of art and cultural characteristics which displays European fashion influence with composition of local element.[29] As it displays in the pictures of the Partap Singh,[30] Amar Singh[31] and Ram Singh.[32] They have been displayed wearing a white colour of turban of Rajputana (Mewar) style and maroon colour coats embroidered with yellow thread, black colour pant and a sky blue gown, display western influences. In the place of the necklaces, they wore gold medals which came into existence with the establishment of the Britisher empire in India in place of ornaments. Hairstyle appears like Rajputana (Mewar) clean shaven beard, long bow type moustaches and heads have been covered by the turbans. The background of the pictures depict dark primary colours i.e., red, yellow, blue, black and white which have been also depicted in the ancient literature of India i.e., *Chitrasutra of Vishudharmothara*, etc. The colour treatment of the picture display characteristics of the society i.e., physical, mental and emotions and social conditions. The facial elements of the pictures display alertness and exquisite lining drawing (Figs. 2, 3 and 4).

There are some miniature paintings which include the name of various painters who worked in the Jammu atelier in the 19th century known as Hari Chand,[32] Jagat Ram Chunnia,[33] Channu[34] and Ruldu.[35] Nand Lal from Kangra also brought to Jammu in early 19th century his two sons Channu and Ruldoo, both artists,[36] who worked for Gulab Singh (1847-1857 A.D.). During the time of Maharaja Ranbir Singh (1857-1885), Hari Chand son of Channu was a top-ranking artist of his time.[37] Jagat Ram, nick-name Chunnia son of Shiva Ram from Bhado Kishenpore was contemporary of Hari Chand.[38] Hari Chand's style was a mixture of indigenous style of Jammu and that of Kangra school.[39] Maharaja created and prepared liberal ground for artists to come in Jammu. Narotam, an artist from Guler, who found employment with Raja Ram Singh, a son of Maharaja Ranbir Singh.[40] It is said that all the painters who were employed in the atelier, were the members of the lower castes and hardly ever rose above the status of artisan. [41]

Pahari painters known as Nainsukh, Manak (Manaku) were the sons of a carpenter (*tarkan*) Seu. According to Mukhandi Lal the most of the artists, particularly of the Rajput and *Pahari* school belonged to the *sunar* (goldsmith) caste. Unfortunately in our country, artisans were assigned a lower status inspite of their considerable contribution in the society.[42]

From the above study it is evident that with the establishment of the Mughal rule in Indian a new style of art and culture has flourished in India. Basohli style of art and culture was a new development in this field with the composition of Rajputana (Mewar) and Mughal influences. It also appears that painter known as Devidasa who got training in the Mughal atelier prior to the Aurangzeb period. The Mughal painters, in India used to live in a different environment then Persia. The Mughal emperors of India had made a permanent arrangement of painters in the courts and they in a sense were courtier. Their direct employment in the atelier, was a unique work that they lead their work according to the command of their patron. Painter was not a paid servant, he always gave a substantial surprise on the production of his good piece of paintings. Those painters who were not prefect in this profession or commands, they were turned out from the atelier. It appears that Mughal emperors used to show personal interest in the art of painting. On the other hand, the conditions of the Rajput painters (*Pahari*) were worsened than the Mughal, because of the Indian communal fabric. As we learnt from the various texts that the status of the artisans in Rajput principalities were lower. They were degraded on the basis of religion hatred. Most of these artisans, belonged to the lower strata of society and were pushed to peripheral village system. Moreover, their economic conditions were not satisfactory and they also were not permanently employed to produce a picture of religious subjects. They were forced to lead an ordinary life. Even though, they were not supposed to demand the actual price of the work. Therefore, it is natural that a great movement in the field of art of the *Pahari* principalities, was discouraged inspite of painters regours training of the new style from time to time.

Theme

Jammu painters have displayed variety of themes in their paintings. The Sanskrit texts like *Ramayana*, *Mahabharata*, *Bhagavata-Purana*, *Rasamanjari* and *Gita-Govinda* were popularly painted by the Jammu painters on the murals and papers. Besides, Sanskrit texts, the Hindi texts known as *Bihari-Sat-Saiya* and *Baramasa* were also painted on papers called miniature paintings. Moreover, Jammu painters have also painted every socio-religious and political aspect of the society. Some scenes of ruling elite appear with their hobbies like hunting, catching, music, dance, songs, etc. Study also shows that colourful ceremonies like marriage and festivals have also been painted as a theme by the Jammu painters. All this reveal the colourful scenes of the society and the socio-cultural history of the areas. Most of the portrayals, we find in the royal palaces, the Dogra rulers who appear to be the great patrons of art and architecture contributed painting gifts to city mandirs. There is a treasure of wall-paintings in Jammu temples of Purani Mandi, Miran Sahib, Bhurja, Sui-Simble, Mansear, Purmandal, Ramnagar Palace, etc. All were erected by the nobility and are worth seeing for their graceful architecture and decoration. C. Sivaramamurti commendably describes that murals were highly valued aesthetic, decorative and educational factors. Royal palaces and houses of noble men, the *prasadas* or temples were also decorated with paintings. Paintings of public importance were forbidden in private residential buildings and specially were recommended for public halls, palaces and temples. The theme of these paintings were appropriately chosen representing households mansions as well as temples, for special purpose.[43]

There are variety of themes which have been painted by the Jammu painters. A discussion about them is as under:

Ragamala

The miniature as well as wall paintings of the Jammu region, have the theme of *Ragas* and *Raginis*. It appears that most of them deal with the visual depiction of the musical modes called as the *Ragamala*. *Ragas* and *Raginis* display the seasonal music of the life. According to Pratapadity Pal the *Ragamala* was a popular subject for both Hindus and Muslims. The expression of the *Ragamala* literally means a 'garland of *raga*', it is the Sanskrit word for a musical mode. Each mode has a distinct mood and a personality in turn provide the iconography for the painter.[44] Such examples of the *ragas* and *raginis* were also a theme of the Jammu painters. They painted the pictures of *Raga Shubha*[45], *Raga Pancham Srinuk*,[46] *Raga Deepak*,[47] *Raga Bibhas*,[48] *Raga Chandra-kans*,[49] *Raga madhur*,[50] *Raga Malakuns*,[51] *Raga khokhar*,[52] *Raga Binodas*,[53] *Raga Basant*,[54] *Natraga*,[55] they are available in the Dogra Art Gallery Jammu and in other museum of India. Whereas the *Raginis* known as *Ragini Bangali*,[56] *Ragini Asavari*,[57] *Ragini Basant*,[58] *Ragini Sindhuri* of Hindol,[59] *Ragini Karnataki*,[60] *Ragini Ramkali*,[61] *Ragini Dowhri* of Hindole,[62] *Ragini Gaund* Malkauns[63] have also been painted and are available in the Dogra Art Gallery of Jammu. It appears from these pictures that *rasa* theory has been superbly applied as adjunct for *ragas* and *raginis* with depiction in colour, though it is also an independent as well as an integral and vital feature of the art of paintings. It is a fact that *chitra* is based on *natya*. The critics applied the *rasa* theory of *natya* and *kavya* to *chitra* as well. As a matter of fact that *rasa* theory applies to all art. Thus, while speaking about the various kinds of pictures sanction on painting in his *Abhilasitarthacintamani* (Mysore, ed.) by a king, Somesvara speaks about a picture called *bhava-citra*:

श्रड.ारादिरसों यत्र दर्शनादेव गम्यते।

भाबचित्र तदाख्याते चित्रकौ तुककार कसू।

Jayadeva, author of the Candraloka and his commentator, *Payagunda* Vaidyanatha apply the *rasa* theory to *citra*:

काव्ये नाट्य च कायें चविभावाद्यौ विभावितः।

आस्वाद्यमानैकतनुः स्थायी भावो रसः स्मृतः।।[64]

The *rasa* theory to *chitra*, for example, *Pahari Ragini*.[65] She has been painted with emotions, close to the nature and her soul has been fully evolved in her divinities (Fig. 1). It is also believed that application of the *Rasa* theory of drama and poetry to picture means that in pictures also *rasa* is to be depicted by conditions which arouse among them, viz., the objects of emotions, the excitements of emotions; the effects of the emotions and the minor emotions which can be called fleeting and accessory to the major emotional mood. This means that application of the *Dhvani* theory was also incorporated to *citra*. For, an artistic presentation, it was included to represent the artistic expressions. This can also be proved by the canons used in the *Vishnudharmottara* for depicting things like evening, night scenes etc. A perusal of the verses in Chapter 24, shows, how mountains, sky, earth, etc. were depicted.[66]

Nayaka and Nayika

It is from the time immorial that a painter has painted the picture of a *nayaka* and *nayika* as the theme in his art. He painted the young men and women pre-occupied with love in its different forms. Such pictures have also been painted by the Jammu painters in different forms with different emotions, like the *Patar Lekhni Nayika.*[67] She has been portraited writing a letter to her *nayaka*, who had gone out for business for a long period. She has been displayed with her emotions, which appear, from her facial expression and the dress. She is waiting to her life partner that when he will come back and they shall share their married life. Her maid-servant has been shown waiting for her letter's so as to send message to her husband (Fig. 3). Besides this picture, Jammu painter had other theme known as *Chatrain*,[68] *Hastni*,[69] a lady near the spring,[70] a *nayika Yawning*,[71] *Muor Priya Nayika*,[72] etc.

The *Rasamanjari* series of paintings of Basohli School known as Devidasa also display the theme of *nayaka* and *nayika* or hero and heroin in the different emotions. For instance the picture known as 'dilemma of the heroine'.[73] It appears that she is looking towards her husband very eagerly, who is taking a sound sleep. *Nayika* has been painted by wearing a *dupatta* around the naked body and waiting for the cajoling. The picture shows the night scene of the social life of the Dogras. In this picture, painter has painted the romantic emotions of the Dogra's lifestyle (Fig. 1). There are several other portraits of *Rasamanjari* which also reveal the various aspects of the Dogras romanticism in the form of a *nayaka* and *nayika* as 'love in union',[74] '*waiting for the lover*',[75] *on the way to the tryst*,[76] *Parakiya Vasaka Sajja nayika*,[77] why *this hesitation, my love*?[78] *On the threshold of youth*,[79] etc. According to Krishna Chaitanya the thematic analysis of the Mughal painting, the most significant contrast with Rajput painting evolving as a parallel tradition, though in Mughal paintings their is the lack of romantic fervour and when confronted with women, the Mughal artists not willing to surrender to poetic warmth and feelings. They rejects exalted raptures and undertakes a cool assessment of feminine charms, which is primarily sepia show. Rajput themes like the *nayaka* and *nayika*, Radha-Krishna episodes are utilized, but in the spirit of sensual sentimentality, not as a great emphoric exaltation of spirit (P. 53).[80] It appears that *nayikas* and *nayakas* had various characteristics, moods, sentiments and behaviour. *Nayikas* were divided into ten categories by the Hindi poets under *nayikabheda*. This classification is based on classical Sanskrit work on the *rasas*:

(i) *Basakasayya* : (One who sits, dress up, waiting to meet her lover).

(ii) *Utkanthita* : (One who is distressed by separation).

(iii) *Svadhinaptika* : (One who dominates over her lover).

(iv) *Kalahantarita* : (One who is separated from her lover by a quarrel).

(v) *Khandita* : (One who is enraged with her lover).

(vi) *Vipralabdha* : (One who goes to the tryst and is distressed at not finding her lover there).

(vii) *Proshitpatika* : (One whose husband is away on a sojourn).

(viii) *Abhisarika* : (One who is on her way to meet her lover).

(ix) *Pravatsyatpatika* : (One whose husband intends to go on journey).

(x) *Agatpatika* : (One whose husband is returning home after a long absence from foreign[81]).

Nayakas or hero's can also be divided into following categories :

(i) *Pati* : (The husband).

(ii) *Upapati* : (The paranour as Krishna is with Radha).

(iii) *Vaisika* : (The ladies man well acquainted with the ways of women).

(iv) *Satha* : (The false and heartless lover).

(v) *Manisatha* : (The false lover enraged the rejection of his false protestations).

(vi) *Dharista* : (The hero who has neither shame or pity[82]).

Radha-Krishna

In the *Gita Govinda* painting, Lord Krishna has been painted as a supreme *nayaka* and Radha as a *nayika* which demonstrate the theme of the Dogras life styles in different forms and emotions as a '*Divine Theory of Rasa*'. The work was composed in the 12th century A.D. by a poet Jayadeve in the praise of Krishna. It also is a collection of songs of the divine love of Radha and Krishna. It has been popularly painted by the *Pahari* or Jammu painter's in the 18th century A.D. In some scenes Gopies and Sakhas are displayed in a manner as Krishna was their master soul and they have submitted their life to him as a king. Every aspects of the social, romantic, political, economic and cultural life of the Dogra society has been painted in the *Gita Govinda* series of paintings by the Jammu painters. As we take up the example of the ecstray of love with Radha[83] in the lawn her two Sakhis are awaiting in the corridor. They left the tray of wine on the selph. Scene displays the night habit of the Dogra society, that they used to take wine at night to enjoy the night life (Fig. 1). The other episodes of this legend reveal the varieties of themes of the Dogra society; i.e. social and cultural engagement, etc. Yet other pictures of the same work expresses the socio-cultural, spiritual, etc, life of the royal families in different form and different emotion such as sports of Krishna during spring season,[84] how Krishna wanton in the wood,[85] enter to the power of love, O Beautiful,[86] etc. have been painted by the painter keeping in view the every aspects of the Dogras life-style.

There are many other portraits of the Radha and Krishna which have been painted by the Jammu painters revealing the various social spherical theme of the Dogras life-style. These portraits have been known by the title of Krishna pulls Radha in a cloudy scene,[87] Radha Krishna,[88] Radha offering garland to Krishna,[89] Sri Krishna with umbrella,[90] Krishna and Radha, a love scene,[91] Krishna play on a flute for Radha,[92] Krishna combing Radha's hair.[93] Krishna and Radha be size a cow.[94] Krishna applying *tikka* to Radha,[95] Krishna and Radha sitting in a window,[96] Krishna Radha standing in a porch,[97] etc.

Shiva

In the paintings of the period, we also learn that Jammu painter made the theme of Lord Shiva as the supreme deity of the Dogras of Hindus who manifests in three characteristics, the Creator, Preserver and Destroyer. There have been embodied in Hindu mythology in the form of Brahma the Creator, Vishnu the Preserver and Lord Shiva the Destroyer. The most powerful of them is Lord Shiva. It is said that he (Shiva) derived his energy (power) from the practice of austerities. In one of the picture,[98] Shiva has been painted by the painter along with the Parvati, who is shown seated on his right side and Ganesh on his left leg, seated on a tiger-skin. Here, we see Lord Shiva wears a short piece of cloth which covers the very private part of his body as a lower garment known as *langoti* or *rumali* in the local language of Dogras. His matted hair has been parted from the middle falling back. Parvati has been shown wearing a Iranian *peswaj* and *dupatta* of traditional Indian dress and watering to Ganesh. Shiva has been also shown wearing a spotted-deer-skin which also was wrapped by the Sadhu or a *Yogi* (Fig. 3).

Vishnu

In the *Bhagawat-Purana's* painting, Jammu painter prefer the theme of Vishnu, the Preserver embodied in the Hindu mythology in the form of goodness and mercy. He is identified with cosmic energy which he maintains and preserves, alongwith the rhythm of the physical and the cosmic order. His spouse, Lakshmi; is depicted as the goddess of the good by the painter. For example, the picture of adoration of Vishnu;[99] he and his wife Lakshmi; have been displayed sitting on a lotus flower projected or springed from the *sheshnag* (snake). Lord Krishna, the representative of Lord Shiva, etc., with cows have been shown offering regards to Vishnu and Lakshmi from their core of the hearts. He has been displayed with four-hands having conch-shell, lotus flower, wheel and a club in his each hand. He wore a golden pointed yellow *dhoti*, and a beautiful golden needled worked scarf and a *mukata* on the head. This picture shows religious life and history of the Dogras that they used to believe on the Hinduism i.e. their gods and goddess (Fig. 3). In another picture Vishnu and Lakshmi[100] have been painted on the *sheshnag* (snake). Lakshmi has been shown sitting in the side of the Vishnu's feet and Vishnu has been displayed taking the position of sleeping and discussing an issue for the welfare of the society. Here, he has been again show depicted wearing a traditional *dhoti* of the Hindus, a *mukata* on the head and holding lotus flower in one of his hand (Fig. 2).

Bhagawat-Purana

As commonly believed that the Lord Krishna is the eight incarnation of Vishnu who was incarnated for the destruction of his perverted uncle king Kansa of Mathura. Krishna is known as the best lover among the Hindu gods, he inspired love and affection rather reverence. The painters of the Jammu region have painted his life story since birth to death. His various scenes in the *Bhagawata Purana* paintings show the lifestyle of the Dogras in the various forms i.e. hero or *nayaka*, god, etc. Through the medium of Lord Krishna, painters also expressed the sentiments of the Dogra kings to improve the economic life of the people. As in evident from one of the picture about the diversion of the Jumana,[101] even Sudama has shown pulling a *hal*. It shows that the king of Basohli in 18th century had an idea to construct a canal for the agricultural development in order to improve the economic condition of the people. The picture also shows that Dogra society was a rural society and they used to rear animals as it was the part of their economy (Fig. 1).

The picture of *Krishna bringing the Parijata from Indra's heaven*[102] shows his godly powers. He has shown along with Radha on the guard wearing yellow *dhoti*, a beautiful *mukata* on the head having four hands keeps a wheel, lotus flower, conch-shell and a club. Radha has shown wearing a *ghaghra*, *choli* and *dupatta* as a dress (Fig. 3). As a *nayaka* of the *sakhas Krishna swallows the forest* fire.[103] He has been shown wearing a *kacha* of vertical living design and a scarf of needled work. Whereas the *Sakhas* of Krishnas have been painted with inferior clothes along with a conical cap on the head, but Krishna wears a golden *mukata*. The sakhas have been displayed weeping on this event along with the cows (Fig. 2).

The Krishna Legend

It appears from the study that cult of Krishna is as old as Christianity. The various portraits which are at our disposal indicate the repository of the Krishna legend. As in one of the picture *Radha giving butter-milk to Krishna*[104] from the pot and his amorous dalliances as a young man have been the subject of devotional songs for centuries. It has been painted by the Jammu painter. He wears yellow *dhoti*, a scarf and beautiful ornaments (Fig. 4). In another picture, Krishna has been displayed *stealing the cloth of gopias*[105] and hidden in the tree looking on the ladies who have been shown taking bath in the pond. In this picture, we learn that *bhakti* cult of which Krishna was the main inspiration, called for love rather than severe austerities and endears to every Indians heart. He was a cowherds god of the Hindus (Fig. 1).

The Mahabharata

There are two great epics of Indians called as *Mahabharata* and *Ramayana*. The central theme of the *Mahabharata* is a great historical battle fought between the cousins at the historical place known as Kurukshetra. The five Pandavas and the one hundred Kauravas, this symbolizing bad against the good composed by Rishi Veda Vyasa about 3000 B.C. *Mahabharata* contains many stories besides this war which appears to be mythical and legendary. Its cultural importance can also be visualised from the fact that *Bhagvata Gita* is a part of the great work. The various events and emotions of the *Mahabharata* were the favourite of the Jammu painters which are available in the Dogra Art Gallery known as Sri Krishna *chatur-bhuja roopa* to Arjun,[106] Sanjay relating the *Mahabharata* to Daratrashtra,[107] Arjun approaches Sri Krishna,[108] Sri Krishna and Arjun,[109] Sri-Krishna teaches Arjun,[110] Sri Krishna and Arjun move towards battlefield,[111] etc.

The Ramayana

The oldest Sanskrit epic known as *Ramayana* was composed by Rishi Valmiki. In 16th century A.D. Tulsidas wrote *Ramayana* in Hindi which is popular to this day. It is the story of Raja Dashratha, the rules of Ayodhya. He married three queens, who gave birth to four sons, Rama was the eldest among them and sons of Kaushalya, the chief queen of Raja Dashratha abiding by his promise to give throne to his son Bharata and an exile of 14 years for Rama. During this period of exile Rama faced numerous odds with his wife Sita and Lakshmana.

In this epic story, Rama Chandra, generally called Rama, the 7th Avatar of Vishnu, appeared and Parsurama became jealous of him. Their conflicts forms the two great epics i.e. *Mahabharata* and *Ramayana*.

The central theme of this epics is that Dashratha was interested to hand over his kingdom to the eldest son Rama, but his wife Kaikeyi was not in the favour of Rama, she stirred up to make the king Rama. She was interested to place her son Bharat on the throne while Rama was exiled for fourteen years. In the exile Lakshmana and Sita accompanied Rama in the forest. The most of the Indian artists have been inspired by its many incidents and they painted its copies as a theme in a large extent. Such type of incidents were frequently portraited on wall painting of Purani Mandi temple. In one of the scene Rama and Sita[112] displayed sitting outside of their hut (*ashram*) and Lakshmana has been shown killing and threatening a lady *rakashes* (evil spirit). It shows the exiled life of the Rama, Sita and Lakshmana in a forest (Fig. 1). Besides this picture of *Ramayana*, there is a another picture of this epic which reveals that in forest Rama was attracted in the romantic manner by Ravanas sister Surpanakha, when her entreaties were rebuffed, she tried to attack Sita and intended to swallow her, but Lakshmana cut of her nose, ear and breast. She rushed to her younger brother Khara, to revenge. When Khara's huge army was destroyed Surpanakha went to Ravana. Ravana while seeing Sita was magnetized by the Sita's beauty. During the absence of Rama and Lakshmana, Ravana abducted Sita. Whereas, Rama set a plan to recover Sita along with huge army of monkeys and bears led by Hanuman. Lakshmana and Rama were injured twice during war with Ravana, but were saved by the herb brought by Hanuman all the way from Himalayas. The result was that the war was won by Rama and Ravana was killed. Sita returned to Rama. On their return to Ayodhya[113] a scene of this event has been painted by the Jammu painter at the wall-painting of the Bhurj temple. At this event the people are displayed along with Sadhus celebrating victory and rejoiced return to Ayodhya (Fig. 3).

The Seasons

The painting of the period indicate that Jammu people used to live very close to the nature and the change of seasons fascinated them. The painting of 12 months or *Baramasa* of the 16th century poet Kesava Das has enriched Hindi, literature with its commendable account about the people of Jammu and the rituals and ceremonies of the various seasons. It remained the popular theme. As in one of the paintings, physical features and seasonal change have been made by the painter communicating the *sawan* is the month of lovers[114] as a theme, in this study painter also corporate the music, fruits and birds of the areas. This work shows the visual life of the Dogra society through the medium of Radha-Krishna as a metaphysical hero along with the musician's party (Fig. 2).

Battle-Scenes

The Jammu painters also preferred battle scene as a theme which display military life of the Dogras Generals. As one of the pictures Maharaja Gulab Singh has been painted with his military strength proceeding in a war procession[115] with his Generals, and war equipment's (Fig. 1). In another picture the strength of Raja Suchet Singh's[116] army has been painted by the painter. He is also shown proceeding along with this force as a Chief (Fig. 1).

Social and Cultural Theme

The painting of Jammu region cover a considerable range of themes. As it is often appeared in most of the Pahari paintings that the subject matter of the and the form of art alike were derived by the Jammu painters from the selection of myths and metaphysics as well as from the contemporary environment of the society which reveal the socio-cultural life of the region. As it indicates in the picture of Raja Kirpal Pal[117] (1690-1693 A.D.). He seated on a beautiful carpet and smoking a *hookah*. Two female attendants are shown attending him: One is displayed *chouri-bearer* standing behind him: another is serving by putting fire on the cap of the smoking *hookah*. This picture demonstrates the domestic life of the royal houses of the Dogras (Fig. 1). In another picture Raja Dhiraj Pal[118] (1720-1725 A.D.) is shown seating on a beautiful carpet and smoking a *hookah* and having *mala* in his hand. Picture shows the domestic life of the royal houses that they use to pray and start the day business (Fig. 2).

There is another picture which display socio-cultural life of the Dogra, as in one of the scene Raja Suchet Singh[119] has been shown sitting on a beautiful stage smoking a *hookah* and most of his security men. They are displayed in sitting and standing position. In the front of the dice, his court dancers, drummers, are singing and dancing and he is enjoying this cultural programmes (Fig. 2). There many examples of the cultural activities of the rulers of the area. Nainsukhs technical accomplishment suggest that he may have received a training at Delhi before the invasion of Nadir Shah. During the 1740's and 1750's, he worked for Raja Balwant Singh of Jammu recording the ritual observances and habitual pastimes of this patrons daily life in superbly drawn pictures which are exceptional in Indian portraiture for their informal elements of pathos and humour. He depicts Balwant Singh hunting, listing of music, inspecting horses and paintings and writing, performing his devotion or more quirkishly as a tiny solitary figure in window or standing on the roof of the huge palace. Nainsukhs delicate colour sense appears in his painting of a Jasrota prince riding through a field of mustard flowers against a cool blue green background (Fig. 192).[120] The hunting scene of Raja Suchet Singh[121] displayed a glimpse of the Dogra culture and pastime activity (Fig. 1).

Marriage

In the wall painting of Ramnagar, the painter was very close to the Dogra society, he painted a marriages scene of Raja Suchet Singh.[122] In this picture, the rites and rituals of the marriage ceremony Dogra society have been highlighted. Women have been shown wearing colourful dress. Few ladies and a man are shown awaiting to receive the bride and bridegroom to perform the ritual at that time (Fig. 3).

Ritual

Ritual scene has also been painted by the Jammu painter, Raja Suchet Singh[123] has been shown proceeding on a war procession. Before the departure, religious ceremony is shown performed by the religious guru of the Raja's. Most of the people are shown assembled near the *hawankund*, they are praying for the safety and victory of Raja Suchet Singh (Fig. 3).

Sati-System

In the picture of a *sati-parikashin*,[124] it appears that *sati-system* practice was also therein the Dogra society early in the 18th century A.D. In this procession most of the Sadhu have been shown assembled near the funeral pyre of a lady's husband chanting their religious rite to become her *sati* and pulling her in his pyre (Fig. 1).

The Animals and Birds of Mythology

From the painting of the period in general it displays that Jammu painters have made their myths and legends showing the religious aspects of the animals and birds. The birds and animals deities have been painted with love and full esteem by the artists with great characteristic. These animals and birds are elephant,[125] cow,[126] bull,[127] monkey,[128] horse,[129] dog,[130] snake,[131] peacock,[132] coku[133] (kojal), chakor,[134] etc. These are portrayed with special characteristics in the Dogra culture.

From the above discussion, the role of religion in the evolution of the Jammu art paintings has been pivotal and it was the primary sources and imbibing force beneath the artistic, creativeness of Jammu people. Thus, the theme was pregnant with a large variety of representation of man's romantic relations i.e. *nayaka* and *nayika*. Yet there was a scope of sublimating the representation by substituting the divine pair, Radha and Krishna, for human relationship with an aura of spirituality about it. The artists of the Rajput school of painting at Jammu recognized this highly expressive appealing potentiality of

Vaishnava themes. The devotional mind, charged with subtle, but spontaneous visualization, and the themes of life is imaginative demonstration of the art of paintings. However, the paintings are an effective medium of demonstration of the fundamental values of the Dugger region. For its proper understanding, one must have to analyses the social, cultural, religious and military life of the Dogra's from primitive to the modern age.

Area

The areas of Jammu paintings roughly comprises Basohli, Jammu itself, Mankot, Ramnagar, Poonch, Parmandal, Mansar, Miran Sahib, Bhurja, Sui-Simbli, etc. and painting got the patronage of local Chief's who were mostly Rajput. The first and foremost example of this work was at Basohli minor Pahari atelier. The following centres of painting of the Jammu region are as under:

Basohli

The story of the Pahari art of painting begins from Basohli. The town of Basohli is situated on the right bank of river Ravi at the latitude of 32°30', longitude 75°51', and the elevation of 2,170 feet high from the sea level. It bounded twenty miles by fifteen miles from the south by Lakhanpur, on the West Jasrota and Mankot, on the north-west by the Bandralta (Ramnagar), on the north by Bhadrawaha, on the east by Chamba on the south-east by Nurpur. It was a tiny state consisted of only 74 villages.[135] The first time '*the Basohli School of Hill Painting*' occurs in the annual report of the Archaeological Survey of India for the year 1918-1919 and published in 1921. It gave birth to the famous Pahari miniatures which were famous world over and have formed pride of place in the international museums and galleries. This art is in its truest tradition is of great Ajanta art. The influence of Basohli atelier had spread to many other areas of Jammu region giving birth to several local schools and also in neighbouring parts of the Himachal Pradesh. This school has played an exceptional role in migrating the art of Malwa and Udaipur, the early Rajput art. The artists from Malwa an Udaipur came to Basohli at Nurpur which was easily approachable from Pathankot. Their descendants confined their artistic activities within Basohli.[136]

It is said that Basohli Raja's claimed to be a descendant of the Pandavas. He hailed from eastern India i.e., Prayag or Allahabad, and may have been related to the Pala of Bengal.[137] Bhog Pal founded this state in (765 A.D.) a son of a Raja of Kulu valley, who had subdued Rana Billo, a feudal chief who once had ruled this area. Bhog Pal founded Balaur, the ancient capital of Basohli.[138] Vallapur modern Balour, on a plateau overlooking the Bini river. The name of the ruling house, Balouria, is derived from that of the old capital Balor. In the eleventh century the capital was shifted to Vivasthali (Basohli) on the Iravati (Ravi). The original site of the town was close to the right bank of the Ravi and its ruins were visible some years ago, but they have now been entirely washed away by the river.[139] A decendent Bhupat Pal (1598-1635) had a turbulent character, who was a contemporary of Shah Jahan, shifted the capital on the Ravi, Bhupat Pal, a man of giant stature, sustained his great frame by consuming mammoth quantities of goats flesh and rice. There was rivalry between the Basohli and neighbouring states in the course of endless warfare, they nibbled compulsively at each other territory.[140] He conquered Bhadu, Bhadrawaha, Kishtwar and Nurpur in 1630. The river side capital town proved strategically more insecure in their scuffles and, therefore, Bhupat Pal moved up the town in 1635 to the present site, further away from the river.[141] Eventually, Jagat Singh, Raja of Nurpur a favourite of Shah Jahan and an accomplished intrigant, managed to have the last Bhupat Pal imprisoned. Jagat Singh then occupied Basohli from Nurpur garrison and in 1635, Jagat Singh was able to have assassinated Bhupat Pal[142] at the ripe age of sixty-two.

After the assassination of Raja Bhupat Pal his son became the ruler of Basohli, who occupied the thorn from 1635 to 1673 A.D. Sangram Pal was invited to the court of Delhi, the queen of Shah Jahan, on hearing, his beauty expressed a desire to see him. So, he was taken to the female apartment by Dara Shikoh, and since he was strictly only on exhibit, a napkin was tied over his eyes. The queens saw the prince and saying with exaggerated, that the beauty be observed with momlay eyes and bandage be removed. This was done and she was delighted. After loading him with presents, they allowed him to leave for Basohli. He was succeeded by his younger brother Hindal Pal, an imbecile.[143]

It is mentioned that the construction of the collapsed palace of Basohli was started by Raja Bhupat Pal in 1635 and was enlarged by his successors. Once it was the wonder of the hills G.P. Vigna, the English traveller who passed the Basohli in 1835 A.D. was struck by its grandeur and thought it one of the finest building, he had seen in the east.[144]

It makes crystal clear from the study that reigns of Raja Sangram Pal, Hindal Pal (1673-1678) ; Kripal Pal (1678-1693); Dhiraj Pal (1693-1725) and Medini Pal (1725-1736) formed a golden period of Basohli and the Basohli style of art and painting from the 17th century to onward.

Jit Pal (1736-1757)

Medini Pal was succeeding by Jit Pal who ruled 21 years and died in 1757. He annexed Bhadu state of Basohli. During this period,

Jammu had become a prominent State, and Maharaja Dhruv Dev of Jammu has also achieved considerable importance among the Raja's of Jammu hills.

Amrit Pal (1757-1776)

Amrit Pal was born in 1748 A.D. and became Raja of Basohli in 1757. He married a daughter of Maharaja Ranjit Dev of Jammu in 1758. Basohli State to a large extent came under a control of Jammu Chief on account of unsettled conditions in the plain of Punjab, following the invasion of Ahmad Shah Durrani and the rise of Sikhs, the trade between in India and Kashmir was carried through the outer hills. The trade route ran via Nahan Bilaspur, Haripur-Guler, Nurpur and Basohli to Jammu. The Basohli Raja levied toll-tax on all the merchandize passing through their territory, and thus the State became quit prosperous during the reign of Amrit Pal. Amrit Pal made a considerable addition to a palace at Basohli. Considering the prosperity which the place enjoyed it appears vary probable that during reign of Amrit Pal, Basohli remained a busy centre of painting it also appears that Kangra style of painting had replaced the Basohli style of art of painting even in Basohli itself during his reign.

Vijay Pal (1776-1806)

Vijay Pal was born in 1763 and he became Raja of Basohli at the age of 13 in 1776.[145] State was systematically looted by the Sikh free booters, and in 1836 ultimately became a fief of Raja Suchet Singh, a brother of Maharaja Gulab Singh, the founder of Jammu and Kashmir State.[146] In 1782, it was invaded by Raj Singh of Chamba with the help of Sikh's army.

Mehendra Pal (1806-1813)

He was also the great lover of the pattern of arts. His two portraits in Kangra style are known: One of them is in the family of Baroo Brahman of Basohli; the another with Kunj Lal dated 1803, shows a darbar scene in celebration of *Basant Panchami*. He married the daughter of Maharaja Ajeeb Singh of Jasrota. In 1809, all the Hill States, including Basohli, came under the control of Maharaja Ranjit Singh. The hilly Rajas were required to go frequently to Lahore, where they attended the court of Maharaja. During one of the trips in 1813, he fell-ill at Amritsar where he died.

Bhuperidra Pal (1813-1834)

Bhuperidra Pal became Raja in 1813, when he was only seven years of old. He was also require, like his father to attend the court of Maharaja Ranjit Singh at Lahore. He too died at Amritsar in 1834 after reigning of 21 years.[147]

Kalyan Pal (1845-1857)

He was the last ruler of Basohli. On account of the misrule, during his minority, Maharaja Ranjit Singh gave the Basohli State in *jagir* to Raja Hira Singh of Jammu in 1836. It was during the minority of Kalyan Pal that the treasures of Basohli Raj, including paintings, came into the possession of a Brahmana family of Basohli. In 1845, when the Sikh war was fought, a Balauria Rajputs, finding a favourable opportunity, expelled the Sikh garrison from Basohli and seated Kalayan Pal, who was aged 11 years, on the *gaddi*. However, in 1846, Maharaja Gulab Singh of Jammu became the paramount Chief of the Jammu and Kashmir State. He assigned a pension to Kalyan Pal. In 1850, Kalyan Pal married a princess of Sirmur and later on a daughter of Chhatar Singh, exiled Raja of Mankot, who was living in Salongri. He died issueless in 1857, and thus, the Basohli dynasty came to an end.[148]

It is evident in the painting of the period that the most popular theme of Basohli painting was from Bhanu Datta's "*Rasamanjari*" or "Banquet of Delight". Datta was a Maithil Brahaman, who used to live in the 16th century in the Tirhut area of Bihar, written in Sanskrit, his *Rasamanjari* deals with *nayakas* and *nayikas* and lovers and sweethearts and classified than in accordance with the age, experience, physical mental and emotional characteristics. It appears that Basohli school of painting is entirely different from other Pahari school of painting in technique, colours, features of men and women with oblong protruding eyes and pointed long triangular noses and Rajasthani dresses, Basohli artists with the passage of time diminished at the end of 10th century owing to the potent want of patronage, whereas, Guler, Kangra and Garhwal schools of paintings continued upto the mid-nineteenth century.[148]

Ananda K. Coomaraswamy has rightly remarked that Pahari art school of paintings can be classified into two groups: a Northern series, and the school of Jammu which may be called the school of Kangra and extended upto Garhwal.

Jammu

Jammu province lying between latitude of 32°-20' and 33°-10', longitude of 74°-45' and 75°-55' and at an elevation of 1200 feet high above from the sea-level. It is bounded on the north by the Chenab river and Bhadarwa, on the south by the Punjab, on the east by the hill state of Chamba, and on the west by the Punjab and Noshera.[150] At present, it covers an area of 26,370 sq kms. Most of its area is mountainous and is criss-crossed by a number of tributaries of the Chenab. Physically, administratively and socially, the province is divided into two main regions, namely Doda, Kishtwar, Bhadrawa region and Jammu, Kathua, Udhampur, Poonch, Rajouri region. These two region covers 44% and 56% of the area of the province respectively.

Rajatarangini of Kalhana, the most important and famous work in Sanskrit is quite about the origin of City of Temples. It has been stated that Jammu was one of the warriors in the Rama's army who used to practise penance in the cave which still is called Jammu Raj. According to its family legend traces its descent to a scion of solar dynasty named Agnigiri, who in olden days came from Ajodhya. Jammu existed as a city or a settlement at that time Sofi, the author of 'Kashir', refers that Vayu Sarva son of Raja Agnivarna (the Raja of Parol) first extended his territory from Kathua to foothill of Jammu Tawi. He extended the construction of a fort of Bahu to Bahu Lochan, who was the son of Raja Agnigarbha—a Raja fifth in succession after Raja Vayu Sarva. This indicated that there was no settlement as such on Tawi on its right bank in the period of Bahu Lochan. His brother Jambu Lochan, who succeeded him laid the foundation off Jammu city. Local legendary story of a goat and lion drinking the water in a pond together attributed to Jamboo Lochan. The origin of the Temple of City has significance in so far as the sight of the pond is concerned. This pond should have formed the settlement of Shivahlika hill and have grown on nallah banks and around the natural ditches.

It is said the Jamboo-Lochan ruled over Jammu in about 1350 B.C. and Dhruv Dev laid down the foundation of the Jamwal clan in 1703 A.D. He ruled upto (1703-1735) A.D., but rose to eminence under his son Ranjit Dev (1735-1781 A.D.) G. Forster an English traveller, gave a detailed information of the political conditions of Jammu under Ranjit Dev. According to him Jammu was a strong power. Inspite of the petty warfare, feudatory Chiefs were paying tribute to Ranjit Dev and stayed at Jammu. G. Forster also refers the political lawlessness in this state and tells how Ranjit Dev's son Braj Dev killed his brother and revolted against his father. The latter was kept in captivity for twelve years of Lahore by Zakaria Khan, Mughal Governor of the Punjab, who suspected his loyalty. His brother Ghansar Dev, acted as agent during his captivity. Ranjit Dev was released on payment of ransom about 1747 on the intervention of Adina Beg, Mughals of Jalandhar. He supported Ahamd Shah Durrani during the latter's invasion of the Punjab, and on its cession by the Mughals in 1752, received favours from Ahmad Shah. Ranjit Dev was able to bring under his control many neighbouring states like Basohli, Kishtwar, Bhadrawah, Akhnur, Dalpatpur, Riasi, Bhoti, Bandralta and Sambha.[151]

It is narrated that Nadir Shah's sack of Delhi in 1739, induced many affluent people, nobles as wells traders, to seek security in

Jammu. Malka Zamani consort of emperor Muhammad Shah, and the widow of Mir Mannu, Mughal Governor of Lahore, were among such Mughal nobility. The traveller Forster has recorded that due to the raids of the Persians, Afghans and Sikhs, the Kashmir trade was diverted from the old route via Sirhind and Lahore and Jammu became the new channel where many branch firms were established.[152] In 1781, Ranjit Dev passed away his son Braj Dev became the ruler of Jammu (1781-1787 A.D.). He killed his brother and nephew treacherously to obtain the throne of Jammu. He was killed in the battle against the Sikhs, who deposed the line at last in 1812. Jammu was granted as a *Jagir* to Kharak Singh son of Maharaja Ranjit Singh. But Gulab Singh (1820-1857), who was descended from Surat Singh, the brother of Ranjit Dev, tool service with Ranjit Singh, rose to eminence at the Sikh court and regained Jammu as fief from the Sikh in 1820. Through legally as vassal of the Sikhs, Gulab Singh was practically got independent in 1846 and he soon gained control of many hill States like Mankot, Kishtwar, Bandralta, Jasrota, Chanehni, etc.

Many sites in Jammu region have yield rich treasures in term of fresco-painting as well as miniature paintings dating from 17th to 19th century A.D. very often have their inscriptions in the '*Takri*' aspects peculiar to Dogra hills[153] States. It makes clear from the study the most of the Kangra set of painting on various religious and *sringara* (erotic) themes may be attributed to a single family of artists, the descendents of Pandit Seu of Guler. Pandit Seu has two sons Manak (Manku) and Nainsukh. Nainsukh worked in Jammu Court for Ranjit Dev and Raja Balwant Singh, probably upto the latter's death in 1763 A.D. Manak seems to have worked at Haripur Guler for Raja Dalip Singh. Later, Nainsukh also seems to have joined his brother Manak at Guler after the death of his first patronage Raja Balwant Singh.

The later history of Jammu is lined with three brothers of the Jamwal family and descended from Surat Singh, the third brother of Ranjit Dev. These were known by the names of Gulab Singh and Suchet Singh. Gulab Singh retired to Lahore about 1810-1812, and entered the Sikh army. Before that, he was in the service of the Raja's of Kishtwar and Rajouri. Gulab Singh then called his two brothers from Jammu and enrolled them in the Sikh army.

Maharaja Gulab Singh's character has also been portrayed by the Jammu painters in multi-colours. Jacquement, who visited in his hill principality in 1831, described him as about forty, very handsome, a lion in courage, but with the plainest, mildest and most elegant manners [154]

About the same title of 'Raja', Dhian Singh was granted the principality of Punch, after expelling the old Rajas. Suchet Singh received the State of Bandralta (Ramnagar) from the Sikhs. After the death of Maharaja Gulab Singh in 1857, he was succeeded by his son, Maharaja Ranbir Singh, who died in 1885 and was followed by Maharaja Pratap Singh.

Mankot

Mankot, a very small state about twenty-five kilometers by fifteen kilometers lying between Jammu and Basohli, now called Ramkot. It is situated on the bank of Mandal stream in the Jasrota district of Kathua at the latitude 33°-38' and longitude of 70°-6'. As a State, it was bound on the north by Bandralta, in the east by Bhadir and Balor, on the south by the Karaidari range, separating it from Sambha and Jasrota, and on the west by Bhoti.

The ruling dynasty has an offshoot from Jammu clan named Mankotia. They claim descent from Raja Bhuj Dev of Jammu about 1150 A.D. and on his death his eldest son, Bharurak Dev, who was feeble minded, was regarded as unfit for rule in those troubles times, and was set aside in favour of his younger brother, and settled down in the Dansal Dun. His descendant in the fifth generation, named Manak Dev, conquered some villages near the present town of Ramkot, probably from the petty Chief's, called Ranas. Above the village is a fort was the throne of Mankotia Raja Manak Dev. The state was always small and more or less in touch with Jammu. The early Rajas were: Bir Dev, Kirpal Dev and Ahl Dev. There were twenty-three Rajas in all from the foundation of the State to its extinction in 1820, ruled an average of about twenty-five years to each. The names of the later Raja were: Manak Dev; Udai Dev; Nagar Dev; Uttam Dev; Hari Chand Dev; Ajmal Dev; Kalas Dev; Biram Dev; Sarwar Dev and Pratap Dev.

Like the other Hill States market came under the control of Ranjit Dev of Jammu in the latter half of the 18th century. In 1809 the State known Mankot came under the control of Raja Ranjit Singh and was annexed to the Sikh Kingdom in 1820 and the ruling family then retired to Kutlehr in Kangra, fixed their residence at Salangari.

The theme of the Mankot school of art of painting is religious in nature which belongs to the *Ramayana* and the *Bhagawata-Purana* series, mostly probably belonging to the first decade of the 18th century A.D. and the intense expressionism of Basohli is not achieved by the Mankot painters. The style of painting have been relaxed a swifter episodic narration. With larger strides and wide-flung arms, the gestural drama in these pictures is spirited, but it cannot by claimed the Mankot managed as distinctive and effective a modulation on the Basohli style as Bilaspur managed on the Kangra idiom,[155] according to Krishna Chaitanya.

Ramnagar

The capital of erstwhile state of Bandralta was situated at the latitude of 32°-48' and longitude of 75°-48' from the a sea level and about 105 kms from the Jammu and 38 kms on the west by Udhampur, towards to Dhar Road, to the south of Chanehni and it was bounded on the east by Bhadrawah, on the south by Mankot or open space on the left bank of the Ramnagar *kad* and junction with the Tawi. Between the Tawi and Ramnagar in particular, they dip usually out an angle of about 45 degrees with a steep abutment on the north. The capital was originally called nagar, as being the only town in the principality. and the ruling family took their dynasty of Bandralta from the name of the tract. It was founded by the royal family of Chamba belong to the Chand dynasty about 1000-1020 A.D. The *Vansavali* contains only twenty-one names down to the extinction of the state in 1822, giving an average of nearly forty years to each, which is very improbably. We must, therefore, conclude that many names have been omitted in copying. During the same period, there are thirty names in the Chamba roll of Rajas.[156]

It is said a tradition of a *Thakuraian* period in ancient times, and much the same reason is given for the invasion of the tract as in the case of other States, viz., tyranny and oppression of their subject by the Ranas and Thakurs. As a result, some of the *zamindars* went to Chamba to ask help. Vichittar Verma (980-1000 A.D.) was then in power, and unable to go himself, he sent his younger brother, who vanquished the Ranas and made himself ruler. A tradition is current which throws light on the methods employed to get rid of troublesome opponents. It is to the effect that the Raja and the local Rana both availed themselves of the services of the some barber, who was bribed to cut the Rana's the throat while shaving him. In this way a powerful rival was removed. Seventy-two petty Chiefs are said to have been overcome by one means or another and the Raja then assumed the name Bahattar to mark the fact.[157]

With the rise of the Sikh power in the Punjab, Ramnagar fell into the hands of the Sikh forces in 1822 A.D. thus, the Bandral dynasty was ended. The hill state was bestowed upon Raja Suchet Singh, brother of Gulab Singh by Ranjit Singh, the tract was made over to him in *jagir*. The ancient line was then deposed but allowed to remain for a time. This, however, was soon found to be awkward, as an attempt made to recover the territory, and they were finally exiled from the State. They first retired to Kangra, where they resided for some time under the protection of Raja Sansar Chand, but afterwards went of Tehri-Garhwal and finally settled at Shahzadpur in the Ambala district. The last Raja to exercise ruling power was Bhupdhar Dev, who died at Shahzadpur. He had been assigned a pension of Rs. 3000 by Government, which is still paid to the family.[158] Raja Suchet Singh took much interest in Ramnager, became the ruler of Bandralta from 1822. A.D., to 1844 A.D. i.e. more than a score of years, who renamed Bandralta as Ramnagar.

Ramnagar palaces were constructed by the Bandral lords but they were renovated and reconstructed by Raja Suchet Singh, where he used to reside and also a fort on the *chaugan* which was held by a garrison. On his death in Lahore in 1844 A.D. his *ranis* became *sati*, and the spot was marked by a garden. As he died issueless the *jagir* reverted to Jammu. At a later time it was granted as a Chief to Raja Ram Singh, second son of Maharaja Ranbir Singh, and on his demise without the male heir, it again became merged in the Jammu State. The paintings of the palaces demonstrate that Raja Suchet Singh like Raja Sansar Chand II of Kangra, was a connoisseur of Bandral school of Pahari paintings. The wall-paintings of the palaces reveal the socio-cultural, religious, political and economic history of the areas. Moreover, paintings depict the military achievement of the Raja Suchet Singh and his lifestyle.

Poonch

Poonch State, in ancient times, was situated in the valley of the Poonch Tawi and its tributaries at the latitude of 32°-44', longitude of 74°-55' and to the elevation 3,300 feet from the sea level. It was bounded on the north by the Pir Panjal range, on the west by the Jhelam, on the south probably by the plains and on the east by Rajouri (Rajapuri) and 240 kms. away from the Jammu. The original name of the state was *Parnotsa*,[159] of which Poonch is a derivation; and the original capital was at Lohara, the present Loharin to the north-east of the town of Poonch.

So far the history of Poonch painting is concerned, as the western most extremity of the Punjab Hills, shows several unusual features. The State was founded by a branch of the Rathor Rajput houses that ruled Jodhpur. But in the Jahangir's time the ruler adopted Islam. The countryside were Muslims, Poonch town retained a Hindu character through its merchants and traders, the court was originally Hindu, later Muslim. The State was under Mughal suzerainty from about 1586 to 1752 A.D. and thereafter the Durranis.[160]

From 1752 A.D. to 1818 A.D. Poonch was under the Durrains rule. In 1810, Bhimbar and Rajouri were reduced and 1812 after much hard fighting and in 1814, the Sikh army advanced to Poonch, led by the Maharaja in person. The Raja of Poonch at that time was Ruhallah Khan and his sympathies were with the Afghans. But in 1819, the Sikh's expelled the Muslim dynasty and made Dhian Singh the Raja of Poonch.

Raja Dhian Singh continued to rule the State till 15th September 1843, when he was assassinated, on the same day as Maharaja Sher Singh, by the Sindhianwala Sirdars. He was succeeded by his eldest son, Raja Hira Singh, who in his turn was also assassinated on 22nd December 1844 A.D. He was followed by his younger brother, Raja Jawahir Singh.[161]

After the first Sikh war, in March 1846, the hill tracts including Poonch, were made over to Raja Gulab Singh, but in the treaty no provision was made for the separate autonomy of Poonch, which thus became a part of Jammu and Kashmir State. This and other censor aroused strong feeling between Raja Jawahir Singh and his uncle which lasted for some years. At last, in 1859, sometimes after Maharaja Gulab Singh death, an arrangement was come to under which Raja Jawahir Singh agreed to abdicated in favour of his younger brother, Raja Moti Singh, on condition of that he should receive an annual allowance of one lakh of rupees and reside in the Punjab beyond Ambala. Raja Moti Singh continued to rule the State till 1897, and was succeeded by his son, Raja Baldev Singh, who died in 1918. The present ruler in Raja Sukhdev Singh.[162]

In 1922, J.C. French, during a visit to Poonch noticed a number of wall-paintings in the Pahari idiom on the interior walls of the palace. But he himself felt certain that they were post-1820. Therefore, they cannot throw much light on the situation earlier, in the 18th century. Now, they have been white washed.

Purmandal

Purmandal presents sight of a strange collection of buildings is situated in a nook among the low hills about thirty-six kms away from the Jammu to the north-east on the banks of river Devaka. According to the local traditional of this right, a stone has been discovered here about a thousand year ago by a Raja Beni Dutta of Amantipur, who told in a dream that he should construct a temple for it. He erected the *Kasivisvanath* temple. Subsequently, Purmandal became a famous place of Hindu's pilgrimage, who visit there for the purpose of obtaining a moral cleaning by taking bath in its water. The whole complex of the *mandir* along with the *dharamsala* came into being on both sides of the stream Devaka. It is known to us that Raja Man Singh of Jaipur (Amber) prayed here before going to Kabul to fight for the Mughals and promised that he would built up a *mandir* of Shiva at this sight, if he would return back alive from the Kabul. Accordingly, he constructed Uma Mahapati temple with a Shiva-ling.[163]

The glorious sovereign Maharaja Ranjit Singh Sahib Bahadur set up his exalted camp at the holy abode of Purmandal on the occasion of '*ashnan*' (holy bath) and distributed among the poor rich charities.[164] He arrived Purmandal on 11th Chet 1895 B.E. (22nd March 1838) and on 12th, he entered the town. It has been rightly informed by Mira Seth that Maharaja Ranjit Singh was attached to this place and occasionally, he used to visit there. He had the dome of the Uma Mahapati temple painted gold and also built the Eklingaonkar temple here. He denoted 1300 *gumoons* (10400 *Kanal*) land to Mahanta Motigar Ji, a Saiva *sanyasi* for its maintenance. According to Drew, many of his courtiers also built temples and houses at this place. Maharaja Gulab Singh of Jammu also donated land to the Kasi-Visvanath temple. This images in the iconographically in the typical Pahari mould (Fig. 50). Shiva even has a moustache which he generally does not have in Indian sculptural iconography. Suchet Singh, Gulab Singh brother, built a *dharamsala* here; Maharaja Ranbir Singh was known to have specially liked this palace where he built several small temples. Rich businessman also put up temples here, for instance, the Shah family who originally came from Gujarat, built the Radha-Krishna temple.[165]

Sohan Lal Suri mentions that Raja Gulab Singh offered to Maharaja Ranjit Singh the following articles: Fine garments, 11 horses with gold and silvers saddles and seven plain ones, and for the Maharaja especially five gold, two silver and two plain ones. Besides these, he presented two elephants, one with golden seat and the other with silver seat. Rupees 51000 in cash, rare garments 101, articles of jewellery 5, consisting of a pearl necklace, an armlet and under turban, a pair of gold bangles, and a diamond ring and 2 falcons.[166]

Mansar

A journey of few miles from Purmandal, but by a rugged path over difficult hills which brings the two small lakes named Mansar and Saruin-Sar. They are 9 to 10 miles apart. Mansar is a small village containing more than eighty houses. It is situated at the latitude of 70°11' at the elevation of about 2000 to 2200 feet above the sea level. It is in Ramnagar's tehsil, thirty-five kms east of Udhampur. There is a large lake. It lies a mid-low hills and about a mile long and half a mile broad. This lake has been considered a very holy lake for the Hindus came from afar to their vows and perform, their abutions in its water.

The village has a big *matha* belong to Saiva *sanyasins* (monks). According to the present *mahanta*, Raj Kumar Parbat, the *matha* first contained only the Nar Singh Ji *mandir* built by Baba Khobal Ji Parbat, who lived here in 1300 A.D. It appears from the present temple and the other buildings that its walls were covered with wall-paintings and now they have been white washed. Its one of the room is now used as a handicraft centre for the women. According to Mira Seth one of its room was originally used as a *baithak* by the *mahanta*, and is now kept locked because of its dilapidated State. This room had painting on walls. Of the originally fifty panels, thirty-seven are still distinct. According to the present *mahanta*, Maharaja Partap Singh was the donor of these paintings. The room is aesthetically located as it overlooks the beautiful panorama of the Mansar lake with its woods.[167] The paintings show the religious tales of the Hindu mythological ones.

Bhurj

It is a small village of more than 65 houses. It is situated in the Jammu district in Jammu tehsil, about 20 kilometers, north-west of the Jammu city. According to local tradition as told by the present priest, Ram Lakhaman Ji, this temple has been erected more than twelve hundred years ago and had donated by the Prithvi Raj Chouhan and said that Maharaja Gulab Singh had also used to visit in this temple occasionally.

Sui-Simble

It is located one and half kilometers north of Bhurj. It is also a small village. According to the present *mahanta*, Prakash Das Ji, Maharaja Gulab Singh of Jammu and Kashmir was devoted to Baba Prem Das Ji of Sui-Simble as the latter had given him the *vardan* or boon that he would one day be a powerful Raja. Gulab Singh built the Raghunath Ji temple and Prem Das Ji Samadhi at Sui-Simble. Architecturally they are both unostentatious but graceful buildings in the style of Rajasthani temples.[168]

Purani Mandi

The Raghunath Mandir at Purani Mandi called "Maharani Ka Mandir" was built by the Maharani Bandhrali[169] wife of Maharaja Rambir Singh (named Ishwari Devi). She was the daughter of a *jagirdar* of Bandral, (Ramnagar) who was married to Maharaja Ranbir Singh of Jammu in V.S. 1938 (1880) at the age of thirteen and widowed at the age of seventeen in V.S. 1942 (1884) (Fig. 3). She started building this temple after her husband's death, using the golden bangles given at the time of her wedding by her parents and donated the temple to Baba Pushkar Das, her *istadevata* on the fourteenth *Jeysth*, V.S.; 1947 (June A.D. 1889). Baba Pushkar Das, a Dogra by birth, was a *vairage* and came from the village of Choboti, tehsil Jammu. The Maharani lived for sometime in the temple precincts and used its painted *baithak*, which still exists. She was so punctilious that she paid twenty-five rupees per month as rent to Baba Pushkar Das whenever she stayed there. The *mahanta* considered himself a caretaker of the place at which all itinerant Sadhus could get free board and lodging. Just before she died, the Maharani gifted the entire property to him in a letter. After the *samadhi* of Baba Pushkar Das the temple together with ten acres of land came under the ownership of the Ramananda Sampradaya. The succeeding gurus to the *gaddi*-Ananta Ram. Thakur Das and the present *mahanta* have been caretakers for Sri Vaisnav. The temple and residence for the *mahanta* their followers and travelling Sadhus, are all part of a closely-knit complex with a single entrance. It has been built in the 19th century style of hill architecture with some Rajasthani influence. It is simple, yet elegant building somewhat reminiscent of Florentine Renaissance architecture—a severe exterior and elegant interiors. The main temples does not have any ornamentation. The living quarters are starkly simple. Besides the main temple of Raghunath Ji containing the images of Rama, Sita and Lakshmana, there are seven smaller temples of Shankar, Natwar Sarikar, Durga, Badri Narayana, Laxmi Narayana, Maharaja Dharam Raj and Hammuana, as well as the *Samadhi* of Pushkar Das.[176]

Miran Sahib

Miran Sahib is situated in south-west of Jammu at about 15 kms. There is a temple of Radha-Krishna. It was built by Diwan Anant Ram of the family of the *diwans* of the Jammu darbar about 1830. Gulab Singh also used to visit there. It is a small temple which was endowed with thirty-two acres of land and given to Pandit Lakhi Ram to run on behalf of the Diwans family of hereditary *pujari*. The style of the paintings in this temple suggests that it is a construction belonging to the mid-nineteenth century. It contains very few panels, but they are good. The entrance *verandah* before the *parikrams* is decorated with two brief panels illustrating on the right, Ganesa with *Ridhi* and *Siddhi* and *Shiva*, and in another panel Shiva and Parvati. On the left Ram and Sita are on a throne and a small panel illustration *Krsna's virap-rup*.[171] Radha-Krishna with a flute under a tree[172] (Fig. 2) and portrait of Maharaja Gulab Singh[173] as a soldier have also been portrayed there on the panels (Fig. 3).

The above-mentioned areas of the school of paintings reveal the details of the creative history of the Duggar society and their visionary life. The analytical study of both the miniatures and wall-paintings not only expose the fashion influence of the Rajputs, Mughals, Sikhs and European (English), but also demonstrate local tradition, standard of living and cultural life of the areas. Nonetheless, study also indicates that Dogra[174] society was a religious society and its Chiefs had to brought a religious fervour in this field by painting the pictures of *Ramayana, Mahabharata, Vishnu, Shiva, Gita-Govinda, Brahma, Krishna-Lila*, etc. from the ancient Hindu literature to present age.

Notes and References

1. Plate 1; Portrait of Raja Kirpal Pal; Basohli, circa 1690-93 A.D. Pb. Mm. Patiala, See Chapter 2.

2. Plate VIII; Portrait on the way to the Tryst; Illustration to the *Rasamanjari* Basohli; circa 1690-1695 A.D. D.A.G.J. See Chapter 2. Plate VI Figs. 1. Also see Plate IX, Figs. 1, 2 and 3; Illustration to the *Gita Govinda*, Basohli circa 1730 A.D.

3. Plate VIII; Portrait 'The way to the Tryst'. Illustration to the *Rasamanjari* Basohli circa (1690-1695 A.D.). D.A.G.J. See Chapter 2.

4. Percy Brown; *Indian Painting*, New Delhi; 1962; p. 96. Hereafter cited as *I.P.*

5. Plate 1, Portrait of Raja Dhiraj Pal; Basohli circa (1720-1725 A.D.) Pb. Mm. Patiala. See Chapter 2.

6. Plate II; Portrait of Raja Medini Pal, Basohli circa (1725-1736 A.D.) D.A.G. J. See Chapter 2.

7. Plate IV; The birth of Krishna; Illustration to the *Bhagawata Purana*; Mankot. Early 18th century; Pb. Mm. Patiala. See Chapter 2.

8. Plate V; Krishna 'Swallows the forest fire'. Illustration to the *Bhagawata Purana*; Tira-Sujanpur; Early 18th century. See Chapter 2.

9. *Ibid*, Krishna Bringing the Parijata from Indra's Heaven. Illustration to the *Bhagawata Purana*; Tira-Sujanpur, circa 1780 A.D. See Chapter 2.

10. *Ibid*, Krishna lifting the mountain *Govardhana*; Illustration to the *Bhagawata Purana*; *Tira-Sujanpur*; Early 18th century. *Tira-Sujanpur*: The contemporary ruler of Ranjit Dev Raja Ghamnd Chand (1751-1774 A.D.) of Kangra. In 1758, he was appointed governor of the whole Trigarta region by Ahmad Shah Durrani, over which he exercised his control with the help of a large army of Muslim mercenaries. He founded the town of Tira-Sujanpur, just located above Nadaun on the river Beas.

11. M.S. Randhawa and D.S. Randhawa; *Guler Painting*; New Delhi; 1982; p. 19. Hereafter referred as *G.P.*

13. Douglas and Barrett and Basil Gray; *Treasures of Asia Painting of India*. New Delhi; 1963, pp. 172, 174. Hereafter referred as *T.A.P.I.*

14. J.N. Ganhar; *Jammu Shrines and Pilgrimages*; New Delhi, 1973; p. 172. Hereafter cited as *J.S.P.*

15. C. Sivaramamurti; *Citra-sutra of Vishnudharmottara*; New Delhi, 1978; p. 2. Hereafter wrote as *C.V.*

16. D.A.G.J; Acc. No. 167/214; Portrait of Raja Ghansar Dev; Artist; Nainsukh. 18th century A.D. Jammu. *Note:* Raja Ghansar Dev: He was the son of Raja Dhruv Dev of Jammu, brother of Raja Ranjit Dev.

17. C. Sivaramanmurti; *Indian Painting*; New Delhi; 1970 p. 13. Hereafter cited as *I.P.*

18. Balwant Singh : He was the son of Raja Dhurv Dev the youngest brother of Raja Ranjit Dev (1735-1781 A.D.). He was the ruler of the small principalities of Jasrota.

19. Plate XXXXVIII; D.A.G.J.; Acc. No. 22/69; 'Reclining, A Women in Yellow Dress' Artist; Channu; 18th century A.D. Jammu. See Chapter 2.

20. M.S. Randhawa and D.S. Randhawa; *G.P.*; p. 22.

21. *Ibid.*; p. 20.

22. (Based on R.P.N. Singh's book). Quoted from S.P. Srivastava; *Art and Cultural Heritage of Patiala*; Delhi 1991; p. 104. Hereafter the title of this book described as *A.C.H.P.*

23. (Based on Dr. B.N. Goswamy's paintings at Sikh court). Quoted from S.P. Srivastava; *A.C.H.P.*; p. 105.

24. Partapaditya Pal; *Court Painting of India* 16th to 19th centuries; New Delhi 1983, p. 8. Hereafter cited as *C.P.I.*

25. Plate X; Portrait of Maharaja Gulab Singh in a War procession; 19th century A.D. Jammu. See Chapter 2.

26. M.S. Randhawa and Krishna Chaitanya; Editor Jyotis Bhattacherya; *Roopa-Lekh*; Vol. XXX Nos. 1&2; New Delhi; July 1959; p. 9.

27. Plate XI; D.A.G.J.; Acc. No. 314; *Panchvakta*; Artist; Aziz; 19th century A.D. Jammu.

28. Plate XVIII; Portrait of Prince Partap Singh on Horse back. See Chapter 2.

29. *Ibid*, Portrait of Partap Singh, (Fig. 2). See Chapter 2.

30. *Ibid*, Portrait of Amar Singh (Fig. 3). See Chapter 2.

31. *Ibid*, Portrait of Ram Singh (Fig. 4). See Chapter 2.

32. (a). D.A.G.J.; Acc. No.83/130; Portrait Arjun Warn To His Uncle Untoward Steps and Serious Consequences; Artist, Hari Chand, Early 20th century A.D. Jammu.

(b) D.A.G.J.; Acc. No. 170/219; Portrait Maharaja Ranbir Singh with his attendances; Artist, Hari Chand; 19th century A.D. Jammu.

33. (a). D.A.G.J.; Acc. No. 71/118; Portrait of Khwaja Khizzer; Artist, Jagat Ram Chunia; 19th century A.D. Jammu. Plate XIII, (Fig. 4). See Chapter 2.

(b) D.A.G.J.; Acc. No. 53/2; Portrait; Rama Panchyat; Artist; Jagat Ram Chunia; 19th century A.D. Jammu. See Chapter 2 Plate XVI (Fig. 2).

34. (a). D.A.G.J.; Acc. No. 12/59; Portrait of Nao-Nihal Singh; Artist; Chananu; 19th century A.D. Jammu. See Chapter 2, Plate XII (Fig. 4).

(b) D.A.G.J.; Acc. No. 13/60; Portrait of Maharja Gulab Singh; Artist; Chananu; 19trh century A.D. Jammu. See Chapter 2 Plate XIII (Fig. 1).

35. (a) D.A.G.J.; Acc. NO. 5/52; Portrait of *Ragini* Gaund Malkauns; Artist; Ruldoo; 19th century A.D. Jammu.

(b) D.A.G.J.; Acc. No. 50/97; Portrait of Krishna applying Tikka to Radha; Artist; Ruldoo; 19th century A.D. Jammu.

36. Lakshmi Narain and Sansar Chand, *Dogri Folk Literature and Pahari Art*; Jammu, 1965; p. 122.

37. *Ibid.*

38. *Ibid.*, p. 123.

39. *Ibid.*

40. *Ibid.*, p. 122.

41. Lubor Hajek; *Indian Miniatures of the Moghul School*; London; 1960 p. 60; Hereafter cited as *IMMS.*

42. Mukandi Lal, *Garwal Painting*; New Delhi, First published 1968; Reprinted 1982; p. 20. Hereafter wrote as *G.P.*

43. C. Sivaramamurti; *C.V.*; p. 13.

44. Pratapadity Pal; *C.P.I.*; p. 46.

45. D.A.G.J.; Acc. No. 33/80; Portrait of *Raga Shubha*; 18th century A.D. Jammu.

46. *Ibid.*, Acc. No. 223/270; Portrait of *Raga Pancham Srinuk*; 19th century A.D. Jammu.

47. *Ibid.*, Acc. No. 38/85; Portrait of *Raga Deepak*; 19th century A.D. Jammu.

48. *Ibid.*, Acc. No. 73; Portrait of Raga Bibhas; 19th century A.D. Jammu.

49. *Ibid.*, Acc. No. 41/88; Portrait of *Raga-Chandra-Kans*; 18th century A.D. Jammu.

50. *Ibid.*, Acc. No. 211/258; Portrait of *Raga Madhur*; 19th century A.D. Jammu. See Plate XV; (Fig. 1) Chapter 2.

51. *Ibid.*, Acc. No.174/221; Portrait of *Raga Malakuns*; 19th century A.D. Jammu.

52. Acc. No. 35/82; Portrait of *Raga Khokhar*; 18th century A.D. Jammu. Chapter 2, plate XVIII, (Fig. 2).

53. *Ibid.*, Acc. No. 187/234; Portrait of *Raga Binodas*; 19th century A.D. Jammu.

54. *Ibid.*, Acc. No. 212/256; Portrait of *Raga Basant*; 18th century A.D. Jammu.

55. Portrait; *Natraga*; Basohli; circa (1700-1720 A.D.). Bharat Kala Bhavan; Banaras. See Chapter 2; Plate XXIX, Fig. 3.

56. D.A.G.J.; Acc. No. 425; Portrait of *Ragini Bengali*; 19th century A.D. Jammu.

57. *Ibid.*, Acc. No. 385/406; Portrait of *Ragini Asavari*; 19th century A.D. Jammu.

58. *Ibid.*, Acc. No. 251/289; Portrait of *Ragini Basant*; 19th century A.D. Jammu.

59. *Ibid.*, Acc. No. 36/83; Portrait of *Ragini Sindhuri* of HIndol; 19th century A.D. Jammu.

60. *Ibid.*, Acc. No. 210/256; Portrait of *Ragini Karanataki*; 18th century A.D. Jammu.

61. *Ibid.*, Acc. No. 276/319; Portrait of *Ragini Ramkali*; 18th century A.D. Jammu.

62. *Ibid.*, Acc. No. 32/79; Portrait of *Ragini Dowhri of Hindole*; 18th century A.D. Jammu.

63. *Ibid.*, Acc. No. 5/52; Portrait of *Ragini Gaund Malkauns*; 19th century A.D. Jammu, Artist; Ruldoo. *Note:* In spite of the miniature painting *ragas* and *raginis* picture have also been painted by the Jammu painters on the wall-painting too. See Chapter 2. Plate XXXIV, Fig. 1. Portrait of *Ragini*, etc. A classification of all the *raga* and *ragini* is provided at the end of Guru *Granth Sahab* the sacred book of Sikh compiled by Guru Arjun Dev (1591-1606). The six principal *raga* are depicted as having five wife and eight sons each, which means that the scale of twenty-two notes can be manipulated in eighty four different ways to produce identifiably different melodies. The six main *raga* throughout India are the same–Bhairava, Malkaus, Hindola, Deepak, Shree and Megha–but the *ragini* associated with them very regionally. For instance, the *Granth Sahab* associates *Bhairva Raga* with the *ragini Bhairavi, Bilwali, Puniyaki, Bangali*, and *Aslekhi*, while in

Rajastani music it is associated with *Bhairvi*, *Nata malvi*, *Patmanjari* and *Lalita*. *Note : Shree Raga* has four wives *Bhairvi*, *Karnati*, *Gauri*, and *Sindhvi*, according to the *Granth Sahab* but in Rajasthan, five wives are mentioned: *Pancham*, *Asavari*, *Sita*, *Malhar*, *Kedar* and *Kumudini*. Apart from the season, the *raga* are also related to different parts of the day and night.

64. D.N. Shukla; *Royal Arts;* Faizabad (U.P.), India, Sept. 4, 1969; pp. 144-45. Hereafter referred as *R.A.*

65. Plate XXXIX; Portrait of a *Pahari Ragini*; Wall-painting of Ramnagar Palace. See Chapter 2

66. D.N. Shukla; *R.A.;* p. 145.

67. Plate XXII; D.A.G.J.; Acc. No.154; Portrait of *Pater Lekni Nayika*; 19th century A.D. Jammu. See Chapter 2.

68. D.A.G.J.; Acc. No. 158/205; Portrait of a *Chatrani Nayika*; 19th century A.D. Jammu.

69. *Ibid.*, Acc. No. 159/206; Portrait of a *Nayika Hastni*; 19th century A.D. Jammu.

70. *Ibid.*, Acc. No. 288/275; Portrait of a lady near a Spring; 20th century A.D. Jammu, See Chapter 2, Plate XXIII (Fig. 2).

71. *Ibid.*, Acc. No. 59/106; Portrait of a *Nayika Yawning* 19th century A.D. Jammu.

72. *Ibid.*, Acc. No.18/05; Portrait of a *Muor Priya Nayika*; 19th century A.D. Jammu. *Note:-* Women are classified into four types: The lotus (*Padmini*), the variegated (*Chitrini*), the conch-like (*Sankhini*) and elephant like (*Hestini*).

73. Plate VII; The Dilemma of the Heroine; Illustration *Rasamanjari*; Basohli; circa (1695 A.D.); D.A.G. Jammu.

74. *Ibid.*, See Chapter 2, (Fig. 2).

75. *Ibid.*, See Chapter 2, (Fig. 3).

76. Plate VII, See Chapter 2, (Fig. 1). On the Way to the Tryst; Illustration to the *Rasamanjari*; Basohli; (1690-1695 A.D.); D.A.G. Jammu.

77. Plate VI, *Parakiya Vasakasajja Nayaka*; Illustration to the *Rasamanjari*; Basohli (1760-1770 A.D.); D.A.G. Jammu, See Chapter 2, (Fig. 1).

78. *Ibid.*, Why This Hesitation My Love? Illustration to the Rasamanjari Basohli (1690-1695 A.D.); DAG Jammu, See Chapter 2, (Fig. 2).

79. *Ibid.*, On the Threshold Youth; Illustration to the *Rasamanjari*; Basohli, circa (1695 A.D.); D.A.G. Jammu. Why This Hesitation My Love? Illustration to the *Rasamanjari* Basohli (1690-1695 A.D.); D.A.G. Jammu, See Chapter 2, (Fig. 3).

80. Krishna Caitayana; *A History of the Indian Painting*: The Mughal Tradition; New Delhi; 1976; p. 62. Hereafter referred as *H.I.P.*

81. Mukandi Lal; *G.P.*; p. 23.

82. *Ibid.*, Why this Hesitation my love? Illustration to the Rasamanjari Basohli 1690-1695 A.D.; D.A.G. Jammu, See Chapter 2, Plate VI, (Fig. 2).

78. S.S.Charak; *Jammu Ragamala Painting*; New Delhi, 1998; pp. 39-40. Hereafter cited as J.R.P.

83. Plate IX. The Ecstray of love; illustration to the *Gita Govinda*; Basohli; 1730 A.D. Pb. Mm. Patiala, See Chapter 2, (Fig. 1).

84. Plate VIII; Sports of Krishna in Spring Time; illustration in the *Gita-Govinda*; Basohli; 1730 A.D. National Museum Delhi. See Chapter 2, (Fig. 3).

85. *Ibid.*, How Krishna wantoned in the wood; illustration to *Gita-Govinda* Basohli; 1730 A.D. National Museum Delhi. See Chapter 2, (Fig. 2).

86. Plato IX, Enter the power of love; O Beautiful; illustration to the *Gita-Govinda*; Basohli 1730 A.D; D.A.G. Jammu, See Chapter 2, (Fig. 2).

87. D.A.G.J; Acc. No. 54/101; Portrait of Krishna pulls Radha in a Cloudy Scene; 19th century A.D. Jammu.

88. *Ibid*; Acc. No 396; Portrait of Radha Krishna; 19th century A.D.; Jammu.

89. *Ibid*; Acc. No. 61/108, Portrait of Radha offering garland to Krishna; 19th century A.D. Jammu.

90. *Ibid*; Acc. No. 117/160; Portrait: Sri Krishna with umberalla; 19th century A.D.

91. *Ibid.*, Acc. No. 52/99; Portrait; Krishna and Radha, a love scene; 19th century A.D; Jammu. Also see Chapter 2, Plate XXIV; Fig. 3.

92. *Ibid*; Acc. No. 51/98; Krishna play on flute for Radha; 19th century A.D. Jammu. *Note:* This scene has also been painted on wall; see Plate XXVIII Figs. 1, Chapter 2, Painting of Miran Sahib Temple.

93. *Ibid*; Acc. No. 364/405, Portrait; Krishna combing Radha's hair; 19th century A.D Jammu. Note: This theme also known to this in the wall painting of Purmandal Temple; See Chapter 2, Plate XXXI (Fig. 2).

94. *Ibid*; Acc. No. 55/102; Radha and Krishna besize a cow;19th century A.D. Jammu.

95. *Ibid*; Acc. No. 50/97; Portrait; Krishna applying Tika to Radha. 19th century A.D. Jammu; Artist; Ruldoo.

96. *Ibid.*, Acc. No. 49/96; Portrait; Krishna and Radha sitting in a window; 19th century A.D.

97. *Ibid.*, Acc. No. 48/95; Krishna-Radha standing in a porch;18th century A.D. Jammu.

98. Plate XVI, D.A.G.J, Acc. No 138; Portrait Shiva and Parvati; Early 20th century A.D. Jammu, See Chapter 2.

99. Plate II; *The adoration of Vishnu*; illustration to *Bhagawat-Purana,* Basohli; early 18th century. Pb. Mm. Patiala. See Chapter 2.

100. Plate XXXXVI; Vishnu and Lakshmi; wall-painting of Saiva Math Mansear.

101. Plate IV; The diversion of the Jamuna; illustration to the *Bhagawat-Purana*; Basohli 1730 A.D. Pb. Mm. Patiala, See Chapter 2.

102. Plate V; *Krishna bringing the Parijata* from *Indra's heaven*; Illustration to the *Bhagawat-Purana* Tira-Sujanpur; 1780 A.D. See Chapter 2.

103. *Ibid.*, *Krishna swallows the forest fire*, Illustration to *Bhagawat–Purana*; Tira-Sujanpur; Early 18th century A.D. See Chapter 2.

104. Plate III, *Radha giving butter-milk* to Krishan; *Illustration to Bihari Sat Saiya*; Basohli 1690 A.D. Bharat Kala Bhawan Banaras. See Chapter 2.

105. Plate III; Krishna stealing the clothes of Gopies; Basohli: Also see plate XXXXIII Fig. 1, Chapter 2.

106. Dogra art Gallery Jammu; Acc. No. 80/127; Sri Krishna Chatur-Bhuja Roop appear to Arjuan; 19th century A.D. Jammu.

107. *Ibid*; Acc. No. 85/132; *Sanjaya relating the Mahabharata* to *Daratrashtra*; 19th century A.D. Jammu, See Chapter 2 Plate XXV; Fig. 1.

108. *Ibid*; Acc. No. 86/133; *Arjuna Approaches Sri-Krishna*, 19th century A.D. Jammu.

109. *Ibid*; Acc. No. 87/134; *Sri-Krishna and Arjuna*, 19th century A.D. Jammu.

110. *Ibid*; Acc. No. 89/136; Sri-Krishna teahes Arjun; 19th century A.D. Jammu.

111. *Ibid*; Acc. No. 101/148; *Sri Krishna and Arjun* move *towards battlefield*; 19th century A.D. Jammu.

112. Plate XXVII; Rama, Sita and Lakshmana in a forest; Wall-painting Purani-Mandi Temple, See Chapter 2.

113. Plate XXVI; Rama and Lakshmana returning to Ayodhya; wall-painting of Bhurj Temple. See Chapter 2.

114. Plate III, 'Sawan is the month of lover', illustration to the *Baramasa*; Early 18th century A.D. D.A.G. Jammu, See Chapter 2.

115. Plate X; D.A.G. Jammu, Acc. No. 445; Maharaja Gulab Singh a war procession; 19th century A.D. Jammu. See Chapter 2.

116. Plate XXXIII; Wall-Painting of Ramnagar Palace; Suchet Singh in a war procession. See Chapter 2.

117. Plate I; Raja Kirpal-l; Basohli (1690-1693) A.D. Pb. Mm. Patiala. See Chapter 2.

118. *Ibid*. Raja Dhiraj-Pal (1720-25 A.D.). *Ibid*.

119. Plate XXXV; A Cultural Scene attended by Raja Suchet Singh; Wall Painting of Ramnagar Palace. See Chapter 2.

120. Basil Gray; *Art in Islamic Period*, New Delhi 1981; pp. 173, 175, Hereafter referred as *A.I.P.*

121. Plate XXXVII; A Festival scene, Suchet-Singh's. Wall Painting of Ramnagar Palace. See Chapter 2.

122. Plate XXXVIII; A Marriage scene of Raja Suchet Singh, Wall Painting of Ramnagar Palace. See Chapter 2.

123. Plate XXXV; Raja Suchet Singh; a preparatory war Scene; Wall Painting of Ramnagar Palace. See Chapter 2.

124. Plate XXIV D.A.G.J; Acc. No. 105/52; *Sati Parikashan*, 18th century A.D. Jammu. See Chapter 2.

125. Plate V; Krishna Bringing the Parijata from Indra's Heaven; Illustration to the *Bhagwata Purana*; Tira-Sujanpur; 1780 A.D. See Chapter 2.

126. *Ibid*; Fig. 2.

127. Plate XVI; D.A.J.A; Acc. No. 138; Siva and Parvati; 20th century A.D. Jammu. See Chapter 2.

128. Plate XXII; D.A.G.J; Acc. No. 144/191, Invasion of the Monkey; 18th century A.D. Jammu. See Chapter 2

129. Plate XVII; Partap Singh on Horse Back; 19th century A.D. Jammu. See Chapter 2.

130. Plate XXXVIII; Suchet Singh on horse back, a Hunting scene, Wall Painting of Ramnagar Palace. See Chapter 2.

131. Plate XXXXVI; Vishnu & Laxmi, Saiva Math, Mansar Temple. See Chapter 2, Fig. 2.

132. Plate III; Sawan is the month of Lovers'; Illustration to *Baramasa*. Early 18th century A.D. D.A.G. Jammu. See Chapter 2 (Fig. 2).

133. *Ibid.*

134. *Ibid.*

135. M.S. Randhawa; *B.P.* p.17.

136. Mukandi Lal; *G.P.* p.19

137. Krishna Chaitanya; *A History of Indian Painting,* Pahari Tradition; New Delhi 1984; p. 5. Hereafter explained as *H.I.P.*

138. M.S. Randhawa & J.K. Galbraith; *Indian Painting*; New Delhi; 1968; p. 122. Hereafter referred as *I.P.*

139. Krishna Chaitanya; *H.I.P.*; p. 5.

140. M.S. Randhawa & J.K. Galbraith; *I.P.*; p. 122.

141. Krishna Chaitanya; *H.I.P.;* p. 5.

142. M.S. Randhawa & J.K. Galbraith; *I.P.*; p. 122.

143. *Ibid.*

144. *Ibid.*

145. M.S. Randhawa; *B.P.*; p. 19.

146. H. Goetz; *The Background of pahari Rajput Painting; (Roopa-Lekha)*; Vol. XXII No.1, Delhi April, 1951; p. 6.

147. M.S. Randnawa; *B.P.*; p. 19

148. *Ibid*; p. 20

149. Mukandi Lal; *G.P.*; p. 19

150. Charles Ellison Bates & Brevet, *A Gazetteer of Kashmir*; New Delhi, 1980; p. 214.

151. Krishna Chaitanya; *H.I.P.* p. 114.

152. *Ibid*; pp. 114-115.

153. Anand K. Coomaraswamy; *Introduction To the Indian Art*; New Delhi1931, 1969, p. 75. Hereafter explained as *I.I.A.*

154. J. Hutchison & J.Ph. Vogel; *History of the Punjab Hill States*; Reprinted, 1982; (Himachal Pradesh), p. 550. Hereafter wrote *as H.P.H.S.*

155. Krishna Chaitanya; *H.I.P.* pp. 121-122.

156. J. Hutchison and J. Ph. Vogel; *H.P.H.S.*, p. 585.

157. *Ibid.*

158. *Ibid.*, p. 586.

159. It was the ancient name of the Poonch Town describes in the Kalahan's *Rajatarangini* by M.A. Stein.

160. J. Hutchison and J. Ph. Vogel; *H.P.H.S.*, p. 724.

161. *Ibid.*

162. *Ibid.*

163. It has been discussed with the present *Kathabachak* (priest) on January 22, 2001.

164. *Gulabnama*, of Diwan Kripa Ram; From Persian to English Tr. by S.S. Charak; pp. 164-65. Hereafter cited as *G.N.*

165. Stated by the present priest of this temple in the March 1979 and by Shri Koushal Kumar, Raghunath Chowk Jammu, who is a descendent of

this family. (Mira Seth; *Dogra Wall Painting in Jammu and Kashmir*, Bombay, 1987, pp. 16-17, Hereafter wrote *as D.W.P.J.K.).*

166. *G.N.*; p. 166.

167. Mira Seth; *D.W.P.J.K.*; p. 26.

168. *Ibid.*, p. 14.

169. Plate XXVII; Rani Bhandrali, Purani Mandi Temple; Jammu. See Chapter 2.

170. Mira Seth; *D.W.P.J.K.*; pp. 18-19.

171. *Ibid*; p. 23.

172. Plate; XXVIII; Portrait of Krishna, fluting under a tree; Wall-Painting Miran Sahib Temple.

173. *Ibid.*, Portrait of Maharaja Gulab Singh as a Soldier; *Ibid.*

174. *Note:* Term '*Dogra*' is composed of three English and Hindi words i.e., Do + g + ra. So far its connotation is concerned. 'Do' in Hindi and two in English soothed of two alphabets i.e., D + O, 'D' stands for destroyers or injurious or Dasa i.e., real living *man* and 'O' stands for '*infinite*', i.e., 'God', 'Nam', 'Nad' or '*Kalma*'; 'G' stands for 'good' and 'ra' means '*way*' or '*thought*'. Thus, term 'Bahu' has also spiritually meaning which is put together at two Arabic words i.e., Ba + hu, 'Ba' means associate of 'God' i.e., 'Nam' kalma or spirit 'hu' also means 'God' which gives delight. And term 'Jambu' which is made of three Arabic words Ja + m + bu; 'Ja' means living being, 'm' stands for living *man* and 'bu' means smell out. Therefore, term '*Jambu*' is associated with *man* or rather living *man*, which is untrue and destructive one. There is a common term between the two that it '*Lochan*' which has been complied of two *Dogri* or Hindi words i.e., Lo + chan, 'Lo' means 'Light' and '*Chan*' means '*Pati*'. Hence, light or 'Nam' or 'God' 'Nad' is the father of all. (For the detail information kindly study the book of the same author entitled '*History of the Brahamans*'). *Note :* Term '*Kashmir*' is made of four English words that is Ka + sh + mi + r, the one hundred and twenty first hymn of the tenth book of the Rig-Veda has as the refrain of each of first nine verses: What god shall we adore with our oblation?

The word 'Ka' is the Sanskrit interrogative pronoun 'what 2'. In later times this interrogative was treated as a proper name, the question became an assertion, and the refrain of the hymn reads:

'Ka' is the god whom we shall adore with our oblation. 'Sh' stands for 'stainthood', 'mi', stands for living *man*, rather man and 'r' stands for 'way' or 'thought', that is 'father'.

In later Vedic literature 'Ka' is a synonym for Prajapati, Brahma, Vishnu and other gods. In the Puranas, 'Ka' appears as a recognised god, as a supreme god, with a genealogy of his own, perhaps even with wife. The Mahabharata identifies 'Ka' with Daksha, and the Bhagavata Purana applies the term to '*Kasyapa*' *Rishi* (A.C. Clayton; *The Rig Veda and Vedic Religion*; New Delhi, 1913, 1981).

2

Dresses

From seventeenth century onwards the paintings drawn by Dogra artists highlight the social, political, economic and aesthetic aspects of Dogra way of life. The artists spectacularly used brush and colour combinations in order to reflect Dogra royalty and the urban panorama. The paintings include the twinkling use of colour for ornaments, hairstyles and of dresses. The Dogras, as is evident from various paintings used to wear turban or caps of various styles. The costumes for the upper and lower part of the body included a simple and printed *jama* or *gheredar-jama* or side fastening *frack-coat* with a simple and beautiful sash or girdle round with waist. Paintings reveal that they also weared *achkan, farji, kameez* or *kurta, coat, dhoti, lungi, paijama, pant*, etc. Among Dogra female *choli* or blouse or bodice, *peswaj, kameez, dupattas* or *odhani, ghaghra* (*lengha*), *paijama, salwar* (drawer), etc. were very common. These dresses beared Rajputs, Mughals, Sikhs and European fashion together local varieties. For example, the portrait depicting '*sawan the month of lovers*'[1] of the early 18th century by *Baramasa*. Krishna has been displayed wearing an orange colour *jama* of Mughalian style. Whereas Radha is shown wearing a light-purple colour of *choli* or bodice and red gold *ghaghra* of Rajasthani style. This painting also contain a party of the female musician wearing inferior kind of dress incomparison to Radha (Fig. 2). This painting reflects the existence of composite Mughal and Rajasthani fashion in Dogra life. Another example of the composite fashion is of *Radha giving butter-milk to Krishna*.[2] In this picture, Krishna is wearing a scarf and ornaments on the upper part of the body. While Radha's upper part of the body is half naked and the her lower part of the body is displayed as wearing a transparent white *ghaghra* of Rajasthani style over the Mughalian red and black *paijama* with lining design (Fig. 4).

Again the war procession portrait of Maharaja Gulab Singh[3] demonstrates that Gulab Singh, Suchet Singh and other Generals of army together with the soldiers of Gulab Singh are wearing a Sikh style of aggressive turbans. Turbans of various styles explicity reveal the status of the high and low rank soldiers, e.g. Gulab Singh has been shown wearing superior kind of *pag* along with a *kalagi*, and rest of his Generals were displayed without *kalagi* and his army personals are shown wearing inferior kind of turban. Same is the case, with the upper and lower garments, Gulab Singh has been shown wearing more superior kind of garments than his Generals, and Generals have been displayed wearing more superior incomparison with the army personels (Fig. 1). The European fashion influence, can be trace out from the picture of Raja Suchet Singh as a soldier.[4] He has been displayed wearing an European style of jacket, pant and boot (Fig. 1). Moreover, European fashion influence is also indicated in the picture of Raja Partap Singh[5] (Fig. 2).

Since Vedic age, certain religious customs are elaborated in the *Girhya-Sutras, Kandika,* 10-Rule, 7 and 12 that on the depicting day on which the student is going to receive the first initiation. On that day, early in the morning, parents give him to eat, cut his hair, wash him, deck him with ornaments, and put on him a (new) garments[6] of a Vaisya, of wool.[7] It appears that costume from the earliest Vedic era to the first century B.C. played a very important role in expressing the advancement of the material culture among human race. In India owing to its warm climate the article of clothing in the beginning were quite simple like *dhoti, dupattas, safa, kamarband, sari* and *odhani* with exuberance of ornaments were sufficient for the women. Their simple articles of dress were, however, worn in different styles in order retain aesthetics and touch.[8] In the *Yuan-Chwang*, the inner clothing and outward attire of the both male and female (people) was not tailored at all. The men wind a strip of cloth round the waist and upto the armpits and leave the right shoulders bare. The women wear a long robe which covers both shoulders and falls down loose.[9] After 7th century the costumes and the ornaments as depicted in sculptures and paintings assume conventionalized character and hence are not of much importance to the history of the costume.[10] The reign of Harsha (1089-1101 A.D.) is a high watermark figure in the history of Kashmir for several innovations. Kalhana's[11] *Rajatarangini,* mentions that nobody in court was allowed without patterned garment (*acitravastrah*) and scantily dressed (*alpaparicchadah*) and nobody dared to enter the royal places without a turban (*vigtosnisah*).[12] Ear-rings were the sole privilege of the kings and who dared to infringe were punished.[13] Gradually, such customary restrictions were relaxed and the masses were allowed to wear parel and ornaments of their taste.[13] Ladies, too, were encouraged to use floral ornament, collyrium, short-jackets and the typically long leather garments like a *lahanga*.[14] The impact of the Islamic invasions on Indian dress was extensive and during the reign of the Timurid dynasty the upper strata of all over the northern India and in Deccan, from palace servants to Rajputs warriors and to well-to-do merchants to princes, gradually adopted some variation of *jama*, the buttoned coat of the Mughals were buttoned coats with any description were formerly unknown in India. The women of India, much more conservative than their menfolk, wore the three-piece costume of Rajasthani style i.e., skirt (*ghaghra*), the bodice (*choli*) and the handkerchief (*odhani* or *dupatta*). But the men dressed themselves in imitation of court wears. The heroes in contemporary miniatures of *Ramayana* and the *Mahabharata*, and the lover in the delectably *nayika-nayaka* series (love affairs in picture) are dressed in an elegant Mughal court turbans and the latest fashions in buttoned coats. (CP, Plates XXII, XXIX, XXVII).[15]

In the time of Babur, cloak (*pyrahan*)[16] was also used by the people of India. The contribution of the Mughals, for example, *Akbarnama*, mentions that on the way back to conquered India, the governor of Herat invested his troops to Humayun with handsome *khilat's*[17] of satin and brocade (*kamkhab*) made from Yezd, and silk (*dara'tha*) made of Mashhad and Khaf, alongwith velvet cloaks (*balaposh*)[18] to every soldier and servants with *Tabriz tumaan*,[19] for his daily expenses.[20] In *Tusz-I-Jahangiri*, it is mentioned that an old turban (*sar-band*),[21] a coat (*qaba*),[22] a *farji*,[23] a shawl (*parmnarm*)[24] drawers (*izar*),[25] etc. were the common dresses of Indian people. The presents of special robes were also presented to Humayun turban fitted with a jewels and ornament, besides a horse and an elephant[26] by the Chief Haret.

Sikh rules, particularly Maharaja Ranjit Singh, besides, the traditional *pagri,* in cold weather, used a *angraka* (coat) which was tied over the chest and reached to the knees, the trousers fell in many folds down to the ancle. On the whole he worn a mantle lined with skins. The entire costume was, as yellow green *pashmina* worn by him. In summer, he wore a white muslin. During festival of Basant he used straw-coloured dress, he wrote with a slight intermixture of green. In earlier days of his rule, he used to appear in silver ornaments. But in later days he never wore any embroidery, brocade, or rich ornaments of any sort.[27]

In Jammu tradition, paintings also have copious references of the costumes which were used in different seasons. The portrait of '*a woman in yellow dress*'[28] demonstrates the spring season which has commenced. The woman is shown with a waving handfan (Fig. 1). The painting of a '*women with sitar*'[29] displays the condition of the areas in 18th century A.D. The background colour, depicts in Jammu great lawlessness and a great need was to establish a strong and peaceful empire. It shows that Sikh rule was at declining stage, at that time (Fig. 2). There is another picture, for example which displays the winter season of the Jammu region. In this picture Maharaja Ranbir Singh[30] wore a woollen jacket over the dress (Fig. 1). With the establishment of Dogra rule (1846 to 1947 A.D.), the common people mostly used plain cotton clothes almost similar to that of counterparts in the neighbouring plains. The dress-habits of the people of this area have undergone a radical change under the consumeristic pressure of readymade clothes from the markets in the plains which were freely available in the village shops and were being increasingly preferred by the people, as being cheaper and of wide variety from the traditional tailor-made.[31]

A beautiful example of Dogra folk song pertaining to the dresses and the ornaments preferably work by the Dogra rulers during 18th and 19th centuries elaborates a picture of Dogra royalty. It follows as under:

Dogri Lok Geet

"जम्मुआं मोरू दे मैहल बने ते,
कटडै बने चबारे।
मैहल मोरू दै फिरै सफेदा,
गासै दा त्रुट्टी पौन्दे तारे।
पंज सत्त मोरू दियां मंजां सुन चन
होर सनै लगामै घोडे।
शिड़का मोरू दे घोडे चलदे,
टुप टुप सुम्बे मारे।
गल मोरू दै कैंठा सोब्बै,
कन्नै सोब्बन बाले।
मखमली मोरू पुशाक लान्दा
साफै दे बुम्बल चबारे।
चंगी मोरू पुशाक लान्दा
जोडैगी जड़ेदे सतारे।
चोर गलै दा बिजली लिश्कै,
अम्बरै दा त्रुट्टी पौन्दे तारे।
मोरू बचारा ऐ शकीनी,
अस विपदा दे मारे।"[32]

Tr. into English:

"Raja having the construction of Mahal in Jammu.

Kataray having double storey building.
Now Mahal became white,
As it looks like that a star shattered from the sky.
Raja having five to seven buffaloes.
Besides these, Raja having the horse along with saddles.
Raja's horses run on road, making the sound of feet's, tup, tup,
Raja having beautiful *kantha* around the neck,
Having smart ear ring's (*balu*),
Raja wears *Makmali* (*kurta*) tunic.
Safa having long tuft,
Raja wears a beautiful *kurta* (*tunic*)
Pair of shoes having beautiful stars.
Thundering light is twinkling as from the unknown track.
As stars shattered from the sky,
Raja only keeps his liking, but we are the affordless people".

Male-Dresses

On the basis of the available paintings Dogra dresses (of the men only) can be divided into two parts:

1. Traditional Dogra dresses, and
2. The dresses depicting foreign influence.

Head-Dresses

18th and 19th centuries paintings demonstrate that Dogras both men and women covered their heads with a garment, a *dupatta* or a *pag* or a *cap*. Here, we see head-dress does not only covers the head against the warm or cold climate, but it had some socio-religions significance also. For example, the portrait of *Panchvakta*[33] Raja Ranbir Singh is shown worshipping his deity. His head has been shown covered by a loose style of turban of yellow and black colour above the red *patka*. It shows that he is praying for the power from the deity; as he had certain problem in the area, as is indicated from the colour scheme of the head dress though shown as a stunch follower of Hinduism (Fig. 4). Another example, shows social and military status of a person, as the picture of Gulab Singh with his army personels in a war *procession*. Where all, the king, the Generals and soldiers are wearing a head dress of its status and economic position.[34] The style of head-dress displays a token of respect and status. In this plate, one can observe that Gulab Singh has worn an aggressive Sikh style of *pag* which shows the martial spirit of a soldier. Above the turban, a beautiful *kalagi* has been wornr by him, and his Generals, including. Suchet Singh and kings youngster son Ranbir Singh, have been shown with simple *kalagi* as a head-dress in comparison with Gulab Singh. On the other hand, soldiers have been shown wearing less attractive head-dress of different colours. Thus, Dogra head-dress does not only protect heads in the battlefield, but it also was used as a protection from the cold climate of the region. In addition, head-dress demonstrate the rank of the wearer. Gulab Singh is shown wearing a costly turban. It also appears that he has not only displayed himself as a great General, but also as a responsible ruler (Fig. 1). In spite of the socio-religious factor, head-dress demonstrates class and cultural identity of the region. As mentioned earlier the style of the turbans of Dogra army indicate that they directly worked under the command of Maharaja Ranbir Singh of Jammu and Kashmir State.[35] Moreover, turban was thought as a symbol of good fortune, as it has been superbly remarked in the *Akbarnama*. When in a grand function, the brother of Humayun Muhammad Hindaal in a perfect reverence; took off his own fortune cap (*taj*) in the midst of the crowd and placed it on the star-brushing head of Akbar.[36] The head-dress known as cap was generally also used by Mughals as a token of honour, respect and reverence in played an religious function.

Turbans

Paintings also depicting *dastar-bandi* played an auspicious role from time to time. It was a coronation of a ruler or in other auspicious functions of the society. It always was a sign of respect. The custom of wearing the *pagri* or a turban was in vogue even in the Satavahana period.[37] It has two names *pag* or *pagri*.

Basically, the head-dress made from fabric as distinguish worn by Hindu deities came to literature and paintings and took the form of a turban of an unstitched kind. There are many names that one comes across including *ushmisha, kirita, patta, vestans, veshtanapatta, shiroveshtani.*[38] The style of wearing the turban evidently varied as much as in ancient and medieval India. In the relief's of the Bharhut of the Sunga period turban was phased twice in front of the forehead in order to cover the bun-shaped hair-do and two ends of the turban were tucked into it. In the second style the whole head was covered with a heavy[39] and a stone head from the Sarnatha who wears a *pagri* of the same style as found in Mughal paintings.[40] It is said that Firoz Shah Tughlaq and his courtiers the effected dress reforms. He also have worn *kulah,* costing a lac of *tanka* which belonged to his predecessors[41] and at the Idd festival the royal court musicians wore yellow robes and red turbans *tanka.*[42] In the time of Babar and after the Babar turbans were modified and took the shape of *kuka* (a kind of pointed skull-up). It is very tall styled cap since Humayun's days[43] (1530-1540 A.D.). From 1555 to 1556 A.D. a typical Akbari shape turban became simpler than Jahangir's times.[44] In the time of

Shahjahan (1627-1659 A.D.), the turban was made of three different patterned pieces of gold, a much more modified form.[45]

When he was in his forties Maharaja Ranjit Singh (1809-1846 A.D.), had rich costume, though they were simple and soldierly; a little white turban of the finest muslin carefully tied and brought down over the left ear[46] known as *safa*. However, a great multi-coloured turban, in Sikh style surmounts his head, his keen eyes shrewdly turned to the right as if to sense a lurking of threat[47] about a situation in which Jammu was badly effected with lawlessness. At that time a cap or a *pagri* that traveller might wear as enough for the temptation to plunder and violence.[48] It is also elaborated that Dogra rulers were used to wear a sort of cloth helmet flowing down back of the head. This had the effect a flattening the top of the head and was probably used to hide the long hair of Sikh males before it became fashionable to put it into a bun at the top of the head. The faces shown in the painting were of modern Sikh and the style is European.[49] The turbans of the royal classes were often decorated with a jewelled ornament holding a plume. Raja's sometimes also used to wore fresh flowers in the turban.[50] According to F.S. Ajjazuddin Raja, Hira Singh wore a profusion of jewel in his turban and around his neck and carriers a black shield across his back.[52]

The head-dress of the people was generally a skull-cap, but Rajput rules used two or more turbans of different colours. One immediately surrounded around the head a cap called *pagri* the other tied in heavy folds over to the right ears was called the *safa* and dyed in various colours, and was further ornamented by the narrow bands of gold and silver tinsel.[53] It is said that a special *darbar* was held by the Maharaja on the Basant Panchmi to honour the coming of spring, everyone on that day wore yellow, dressed wholly in that colour.[53] Ananda K. Coomaraswamy narrates, that effects of white or flowered costumes and the white often delicately relieved by the back dots of rosary. (Plate XXXIII) almost all placed in their turbans a flower or a peacock feather, a custom still prevailing in the hills.[54] It is a custom adhered only to the Dogra families to wear a saffron colour of *pag* or *pagri* for wedding guests (*baratis*). Some people also use a white turban muslin *safa* or mica-starched *pagri* with its one end made into upright tuft and other falling on the back like a pig-tail.[55]

Varieties of the turbans as depicted in the paintings of the period are discussed as under:

1. One variety of the head-dress is detected from the picture of *Raga Khokhar*.[56] Portrait shows that a sitar bearer musician wore a readymade white compact turban alongwith a plume in tuft manner. It is an Indian turban, worn in Gujarat. The making of the turban

shows that artist had a mastery over his art and had enjoyed reputation among people (Fig. 2).

2. There is another distinguished variety of the turban, made by the same artist on the same picture.[57] Portrait displays that a drummer has worn an elegant type of *pataka* of red and white colour, tied by the unusual strings. It bears Marwar fashion influence. No doubt, turban is of inferior cloth, but the colour combination of the turban has given it a majestic view and explicitly shows artists mastery (Fig. 2).

3. The picture of Babur[58] displays his deep concentration for the future ambition. He wears a Turkish style of head-dress known as *kulha*, a type of *pagri*. The tiers of the turban have been beautifully arranged around the cap. Cap is displayed as it is coming out from the tiers of the turban. The expression of turban shows that he had an idea to establish an empire. *Pag* shows Turkish fashion influence (Fig. 1).

4. Another distinguish variety of the head-dress is called turban or *pag* as depicted in the picture of Khwaja Khizer.[59] It appears that a red cap (*kulah*) over which a turban's cloth of parrot green has been arranged in a artistic way. The pattern of the turban looks like a hand-made paper boat. The colour scheme of the turban provides an image that he has come down from snowfall areas and now has arrived in the lush green areas and lays down the foundation stone of his empire in India. He was the son-in-law of Babar. *Pag* shows Persian fashion influence (Fig. 4).

5. The picture of Sultan-Abu-Said[60] demonstrated another variety of head-dress. It appears that he used to prefer a white Turkish turban. The cloth of the turban is arranged around the cap (*kulah*) in upward twisted manner. Turban has been made of white cotton cloth and peacock feathers are placed on it. The colour of the turban makes one to understand that he is facing tough time though have a desire to establish a peaceful empire. *Pag* shows Turkish fashion influence (Fig. 4).

6. This variety of the head-dress is also present in the picture of Umar-Sheikh-Mirza.[61] He wears blue (*Krsna*) and white colour of printed *pagri* in twisted manners around the cap (*kulah*) with peacock feathers a Turkish traditional head-dress. The colour combination of turban and its expressions shows explicitly explains that he is removing eco-political barriers so that peace for economic development in restored (Fig. 2).

7. The picture of Rai Raodeh Dharmasalwala on camel back[62] displayed another kind of the *pagri* which is made of cotton. It is a simple turban. The pattern of the head-dress has been shown over lapping layers. It is a traditional Dogra style. The portrait is of the picture of the ship in the desert and the reflection of the *pag* show that

he had to proceeded towards the Rajputana States for acquiring economic as well as military help against the Mughal (Fig. 1).

8. The distinguish variety of the turban, is detected in the picture of Raja Jagat Singh.[63] In this picture he has been shown in all his glory. He wears a superior kind of *pagri* as that of the Jahangir. Its pattern is a stylistic and its lower end is terminating by an ornamental band with peacock feathers in whisk style. The turban is placed on the head in a way that he challenges the Mughal power and is ready to face any kind of eventuality. *Pagri* shows Mughalian fashion influence (Fig. 1).

9. This style of turban or *pag* explored from the picture of Raja Kirpal Pal[64] of Basohli. Who wears a simple kind white turban made of superior cotton, tied in a criss-cross ways in backward slopping over a cap, without *kalagi*, or a plume. Two female, one *chouri*-bearer and another the attendant are serving to fire the smoking *hookah* and one as a security personel. He is seated comfortably. His style of seating and simple style of white turban reflects the message that Raja Kirpal Pal is pondering about the future plans for the development of his kingdom. Turban shows Mughalian fashion influence (Fig. 1).

10. Another variety of the head-dress is detected in the picture of Raja Dhiraj Pal.[65] He was the contemporary of Raja Udai Singh of Chamba. He wears an artistic style of white turban, tied by a orange piece of cloth. He has been displayed having a *mala* in his hand a pointed mark on the forehead below the three horizontal lining of the ashes and an orange piece of cloth has been placed to tie the turban. The colour scheme of the head-dress shows that he is meditating on some *mantras* of the Hindu religions philosophy expecting happiness and contentment. To some extent the pattern of the turban appears like the modern cap of the army officer. *Pag* shows Mughalian fashion influence (Fig. 2).

11. The portrait of the Rafi-ud-Darjat[66] demonstrates another Mughalian style of turban made of a fine piece of cloth of white and blue colour. It has backward slopping, with separate piece of cloth. The cloth of the *pag* has lining design both vertical and horizontal. Emperor has a white rose in his hand, which yet has to open its mouth. Moreover, he has a dagger in his *kamarband*. The expressions of the colour scheme show that he has laid down his empire, but there were number of barriers in his way. The white *jama* shows, after removing the barriers, a peaceful empire could be established and then can proceed a progress and prosperity in the state (Fig. 3).

12. Another variety of the turban can be found in the picture of Raja Kishan Singh.[67] It appears that he wears Mughalian style of turban having backward slopping, but pressed in projection and wrapped on a cap. An ornamental fillet decorated with multi-colour jewels in floral

design has been tied round it for its beautification. The theme of turban and his dress demonstrates that he was a dauntless man, and challenges the Mughal power as reflected from the postures of his shield and sword. *Pagri* also shows Mughalian fashion influence (Fig. 3).

13. The painting of Raja Jai Singh[68] demonstrates another kind of the turban. He wears an artistic style of turban of chocolate colour having upward projected design. It has been decorated by a beautiful head-ornament having white plume and peacock feather as in the form of *kalagi*. It shows Katoch (Kangra) fashion influence (a tribe of the Rajput clan used to live in Bhadrawha area also). The reflection of the turban shows that he had decided to live a peaceful life. It also reflects a Dogra traditional head-dress (Fig. 2).

14. Another variety of the *pagri* is delineated in the picture of Raja Hataf Bandral.[69] It appears that a fine piece of cloth has been tied round the conical cap (*kulha*) over which a turban is tied. It is a backward slopping type of *pagri*. Instead of a fine piece of cloth, a conical slopping cap has been decorated with floral design of pearls and diamonds, and the fine piece of cloth is ties to the turban, and decorated with switching beads of glass. The mode of the turban demonstrates that he was a powerful ruler and had a will to challenge Sikh state. *Pag* shows Mughalian fashion influence (Fig. 1).

A Dogri writer has commendably described the colours of the Dogra turban in the following folk song depicting an orthodox beliefs of Dogras.

"जे सिपाई पग्गां बनदे, ते रग गुट्टिऐ दा।
के भरोसा करना, नाजो खुट्टिएँ दा?
जे सिपाई पग्गां बनदे, वे रग अम्मिएं दा।
के भरोसा करना नाजों, लम्मिएं दा?
जे सिपाई पग्गां बनदे, बे रग किक्करैं दा।
के भरोसा करना, सक्के मित्तरैं दा?
जे सिपाई पग्गां बनदे, वे रग धाइए दा।
के भरोसा करना? सक्के भाइऐं दा।"[70]

Tr. into English:

It is a chat between the husband and a wife. Husband says to his wife:

"If the soldiers wear the turban of *gutta* (it has different colours i.e., yellow, orange, mahroom, etc.).
I don't have a trust on the fickle minded lady.
If the soldiers wear the turban of mango colour
I don't have a trust on the moment.
If the soldiers wear the turban of Kikkar.[71]
I don't have a trust on the fast friend.

If the soldiers wear the turban of whey (white colour)
I don't have a trust on the real brother."

15. A distinguish kind of the head-dress is observed in the picture of Raja Kharaq Singh.[72] His compact turban, projected like a hook from the backside is a light turban of its own style (i.e. Sikh) decorated with a head-plate. Picture shows that had he an idea of extending his empire upto the Silah territory (Fig. 2).

16. The another typical variety of the head-dress is detected in the painting of Sher Singh.[73] He is wearing a compact light colour turban. Above the turban, a scarf type of a white piece of cloth having ornamental border, is shown covering the nape of neck dangling over the shoulders in a wrapped form. A beautiful head-plate has been placed on it, along with a plume or peacock feather. The reflection of white turban shows that he was pondering how to control the borders of the Sikh empire (Fig. 3).

17. The portrait of Naunihal Singh[74] exhibited different kind of the head-dress. He wears an artistic style of turban, which has been arranged in a lose manner and it's one end is shown coming out from the nape of the neck falling on the back. A beautiful head-ornament has been placed on it, along with a peacock feather. It was a Sikh style of head-dress. Picture shows that he was an angry man (Fig. 4).

18. Another variety of the head-dress known as turban is located from the picture of a *nayaka*[75] of the *Rasamanjari*. It appears that *nayaka* wears a beautiful backward slopping high turban of henna colour. The tiers of the *pag* have been arranged in overlapping manners in circular shape. A beautiful head-plate with peacock feather has also been tied on the turban by a white beaded chain of strings. *Nayika* wears a blue (*Krsna*) colour of dress which demonstrates, that she was coying to her lover. *Pag* also shows Mughalian fashion influence (Fig. 2).

19. The picture of a Rajput prince[76] demonstrates another but different kind of the turban. It displays that a costly piece of cloth has been tied round a cap (*kulah*) over which a turban is bound. A cap (*kulah*) is shown supported with a flanked type of a fine piece of a cardboard at the nape of the head. It has been decorated with a peacock feather, on the frontial top, three beautiful card of golden tinsels are attached to it, and have been shown dangling on the right side below the shoulder. The reflection of the turban displays that he was accumulating his power. It shows Balochistani Pathan's fashion influence (Fig. 2).

20. Another portrait of a *nayaka*[77] presents another beautiful kind of *pag*. It is a Mughalian style of turban of backward slopping, tied by an ornamental piece of cloth. The colour combination of the turban is a sign of a happy and prospers life (Fig. 1).

21. One more distinguish variety of the *pagri* is emanated in the picture of another *nayaka*.[78] He wears a Mughalian style of *pag*. It shows that a pinkish (*piyazi*) piece of cloth has been tied by a ornamental band, decorated by placing the *kalagi* on it. The colour scheme of the head-dress is a sign of health and wealth. He wears a blood colour of *jama* of floral design. It appears that he was a young, enthusiastic and powerful man of the areas. Turban shows Mughalian fashion influence (Fig. 2).

22. A peculiar variety of the head-dress can be found in the picture of physician[79] (*hakeem*). He wears a readymade turban[80] of parrot colour in scorpion style. It appears that he is inquiring and checking a lady and prescribing her. Her mother-in-law is listening about the treatment carefully from the physician. The colour of the turban and its style, of a patient, who is in pain, after getting the dose of medicine patient has got relief as is shown in the picture's expression. *Pag* shows Gujarati[81] fashion influence (Fig. 2).

23. The portrait of '*birth of Krishna*'[82] show that Yashoda intended to migrate so as to save the life of Krishna form his *mama* (Kans). One of her attendant is shown making the request to Yashoda not to migrate. She has been shown turning down his request. Her security personals and the animals (dogs) have also been shown so sad on this news. The colour scheme of the picture i.e., blood red, pinkish, chocolate, black (*Krsna*), white, black, etc. show that this moment is for joy and sorrow. On as the birth of Krishna, they are shown happy, but on the issue of migration of Yashoda along with Krishan, they are displayed so sad. Here, we see security personels of Yashoda wear backward slopping turbans, made of inferior kind of stuff incomparison with the Chiefs mentioned above; there is one more variety of the head-dress or turban which has been worn by the attendances of Yashoda. They wore simple backward pressed style of Mughalian turban. It shows Mughalian fashion influence (Fig. 2).

24. The portrait of the Gulab Singh in a war procession[83] exhibits that he had to wear multi-colours of turban, i.e. red, white and green of Sikh style in forward slopping , decorated by putting a plume on the turban. It demarcates the status of a Chief, Generals and soldiers. It depicts that as soon as Gulab Singh occupied the throne of Jammu and Kashmir state. There was an uproar around the borders. He suppressed it. The face expressions as well as the aggressive style of turban conveys the message. Moreover, the colour combination of the turban is conveying to adjoining countries, a message for mutual co-existence with an intension to exploit natural resources for the economic development. The picture of Ranbir Singh displays a yellow dress which impresses that the Sikh power was fading and the power was above to

be transferred into the hands of Gulab Singh. Turban shows Sikh's fashion influence (Fig. 1).

25. Another kind of turban was weared by Gulab Singh.[84] It was of green and gold colour, over the red *pataka* in a loose manner having rolling tiers and decorated by a head-plate. The colour combination of the wearing turban displays that Jammu and Kashmir state was under his complete sway and his territorial expansion was in full swing with powerful administrative skill. It shows that he had established a strong empire, and there was no threat form the outside. *Pag* also displays Sikh fashion influence (Fig. 1).

26. One more variety of the turban is located in the picture of Gulab Singh as a soldier.[85] It was a coca-cola colour of *pag* having rolling tiers, decorated by *kalagi* (peacock feather) on it. The expression of the turban as well as the whole dress shows that before proceeding to war, Gulab Singh used to worship god or goddesses i.e. Radha and Krishna, etc. for the stake of accumulation of power and honours. The colour of the turban messages that at that time Jammu and Kashmir state was in dark phase. *Pag* shows Sikh fashion influence (Fig. 3).

27. A *darbar* scene of the Maharaja Gulab Singh[86] displayed a new style of the turban. The portrait to some extent has been damaged, however; by a close observation one can hardly see three different styles of turbans. In the first place: a different style of Maharaja Gulab Singh turban, is a loose style of turban or *pag* and its one end is hanging over the right side of the chest. The pinkish (*pyazi*) colour of turban and its layers show that the *darbar* has been held for the future plans of the state with an intension to make his administration more effective. Red colour of the *pagri* or *safa* demonstrates the desire to make the state a powerful state. Turban shows Sikh fashion influence (Fig. 1).

28. This style of the head-dress is detected in the picture of Gulab Singh's subordinate.[87] The turban has loose style, but its folds have been swathed in different manners having crescent pattern of design and its one end is displayed hanging over the right side of the chest. Ordinarily, it seems that the princes wore turban with hanging end called *safa*. The pinkish (*pyazi*) colour demonstrates the happiness of the state and will to introduce considered programme for future development of the State. It shows Sikh fashion influence (Fig. 1).

29. Another *darbari* of Maharaja Gulab Singh[88] wears a red colour *pagri*. The one end of the turban's cloth is shown sprouting out from the top as a tuft (*wunmbal*) and dangling on the nape of the neck. It was a Dogra's traditional head-dress known as *safa*. Tuft and colour of the turban shows that the power of the Gulab Singh was increasing and becoming strong day by day. He had also a great ambition to

strengthen his country (Fig. 1). As a Dogri writer in a local folk song explains the dignity and status of the turban of a Rajput of the areas under the Dogra rule (1846-1947) in the following few lines:

"साफा बन्नी मियां घोडी जे चडेया,
लोग कैहन्दे पिण्डै दा पटबारी"[89]

Tr. into English:

"Turban tied on head, *mian* rode on a horse
People call him as a *patwari* of the village"

30. In the painting of Gulab Singh[90] in a war procession, soldiers have been displayed wearing different colours of head-dress i.e., yellow, light pinkish (*pyazi*), blue (*krsna*) and white. The folds of the turban's cloth are shown as have been arranged in an artistic ways and its one end is shown coming out, form the back falling on the shoulder. It was called as *safa*. The colour combination of the turban shows that there was a political problem, but they were determined to fight with full strength for the peace and happiness of the area. It was also a Dogra's traditional head-dress or *pag* (Fig. 1).

31. A typical variety of the head-dress we trace out in the picture of Raja Suchet Singh.[91] He wears white and green colour of *pagri* and it has been arranged in a stylistic manners. It has been shown circular in manner from the above and its one end is displayed coming out from the neck falling on the left shoulder, decorated with a head-plate. It is a variety of the *safa* but it shows Sikh fashion influence. The pattern of his wearing and its colour scheme shows that there was certain a problem in his relationship of Gulab Singh. The style of holding the sword shows that he was not in a mood to fight against him, but he is shown considering over it and tolerating that in the days to come good-relation will be cultivated between them (Fig. 2).

32. The head-dress known as *pataka*, depicted in the picture of Raja Suchet Singh.[92] It was a simple kind of head-dress of read colour likely to be a cap. A beautiful head-plate along with peacock feather has been placed on it. The style of wearing the *pataka* and its colour displays that he was leading a peaceful and happy life at that time. Plate XXXII, Fig. 1, a *darbar* scene of his time shows that it was a popular dress in the areas. His army personels are shown wearing a simple *pataka* without *kalagi*. It was a compact head-dress and shows Sikh fashion influence (Fig. 1).

33. The portrait of Raja Ranbir Singh[93] demonstrated another variety of the *pag*. It shows that it was a high turban, made of superior kind of cloth of gold and white colour, and has been worn over the black *pataka's*, *kalagi* has also been placed on it. Turban has rolling tiers and Ranbir Singh has shown an aged man. The colour scheme of the turban and its rolling tiers display that Jammu and Kashmir

State at that time was prospering and there was a peace in the area. But black colour of *pataka* is indicating that there were certain rebellion because the western influences. Turban depicts Sikh fashion influence. Yellow colour of the jacket is indicated that a change is going to take place in near future (Fig. 1).

A beautiful example of a full-dress is given by a Dogri writers which was preferred by the Dogra elites from 17th century onwards as discussed in the following local folk verses:

Writer Express:

"ल०भा जम्मुआँ जनेहा नेइयी शैहर मिकी,
इस देसे जनेहा देस नेई, इस भैसे,
जनेहा भेस नेई, चुडी घटन्ने दा ते,
पग्गा–साफे दा रलदा पलेस नेई।
चगां लग्गा ई चोगा तिल्लेदार मिकी"[94]

Tr. into English:

"They elaborated:
There is no city incomparison to Jammu,
There is no other country like this,
Having nor any dress like it.
The pleats of the *suthan* and the tiers of the *pag, safa* are matchless.
Looking nice *achkan* to me."

34. Yet another variety of the head-dress known as turban, is uncovered in the picture of Raja[95] likely to be Ranbir Singh. The layers of the *pag* have been arranged in overlapping formation one after another in the golden lines. The reflection of the turban shows that he was a young man, leading a happy life and having good economic status. It is a blood-red colour of *pag*. *Pag* depicts Sikh fashion influence (Fig. 3).

35. The picture of *panchvakta*[96] man in appearance with Maharaja Ranbir Singh. He has been shown worshipping a deity for the accumulation of power before going for a war. He has yellow and black colour of *pagri*, above the red *pataka's*. He has vertical lining marks on the forehead. He wears a loose style of turban as usually worn at home. However, the colours scheme of the turban demonstrates that he is a follower of Hinduism and there were certain problems in the country and red colour *pataka* is being displayed that he is praying for the accumulation of energy. *Pagri* shows Sikh fashion influence (Fig. 4).

36. This variety of the turban or *pagri*, in the picture of Maharaja Partap Singh[97] on horse back, presents a yellow colour of *pagri* and is decorated by a head-plate with peacock feather. This is a high turban of a young man. The layers of the turban have been swathed in

overlapping formation one after another. The colour of the turban with yellow dress show that transfer of power has been taken place from Ranbir Singh to Partap Singh. But the general concept of the dress demonstrates that a change is going on in the society, because at that time national movement of India has been launched throughout India and Western ideological influences have been fully permeated in India. Moreover, oneness colours of the dress depicts that at that time there was a great unity to fight against the foreign yoke for the sake of the dignity and honour of the country itself (Fig. 1).

37. One more example of the head-dress which is different in style in another picture of Maharaja Partap Singh.[98] He wears a heavy turban of white colour. It has been arranged in overlapping pattern. It shows at that time national movement of India was in full swing and foreigner (Britisher), were committing crimes and were fully interested in suppressing the freedom movement. The colour of the turban shows that it was the time to be patient and fight rigorously against the foreigner for the sake of the India from the foreign rule. Turban shows Rajasthani fashion influence (Fig. 2).

38. The picture of the Raja Ram Singh[99] displayed another variety of the head-dress, but it has its meaning of its time. He wears a simple white colour of turban, made of superior kind of cotton cloth, arranged in overlapping manner, over the blue *pataka*. It was a high turban and its height indicates that tolerance against the Britisher government, and an urge to get rid from slavery. Picture also represents the past history of the Indian people. It shows Marwari fashion influence (Fig. 1).

39. This variety of the head-dress, detected in the picture of Raja Amar Singh.[100] He wears a medium size of white colour turban above the blue *pataka*. The theme of this turban is the same as mentioned above in the picture of Raja Ram Singh. The only difference the *pag* displays is Rajasthani fashion influence (Fig. 2).

40. The picture of the toy-seller[101] demonstrates another simple variety of head-dress. It is a loose kind of head-dress just like a *pataka* of light brownish colour. His dress shows poor economic background of the man. It also is a inferior kind of head-dress. Moreover, he wears *pataka* against the warm climate of the areas. But he is shown expert in his profession and enjoys a contended life. Head-dress shows Mughal fashion influence (Fig. 3).

Thus, similar kind of head-dresses or turbans worn in other parts of India.[102]

Caps or '*Topi*'

There are, apart form the turban or *pag*, head-dresses of different types used by the Dogra men. The paintings of the period discloses that caps of various kinds were customary all communities of the Jammu region. They were commonly called as '*topi*' in the local language as was also named in other parts of India. They had been used against the sharp heat of the sun in summer and woollen caps were also used against the cold of winter. Sometimes, it had been used at the auspicious occasions like religious function, marriage ceremony, etc. It is also a fact that caps were generally worn by the foreigners.[103] It has some local and other non-local names like *natio, moshlo, topi, kulah, kantop.*[104] The male idol figures of the Harappa and Mohenjo-Daro culture also has a conical cap fastened with a ribbon and tilted to one side.[105] In 150-200 A.D. a skull cap like head-dress[106] was a fashion among the males. The Mathura sculpture of the Saka kings and soldiers also have conical and hemispherical caps.[107] In the Gupta period, the relief of the temple at Bhumara, a picture of the musician playing the trumpet wears a conical cap tilted at the top,[108] and another musician playing on an hour-glass-shaped drum wears a conical cap.[109] The dancer's cap has fringed end (Fig. 84).[110] Ksemendra, (1000-1065 A.D.), a great Kashmiri author, observes the condition of a miser shopkeeper of Kashmir and mentions: "He wore a mis-shapen cap (*tuppika*) gnawed by rats[111] and the official, dress of the high and low ruling elite was made of many tiny pieces (of felt) and was high at the borders.[112] In the *Akbarnama*, it is mentioned that *taqiya* is properly the skull-cap worn under the turban, but perhaps this was all the child was wearing.[113] In the middle mountains of the Jammu region the woollen cap of different shape as a head-dress of the poorer classes was generally a skull-cap,[114] and sometimes they used to wear a low round cap.[115] In the winter, not unoften hardly Dogras wearing huge turban or *kantopa* (skull-cap's reaching down the neck) was also worn by the men and carried a *hookah* to relieve the tedium of the journey. The traditional male dress was also constituted with a simple white cotton made boat-cap, called *kishti-numa-topi.*[116]

The following varieties of the caps are depicted in the paintings of the period which were customary among male is discussed as under:

1. A dancer of Raga *kokhar*[117] wore a brimming woollen red colour skull-cap, the cap is decorate with a pair of fresh flower's garlands of white colour. The cap was used in the cold weather. The combination of the colour i.e. white flower and red cap demonstrate the profession of these people was to entertain people through their art, i.e. music, dance, singing etc. This beautiful type of head-dress shows Persian fashion influence (Fig. 2).

2. The portrait of Mirza Rustam Qandahari[118] displayed another typical variety of head-dress. He wears a pointed cap of white colour, made of wool. It appears like a cat above the drapped scarf or handkerchief of liquid henna colour, which covers the back. It is a

head-dress worn in the cold climate. The colour scheme and pattern of wearing indicates that the Eastern Himalayan Rajputana States at that time was under unification against the Mughal yoke. But its replica of the cat shows that Mughal army was aware, waiting and watching the feeble movement of the Rajputana States. And was ready to attack them like a cat who captures the rat. Head-dress shows Persian fashion influence (Fig. 3).

3. This variety of the head-dress we located in the picture of Maharaja Ranjit Singh.[119] He wears *kantopa* type of head-dress, made of yellow and parrot colour of wool, and was used in the cold weather. Besides, painter informs us through the colour combination of yellow and parrot that his rule was declining, but parrot colour indicates that he had still hope for its survival. Head-dress shows foreign fashion influence (Fig. 1).

4. The portrait of 'the diversion of Jamuna'[120] displays the pointed cap made of pinkish and red colours of wool, over which a fine piece of cloth of white and gold colours was tied and worn by the *gopas* of Krishna. Besides the social life of the people, seasons and the profession of the areas i.e., agriculture as the *hal* has been shown driven by Sudama.[121] The theme of the picture shed light that there was a great need of the canal for the agriculture development so as to improve the economic conditions of the people. Krishna is shown as a ruler and had an idea for the welfare of the public. Head-dress shows Persians fashion influence (Fig. 1).

5. This variety of the head-dress we discovered in the picture of Lord Krishna.[122] He wears beautiful grey colour cap (helmet) of tomb shape, which has been tied by a beautiful piece of cloth of white and gold colours. It was a *Mahabharata*'s scene of Krishna. The helmet has a peacock feather at the top. It appears that Dogra society was a religious society; they used to decorate their gods and goddess with precious ornament. Moreover, such type of head-dresses were used to wear in the battlefield for the protection of the head and worn by the military Generals. It shows Persian fashion influence (Fig. 3).

6. Perhaps a bowl type of Himachali cap was also worn by the Sadhus of the Jammu region as displayed in the picture of *Sati Parikashan*.[123] The cap is made of wool. At the forehead, it has parrot colour strip and rest of the area of the cap has been shown in orange colour. The cap is used in the cold climate of the area. The colour scheme of the dress depicts that he enjoys contentment after performing his duty as a successful religious priest. It shows Himachalian fashion influence (Fig. 1).

7. This variety of the head-dress is discovered in the picture of Gulab Singh's *darbaris*.[124] He appears like a military Chief. He wears a cylinderical cap (helmet) of grey colour, over which a white short

piece of cloth is tied and another piece of cloth covers the nape of the neck in the pattern of a curtain falling over the back. Moreover, three aigrettes are shown placed on it in interval manner, one, on the top of the cylindrical cap and other two are shown placed on its one side. The head-dress is looking gorgeous with the installation of the peacock feather on it. It appears that it had been used for the protection of head in the battlefield. Head-dress shows Persian fashion influence (Fig. 1).

8. A battle scene of Rama and Laxmana[125] against Ravana demonstrated a typical variety of the head-dress as a garment. It appears that a rectangular piece of cloth known as (*chadar*) or scarf little bit modified in the shape of a garment. Its one end has been displayed stitched up which take the shape of a cylindrical cap and covers the head of the wearer and its opposite side is shown as usual as a *chadar* or scarf which covers the back side of the body and reaches to the waist, and tied round the waist and knotted at the neval. It was a Dogra's originated garment worn also by the Hanuman as well as by the Rama's army personels. It shows that poor people used to wear such type of garment in Jammu region (Fig. 1).

The comparative example of the head-dress i.e. caps, we also find in the other States[126] of the Indian territories.

The traditional Dogra costumes i.e. the *uttariya* (the upper garment) and the *adhovastra* (the lower garment) were both sewn and unsewn pieces of clothes. They were worn in different ways in conformity with the seasons. They were of various fashions with a view to bring about a change in their dresses. In most of the paintings the lower and upper-garment of male has been depicted, discussed as under:

Upper-Garments (*uttariya*)

The paintings of the period throw a flood of light on the attire of the Dogra male. It consisted of both stitched and unstitched garments.[127] The apparel known as *kurta, jama, farji,* or jacket, gown, coats, etc. were in fashion among the males in different style as portrayed in the Jammu paintings. The rich people are shown, with superior embroidered clothes, whereas the poor are displayed with inferior type of cotton cloth. In the *Grihya-Sutras, kandika 8, rule 10*, it is mentioned that in Hindu society there was a custom on the eve of newly born child. The mother dressed the son in clean garment, turning him, from south to north, with his face to the north, to the performer (of the ceremony[128]), and the upper part of the body of men was covered by the garment called either a wrapper *upavasana, paryanahana,* or *adhivasa*, or a jacket.[129] In *Yuan-Chwangs* it has been explained the clerical costume of the *Sha-men* (*Sramanas*) is only the three robes and the *Seng-kio-ki* and *Ni-po-so-na*. As to the three robes the schools adhere to different styles having broad or narrow fringes with small or large folds. The *Seng-kio-ki* goes over the left shoulder covering the armpits and joined on the right and opens on the left side. It length reached below to waist. As to the *Ni-pu-so-na*, since no belt is worn when it is put on, it is gathered into plaits and secured by one of these, the size and colour of the plaits vary from school to schools.[130] In *Akbarnama*, it is mentioned that Akbar had 120 suits in his wardrobe, four hundred pieces of velvets and satin from Europe and Yezd hundred and twenty coats were always ready for the king's special use.[131] In the Dogra wall-painting Vishnu in his various incarnation is always seen wearing an upper garment which is like the *angavastra* worn even now by men in southern India.[132]

The main types of the upper garments which were preferred by the Dogra male, are depicted in the paintings of the period and discussed as under:

Kurta

The garment that clothed the upper part of the male body is generally known as *kurta* or *kameez* in the local language of the Dogras as it is generally called in the other parts of India. So for the auspicious and festival occasions are concerned, the *kurta* or *kameez* of various colours were used by both the rich and the poor class of the Dogras. Paintings displayed that the rulers of the areas weared superior kind of *kameez* and the attendants weared inferior kind of cotton *kurta* and it was a common wear in Northern India.[133] In the Sunga period tunic (*kurta*) was occasionally worn. One of the soldiers represented on the railing of Stupa II at Sanchi fighting with a lion wears a half-sleeved tunic reaching to the knees fastened round the waist with a *kamarband*.[134] The origin of it is in the mist of obscurity. The paintings of the 16th to 19th centuries display that *kurta* or *kameez* were the popular article of dress in Jammu region. A white *kurta* or *kameez* or chintz, shirt which reached the knees was worn by the agriculture class and loose shirts by the poor masses. There was a common practice even in the villages of the Dogras region to dye their white clothes with indigo colour. A plain shirt or *kameez* with or without collar made of cheap mill-made cotton[135] or mixed fabric[136] was also a common dress wear among the Dogra people and is due course of time it became a traditional costume.

At the religious and ceremonial occasions, so the Rajput clad in *gulnar* dress, with embroidered cloth wrapped on heads, saffron-coloured marks on fore head, uttering 'Ram Ram' and carrying *swords* in hands.[137]

The main types it were preferred by the men, as depicted in the paintings of the period like,

1. The portrait of Gulab Singh as a soldier[138] displayed that he wears a coco-cola colour of skirt type of *kameez*, opened from the front. It is well-fitted to the upper-part of the body and flaired from the waist, having tight-fitting full sleeves, without collar, reaching below the knees. The expressions of the portrait and the colour of the shirt impresses that he was aware of the political uprising in the state and was ready to sacrifice his life for the sake of his domain i.e. Jammu and Kashmir state to retain it. He wore a Dogra traditional *kameez* (Fig. 3).

2. This variety of the upper garment i.e. *kameez* is detected in the picture of a dancer of *Raga khokhar*.[139] He wears a full-sleeved frock type of long shirt reaching below the knees. It is a cotton made shirt of white colour without collar. The colour mixing of the shirt indicates that people of the areas were leading a peaceful and prosperous life. It was a Dogra traditional *kameez* (Fig. 3).

3. There is another variety of the Dogra traditional *kurta* can be explored from the picture of Dharamsawala on camel back.[140] He wears a simple loose-full-sleeved collarless *kurta* upto the knees. It is white cotton *kurta*. The white colour symbolizes that they were leading a peaceful life and someone was disrupt them (Fig. 1).

4. This kind of the *kurta* one finds in the picture of Raja Ranbir Singh.[141] He wears full tighten-sleeved, collarless flair type of white *kurta* open from the front. It was a Dogra traditional *kameez* worn by Ranbir Singh under the silken *chogha*. The colour of the shirt shows that Ranbir Singh was leading a peaceful and prosperous life (Fig. 4).

5. This garment was used to dress the upper part of the body and known as *kameez* or shirt. The picture of Gulab Singh's army commanders[142] particularly Suchet Singh etc. In this picture they wear a Dogra traditional (superior white cotton *kurta*). It is well-fitted collarless skirt. From waist they have gold borders. The style of these shirts indicate the ruler i.e., Gulab Singh had a peaceful and prosperous life (Fig. 1).

6. The portrait of a *nayaka*[143] possibly Suchet Singh displays another variety of the *kameez*. He wears a collarless full sleeved skin colour frock type shirt. It reaching below the knees and symbolizes that Suchet Singh was issueless though had a dream of an issue. However, he was having a comfortable life. The dress material weared by him is also a Dogra traditional shirt (Fig. 1).

7. The portrait of Suchet Singh in a war procession shows his army personels[144] wear a tight-fitted, full-sleeved *kameez* of different colours i.e., sky-blue, yellow, white, red, pink, etc. The colour scheme

of the *kameez* symbolizes that Suchet Singh had a problem with his adjoining states. The yellow colour reflects symbolically that he was lossing his control dishearteningly over few areas though of the colours display that he was waiting and expecting improvement in the political and military situation. The uniform of the army personels is Dogras traditional dress (Fig. 3).

A Dogra writer superbly describes a Dogra dress fashion in 17th century A.D. in the following verses of folk song:

"कुर्ता खद्दरे दा लाना,
ते साफा मलमलै दा जी ओ।
अहें–चंगा खाना, चंगा लाना,
बसाहनि यारो पलै दां जी ओ।
तैह्मत लट्ठे दा बन्ना,
ते नुक्क फुम्मनेदार जी ओ।
अहें–जोडना निं किज छोडना निं,
रेही जाने भरे पटार जी ओ।"[145]

Tr. into English:
"To have a *kurta* of the *khaddar* (cotton).
Having a *safa* of *malmal* having (light cotton stuff).
We (the people of Jammu): take nice dishes, and have nice dress.
Also have a *tehmet* wrap round the waist of
Latha (variety of cotton cloth).
Also having a nice shoes of whisk.
We (the people Jammu): Nothing to accumulate, nothing to leave behind.
If we accumulate, it will remained there after the demise.".

8. The picture of an umbrella bearer of Suchet Singh[146] depicts another variety of the *kameez*. He wears a red cotton colour shirt of floral design. It is full-sleeved shirt, well-fitted and reaching above the knees. The traditional *kurta* significes of the Dogra's shows that this area was flourishing under the rule of Suchet Singh (Fig. 1).

The same varieties of the *kurta's* mentioned above, were popular in the other parts of the Indian[147] territory.

Jama (*Angarakha*)

Paintings displayed that a full-sleeved upper garment known as *jama* or *angarakha* of various types were popular in the Jammu region. In the local languages it was also known as *angarakha* as generally named in the other parts of India. During the reign of Timurid dynasty, a simple Persian originated *jama* was the elite dress.[148]

With the establishment of the Mughal rule, political, business and military elites preferred to wear bright colours, which were rich in designs and multiple in variety, especially of brocades were enticed among the non-Mughal people particularly the Rajputs of the plains and the Punjab Hill States. Towards the end of the 16th century, when diaphanous *jamas* and skirts became a fashion at court, the gentlemen of Rajasthan wore the same dress. (This went out of fashion are around 1610 A.D., when transparent skirts were worn only by entertainers, whilst gentlemen and ladies who wore opaque material[149]). Gradually they adopted some variation in *jama*, i.e., the buttoned coats. Before the Mughal, button coats of any description were formerly unknown in India. In the Sikh reign the *jama* was no longer flowing, but shorter and often tucked up around the waist to allow freedom of movement.[150] This dress was also worn by the Dogra chiefs. The Jammu paintings also displayed the popularily of this dress. Most of the *nayakas* weared plain, bright, brocade bright, printed *jama*; though transparent white, green robe with small floral design was also a fashion among the rulers of the areas.

The following varieties of the *jamas* or *angarakhas* which were depicted in the paintings of the period are as under:

1. The *jama* depicted in the picture of Sultan Abu Said[151] is full-sleeved, collarless long *jama* of golden colour. It has buttons in the front. Over the *jama*, he wears a *chogha* of *lapis lazuli* colour. The colour scheme of the dress, its style of wearing and sitting posture in the chair with smiling face symbolizes his intension to laid down a strong and powerful empire. No doubt, dress is above weared against the cold climate. Though colour of the *chogha* reflects that he had certain political problem and is unhappy in Persia. The open face of the *chogha* signifies his strong desire to leave the Persia and to set up a strong and permanent empire somewhere else. His dress shows Persian fashion influence (Fig. 4).

2. Another variety of the garment known as *jama* is displayed in the picture of Babur.[152] He wears a self-printed full-sleeved long silken collared *jama* of pinkish colour and buttoned from the front in an artistic ways. The vibration of the colour and his sitting style displayed that he was enticed to see the Indian territory incomparison to Persian land. He in this picture is shown as considering for lying down his empire in India. *Jama* shows Turkish fashion influence (Fig. 1).

3. The portrait of Rafi-Ud-Darjat[153] demonstrated another kind of the *jama*. It displays side-fastened, full-sleeved silken long *jama* of white colour with gold print. He has also a *rose flower* in his hand. The style of the turban shows that, he had certain criss-cross political problem in Indian. But the colour scheme of the *jama*, and his sitting style on a gold chair, having a flower in his hand depict that he had a strong will to overpower all states of India to laid down a peaceful and powerful empire. Dress shows Turkish fashion influence (Fig. 3).

4. The portrait of Raja Jagat Singh[154] displayed another different kind of *jama*. He wears a side fastened frock type of pointed *jama* of full-sleeves. It is a transparent white *jama* tied by a *kamarband*. His head-dress shows at one time he was a powerful Dogra chief, but his pointed ended *jama* and style of holding the sword in downward depicts that his power has declined. *Jama* shows Persian fashion influence (Fig. 2).

5. There is another variety of the *jama* we detected in the picture of Raja Kishan Singh.[155] He wears a side fastened, full-sleeved frock type of *gheredar jama* of green colour having golden print and reaching below the knees, tied by a *kamarband*. It shows that he was leading a prosperous and peaceful life. The style of holding the sword and shield show that he was always alert to face any eventuality at any time for the sake of his kingdom. It also displays that he was a powerful and strong ruler of his areas. *Jama* shows Mughalian fashion influence (Fig. 3).

6. The picture of Raja Jai Singh[156] delineates another variety of the *jama*. He wears a full-sleeved, also a side-fastened *gheredar* or frock type of white *jama*, reaching below the knees having golden border with attached piece of cloth is shown hanging from the left armpit. It appears that he had surrendered his kingdom to someone else and is shown in a peaceful state. *Jama* shows Mughalian fashion influence (Fig. 2).

7. This variety of *jama* in the picture of Raja Kirpal Pal[157] is white colour full-sleeved *jama* and is attached with a piece of cloth hanging from the right armpit. It narrates that he had a desire to lead a peaceful life *jama* shows Mughalian fashion influence (Fig. 1).

8. The same kind of *jama* mentioned above, has also been worn by Raja Medini Pal.[158] His body language impresses that he was a strong ruler than Raja Kirpal Pal (Fig. 2).

9. The painting of Raja Dhiraj Pal[159] displays that he used to wear a same pattern of *jama* of Raja Kirpal Pal, but it is a green printed *jama*. Its colour combination shows that he was leading a peaceful and prosperous life. *Jama* shows Mughalian fashion influence (Fig. 1).

10. The portrait of Sanjaya of *Mahabharata*[160] to Darashtra displayed that he wears a parrot colour of superior cotton *jama*. It is a side-fasten; full-sleeved skirt type of upper garment with Mughalian fashion influence. It appears that garment was not popular among the rulers of the areas though artist has portrayaled the picture of Hindu religious gods i.e., Krishna[161] and Rama[162] in the same fashion garment in the orange and pinkish colours (Fig. 1).

11. This variety of the upper-garment is unearthed in the picture of the security personels[163] of Raja Dhian Singh. It appears that they

also to weared the same[164] kind of *jama*, but it was an inferior kind of cotton garment in blood-red colour. Colour of clothes symbolizes that they were the healthy army personels. It shows Mughalian fashion influence (Fig. 2).

12. The picture of an attendant[165] of a Dogra Rajput Prince displays another different variety of the upper garment also known as *jama*. It is right side fastened full sleeved skirt type of upper garment reaching below the knees and tied by a girdle from the waist. It is a cotton garment likely to be red colour. Colour shows the good physical health of man (Fig. 3).

13. This different colour of *jama* is seen in the picture of a *chouri-bearer* of Raja Medini Pal.[166] He wears vertical lining design of side-fasten frock type of upper garment of sky and saffron colour. It is a full-sleeves *jama*. It narrates that it has been made out of a light cotton stuff known as *patya*. It was an inferior kind of cloth. The colour scheme of the dress shows that he is a most submissive manner talks with the Raja, and had a good deal. *Jama* shows Mughalian fashion influence (Fig. 1).

The same dress was a fashion in other region of the Indian[167] territories.

Chogha (*Choga*)

In the paintings of the period, *chogha* was a long loose, half and full-sleeved type of an outer-garment, worn over an inner garment. It was made of wool or silk kind of stuff usually wear on the ceremonial occasions, especially by the Dogra's rulers and their courtiers. In the cold climate of the region, they used woollen made *chogha*. Whereas in the summer, they weared transparent silken *chogha*. It was a Turkish originated upper and outer garment less flared then the *jama*. It also was called as *chogha* in the local dialects. In Russia *chogha* is known as *shuba* or *shubha*. In the Gandhara sculptures, an overcoat (*chogha*) lined with fur is worn over the tunic[168] by the men. In the *Yuan-Chwang* the "three robes" of the Buddhist monks have *Antaravasaka*, the *Samghati* and the *Uttarasanga*.[169] In the Sultanate period the costumes of the notables of Delhi depicted as: "Most of their Tartar (Tatari) robes are embroidered with gold (*muzarkasa-bi-dhahab*). Some wear garments with both sleeves having a *tiraz* border of gold embroidery (*larkas*). Other, for example the Mongols, place the *tiraz* inscription between the shoulders[170]." In the *Akbarnama*, it is mentioned that in the honour of Akbar, robes of honour of diverse colours were bestowed, and dress namely *khilat* upon *khilat* was presented[171] by their courtiers. The *Tusk-I-Jahangiri* narrates that a *jagirdar's* of the local areas, presented to Raja Suraj Singh ten turbans (*chira*) coats (*qaba*) and ten waistbands.[172] *Chogha* has also some other similar garments known as *aba, qaba, jub*.[173]

The other varieties of the *choghas*, which were popular among in various the rulers courtiers are narrated in the paintings of the period discussed as under:

1. The distinguished variety of the *chogha* is in the picture of Sultan Abu Said.[174] He wears a full-sleeved long *chogha* of *lap lazuli* (blue) colour having golden print and open front. From the colour scheme of his dress and his smiling face one can conclude that he was unhappy in Persia due to certain political problems and he had an eye on Indian territory to setup a strong empire. He wears Turkish origin *chogha* (Fig. 4).

2. The portrait of Umar Sheikih Mirza[175] has same type of *chogha*, but only difference is that he wears half-sleeved kind of *chogha*. The colour scheme of the *chogha* and its half-sleeves show that he was unhappy in Persia as his close relatives had circumscribed his political power. But he had a capacity to setup a strong empire *chogha* shows Turkish fashion influence (Fig. 2).

3. There is another different kind of upper-garment known as coat (*qaba*) in the picture of Mirza Rustam Quandahari.[176] He is wearing it over the shirt like garment. It is also a half sleeved woollen coat (*qaba*) of dark liquid henna colour having sky blue horizontal dots. No doubt, it is not a tropical but the reflection of the colour scheme and half-sleeves of the *qaba* identifies that Akbar had not yet conquered the whole territory of India. Certain Rajput Chiefs at that time, were at rebolt. Same was the case in Dogra region. Akbar dispatched Mirza Rustam Quandahari as a commander of the Mughal force to quell the rebellion of Raja Basu. With little hesitation he attack and ultimately, suppressed the revolt and removed the hurdle of Akbar. Coat (*qaba*) shows Persian fashion influence. It is likely to be the uniform coat of the Mirza Rustam Quandahari (Fig. 3).

4. This variety of the garment which dresses the upper part of the body is known as *chogha* or coat is in the painting of Maharaja Ranjit Singh.[177] He wears a yellow coat or *chogha* having green and brocade borders. It is a half-sleeved coat. The colour combination of the *chogha* and its half-sleeves depicts that his rule is on the decay. His power is declining, even he is struggling very hard for his survival. *Chogha* displays Turkish fashion influence. Moreover it is a climate garment (Fig. 1).

5. This distinct *chogha* or a long coat is in the painting of Raja Kharaq Singh.[178] It was a costly kind of *chogha* or coat, mostly worn by the rulers or the rich people. He wears an orange colour of woollen

brocade *chogha*. It has long and loose sleeves. It is a garment of moderate cold climate. Its colour, wearing and style of shoulders depicted that Sikh rule was gradually fading from Jammu region. Moreover, the downward holding style of the dragon in the one hand of Kharaq Singh. One shows that Sikh empire was at the verge of downfall and the turning point of the Sikh history was above to take place. *Chogha* shows Turkish fashion influence (Fig. 2).

6. The portrait of Raja Sher Singh[179] displayed another variety of the *chogha* or a coat. He wears light orange colour of brocade transparent *chogha* made of silk. It is a half sleeved *chogha* or a coat. The colour scheme, its transparent stuff his thinking posture and sitting style demonstrates that Sikh reign has declined. There is no hope of its revival. *Chogha* shows Turkish fashion influence (Fig. 3).

7. There is one more different kind of the *chogha* in the picture of Gulab Singh in a war procession.[180] He wears an orange colour of gold printed *chogha* of full-sleeves. The colour of the outer-garment shows that his rule has been started in Jammu and Kashmir State and he with great enthusiasm is founding a powerful empire, and is ready to face any lurking threat. Dress also shows status of the wearer. Gulab Singh is shown as a leading man, Suchet Singh and others are shown as subordinates. *Chogha* shows Turkish fashion influence (Fig. 1).

8. The portrait of *Panchvakta* man likely to be Raja Ranbir Singh.[181] He wears a transparent silken *chogha* of green colour having gold print and borders. It is a full-sleeves *chogha*. It shows that his rule was progressing and becoming strong day by day. He has been shown worshipping his deity for the accumulating of energy (power). Though it also reveals that he had minor problems yet to come. *Jama* shows Turkish fashion influence (Fig. 4).

9. This variety of the *chogha* in the picture of Raja Ranbir Singh.[182] He wears a brocade woollen made *chogha* of blackish haldi colour outer-garment. It was a half-sleeves open front *chogha*. The colour scheme and the wearing style signalizes that national movement has started in India and British Government was committing crime against the Indian in order to suppress them. However, British were tactically reforming the governance and new ideas have permeated in the Indian society. *Jama* shows Mughalian fashion influence (Fig. 4).

10. There is another style of garment in the picture of Maharaja Ranbir Singh.[183] He wears a half-sleeved *chogha* or a woollen coat. It is a brocade blackish haldi colour of *chogha*. It has circular neck and have buttons in the front. The colour scheme of the *chogha* shows that national movement has widely spreaded in India. The Indian people are determined to overthrow the foreign yoke. They have an

idea to built-up India a peaceful and powerful nation. *Chogha* shows Mughalian fashion influence (Fig. 1).

11. The picture of Maharaja Partap Singh on horse back[184] displayed a different kind of the upper-garment i.e. known as *chogha* or a long coat. He wears a blackish yellow colour shade brocade full-sleeved long *chogha*. It appears from his dress that princely power was declining at that time and new ideas of the western countries have been permeated in Indian society for the formation of modern society as the spring season is disappeared and summer has to starts. Picture shows that India had great courage to face the foreign yoke. Besides this the garment was used in the cold climate of the region. *Chogha* shows Turkish fashion influence (Fig. 1).

12. This variety of the upper-garment i.e., *chogha* is in the picture of Ranbir Singh's *chouri*-bearer.[185] He wears full-sleeved woollen *chogha* reaching below the knees and also having embroidery on it. This type of dress was used by him in the cold climate of the areas. *Chogha* shows Turkish fashion influence (Fig. 1).

13. This type of the simple *chogha*, is in the picture of Shishu Pala and Jarasand.[186] They used this woollen *chogha* in the cold weather. It has multi-colours. Some have open front and some had been tied by the girdle of different colours. It is a full-sleeved upper-garment. The figures of Shishu Pala and Jarasand have unbuttoned front and are concentrating with others for future course of action. The colours scheme of the dress shows that they were pondering over an important issue of the socio-political issues of the areas. *Chogha* shows Turkish fashion influence (Fig. 2).

The similar kind of *chogha's* mentioned above, was also a fashion in other parts of the Indian states.[187]

Jacket (*Fathuhi*)

In the Jammu paintings, one can find that over the shirt, a very smart sewn jacket or waist coat like, an over garment with or without sleeves but open front or middle is worn. It is a coat made of either silk or coloured cotton, edged with embroidery and lined with fur was also frequently worn by the Dogras during winter. In the Gupta period, besides, the common article of clothing in northern India, where the climate is very cold closely-fitting jackets were worn that resembled the garment of the same pattern was worn by the Tartars (Hu).[188] In the Mughal period, *farji*[189] was also worn by the men as an over-garment. A scene of the Pahari miniatures painting of the 19th century reveals that Sikh predominated Dogra region. And Dogra were influenced the Sikh fashion style. They adopted short-sleeved jackets that was worn over the long-sleeved jackets with knee length shirts.[190]

It is evident that Dogra male in the cold weather weared a waist-coat, usually made of silk in various colours. Dogra peasant generally used to put on a *postin*, or short-sleeved sheep-skin coat, over the shirt, called *sadari*,[191] and short breeches, i.e., *kuch* instead of the trousers and sleeveless jackets instead of the shirt. In Bhadrawha, folk dancers on the day of Baisakhi wear tight *pyjama* and a black jacket with a long robe start dancing in a slow rhythm and go on stepping round the fire.

Normally, the people at home feel ease to wear a home-made cotton *baniyan*, while indoor or working in the field.[192] Whereas the Gujjar male of the Jammu region, they are usually dressed somewhat scantily a colour sheet tugged loose around the waist with a black velvet (*shaneel*) jacket above the shirt.[193] In the dialects of the Dogras, it is called as *baskit, fathuhi, farji* or jacket, etc. as usually called in the other parts of the Indian territory. It is similar garments is known as *sadari, mirzai, farji, fathuhi*.[194]

The following types male jackets depicted in the painting by the male of the period discussed as under:

1. The variety of *farji* or jacket, in the picture of Raja Ranbir Singh.[195] He wears a yellow colour jacket of short sleeves having needle work on its borders, buttoned in the front and worn over the shirt. It was a woollen jacket worn against the cold climate. The wearing style and body language of the painting reveals that princely rule was under stress and strain as new ideas for the formation of the modern society has permeated in society. Jacket shows Turkish fashion influence (Fig. 1).

2. The painting of Raja Suchet Singh as a soldier[196] displayed another gorgeous type of full-sleeved jacket. It has red colour, well-fitted to the body up to the throat known as *band-gala*. It is artistic in nature form the front and has been tied by a long but narrow belt like a *nara* (rope). In the left hand, he has a red rose. The expression of the pictures and the colour scheme shows that he was contented and well build. Again the theme of the picture reflects that he had an idea to set up a strong and powerful empire and had laid down the first stone of his empire. Jacket shows European fashion influence (Fig. 1).

Such type of jackets as discussed above were also worn in other states[197] of India.

Kamarband (Girdle)

In the paintings of the period, *kamarband* or girdle was mostly worn over the *jama* or *peswaj* round the waist to keep the dress on proper position. It also appears that girdle, sash (*pataka*) or belt was one of the most fenced article of clothing into which the ceremonial, knife with dragon shapeholder, etc., was used to put. Its function and use was different from time to time such as in the war it was used to cover the wounds and dead bodies and during peace besides, its usage as belt it was thrown in air at the time of joy. However, it were many fold. It was used to carry domestic articles etc. Though there were many ways to tying the *kamarband* (*kayaband-hana*).[198] As in the *Grihya-Sutras*, it has been described in *patala 1, section, 4 rule 4*, that in the Vedic age girdle was used to wind three times from that left to right round the waist of the boy so that it had to cover the navel. It was tied by the religious teachers with verses[199] as a custom in the Hindus society. Thus *kalavuka* expresses the *kamarband* made of many strings plaited together (Fig. 5); *deddubhaka* was literally 'shaped like a water-serpent's hood' i.e., the knot tapering to one end; *muraja* is 'torn toni' shaped (Fig. 3); girdle with ornaments hanging in it was known as *maddavina*.[200] The fashion of wearing the *patta* arranged in various artistic ways was made of *viliva* (woven bamboo fibres), leather *carmapatta, dhussapatta* (woollen cloth), plaited woollen cloth (*dussaveni*), and fringed clothe (*dussavatti*).[201] In the Akbar's time the palace servant had four buttons on both sides of his chest and two during Babar's and during Humayun's 'uniforms' and a simple *pataka* (sash), into which his dagger was tucked and held by two small chains.[202] This characteristic is also visible in the Jehangir's rich and brocade *jamas* a boldly developed sash, the *kamarband* (the English '*cummerbund*') rather the *pataka*.[203] Besides, the *kamarband*, the Dugger used to wear a country made belt of a woollen rope, usually black round many scores of time round[204] the waist. A beautiful sash hang down to the front to the left of the waist and almost down to the knees at the back, forming a sort of girdle[205] mostly tied round the waist over the *jama* or the *kurta*.

The following styles and their wearings manifest in the paintings of the period, discussed as under:

1. The first mode of wearing is in the picture of Gulab Singh in a war procession.[206] It has been worn by both the army Generals and soldiers. It serves two purposes: One is that it impresses that Maharaja had a well disciplined army with proper kit. Two, the army personnels comfortably carried sufficient weapons and use thin dress as a bag. So far its mode of wearing is concerned, it appears that it was a sort of *chadar* like a piece of cloth, its two lengthwise pointed corner tied round the waist, knotted at the naval and its two opposite ends pass over the left shoulder, knotted on the former knotted of the *chadar* at navel. It has a bag shape on the backside to carry essential weapons of war, etc. Besides the war occasion, it has been also used by the Dogra

people as a fashion in the peacetime. It was also a common feature to warp (Fig. 1).

2. The second variety of the *kamarband*, is in the picture of Raga *Khokhar*.[207] A dancer wears it round the waist to keep up the *kurta* at proper position. It is a simple kind of girdle. It shows Dogra fashion influence (Fig. 2).

3. The portrait of Rafi-Ud-Darjat[208] demonstrated another variety of the *pataka* (sash). It shows that he has worn it keep up the dagger and the *jama* at proper position. It was popular article of dress among the upper class of the people. It was tied round the waist and its two ends were allowed to be free. It shows Persian fashion influence (Fig. 3).

4. This variety of the *kamarband* or waistband is in the picture of Mirza Rustam Quandahari.[209] He wears modern type of belt over the *qaba*. It shows that he has tied the girdle around his stomach for the service of his master (Akbar), who commanded him to defeat the turbulent Raja Basu of the Dogra State. The golden belt of Mirza shows the power of the commander that he was used to belong from a powerful empire. It shows Dogra fashion influence (Fig. 3).

5. The painting of Partap Singh's umbrella-bearer[210] has a typical variety of the *kamarband*. He wears its over the upper and lower garment round the waist. It shows that, he first weared it in the *lungi* (loin-cloth) style and then it was folded in upward direction tied round the waist. It is a yellow *kamarband* and signifies that the era of slavery has end and era of equal right for all has commenced. It was a Dogra's traditional *kamarband* (Fig. 1).

Similar types of the *kamarbands* discussed above were also found in the paintings of other parts of the India.[211]

Chadar (Scarf)

Scarf a piece of cloth of long strip of moderate breadth was used for various purposes. Paintings display, it was very common among elites and without its wearing dress was in complete. It was an unstitched piece of cloth of the Indian origin. In the local dialects it was called as *parana* or hand towel, etc. as generally called in the other parts of India. Another variety of the woollen scarf known as *guluband* was used in winter, for the protection of head by the Dogras. In Punjabi and Hindi languages woollen *chadar* has been called as *dhussa*.[212] In the *Amarakosa*[213] the unsewn Indian garments known as *dupatta* and *chadar* have five names; i.e., *pravara uttarasanga, vrhatika, samvyana* and *uttariya*. In the 3rd century A.D. a prince or a nobleman of the northern India drapery of the dress was a cloak, a *chadar*, a piece of cloth worn in a different ways, one or both shoulders and allowed it to fall over an arm or kept its one end hanging at the back side.[214] In the Gupta period, the costumes of an Iranian style consist of a scarf, tied round the neck. It borders are seen fluttering at the back.[215] The function of the scarf, we can trace out on the back of the drummer holds the drum.[216] In the *Narmamala,*[217] Ksemendra has narrated the costumes of the government official, as the article of the dress of a head-clerk, is described as following: "His head scarf (*sirah-sataka*) had many holes. The woollen *chader* (*tustaka*) dangled by his side". A fragmentary figure of a four-armed Bharapa sculpture of Ramnagar and Basohli displays that the ends of his scarf fly outwards the sides.[218] At Ballpur a sculpture of Ganesh has been displayed wears a scarf covering his body, but his large belly has been shown naked.[219]

During hot climatic condition of the Jammu region *dhoti, dupatta* scarf, *saris* and *chadar* are the most suitable garments from the hygenic point of view. There were different modes of wearing the scarf or a *chadar* or of a woollen *guluband,* which adds grace to the wearer and changed the monotony of the wrapped round white or colourful sheets or scarf in various styles, are represented in the paintings of the period discussed as under:

1. The first mode of wearing the scarf has been expounded in the picture of Maharaja Gulab Singh's soldier.[220] He wears it over the left shoulder and than its one end has been shown passing through the left armpit falling on the cloak (Fig. 1).

2. The second style of wearing the scarf is delineated in the same picture were Maharaja Gulab Singh.[221] Scarf hangs from the neck and knotted its both edges dangling on the chest. It shows that he is more concerned to protect the Jammu and Kashmir State from the foreign invasion and it was his soul responsibility. He was not ready to lost an inch of territory of the Jammu and Kashmir State (Fig. 1).

3. A picture of a dancer of *Raga Khokhar*[222] displayed different mode of wearing the scarf. He hangs it from the neck, allowed its free falling below the waist. It shows the perfection of the art (Fig. 2).

4. The fourth style of wearing the scarf is discovered in the picture of Khwaja Khizar.[223] He wears it round the neck in a loose way, and its one end falls on the back, and other end is hanging on the right side on the front part of the body below the waist. Its green colour symbolizes that India is of greenlands and leads a prosperous life (Fig. 4).

5. This style of wearing the scarf, in the paintings of Gulab Singh[224] on the horseback. It seems that he hanged it from the neck and its both ends have free hanging on the thigh. It shows that Jammu and Kashmir State was progressing day by day (Fig. 1).

6. The picture of *natraga*[225] woollen demonstrated another mode of wearing the *guluband* or *muffular* alongwith a *pataka* or head-dress. It is short in width and long in size, having vertical lining design of white and sky blue colour. Its colour scheme shows that there were certain problem in their profession; and they were under training. Its one end has been displayed hanging like a camel tail (Fig. 3).

7. Another style of wearing the scarf, is in the picture of Daksha Yajan (Birba-Ddra-Usinatting) in Hawan-Kund.[226] The length and width of the scarfs is of a *chadar* which sometimes was used to cover the naked but upper part of the body. The white *chadar* shows the sign of tolerance (Fig. 2).

8. The picture of *sati-parikashan*[227] also demonstrated different mode of wearing of scarf or a *chadar*. Some Sadhus are displayed wearing it over the left shoulder and some are shown wearing it in a ladies style. Who generally cover the breast and its both ends fall to back side. They are shown wearing different colours of *chadar* i.e., white, yellow green, etc. The colour scheme of the *chadar* shows, tolerance, status in religion and perfection of the profession (Fig. 1).

9. In the painting of Sanjaya-relating the *Mahabharata* to Dhritrashtra.[228] Another style of wearing the scarf is dected. It hangs from the neck and its both ends have been shown lying on the right side, and his *chouri*-bearer has also been shown hanging it in a stylistic manner over the right shoulder and tucked its one end in the belt. The white and grey colour of the scarf shows the sign of tolerance and sorrow. (Fig. 1).

10. Another mode of wearing the scarf or a *chadar*, is in the picture of a Brahmin returning from the Muslim court.[229] He hangs it on the left shoulder passing over the thigh and than back to the right side. It shows the decline of Sultan Khan and new empire was in the process of its commencement (Fig. 3).

Same modes of wearing the scarf or a *chadar* were also fashioned in the other States of India.[230]

Achkan

It was a long-sleeves coat, an outer-garment generally worn by males, well-fitted to the upper-part of the body. Its length down to the knees or even lower and buttoned in front-middle. It has metallic wire, often gold or silver embroidery. It was mostly weared by the bridegroom as depicted in the paintings of the period. In the local language of the Dogras, it was also known as *achkan*, as it was called in the other parts of the Indian territory. In the *Harsacaritra*, a word *candataka* is occurred. The compound word *candataka* is made of *canda* and *ataka*; the latter seems to be the form of the Vedic *atka*.[231] It has been identified by Dr. Moti Chandra and Indu Prabha Pandey as *achkan* modern word, was used for a long flowing bright beautiful and embroider coat seems to be originated from the *atka*.

The following variety of the *achkan*, in the paintings of the period are discussed as under:

1. This variety of the coat-like garment known as *achkan* is explored in the painting of a marriage scene.[232] Here, one observes that bridegroom is wearing a well-fitted bright, beautiful and embroidered coat known as modern *achkan*. His lower garment is *churidar-pyjama* of red colour. His head is tied with a *sehara* on the *safa* i.e., turban. Most of the females are shown around the departuring newly weded couple from the lawn. The colour scheme of the dress shows that bride is well build and wealthy. Scene also displays the social-cultural life of the areas. It was a Dogra traditional dress (Fig. 3).

The Dogri scholar depicts beautiful example pertaining to the Dogras traditional dress in the following lines:

"इस पासे गुडडा बैठदा,
उन्न सिलका कुरता लाए दा।
लत्ते पर चुस्त घटन्ना ऐ,
साफे पर सेहरा वन्नेया दा।"[233]

Tr. into English:
It is a scene of the *mandap* (marriage) expressed by a scholar as;
"Having one side bridegroom in the *mandap* used to sit.
He wears a silken *kurta*.
Having smart tight-fitting *suthana* in his legs.
Having a *sehara* tied on the *safa*".
Similar dresses were also a fashion in other Indian States.[234]

Gown

Paintings demonstrate that gown or wide robe was also a royal dress and used on the ceremonial occasions like convocation or coronation of the king. It is a long *chogha* type of garment mostly worn over the dress. In the Gupta period,[235] the costume of the foreigners, probably the Syrians, the so-called Persian embassy scene at Ajanta had a peaked cap of striped silk or broad-cloth and a long green coat (*qaba*) reaching down to ankles, trousers and boots with a curved tips. In the Sultanate period,[236] the dress of the soldiers including the Sultans, Khans, Maliks and other officers, were the gowns (*tatariyat*), *jakalwat* and Islamic *qabas* with embroidered sleeves. The *qaba*[237] was also a fashion in the Mughal period.

The following variety is expressed in the painting of Jammu, described as under:

1. The outer-garment i.e., gown in the picture of Maharaja Partap Singh[238] is of European origin dress for the royal soldier. It has been tightened with the help of a marvellous white tie-cord in an artistic manner near to the chest and its front-middle generally opened. The both end of the tie-card suspend on the thigh. Owing to the spectacular display of tie-cord clasp, the appearance of the gown is gorgeous. It is a sky blue long gown reaching on the anklet. It shows that it has been worn by Partap Singh at the time of his coronation. The colour combination of the gown with the dress demonstrates that in India, there was a large scale grief due to the violent suppressive policies of British government against the national movement of India. Gown as well as his dress shows British fashion influence. He wears a white colour *safa* of Rajasthani style in this painting (Fig. 2).

Similar type of example of the gown were also a fashion in other Indian States.[239]

Coat

In the painting, it appears that dark red (maroon) woollen coats were also used by the Dogra gents in the cold weather. The elites used superior kind of coats made of superior material. Whereas, the poor people weared inferior type of cotton coat. Therefore, it is presume that woollen clothes were available in the area. It was a buttoned-up coat called (*band-gala-wala-coat*) of full-sleeves of waist length. It was an over garment of a dress. In the Gupta period, a *bagal bandi* type of a full-sleeved paddeed coat with fasteners on the left side[240] was fashion among the gents. In Babar's time, a long-sleeved garment, a kind of shirt in a completely different colour, was worn under the short-sleeved coat, and the lapel of the coat was sometimes of gold cloth.[241] In Humayun's reign, the attendants wore an almost uniform-like dress, as shown in (b), in contrasting colour, with the coat ending in two or three flaps hanging from the waist, and a much longer one at the rear.[242] A the end of the Akbar's reign and with the beginning of Jahangir rule, silk and brocades, the diaphanous coat went out of fashion for public occasions,[243] like the marriage ceremony or in other function of the society. In the Shah Jahan's period the collar of the coat up in military fashion[244] move pomp and luxury. In the later Mughal period (1820 A.D. at the court of Delhi) there were two slits in the skirt of the coat on the right and left, with extra lacing, and gold braid (lacing) on the shoulders up to the upper arm as well as on the sleeve. There was a plastron made of different material under the neck of the coat, it did not button over the chest, but has a large V-shaped opened front, ending at the sash, with buttons in the centre.[245] Red coat[246] in the same year was also introduced by the English officer. The western dress particularly the frock-coats and the patent boots adopted the popular fashion among Dogras elites. Mira Seth study reveals that two royal Dogra brother look like a soldiers in Persian miniatures, where, they wear knee length coat and helmet like crown.[247] Whereas a scene of the *darbar* hall painting depicts, *Krsna* wears a long, coat in the panel depicting his abduction of Ruknini (XXXIX).[248] Other art historian name reveals that a close-fitting coat[249] of costly material was also in vogue among the Dogra nobles. According to Fredric Drew the men of the middle mountains dressed themselves in a thick woollen clothe of light-grey colour. But while in some parts they wore short-coat of same cloth. In cold places the coat was long and full one, hitched up by a *kamarband*.[250] The other variety of the coat was fashion among the Dogra people. It was was buttoned-up (*band-gale-wala-coat*) or collared coat made of *khaki* drilling cloth or a woollen coat. But its use was only occasional and not a routine.[251]

The following mentioned coats in the painting of the period were fashion among the Princes and Raja's only.

1. This variety of the British originated red coat is expounded in the picture of Raja Ram Singh.[252] Here he has been displayed wearing a dark red colour a *galati-wala-coat* or *band-gale-wala-coat*. It is a woollen cloth, well-fitted to the body, an over and outer-garment. It seems that it was a royal soldier grament. With the close observation, it makes clear from the picture that it has been imitated from Britishers soldiers (army officers). It has pockets on the chest which carry the medals of the soldier's achievements. The colour of the coat shows that the Indian people were sacrificing their life for the sake of their independence and they are being brutelessly slaughtered by the Britishers (Fig. 4).

The same kind of coats were also worn in the other parts of the Indian union.[253]

Patta

In the paintings of the same period, a *patta* or *patti* type of a grip an article of the upper garment was a fashion among the royal soldier. It has been worn from the left shoulder to the right waist in a crossed manner and appeard to be attached with a waist-belt. The literature about it mentions that it has different meaning, for example, in the *Brhat-Kalpa-Sutra-Bhasya*,[254] it has been described *patta* was woven from that *patta* yarn. It was a cẹrtain kind of silk yarn. Jaina nun's however, tied their costume with a fasteners fixed on its sides, known as *patta*. It was four fingers in width and its length was in accordance with the measurement of the nun's waist.[255] Somesvara encyclopaedic work *Manasollasa*, reveals that during the Western Calukya kings rule who ruled from 1124 to 1138 A.D. The army officers used to wear an upper-garment called as *patti*.[256]

The following variety of royal soldier's in the painting of the period are elaborated as under:

1. This typical variety of the *patta* is discovered in the picture of Maharaja Ranbir Singh shown as a soldier.[257] It appears that *patta* was few inches in width and its length was in accordance with the measurement of the soldier's body. From left shoulder to the right side of the waist in a cross-band formed constituted the dress of a soldier in a particular manner. It has sky blue colour. Colour mixing symbolise that at the time of Maharaja Ranbir Singh, rule in Jammu and Kashmir State nationalism of India was suppressed with heavy hands by the British government. *Patti* or *patta* shows Persian army fashion influence (Fig. 1).

Animal Skin

From the paintings of the period again animal skins were used as an unsewn article of clothing generally worn by the Sadhus and the aboriginal tribes. The skin of antelope, spotted-deer and spotted-tiger was worn by the Sadhu. In the *Grihya-sutras Kandika, section 10 rule 9*, it is mentioned that at the time of initiation of the students, the Brahmana used to wear skin of an antelope, Kshatriya of a spotted deer and a goat's skin by Vaisya.[258] The gods, *munis*, aborigins and *vratyas* also used skin clothing. The Maruts dressed in deer-skins are mentioned. Gods alarm the enemies with coats and shields of such skins (*harinasya-jinena*). *Munis* used to wear brown and tanned skins (*pisanga mala*). The *bratya* chiefs and their followers who used two fold (*dvisamhitani*) skins, one black and the other white (*krsna-valaksa*) so as to form furlined skin wraps, and the aboriginal tribes wore krttis and *dursa* during dances and also used *jinas*.[259] In the first century A.D. to the beginning of the 4th century A.D. a rough kind of animal skin with fur left on, or perhaps heavy woollen coats were exported from north-west India to East-Africa.[260] According to Fredric Drew in the winter, the Dogra peasants generally put on a *postin*, or short-sleeved sheep-skin coat.[261] Goat-skins, sheep-skins were mostly used by the aboriginal tribes, those, who used to live in forest. During dance, it was used as a traditional article of dress. Other varieties of the skins e.g. bears, and deers were used for making the shoes, seat, covers, etc. As we see the modern people wear leather jackets, leather shoes, bags, coats, etc.

The following varieties of the animal skins and their mode of wearing is illustrated in the paintings of the period, discussed as under:

1. The upper-garment of skins or cloth, hung from the shoulder or head, and wound arround the body and tucked under the right shoulder, is displayed in the picture of a Sadhus.[262] This was the '*upavita*' mode invariably adopted at religious rites and rituals for accumulation of knowledge (*vidaya*) and prayer by the badge of *Brahmacharaya* (continence) or concentration to accumulation of spiritual power (energy) (Fig. 2).

2. The '*samvita*' mode used to allow the skin or clothes to hung down on both the sides of the shoulders. This particular mode was used at the time of the initiation of the students of the three respective castes i.e., Brahaman, Kshatriya and Vaisya. They weared different kind of skins as already mentioned above. Sanjay has also worn it while by relating the *Mahabharata* to Daritrashtra the Sanjay.[263] Sanjay (Sadhus) has been displayed wearing an antelope spotted skin on the shoulders. It shows that Sanjay (a Brahmin) was performing his duty as a routine matter of the daily life (to king Daritrashtra). This rite and ritual has started from the Vedic period in the Hindu society (Fig. 1).

3. A painting of a door panel representing, a representative of Lord Shiva.[264] He is shown wearing an antelope spotted skin on the left shoulder hanging below the waist. It shows the spiritual power or energy of the *mantras* while its wearing. He has been shown with four arms having a *trisul*, a *damru*, *a flower* and a *conch-shell* in his hands with a flag. Picture shows the religious belief of the Dogra as the follower of Lord Shiva. A Gurad, a *nandigan*, a *chakor* (bird), a tiger having saddle on the back and two ladies are depicted praying the representative of Lord Shiva (Fig. 2).

Shawls

Shawl is a long sheet like upper-garment which was mostly used in cold climate and wrapped round the upper part of body. From various paintings of the period, it is observed that silken type of printed shawl was fashion in Jammu region among the royal class of the Dogra society. Though the paintings of the period do not exhibit the woollen shawl.[265] The poor class of the Dogra society were contented with white or a colourful white cotton sheets in the winter. The literature makes it clear that woollen fabric was generally made from wool either plain or coloured from the Vedic age.[266] In the *Yuan-Chwang's* accounts, it is referred the clothing materials used by the lay people of India are *Kiao-she-ye* (Kausheya) and muslin (*tieh*) and calico (*pu*), Kausheya being silk from a wild silk worm; *chu* (or *ch, u*)-*mo* (*kshauma*), a kind of linen; *Han* (or *Kan*)-*po-Lo*. (*Kambla*) a texture of fine wool (sheep's wool or goat's hair), *Ho-la-li* (Ral ?) a texture made from the wool of a wild animal—this wool being fine and soft and easily spun and woven was a prized material for clothing.[267] The history of shawl-weaving with which the history of woollen fabric in India is closely associated, is rather in the mist of obscurity. Kashmir is said to have enjoyed a worldwide fame for its elegant shawls from the earliest time. Different scholars expresses strongly that the origin of the shawl-industry in India for first time, was founded by Zain-ul-Abidin (1420-1470 A.D.) in Kashmir, who introduced Turkistan weaver in Kashmir. The technique of Kashmiri shawl weaving was parallel to Persia and Central Asia. Nowhere in Indo-Pakistan continent its weaving has been elaborated by the scholars. With the establishment of Afghan reign in Kashmir valley in 1753, the shawl industry received a boast. It was during this period the Kashmiri shawls were in demand in Iran, Afghanistan and Russia.[268] *Parm-narm*,[269] is a special kind of shawl, named by Akbar, made of soft, fine and rare fabric of ibex wool.[270] The trade of Kashmiri shawl had been flourished under the Sikh rule in the European Market. But the condition of the shawl weavers was not good because, the heavy imposition tax by the government. However, with the arrival of Maharaja Gulab Singh 1846, conditions for the artisans and of the shawl industry worsed. The imposed annual tax levied by the Maharaja on each shawl weaver was Rs. 47.8.[271] The outbreak of the war between France and Germany, the shawl trade suffered and temporarily collapsed, the manufactures and marchants. Though it was averted by the Maharaja who made large purchases to the value of several lakhs of rupees. The depression, obstructions and abuses slowly and gradually were removed, this valuable branch of the industry began to revive. The shawl-weavers at Badrawha, Doda, and Basohli enjoy great advantages, as they were free from many of the burdens and restrictions imposed upon their brethren in the valley of Kashmir.[272] The raw material for this product came from Ladakh and Tibet. During Gulab Singh this product was monopolized by the traders of Amritsar who took and sold it in the Punjab and Bengal and even it to French market, where a brisk demand existed. The export per loom was levied by the Raja. The weaving industry of Basohli owed its origin to the patronage of the then Raja, who imported a few workmen from Kashmir and got it started their. The initiative attracted other workers and the contagion spread in the local inhabitants till the industry throve so well that it counted, 1,400 establishments and shops dealing with shawls.[273] The craft of weaving *pashmina* thrived in Kashmir on imported *pashmina* wool from Ladakh to Tibet. Basohli in present, in Kathua district of Jammu, also used to be an important centre of *pashmina* weaving as it was on the route of marchant travelling from Tibet via Kulu. *Pashmina* being the natural coat of goat---a variety of capricious-living at high altitudes was one of the finest and softest animal fibres used in the textile industry. Besides being utilized in the country for weaving of shawls and scarves, *pashmina* was also exported to foreign countries, the bulk of which went to the USA. The shawls were of different qualities with price varying from Rs. 40 to Rs. 500. In France the price fetched by a good shawl was handsome. But unfortunately for Basohli, France under took to machine manufacture shawls and not only succeeded in meeting its own demand locally but even started exporting shawls to India.[274] This disastrously effected the industry which could not stand the competition of machine made shawls. The patronage of the Raja could not avert the catastrophe and the workers dissatisfied with their lot emigrated to place like Amritsar, Sujanpur, Nurpur, Pathankot, etc. The net result was that industry became extinct.[275]

The following varieties of a shawls preferred by a *nayaka*, in the paintings of period is explained in details as under:

1. This variety of the printed woollen shawl located in the picture of a *nayaka*.[276] He wears it on the shoulders and covered the back reaching the knees frequently. *Nayaka* has been shown in an elegant dress made of superior stuff. He has a parrot in his right hand and a stick to his left hand. The expression of the picture shows that he was a healthy and wealthy man of the area, and shown waiting for the message of his *nayika*, who is absent from the home rather she has gone to her parents home for few days (Fig. 3).

The same kind of shawl mentioned above was also prevalent in other Indian territories.[277]

Kambala or *Patoo* (Blanket)

The paintings of the period makes it very clear that a *kambla* or *pattoo* was a long sheet type cloth, normally used in the winter. It was made of coarse wool of sheeps. It was a common wearing an article of dress either plain or colourful. In the Vedic age *kambala* together with *samulya* formed a part of the ordinary domestic.[278] In the *Yuan-Chwang* account, it is elaborated that *kambala* was allowed to the Buddhist Brethren.[279] In *Akbarnama*, the word called *siyah-gilim*[280] is used for black-blanket. It depicts that black *kambala* was used to wrap in the Mughal period. *Tuzk-I-Jahangiri*, also mention that in Kashmir *pattoo chaddar* was used and made of wool and two chaddars were sewed together, they smooth them into a kind of *saqarlat* (broad-cloth[281]). In Kangra, Dogra peasant generally brought with them *pattoo* or blanket, which in Jammu was replaced by *postin* or short-sleeved sheep-skin coat. The *pattoo* was of home spun texture, woven in alternative square.[282] In Badhrawah and Kishtwar areas, of Jammu region, women weared a long piece of local made *loia* or *pattoo*[283] or blanket[284] which were popular throughout India, round the body coming over the shoulders, fastened by two curious long pins, with a chain connecting them. Sometimes a blanket wound round the loins, a pair of gross shoes used to complete the costume,[285] and men all dress in a light grey thick woollen cloth also called *pattoo* which was made in almost every house.[286] Census Report of India, 1931, describes that woollen blankets and *pattoos* under the Dogras rule (1846-1947) were manufactured in Ramnagar Tehsil and was exported outside. The military department of the State precured the demand of blankets from this Tehsil but due to machine made blankets and *pattoos* with a superior finish and cheaper price this industry began to decay.[287] The collective data of the textile industries as it mentioned in the census report of India, comprise 40 establishments, i.e., 6 woollen carpet factories 24 shawl weaving factories, 4 fringe weaving factories all in Srinagar, 2 silk factories (Jammu 1, Srinagar 1) and one *pattoo* factory in Srinagar. Textiles have given employment to 4,451 persons or nearly 58% of the total skilled population registered at special industrial census. Only 106 were females (including 1 female convict in the Jammu Jail factories). The number of silked workers was 2,885 males and 38 females, and the proportion of adult females employed per 1000 adult males works out at twelve children, however took every thousand adult, there were no less than 341 children.[288]

The following varieties of the *kambala* or blanket which were used by the people of the Jammu region, are depicted in the paintings of the period are elaborated as under:

1. This variety of the *kambala* or *pattoo* like garment is detected in the picture of camel puller[289] of Rai Raodeh Dharmsawal. It has been displayed in a hanging manner on the right shoulder of camel puller by making its one edge gathered in the form of a knot falling below the knees. It used during winter. It is always light cream and garlic in colour as mostly the wool of the sheep is grown. The camel puller in the painting has been shown naked around the upper part of his body. It shows that he was an ordinary man and his financial condition was weak. Colour shows that this tolerating the Mughal power (Fig. 4).

2. The painting of Lord Krishna[290] demonstrated a different variety of the *kambala* (blanket). Lord Krishna hangs it on the left shoulder worn it against the cold. It is a black blanket, made of a special kind

of wool. He has been shown playing with flute and Radha is listening its lyric meticulously. It appears the royalty of the Dogra society used blankets of superior wool. Colour of blanket is the epitome of the sad event as *nayaka* was leaving *nayika* in an isolation owing to his other preoccupations (Fig. 4).

3. Third kind of the *chadar* type of garment known as *pattoo* or *loia* is explored in the picture of a Sadhu.[291] He hangs it on the left shoulder by making a knot like a tent. It shows that it was used in the cold season. He is displayed vibrating a *mala* or *mantra* of the Hindu religious philosophy in front of Radha-Krishna temple of Purmandal. He wears brownish *pattoo* which was mostly preferred by Hindu saints (Fig. 1).

4. This kind of the *chadar* type of garment has also been called by the name of *pattoo* or *kambala* and is explored in the picture of Gulab Singh's Guru.[292] He is seated on the ground, and is wrapping it round the naked body instructing Gulab Singh and with his troops. It is a blood red *pattoo* of Indian origin garment from the Vedic times. (Fig. 3).

The similar kind of *pattoos* were also preferred in other parts of the Indian union.[293]

Lower Garments (*Adhovastra*)

The paintings of the period shed light on the people of Jammu region who attached similar significance to both lower garment (*adhovastra*) and upper garments (*uttariya*). The climatic condition of the Jammu region has provided a unique dress habits to its people according the style of its wearing was adopted. Lower garment provides a cover to the most private part of the human body. In different periods it had different names, including; *antariyavasas*, *kanpina*, *kaupinavasas*, *jati-pattika*, *nivasana*, *nishpravani*, *pata*, *vasana*.[294] Certain paintings indicate that the lower garments made of woollen were also used. In such paintings upper garment is woollen, therefore, possibility is that the lower garment would have remained woollen in winter and cotton in summer. The garment in the shape of trousers were called as *churidar-pyjama*, *tight-reb-dar-pyjama* or *suthan*, *tambi*;[295] *khuli-mohari-wala-pyjama*,[296] etc. The *pyjama* with disimilar switching was a common lower dress among both the men and the women. Besides the said varieties of the trousers, the other lower garments known as *dhoti*, *tehmat*, *kaccha*, *longota*, *lungi*, etc., were also used by the men of Jammu region.

The main features of the lower garments are epitomized in the paintings of same period preferred by the menfolk discussed as under:

Pyjama (*Paijama, Paejama, Pyjamah*)

Pyjama in a lower garment woren in legs. It always had a cotton made string which ties it with the body near the hip and stomach with the help of a knot. It has some similar and related garments called *ghutanna, suthan, salwar, izar*, etc. *Pyjama* is a Persian term which is a compound of two words '*pae + jamni*' = *paejama* means '*leg* or *feet*' and '*jama*' means '*cover*'. Thus, it is signified '*leg clothing*'. In its shape and pattern, *paejama* has tended to vary especially in respect of its girth, length, fitness material and the like. Over a period of time, it became a general dress, and came to be accepted as a popular garment by the menfolk of the Jammu, as has been depicted in the paintings of the period. In Gupta period, trousers was of the loose *salwar* type, but of a *churidar* type[297] *pyjama* was fashion among the kings. In Mughal period, tight *paijamas*[298] and drawers (*izar*)[299] for leggings have also worn by the emperor. A lower garment, short of *pyjama* type, tight and end at the calves, worn by the Punjabi and called as *ghutanna* acquired a measure of populatiry.[300] W.G. Archer mentions that a lower garment known as close-fitted *pyjama*[301] was worn by the Dogra kings. It was worn in many shapes and cut. Such types of *pyjamas* were made of cheap mill-made cotton or *khadar*. People also used to wear *reb-dar-pjama* or *khuli-mohari-ka-pyjama*. A tight *reb-dar-pyjama* was of great choice[302] among Dogras. The *pagri* and *churidar-tight-pyjama* was the court dress[303] of the Dogras along with a (chintze) white shirt or *kameez*.

The following varieties of the lower garment called as *pyjamas* was popular among males, as depicted in the paintings of the period. It elaboration is as under:

1. The first style of the lower garment which has been known as *pyjama* is discovered in the picture of Khwaja Kheizer.[304] It is a green *churidar pyjama* of woollen cloth and well-fitted to the legs. The colour of the lower garment signifies that he was happy to see the plain and lash green area of India after descending the snow fields of Samarkand. It shows Persian fashion influence (Fig. 4).

2. This variety of the tight *pyjama* we expounded in the picture of Raga *Khokhar*.[305] A dancer wears a red and black pointed *churidar-pyjama* which is well-fitted in the legs. Colour scheme of the lower garment shows that he was attempting hard to entertain the audience. However, few remained unhappy with his performances. It shows Persian fashion influence (Fig. 2).

3. The portrait of Raja Kirpal Pal[306] depicts another kind of the lower garment known as tight-*pyjama*. It has red and black linings. Colours reflect that he was determined to set up a strong empire, though he had certain economic or political problems in his way. It

also depicts Mughal fashion influence (Fig. 1).

4. This variety of the tight-*pyjama* is in the picture of Raja Medini Pal.[307] It is well-fitted *pyjama* with red and blue linings. The colour scheme of the *pyjama* indicates that he had a desire to establish strong empire and but was demoralized owing to impending social problems. Same type of lower garment has also been worn by his *chouri*-bearer. He has a cheap cotton-made lower garment. Its stuff is known as *pattya*. It also shows Mughal fashion influence (Fig. 1).

5. The picture of Raja Kishan Singh[308] demonstrated different variety of the lower garment known as tight-*pyjama*. He wears green silken *tight-pyjama* having vertical golden lining, well-fitted in the legs and a silken *kurta*. Colour combination of the lower garment depicts that he was leading a peaceful life and his state was in progress and had light sway over his state. *Pyjama* shows Mughal fashion influence (Fig. 3).

6. This variety of the lower-garment is located in the painting of Raja Jai Singh.[309] He wears fitted-*pyjama* but little bit loose of light pinkish colour having vertical lining with pointed design of grey colour. It has golden border at its lower ends. Colour combination of the lower garment indicates that he was contented man even after pinchits. It was a moderate type of *pyjama* and shows Mughal fashion influence (Fig. 2).

7. This type of the lower-garment is unearthed in the picture of Raja Jagat Singh.[310] He wears it with the white pointed shirt. *Pyjama* has reddish background, floral print and golden borders are at its lower ends. It was a *reb-dar-well-fitted-gehere-dar-pyjama*. Colour scheme of the *pyjama* demonstrated that he enjoyed tight sway over his state was and happy with his performances. It also shows Persian fashion influence (Fig. 2).

8. The piture of Maharaja Gulab Singh[311] demonstrated another variety of the lower garment. He wears an orange colour *tight-pyjama* with lining designs, well-fitted in the legs. Colour and vertical lining design of the lower garment depicts that he had an urge to established a strong and powerful empire. It shows Mughal fashion influence (Fig. 1).

9. Another different kind of the lower garment known as *pyjama* is expounded in the picture of Maharaja Gulab Singh as a soldier.[312] It was a *reb-dar-churi-wala-pyjama* of *haldi* (yellow) colour, well-fitted in legs. Colour scheme shows that Sikh rule has faded and Dogra rule has been established. He is shown in a posture as if he was preparing himself for the governance the Jammu and Kashmir State. *Pyjama* shows Persian fashion influence (Fig. 3).

10. This variety of the lower garment which is known as *pyjama* has been found in the picture of *panchvakta* a man appears like a Maharaja Ranbir Singh.[313] He wears white cotton shirt and an orange colour of tight-*pyjama,* well-fitted in the legs also made of cotton. The colour expression of the lower-garment depicts that he was a powerful ruler of his time. *Pyjama* shows Persian fashion influence (Fig. 4).

11. The picture of Maharaja Partap Singh[314] demonstrated another kind of the *pyjama.* He wears a *haldi* (yellow) *chogha* and same colour tight woollen *pyjama* well-fitted in the legs. Its colour reflects the princely rule gradually fading and new rule is going to set up. *Pyjama* shows Persian fashion influence (Fig. 1).

A beautiful example pertaining to the impact on local fashions dress is of Dogri writer on the eve of Muslim in vasion in India, is in the following few lines of this folk song:

"गन्धै दी शिडकै मत जन्दा,
ते छन्दा मिंजो मन्दा लग्गा ओ।
पटे दी तम्बी मत लांदा,
छन्दा मिंजो मन्दा लग्गा ओ।
पटे दी तम्बी मेरा उमरी दा लाब्बा,
तेरी गल्ला किया छड़डां ओ।
काला कोट मत लांदां,
ते छन्दा मिंजो मन्दा लग्गा ओ।
काला कोट मेरा उमरी दा लाब्बा,
तेरी गल्ला कियां छड़्डां ओ।"[315]

Tr. into English:

In this folk song a Dogri writer highlights the argument of a couple on a dress.

Nayika says: "Don't move on the dirty roads (muddy street).
Dear! it doesn't look nice to me.
Don't try to wear on *tambi* of *pattya's.*
Dear! It doesn't look nice to me.
Nayika replies: *Tambi* of *pattya* is my dress since long period.
Why, I should leave it for your word (saying).
She again says: Don't try to put on a black coat (cloak).
Dear! It doesn't look nice to me.
He replies: Having a black coat (cloak) is my dress since long.
Why, I leave it for your word (saying)."[316]

Dhoti

Most of the portrayals of the period sheds light that legs were mostly tucked by a *dhoti.* It was a traditional garment of the Indian people and was common among the priestly class of the Dogra's (Hindus). It is an unsewn a piece of cloth drapped round the waist in different ways which also covers the legs of the wearer. It appears, that some weared it in a easy form round the waist in skirt shape and some are shown wearing it by putting one end to the cloth on the backside of the loin. It was also used in the warm climate and worn since remote past as Harappa excavations reveal wearing of clining *dhoti*.[317] In Sunga period *dhoti* or loin-cloth was major male costume.[318] On the coins, Gupta kings are wearing *dhoti* and *dupatta* as well as a tunics and trousers.[319] In *Amarakosa* for *dhoti* have four words i.e., *antariya*, *upasamvyana*, *paridhana* and *adhomsuka*.[320] The local dialects of the Dogras it has been also called as *dhoti* as it has been called in other parts of India. In the period between 11th century A.D. to 13th century A.D. it,[321] there was a distinct regional differences in wearing the *dhoti* between the South and North Indian people. The Northern India adopted a wide and voluminous *dhoti* and in Southern of India a tight type of *dhoti* like the trouser was wrapped. In *Kalpasutra*,[322] the 15th century chronical a typical heavily ornamented *dhoti* and a scarf was fashion among males. It is also worn nowaday in various parts of Indian territories.

The following types of the *dhoti's* are found in the paintings of the period and worn by Dogra men explained here as under:

1. The first and common mode of wearing of *dhoti* or loin-cloth is found in the picture of Lord Krishna.[323] He wraps it round the waist and its frontal pleats display the perhaps after times around the waist, it passed between the legs and then it tucked at the back. The cloth wrapped round the waist is having bigger end and is pleated beautifully and tucked at the navel. He wears a yellow *dhoti* and is seated under a shady tree where he is playing flute. Colour simbilizes that he has left the wordly life and intends to lead a spiritual life. *Dhoti* was the traditional dress of Dogras (Indian or Hindus) (Fig. 2).

2. This variety of the *dhoti* is found in the picture of Gulab Singh's army personels,[324] who are shown getting the blessing and instruction from the guru (of Gulab Singh) and other Sadhus along with Gulab Singh before proceeding to war. They wear *ghaghra* type of circular white *dhoti* having the border with smoking colour. Colour scheme of the *dhoti* indicates that on the borders of the Jammu and Kashmir State, foreign armies penetration was disturbing the peace of the Jammu and Kashmir State. Gulab Singh was interested to attack them with heavy hand. It was another different style of the *dhoti*. It was the traditional Indian an article of dress (Fig. 3).

3. Another elegant variety of the *dhoti* is again explored in the picture of Lord Krishna.[325] He wraps it round the waist, and pleats of

the one end of it has been beautifully arranged tucked near the navel and its other end is shown tucked in the back of the waist. It is yellow *dhoti* having lac red lining design in vertical as well as in curved pattern in the form of wrinkles. Moreover, it is decorated by stitching white jewels on the surface of the *dhoti* and on the lower end of the border. It was also an Indian originated lower garment. It is a superior silken *dhoti*. The colour scheme of the *dhoti* shows that he used to get rid of the wordly life, but being in a human he was surrounded with certain responsibilities, of society, its cultural social, political, spiritual and worry of human happiness (Fig. 1).

4. The portrait of a representative of Shiva[326] exposed another typical variety of the *dhoti*. He wears half yellow and half pinkish colour in the same pattern as mentioned above. The colour scheme of the *dhoti* shows that he has left worldly life and shown contended by attaining heights of spirituality. He has liberated himself from the cycle of life and death (Fig. 2).

A traditional *dhoti* of the Dogra (Indian) origin was wrap in different modes. A Dogri writer explains it in the following folk song:

"जीजा तेरी धोती दा,
जीजा तेरी धोती दा केह करां ?
धोती बान्द्रै अग्गैं धरां।
बांदर लेई बडै पर चढै।
बांदर लीरां–लीरां करै।
ते बान्दर पुर्जे–पुर्जे करै।
बान्दर हई–हई....करै।
ते बान्दर हऊ–हऊ–करै।"[327]

Tr. into English:

This is a marriage ceremonial song in the honour of a bridegroom song his sister in-laws and their friends:

Title of the song: "*Jija* (brother-in-law) what we do for your *dhoti*
We put this *dhoti* on the face of monkeys.
Monkey lifted it and climbed a pipal tree.
Monkey tore-tore it,
Monkey make it pieces, pieces.
Monkey will cry haie, haie....
And monkey will do cry hoo-hoo..."

Same types of the *dhoti* we also find in the other States of the Indian territories.[328]

Lungi (Loin-cloth)

Lungi (loin-cloth) fastened on waist has similar garment called *tehmat*, *lacha* and *majhla* in the local language of the Dogras as generally known in ther parts of the Indian region. They have little bit differences in mode of wearing, in length and width. *Lungi* or loin-cloth is short in length and width than the *tehmat* or a *lacha*. It is also an unstitched piece of cloth worn by the Dogra people in the warm climate as a luxury item of the dress as we learn in the paintings of the period. Paintings also shed light that it was mostly made of cotton and was a traditional Indian (Dogra) dress. Its wearing in Indian is ancient. In Sunga period the small loin-cloth (*lungi*) was fastened near waist[329] by horsemen, grooms, etc. In the *Akbarnama*, it was called as *lungi*,[330] a small piece of loin-cloth, was also worn by Akbar while relaxing. In the paintings, it has been displayed that it was popular dress wear in the 19th century A.D. in Jammu region.

The following varieties and style of wearings are found in the paintings of the period and elaborated as under:

1. The first mode of wearing the *lungi* or a small loin found cloth in the picture of Rai Raodeh Dharmsalwala a camel puller.[331] He wraps it round the waist in skirt style knotted at the navel. It cotton made used in the hot season. It was a grey loin-cloth and depicts that there was a problem in the state and the proceeding to Rajasthan to seek the help of Rajput States against Akbar's mightily forces. It was a Dogra's (Indian) traditional garment. The painting depicts the poor economic state of the camel driver (Fig. 1).

2. In painting of Maharaja Partap Singh an umbrella-bearer[332] displays another kind of the loin-cloth which is known as *tehmat*. He wraps it round the waist as usually worn, but he has painted with folded turn and tucked near the navel. He wears it over the *suthan*. It is an *haldi* (yellow) *tehmat*. Colour scheme shows that slavery of the working class is on declining. It was Dogra (Indian) traditional clothing (Fig. 1).

It was also a fashioned among other in various Indian States.[333]

Animals Skin

In the paintings of the period, animal skin was also worn as a lower garment by the Sadhu (Brahmin) who held round the waist. They are shown wearing an antelope lack spotted skin. It shows that it was used to wrap for the accumulation of spiritual strength. As already stated the upper-garment, skin was used during in Vedic times at the time of initiation of the students. It was mostly worn by the *rishi*, *munis*, and *saints* of the Hindu community. The study indicates that coats, jackets and boots were also made of its leather.

The following modes of wearing of animals skin by the Hindu saints are found in the portrays of the period explained as under:

1. The first mode of wearing the animal skin is expounded in the picture of Daksh Yajan (Bribh-addra-usinatting) in Hawan-Kund.[334] In the picture, sadhu is shown wearing an antelope spotted skin knotted round the waist and reaches above the knees and keeps an archery in his hands. Its black and yellow skin shows that Sadhu had a barrier in the attainment of spirituality he had to remove it with the accumulation of divinity. This kind of skin was used by the Brahmin (Sadhu). It was the traditional dress of the Sadhu of a Hindu society (Fig. 2).

Langota or _Kaccha_ (Loin-cloth)

Paintings of the period also demonstrated that *langota, kaccha* or short breech or loin-cloth knotted round the waist were worn in Jammu region by the Sadhus and the Gopas of Lord Krishna. It mostly covered the private part of the body. *Kaccha* or *langota* was mostly used in the rural areas by the labourers and agriculturists. The *langota* not only covered the private part, but it cured hernia or the undescendent of the testies and Sadhu's they used to control the sex and to accumulate spiritual power through Vedic *mantras*. Besides the Sadhus or labourers, it was also used by the wrestler's at the time of wrestling. In the local language of the Dogras, it has been called as *roomali, langar*; etc. In the period between 1st century A.D. to 4th century A.D. a short loin-cloth *janghia*[335] was worn by soldiers *langota*[336] was a common wear of labourers and agriculturist class. In the Gupta period, it became like the wrestler's short (*janghia, mallacalanakrtih*) except that its broad and was firmly tied between the two thighs (*urudvayeca kasavaboddhah*). It resembled sometimes like the modern *langota*.[337] In the painted wooden block of the Jaisalmer Jnana Bhandar army personels a tight-fitting shorts made of striped material is worn.[338] Short breeches,[339] *kuch* or *kaccha*[340] instead of trousers,[341] was also worn by the agriculturist class in Jammu region.

The following modes of wearing the *langota* or *kacchas* preferred by the men of the Jammu region, represented in the portrayals of the period delineated in detail as under:

1. This variety of the lower garment i.e., known as *langota* or *langoti* as a lower garment is found in the picture of Rama's *Panchyat*, worn by Hanuman.[342] It is a stitched *piece* of cloth held round the waist, and is shown passing between the legs which covers private part of his body, and its one end is tucked to the back of the waist, and has a shape of a short breeches called a *langota*. It has been worn in the warm climate of the areas. It was a Dogra (Indian) traditional garment worn as an underwear under the trousers. Hanuman wears it under the *kamarband*. It is pinckish *langota*. Colour shows that he

was happy to attend the duty which has been assigned by the Rama (Fig. 2).

2. Another variety of the *langota,* is in the picture of a Sadhu,[343] who has been shown standing on one leg. It shows that he wears few inches of unstitched cloth held round the waist and then there is another a piece of cloth which tucked at the navel between the legs from the back of the waist. It was also another kind of the *langota* called in the local language of the Dogras. It was worn during the warm climate of the area. The Sadhu wears grey *langota.* Colour shows that he overcomes the problems i.e., *vidya* or *mantras* to accumulate the spiritual power. It was also a Dogra traditional garment (Fig. 2).

3. Third typical variety of the short breaches or *roomali,* a different kind of the *langota* we detected in the picture of soldiers.[344] It appears that an unsewn piece of cloth and cream colour stripped cloth have been arranged in an artistic way that it covers the whole hips of the soldier and its one end has been shown passing between the legs which cover the private part of the soldier. The colour combination of these *langotas* show that they have to show tolerate in the event of war and has to restore peace and happiness. They have worn it in the hot season. It was also a Dogra (Indian) traditional lower garment (Fig. 1).

4. This variety of the short breeches or *kaccha's* is detected in the picture of *Gita-Govinda* repentance of Lord Krishna, worn by Gopas.[345] Here, we see that a group of Gopa's of Lord Krishna wear indigo, pinkish, red and blood red colours of plain short breeches or *kacchas* round the waist. Above the shorts breeches, different *kamarband,* of white, pinkish, grey, etc. have been weared round the waist. It was a sewn garment worn against during the warm climate of the Jammu region. The colours of the shorts demonstrate that when over Krishna intended to shift from one place to another, they have been displayed in a sad mood. Moreover, the scene shows the rural life of the Jammu region that it was tough and poor, that most of the working class, they used short breeches. It also shows the economic condition of the area was not better. It was a Dogra originated garment with the impact of Muslims invasion which contributed the sewing art of clothing in India (Fig. 3).

Pant

Paintings of the period also shed light that wearing of *pant* was also a fashion among the later Dogra political and military elite. Now-a-days it is a common dress among men and the women of the Jammu region. It is has durable material and have sturdier stitching than *pyjama*. It is held at the waist with the help of a belt, hooks or buttons doing away the complication of a string. And, of course, there is the buttons or a zipper in the front provide incomparable convenience. Sometime, it is used in baggy pattern and sometimes, it is fitted to the legs in various colours. The word '*pant*' derived from '*pantaloon*', the clown in Comedia del, Arte, and his characteristic grab, the loose-fitting *pyjamas* of the comic atora crobat. Yet, trousers, of all garments, may claim to have revolutionary significance, adopted by the French revolutionists to replica the privileged breeches of aristocracy. In due, course, the garment evolved into the present day '*pant*'.

The following varieties of the *pant* or *pantaloon* common among elites of the Jammu region, are depicted in the paintings of period explained as under:

1. This variety of the lower garment i.e., known as *pant*, is explored in the pictures of Ram Singh, Amar Singh and Partap Singh.[346] As it appears in the paintings that it brought certain obvious advantage to the wearer than that of the other lower garment of Indian origin. It is loose-fitting type of pant called the beggy or a loose *pyjama*. In the paintings elites wear black pants with lac red coat. The major factor in the popularity of the pant, is its incorporation into the uniforms of the military, schools, police, attendants, security personels, drivers and hosts of the hotel employees. It normally has three pockets. It shows European fashion influence. The black colour symbolizes mournfulness for Indians during British rule as they ruled with monetarism, and committed all crimes against people. As a result there was restless in whole of the Indian territory (Figs. 2, 3 and 4).

2. This variety of the pant, is obtained in the picture of Raja Suchet Singh as a soldier.[347] He wears *khaki* which appears as skin colour of tight-fitted *pant* with a smart red jacket. Such type of *pant* or a lower garment was mostly worn by the British army or police officers. Colour of the *pant* exhibits that he was healthy and powerful man of the area. *Pant* shows British fashion influence (Fig. 1).

Footwear

In the paintings of the period, shoes and sandals of different shapes, patterns, with variety of colours and material formed an important article of dress. It shows that the dress of a man has been taken as incomplete without a shoes. There were important a part of the costume and considered as a luxury item. These were non-traditional among common people. The close study of the portrayals reveal, that, it was not possible for the painter to demonstrate them in many artistic styles. It appears that there were made out of variety of leather. Leather of various kinds was one of the important industry,[348] that provide livelihood and brought to light the talent of the people in the Jammu region. Footwears both ornamental and ordinary were in use. Such sandals and slippers in those days was the fashion and profession of the cobbler (*chamar's*).[349] Leather shoes decorated with woollen fluffing were also a fashion in the Jammu region. In the local language of the Dogras footwear were known as *jora,*[350], *paniyanas,*[351] *nukayana.*[352] The fashion of wearing the shoes and sandals have started in the remote past as in the *Grihya-Sutra*, *Prapathaka* 1, *Kandika* 25, it has been described that in no case sandals[353] were worn by men and in *Prapathaka* III, *Kandika* 25, shoes were worn in the villages also.[354] But, in the period, between 150-100 B.C. sandals among the king were very rare.[355] In the *Yuan-Chwang*, it is discussed that in India most of the people go bare foot and shoes were rare.[356] The Sanskrit lexicons, *Vaijayanti* of 11th century A.D. and *Abhidhanacintamani* of 12th century A.D. recorded the traditional information about the shoes maker (cobbler) who was known as *padukakrt* and *carmakt* (*Abhi*; III, 914). The shoes are classified as *upanat* (shoes) *paduka*, *padar* (sandals), *pannaddha* (*H. panabi*), *padarakasana* (protecting the feet), *pranahita* (enemy), (*Abhi*; III, 915), *anupadina* (according to foot measurement) and *adaddha* (strapped) (*Abhi*; III, 915).[357] In the times of Babar high boots were worn while riding; and the smaller shoes were in use in home or in the camp.[358] The shoes with horn-shaped back and embroidered with gold thread[359] was worn by the emperor Akbar. The shoes without horned back and no heels, of crimsen leather, with a plain black piece across the instep[360] was fashion by emperor Jahangir. The shoes without heels (no horse black) and elaborately embroidered[361] was used by emperior Shah Jahan and heavy-heeled shoes[362] was fashion in the later Mughal period.

In Kishtwar, during the time of Maharaja Ranbir Singh, the footwear of the hill people was grass shoes.[363] The Meghs (a tribe) were cobblers and shoes-maker.[364] But these shoes were merely soles with one broad band between the big and the toes. The band was fastened loosely an both sides with the sole. The heel was also quite loose and unbound. By regular practice, however, the people kept the shoes firmly attached to their feet. It is said that wheat straw woven into fine rope was a fashion into the shoes and decorated with coloured threads on the upper half. These were used in the remote hilly region of Kishtwar, where most of the journeys were undertaken on foot over wet and slippery terrain. Earlier, for out door use, inhabitants of the entire Himalayan region wore different versions of this design in straw shoes. Felt and woollen shoes with straw shoes were worn indoors by both men and women and common footwear was made of local leather and called as *joota*.[365] Whereas, the people from Kishtwar wore ornamental straw shoes with coloured threads and pompoms. There were many differences in dress between the Muslims and Hindus, However, Hindu women unlike their Muslim counterparts, always wore grass sandals, never leather ones.[366] In Basohli, there was a *boali* of *Dhan* having various sculptures of Hindu gods and goddesses, three miles from Thara-Kadwal and on the way to Khun, there is a figure of a standing *yogi* knotted beard. He wears a *dhoti* and a scarf, and has a woollen sandals on his feets.[367]

The following varieties of footwear in the paintings of the period preferred by the Dogra men are elaborated as under:

1. This variety of the footwear is in the picture of Maharaja Gulab Singh[368] in a war procession. Here, Suchet Singh the military General of Maharaja Gulab Singh wears a beautiful shoes made of leather, and have been embroidered with golden wire and decorated with floral design on the face and sides. It is a sharp shape toe at the face. The colour treatment of the single sole shoes shows that Gulab Singh's empire was progressing and becoming strong day by day from the very ground level. Footwear shows Punjabi fashion influence (Fig. 1).

2. There is one more variety of the shoes fashioned amongst the Generals[369] of the Gulab Singh, detected in the same picture mentioned above. But it keeps slight difference from the toe as it is hook shape and made of single sole leather. It appears from its orange colour and the pattern of design that during the Gulab Singh's rule the resources for development in the Jammu and Kashmir were limited, but with his great efforts slowly and gradually, the State was progressing and strengthened. Footwear shows Punjabi fashion influence (Fig. 2).

3. The painting of Maharaja Partap Singh[370] demonstrated another type of the shoes made of leather. Here, he wears a simple kind of footwear made of sky colour. This kind of the shoes or *nukana* was popular among the men folk of the Jammu region. This example is visible in the picture of his umbrella bearer. He wears same kind of shoes, but it has cream colour and simple. The shoes have sharp toes at the face. The colour scheme of the Partap Singh shoes reveals that there was unpleasant time during his period in India as British gevernment was committing crime against the Indian's and lawlessness was the common feature. The colour treatment of the umbrella bearer's shoes show that princely rule is on decline and freedom from the clutches of princes and nawabs is coming. It was a Dogra's traditional footwear (Fig. 3).

4. This kind of the shoes prefered by *nayaka*.[371] It is made of leather and decorated with the golden wire having pointed design. It

is superior kind of shoes in a hook shape toe. It was like a traditional shoes Dogra. It appears that this art during Dogra rule was flourishing the handicraft industry. Colour vibration of the shoes depict that during Dogra rule, development in the economic field was taking place in Jammu (Fig. 4).

5. This variety of the shoes we explored in the picture of Maharaja Jai Singh.[372] He wears single sole slipper type footwear. The upper part of slipper has been made with two joints, one has lac red colour and another has orange colour, and opened from the spur having sharp toe. It was also a Dogra's traditional footwear. The colour combination of the slippers shows that Jai Singh was a powerful emperor, but his rule was slipping out of his hand and Sikh's slowly and gradually. There was no powerful Dogra emperor who could have united the Dogra territory and resisted rising of the Sikh power (Fig. 5).

6. The portrait of Lord Krishna[373] demonstrated another variety of the shoes known as an ankle-shoes or full-boot. He weared it during war of *Mahabharata*. Through the *media* of brush (*kalam*), painter highlighted the military lifestyle of the Dogras rulers who during the war and hunting time for the protection of the naked feets used full-boots. Here, in picture, one finds that this full-boot, has been made of black leather having joint stitched on upper part with double sole, and high heels. The black boot shows the disaster of the period either it was lawlessness or a terrific event was going to taken place. Footwear displays Central Asian fashion influence brought by the Mughal to India (Fig. 6).

7. The pair of the shoes or *jora* is detected in the wall-painting of the Mansar temple.[374] It is a different kind of shoes having distant pattern of design. It was worn by the ordinary man and of animal skin. This shoes has a long hook shape toe. Footwear has a long projection in upward direction from the spur. It has self colour and displays Dogras fashion influence. Colour scheme of the shoes declares that the economic condition of the wearer was not well (Fig. 7).

8. The portrait of a soldier[375] demonstrated another type of footwear known as sandal and made of wood in a pattern of a sole, a short sticked type of button has been placed on it which grip the feet at proper position. It has also a small heel supported by the piece of wood. Such type of sandals were used by the men of the Hindu society in the premises of the temples and in kitchens to avoid the leather shoes. It was also a Dogra's traditional footwear (Fig. 8).

In one of the popular falk song, a Dogri poet describes the beauty of the shoes, dreses and ornaments which has been fashioned during the period of 19th century A.D. discussed in the following manners:

"सज्जने दा घोडा हिन–हनाया सज्जन खडोते आई बाहर।
झट्ट गोरी जाई कोठे पर चढी ऐ कूडा जे रेहई आ पसार।।
सज्जने दे सिर बुंबलू जे सौभे ला भदा ऐ ठानेदार।
सज्जने दे गल काली जे गान्नी, जुत्ती ऐ तिल्लेदार।।
मंजा डाहन्नी आँ सेज बधान्नी आं, बेहई जाओ मेरी जान।
लाम्मियें डीकें जिन्द रूलाई दुनियां नित्त बरान।।
लाम्भियें डीके माही घर आया अक्खीं चा डुल्लेआ नीर।
नेई रो नाजो रानिये, सज्जन घोडी जे आए कश्मीर"।[376]

Tr. into English:

Meeting of the Raja and Rani after a long period:

Rani was waiting her *nayaka* for a long period, who was away to Kashmir from the home for his business. As soon as he appears in the house, Rani expressed her sentiments in the following lines:

"Raja stood on outside the house, Raja's horse have a neigh. Immediately Rani rush on the roof of the house, garbage remains in the corridor or verandhe (she was brooming the house at that occasion).

Raja having a high tuff turban (*pagri*) looking nice, as a police officer. Raja have a black *ganni* in his neck and shoes made of copper-wire embroidery.

Rani: Sheeted on the *cot*, be seated, my sweet heart.

After a long waiting, health became unsound and world always looking barren.

After a long period (Raja) her husband came at home, she keeps weeping. Don't weep my heartly queen, I have left the Kashmir."

9. This variety of the shoes is detected in the picture of a Dogra soldier.[377] He wears *jora* or shoes made of self coloured leather. It was a Dogra traditional shoe having sharp toe and hook type horn on the face in the opposite direction. Shoes have double sole and upward projected spur. The expression on the shoes craft shows that Gulab Singh had a strong military power. But the economic condition of the soliders were not satisfactory (Fig. 9).

10. The variety of the full-boot or ankle shoes, is discovered in the picture of Maharaja Gulab Singh's General possibly Raja Suchet Singh.[378] It was a black shoes made of leather. At the upper end of the anklet it keeps curvature type and stitched chain spots. Such type of boots were used in Central Asia and brought in India by the Mughals. It was mostly worn by the military Chiefs during war and hunting procession. The black shoes symbolizes life in hard and hitting battlefields (Fig. 10).

11. One more the shoes or *jora* we expounded in the picture of another soldier of the Gulab Singh.[379] It is a plain and simple *jora*

having sharp shaped toe, and hooked shape projection, it has short hook. It was also a traditional shoes of the Dogra's called *Desi Jora* and made of animal skin having self colour. This shoe was popular among the Dogra people. Colour scheme of the shoes demonstrate the normal status of the mind of the wearer (Fig. 11).

12. This variety of the shoes is explored in the painting of Raja Man Singh.[380] It is made of white leather and decorated by stitching sky blue colour of leather on the upper surface. Shoe had single sole and sharp shaped toe. From the ankle it has high projection. The colour treatment of the shoe depicts that he had a problem in the beginning of the reign and was feeling unhappy, but he tolerated. Footwear shows Mughalian fashion influence (Fig. 12).

13. The portrait of Raja Suchet Singh[381] demonstrated another variety of the high shoes or full-boot. He wears black shoes made of superior leather. Shoe has circular toe and long as it touches the knees. It was used during war or in hunting procession. Colour scheme of the shoe demonstrate that it was used in the warfare event. Footwear shows European fashion influence (Fig. 13).

The comparative study of the painting reveals period that only a few styles shoes were not prevalent in Dogra society but it had created variety of models and they with great comfort extended them in other parts of the India [382]

Female Dresses

On the basis of the available paintings dresses of the women, like men can also be divided into two parts:

1. Traditional Dogras Dresses, and
2. The Dresses displaying foreign influence.

Head-dress

Inspite of the fact, that head-dress was one of the important men dress wear, but the women of the period also used it with the purpose of beautifying themselves. The Jammu paintings indicate that traditional Dogra head-dress of the women was *dupatta, ordhani* or a *chadar* (an unstitched piece of cloth in rectangular pattern). In the local language of Dogras, it is known as *ordhani, chadar, dupatta* and *saloo* as it is generally called in other parts of the Indian States. Paintings display besides *dupatta* or *ordhani*, etc., used to wrap by the women some caps were also prevent among female. Some pictures of the goddesses also shown *mukuta* (crown) and tiaras. According to Charles Fabres, a scarf of *kerchief* (*dupatta, ordhani*) was worn by the women in the 150-100 B.C. They wore turbans as often as men did, it was not often used for breasts.[383] The *Satvahanas* period, women also cover sheals with *ordhanis* that were decorated with beautiful borders,[384] and in 1127 A.D. *ordhani* (*ordhani*) was frequently worn on the shoulders than on the head. It was a scarf, with a striking variety though the stripe being no longer the most frequently design.[385] For the *dupatta* and *chadar*, five names of it are in the *Amarakosa;* the Sanskrit literature of the Gupta age, as *pravara, uttarasanga, vrhatika, saṁvyana* and *uttariya.*[386] In *Akbarnama*, elaborates that *chadar* was perhaps veils or canopies for the women.[387] A married as well as widows of the Dogra region, under the traditional injuction were forbidden to remain bare-headed However, it was essential for all to wear a *dupatta*, called *chadar*, drawn long over the face,[388] it was significantly called as '*chund*'[389] (*ghungat*) in the local language of the Dogras. Married lady in the presence of the elders, in-laws, in family and the among outsiders of the same locality a *purdah* was maintained. The paintings indicate that Dogra women was not properly encouraged by the Dogra feudalistic set-up, but certain restrictions were imposed on her to cover the head and about the uncovered head it had to believed as a bad omen.[390] *Dupatta* or *chadaru* had different colours used at different occasions for example, at the time of marriages, ladies used colourful head-dresses and at the injunction of death, ceremony they mostly weared white *dupatta*. Paintings demonstrate that it had different colours and made of different stuff. A *chadaru* was made of muslin, dyed at home in plain pastel shade of green yellow or pink. The widows were tabooed to wear coloured *chadaru* in the Dogra society. They wore only unbleached white *chadaru.*[391]

Dupatta (*Chadaru*)

There were various modes and styles of wearing the unsewn *dupatta* or *ordhani* or a *chadaru* which imparted grace to the women after wrapping round the upper-part of the body alongwith the head. In the paintings of the period, many head garment are revealed and discussed as under:

1. The principal garment of the women which covers the upper part of body and head, is in the picture of a marriage scene.[392] In this scene most of the females are shown wearing different colours of *dupatta's* made of *muslin* or other kind of cloth having golden print on the surface and borders. It shows that at the festive occasion various colourful *dupattas* were wrapped. Colour scheme of the *dupattas* show that they were happy and celebrating the marriage ceremony. The close relative of the bride i.e., mother or sister, they have been shown in sad mood after the departuring of the bride as it indicates from this blue (*Krsna*) colour. The golden and red colours show that the wearer were healthy and wealthy. Its was the Dogra traditional head-dress (Fig. 3).

2. This variety of the *ordhani* or a scarf is detected in the picture of a love-lorn lady.[393] She wears it over the head with a stylistic manners and its both ends are shown flowing frequently in the air. It has blue surface, decorated with stitching white jewels in strip manners shows floral design and also having golden borders. It has short width and long as about 2.25 metre. Colour scheme of the *ordhani* declares that she is quite young healthy and wealthy lady. But she has been shown in sad mood as she is feeling the absence of her husband who has gone out for business and sending a message to her husband through the white pigeon. It was also a Dogra traditional head-dress (Fig. 3).

A Dogra poet highlights the traditonal *dupatta* of a village lady fashioned from 17th century onwards in the following folksong lines:

"देआं माए मिकी ओडनू,
कन्नै गौड़नू,
मैं मरूआं गुड्डन जाना,
ओ लोभी मरू ए दा,
देआं माए मिकी ओडनू,
कन्नै गौडनू,
मैं मरूए घुम्वा पानां,
ओ लोभी मरूए दा"[394]

Tr. into English:
Nayaka says: "Mother give me an *oodhanu*[395] and a *goodanu*
(It is a sort of agriculturist tool like the spade).
I have to go for hauling the field.
(Husband) He is greedy to take *maruya* (a kind of the foodgrain)
Mother give me an *oodanu* and a *goodanu*.
I have to sow the *maruya* in the field.
He is like (greedy) to take *maruya*."

3. The portrait of a Pahari *Ragini*[396] demonstrated another kind of the *dupatta* and its mode of wrapping. It has been made of a fine piece of cloth, decorated with needle works from the borders. She draps it on the shoulders and head with an stylistic manners, its one end is displayed falling on the back little above the anklet and another end is shown caught by the right hand dangling little below the knees. She has also been shown, while putting it on the head like a '*chund*' or *ghunghat* (draw). It is an orange *dupatta*. Colour shows that she was a young lady having fine and charming personality. It was also a Dogra traditional head-dress (Fig. 1).

Another Dogri writer gives a beautiful example and praises the beauty of a *dupatta* when it was used to drap by a newly weeded *nayika* after the marriage in the following manners:

The title of the folk song as:

"कासनी टुपट्टा रंगदार गोरिये !
कासनी टुपट्टा रंगदार गोरिये !
लैन नेईं दिन्दे बेइमान गोरिये !
चंदरे चनैहनी दे लोक गोरिये !
अन्दरा नि जान दिन्दे बाहर गोरिये !"[397]

Tr. into English:

Nayika having a coloured *dupatta* of *kansani*

Husband says: *Nayika* having a coloured *dupatta* of *kansani*. *Nayika*, evil minded people did not allow to drop on.

Nayika, the people of Chananni[398] having bad intension.

They don't permit to go out from the house."

4. This variety of the *dupatta* is detected in the picture of Rani Bandrali[399] (the widow of Maharaja Ranbir Singh). She wears white sheet type of *chadar* or *chadaru* made of cotton, drapped round the upper part of the body and on the head. The white *chadar* shows that she is tolerating the death of her husband. She is shown very sad. It appears that in Dogra society widow was not allowed to wear colourful dress as a social binding. She wears Dogra's traditional *chadar* (Fig. 3).

5. This kind of the *uttariya* is explored in the picture of Marig-Priya *nayika*.[400] She simply wears it over the head and gently wrapped on the back, reaching to the hip. It is a silken *chadar or dupatta* having floral design. She has been displayed healthy and beautiful *nayika* having charming personality. It is a red *dupatta* of Dogra traditions (Fig. 2).

One more variety of the *dupatta* has been highlighted by a Dogri writer which was fashion among the Dogra womenfolk during Dogra rule (1846-1947A.D.) and was manufactured in South India. He describes it in the following lines of the folksong:

"कत्थोआं आई शनून,
शनूना बेशर्मी,
खल्ला आई शनून,
--शनूना बेशर्मी,
झुंढ कड्डा रमालै नाल,
शनूनां बेशर्मी।
खल्ला आई शनून,
शनूना बेशर्मी।
लेई के चादर खूहै पर जन्नी आं,
अग्गुआं मिलआ सौहरा।

शनूनां बेशर्मी।
लेई के चादर खुहैपर जन्नी आं,
अग्गुआं मिल आ जेठ।
शनूना बेशर्मी,
खल्ला आई शनून, शनूनां बेशर्मी"[401]

Tr. into English:
"Where from this *sanoon* (transparent cloth) came.
To have the *sanoon* on the head is a shameful.
Sanoon came from Daccan.
To have the *sanoon* on the head is a shameful,
To have a '*chund*' (draw) with *rumal* (hanky).
To have the *sanoon* is a shameful.
Sanoon came from the Daccan.
To drap the *chadar*, I proceed to well,
On the track, my father-in-law met me,
To have a *sanoon* is a shameful.
To have a '*chund*' (draw) with rumal (hanky).
To drap the *chadar*, I proceed to well,
On the track, my elder-brother-in-law met me,
To have a *sanoon* is a shameful.
To have the *sanoon* on head is shameful."

6. This mode of wearing the *dupatta* is detected in the picture of a Ragini Devagiri (Hindole).[402] She is seated on a royal chair smoking a *hookah*. She wears it over the head and shoulder, round the upper part of the body and its one end is displayed passing through inside the right arm flowing in the air. Its left end has been shown on the left leg. It is a transparent and indigo coloured *dupatta* having chocolate borders. Colour scheme of the *dupatta* demonstrates that she had a problem and is worried about it. She wears traditional *dupatta* of the Dogra region (Fig. 1).

7. This variety of the *ordhani* or scarf is explored in the picture of *Rasamanjari* love in union.[403] Here, it is seen *nayika* has been displayed seated in the lap of her *nayaka*. She wears sky colour scarf having golden borders. Its mode of wearing is stylish and she wears it over the head and its one end has been displayed passing over the left arm and falls back on the brocade metress. It has short width and length as usual as it has. The colour treatment of the scarf shows that she is hesitant with her husband, and she has been depicted quite young and healthy (Fig. 2).

8. In the same plate mentioned above, there are two pictures of the ladies. One's[404] displayed carrying a bottle of liquid (wine) and two cups in a tray for the sake of *nayika* and *nayaka*. It shows that in the

royal family both male and female used to drink. This lady wears a red colour scarf having sky blue border. It appears from the colour scheme that she is happy in the core of the heart, but display hesitated expression owing to the societal bindings. Her mode of wearing the *ordhani* or scarf is stylistic, she wores it over the head and its left end dangs below the left knee and another passes through the right armpit and then is placed over the right shoulder flunging on the back. She wears Dogra traditional scarf or *ordhani* (Fig. 2).

9. The another woman[405] wears green shade *ordhani* or scarf having sky blue borders is explored in the same plate discussed above. Her mode of wearing the scarf or *ordhani* is different from the previous one. She wore it over the head, its one end is displayed passing through the back on the right shoulder, and then it from an armpit and thrown over the left elbow reaching on the left knee, and another end of the scarf has been shown flowing back. It was also another variety of the Dogras traditional scarf or a *ordhani* (Fig. 2).

10. One more variety of the scarf or a *ordhani* is detected in the picture of a *nayika* who has been shown waiting to her lover.[406] It is a night scene, she has been displayed in a sleeping posture on the *cot* and waiting for her lover. Her lover might have gone out for state business. She wears a beautiful type of *ordhani* or a scarf having redish background, gold borders and decorated with inlay works of white jewels in beautiful design. Its mode of wearing has been shown touching its one end to the right corner of the *cot*, and another is displayed hanging down at the left upper corner of the *cot*. The colour treatment of the scarf or an *ordhani* demonstrates that she is quite a young lady charming and attractive and waiting for her lover's arrival. At this juncture, she appears to be happy as a flower sprouts from the bud. She wears Dogra's traditional garment (*ordhani*) (Fig. 3).

11. This variety of the *ordhani* or a scarf is explored in the picture of the female attendances of the Raja Kirpal Pal,[407] who have been shown with a *chouri* and a sword. She wears red lac scarf having dark green borders. The mode of her wearing has been displayed in stylistic manners. She wears it over the head and its one end has been displayed hanging on the back and another displayed falling above the right ankle. Colour combination of the *ordhani* or a scarf shows that in the peripheral areas of the Raja Kirpal Pal, there was agricultural development owing to the hard work of the people. It was also a Dogra's traditional garment (Fig. 1).

12. In the same plate discussed above, another variety of the scarf or an *ordhani*.[408] It appears that it has been made of cotton cloth having different design in geometrical pattern. It has dark green background and gold borders. Colour combination of the *ordhani* or a

scarf shows prosperity in the period of Raja Kripal Pal and his country was builting-up stronger and stronger day by day. It was also a Dogra's traditonal head-dress (Fig. 1).

13. This variety of the sky blue transparent *dupatta* with lining design is discovered in the picture of a *nayika*.[409] It was the night scene of the two lovers. Here, *nayika* has covered her private part of the body with the transparent *dupatta* and has naked breasts. Her life partner has been shown in a lying posture comfortably and eagerly attempts to cajole. The colour treatment of the head-dress or *dupatta* demonstrates that she had hesitant nature and gold colour borders of the *dupatta* depicts, she is quite a young, healthy and charming. It was also a traditional *dupatta* of the Dogras (Fig. 1).

14. This variety of the *dupatta* we expounded in the picture of a Ragini Devangiri (Hindola).[410] She has been depicted as if she occasionally weared sky blue *dupatta* of indigo (dark purplish blue) shade having redish borders and golden design. Her mode of wearing covers her head and its one end has been shown touching the back of the chair and its left end is slipping down from her body and falling on the chair. She is talking with her maid-attendant. Colour combination of the *dupatta* highlights the sentiment of the *ragini* that she had a conflict with her husband and she is hesitant to talk him directly. Red colour shows that she was quite young, healthy and happy. She is conveying her message to her husband through the maid-attendant, It was also a Dogra's traditional head-dress (Fig. 1).

15. There is another *chadar* or *dupatta* a type of head-dress and found in the painting of a *pater lakhni nayika*.[411] She wears pinkish (*piyazi*) *chadar* having artistic design of different colours. It has been placed on the head covers the upper part of the body and then its one end has been depicted passing over the left shoulder to back. Colour treatment of the *chadar* highlights that she was a well-built lady and happy with her life partner, but blue colour shows that she was little bit uncomfortable. It appears that her husband had to gone out for State's business, and she is dictating a letter to he maid-attendant for her husband maid is penning down the letter of the *nayika's*. It was also another traditional variety of the Dogra dress (Fig. 3).

A Dogri poet himself excited to see the embellishment of a *dupatta* of a *nayika* and her ornament which was a fashion from 1846-1947 A.D. in Jammu region. He describes these article of wearing in the following folk song:

"राह–राह जंदिये, सूहे सालू आलिये,
कविये दा मन मोहेआ,
राह–राह..........

हत्थें तेरे छापां बांहें चुड़ियां,
आरसू डल्का मारे।
राह्–राह्...........
नक्क तेरे नथली, छोटी जेही मछली,
स्हीरी देऐ लसकारे।
राह्–राह्...........
बाहें तेरे टाडां, सिर चौक बिराजै,
कडिये दे छनकारे।
राह्–राह्...........
हत्थ तेरे मैहंदी, भार नेई सैहन्दी,
सुरमा करै अशारे।
राह्–राह्...........
गलै बिच गान्नी, लगदी सुहामीं,
विंदलू दे चमकारे,
राह्–राह् जांदियें, सुहे सालू आलिये।"[411]

Tr. into English:

"Going on way-way, having red *saloo*.
You have excited the heart of the poets.
Going on way-way..........
Having rings in your hands, *churiyan* at arms.
Aarsoo having movement
Going on way-way.....
Having a *nathli* at your nose, like a small fish.
Also having shining a *chiri*
Going on way-way......
Having *tadana* at your arms, depicting chook on the head.
Having jingling sound of *karyians*.
Having *henna* at your hands, it doesn't permit you to do a heavy work.
Collyrium is giving indication.
Going on way-way......
She also having a *ganni*, round the neck, looking gorgeous along with a shining *bindlu*.
Going on way-way having red *saloo*."

16. The painting of *Ragini* Dowhri of Hindole[412] displayed wearing a pinkish (*piyazi*) *dupatta* or a *chadar* made of cotton cloth having golden borders. She wears it as usually worn by the lady. She has been shown looking her beauty in the mirror. Colour scheme of the *chadar* shows that she was quite young lady and shown happy with her married life. She is decorating herself for the sake of her husband. It was also a Dogra's traditional *chadar* (Fig. 4).

17. This variety of the decorative *dupatta* is detected in the painting of Radha.[413] In one picture, Radha appears with black *dupatta*, decorated with inlay work of white jewels in strips having white and silver colour border or *gota*. In another opposite picture, Radha wears indigo dark purplish blue (*lapis lazuli*) *dupatta*, and is decorated in the same manners as discussed above. The expression of the picture of Krishna shows that he was angry with Radha. The vibration of the colour scheme shows that Radha is saying to Krishna, don't be angry, the result of your anger may cause darkness in the physical world. If there is any mistake in the universal. We shall be responsible and consequences are to be shared by us at the cost of our happiness. Indigo colour depicts, if unfortunate event, occurs we should avert it, for the sake of future. *Dupatta* has been made of light cotton and was a traditional *dupatta* of the Dogra region (Fig. 1).

The comparative study of the period also informs us that *dupatta*, *chadar* or *chadaru*, *ordhanu* or *ordhani* was not only fashioned in Jammu region, but it was also worn in other parts of the Indian terriotries.[414]

Caps (*Topi*)

Apart from the *dupatta* or *ordhani* or a *chadaru*, paintings of the period reveal that caps were worn as a head-dress by the maid-servants of the Dogri *nayikas* in Jammu region. They used to wear skull-cap, long 'Turkish' type of cap, etc. made of cotton or other kind of cloth having brocade design. The detail history of the cap has already been discussed. In the *Kushana* period, the women of Mathura generally did not cover their heads though occasionally they used veils and turban.[415] But in the Gupta age, at Ajanta generally the women of higher status wear tiaras. Some attendants also wear caps.[416] If an ordinary woman did not wear caps, was but the tall, 'Turkish' cap worn by the woman shown in early Mughal paintings, did make its appearance in India and dancing girls displayed wearing caps much like men in the 19th century and in certain parts like Kishtwar, Kashmir, and Churaha in Himachal Pradesh. Women often used to wear a little cap set conquestingly on the head with just a slightest cock to one side[417] B.N. Goswamy describe. There were mostly made of cotton and wool sometimes embroidered with gold or silver wire, decorated with applique work. It was mostly worn by the foreigner ladies.

The following varieties of the different caps were found in the paintings of the period and discussed as under:

1. This variety of the head-dress or a cap we explored in the picture of Sita.[418] She wears a dome shape pointed design green cap on

the head in place of the *dupatta*. Scene shows the wildlife of the Jammu areas. It has been made out of the green leaves of the plants. It indicates that such type of head-dress was weared during the acute heat of the summer. Same type of head-dress has also been worn by the Rama and Lakshmana in this scene. Green colour of the caps indicate there was a peace and prosperity in the time of Maharaja Ranbir Singh. It shows foreign fashion influence (Fig. 1).

2. The portrait of *Ragini* Devagiri (Hindole's maid-servant)[419] demonstrated another variety of the cap. It is 'Turkish' model, i.e., little but high cap. It has been decorated with white jewels and admixture with chocolate background. For its embellishment, three white beads like pendents have been shown flunging on the forehead. Colour scheme of the cap displays that a precious assignment has been assigned to the maid-servant to reconcile both the wife and the husband to make their life happy. It shows Turkish fashion influence (Fig. 1).

3. There is another variety of the head-dress or a cap we explored in the picture of *Pater-Lekhni nayika's* maid-servant.[420] She wears bowl or skull-type of artistic cap over the head and her hair has been shown long loose falling on the back. It has braided design having chocolate colour. Such types of caps most probably are wore by the Gujjar and Bakarwal women. It shows foreign (Persian) fashion influence (Fig. 3).

4. A picture of the female angel[421] with a peacock demonstrates a hat type of high cap, terminated with ornamental band. It shows that her ideas and dreams were high and led a happy life. Cap shows European fashion influence (Fig. 2).

The comparative study of the caps, reveals that similar type of caps were also used in other parts of the India States.[422]

The traditional Dogra garment i.e., the upper garment (*uttariya*) and the lower garment (*ashovastra*) were both sewn and unsewn pieces of cothes. They were weared in different way as the paintings of the period demonstrate in conformity with needs of geographical conditions or variations. Like men, the women were also aware to use various fashionable clothes. In most of the pictures, those garment, has also depicted in the case of women.

Upper Garments (*Uttariya*)

The portrayals reveal that the women of Jammu region irrespective of class status had many ways of wearing the upper garments. viz. *choli*, *kurta* or *kameez*, *peswajs*, etc. It appears that various types of upper garments were used to cover the upper part of the body. In the Vedic age either it was a wrapper *upavasana*, *paryanahana*, or *adhivasa*, or a jacket, bodice or cloak-like *pratidhi*, *drapi* or *atka*.[423] According to B.N. Goswamy several terms for this are used in Sanskrit and Prakrit literature including *uttarasanga*, *uttariua vasana*, *uttariuavasa*, *udaramshuka*, *samvyana*, *stanamshuka*, *stanottariya*.[424]

The following upper-garments (*uttariyas*) are represented in the paintings of the period in these manners:

Choli (*Kanjari, Kanchali, Kanchuki, Kanjuri*)

In the paintings of the period, it is a bodice or blouse-like breast cover, an upper-garment which was popular article of clothing among the women of the Jammu region. It has been worn along with *ghaghra's* and *pyjama's* as a lower-garment. It appears that it was not only used to cover the cups or the upper-part of the body, but it shows that it was worn by women with all its erotic and romantic possibilities. In the study, it also depicts that *choli* or bodice were the popular garments which received best attention by the women and worn as an upper garment along with a *sari* or *dhoti*. Thus, with back-covering or without, fastened with strings or extended cloth-pieces with shaped breast pieces or flat etc. It shows that cups of the blouse or a *choli* have been richly decorated with needle work of fine taste, and some have been ornamented with beads of different colours, gold thread, *tilla* pieces of mica and mirror. The royal women used richly decorated and superior kind of *cholies*. The poor women has been displayed with simple and inferior kinds of *cholies*. In the Vedic period, the *pratidhi* was a breast-cover of a bride made of one or two strips of cloth drawn across or crosswise on the bust and tied at the back.[425] Charles Fabres mentions, the first recorded examples of the *choli*, the bodice or blouse, is found, in the pre-Mughal miniature paintings of Gujarat, mostly Jain religious manuscript illuminations. Though a few of these may well go back to the 10th century A.D., an example has been given in Plate XVI is dated by Prof. Norman Brown at 1127 A.D.[426] It was the great turning point in the history of Indian dress on the investigation of the bodice or blouse. It shows that it has been evolved on the wake of the Mughal invasions and, he, again, says that it is not altogether a foreign garment for no Iranian woman ever wore a *choli*. There early *choles* cover the breasts only while back was bare and a string ties the two ends at the back.[427] It is indicated that word *choli* has been derived from the word '*chola*' and English word 'bodice' has been derived from word '*body*'. It has some similar and related garments; *angia*, *kasani*, *tani*, *phundia*, *kapadu*, *polka*, *kurpara* and *kurpasaka*.[428] In the local language of the Dogras it has been known as *bodi*, blouse, *kangari*, etc. as usually called in other parts of the Indian States.

In the opinions of various scholars, a short type of bodice or *choli*[429] was a popular garment[430] among the womenflok of the Jammu region. It appears that the bossom[431] was covered in a bodice which was short enough to leave the most of part of the body between the breast and the navel uncovered.[432]

The following varieties of the *cholies* are discussed in the available paintings of the period, worn by the women of the Jammu, discussed as under:

1. The first variety of the *choli* we noticed in the picture of Radha[433] with Krishna. She wears a short sleeves bodice or blouse, well-fitted cups and the upper part of the body has V-shaved neck and her body below the cups and the waist has been shown uncovered and displayed in a way she covers the uncovered part of the body with the help of a *dupatta*. The short sleeves of the *choli* have been decorated by tying the bracelets of white beads in strips formation, over the sleeves. It has lead (dull grey) colour admixtured with the maron shade. Colour treatment of the blouse shows that she was unhappy at that time and maroon colour indicates that (Radha says to Krishna) those who did wrong, they would have to pay the price of it latter or sooner, but we have to start the life with new music, and leave the worries. *Choli* shows Rajasthani fashion influence (Fig. 1).

2. This variety of the cotton made *choli* or blouse was detected in the picture of Krishna on the way to the tryst;[434] illustraton to the *Rasamnjari*. Here, the lovers of Krishna wear green and redish blouses of short sleeves and hardly fitted on the cups and on the other part of the body. The short sleeves of the blouses have been ornamented with gold fillet from the borders and same is the case with the lower end of the bodice. Colour scheme of the blouses show that they were quite young, healthy and happy to see the Krishna. Blouse also shows Rajasthani fashion influence (Fig. 1).

3. The same pattern of *choli* or blouse mentioned above, have been worn by another lover[435] of Krishna. It has silken stuff and has been decorated with gold embroidery work over the redish background. Colour scheme shows that she was quite young, healthy and wealthy lady (Fig. 3).

4. The rest of the ladies[436] they have shown wear the same style of blouse described above. It was a popular feature having multi-colours and cotton made (Fig. 2).

5. The painting of *Prem-Lila*[437] of *nayaka* and *nayika* with ladies standing on her door, have demonstrated same pattern of *choli* or blouse as discussed above. The blouses or *cholies* have been decorated with needle work of gold wire in strips type of design. It appears that

it has been made out of silken cloth. It also shows Rajasthani fashion influence (Fig. 3).

The beautiful example about choles is give by the local poet that how a Dogra lady used to decorate herself with the dresses and the ornaments for the sake of her husband in daily life. It shows that such type of dresses and ornaments were used before the arrival of the Muslims in Jammu, writer describes it in the following folklore:

"पैहल्लड़ै शंगार गोरी पैह न लैता हंगिया,
मरो गेडा हंगिया, कट्‌टेया स्याल नंगिना।
दूजडै शंगार गोरी पैहन लैत्ता डोरिया,
मरो गेडा डोरिया ते रोज जन्दा चोरिया।
तीजड़ै शंगार गोरी पैहन लैत्तियाँ डंगिया,
मरन गेडियां डंडिया, मोआ रोज करदा भंडियाँ।
चौथै शंगार गोरी पैहन लैत्तियाँ बालियाँ,
मरन गोडियां बालियाँ, मोआ रोज कडदा गालियाँ
पजमें शंगार गोरी पैहन लैत्तियाँ शल्लियाँ,
मरन गेडियां छल्लियां औं नस्सी मुल्खा चल्लिया।"[438]

Tr. into English:
In the first make-up, she wears *hangia*,
Leave the *hangia*; he has to co-operate with me in winter.
In the second make-up; *nayika* wears a beautiful *doriya* (*dupatta*).
Leave this *dupatta*, he always goes like a thief.
In the third make-up; she wears *dandiyans*
Leave these *dandiyas*; lifeless man always has to advertise;
In the fourth make-up; she wears *baliyans*,
Leave these *baliyans*, lifeless man always calls me names.
In the fifth make-up; *nayika* wears *challiyans*.
Leave these *challiyan*; now, I run away from this nation."

The comparative study of the various scholars narrates that *choli* or bodice was not only fashioned in Jammu region; but its fashion was also extended in the other States[439] of India.

Kurta (*Koorta*)

The word '*kurta*' described in the dictionaries as a shirt or "a tunic, waist coat, etc." The paintings of the period shed light that it was a popular feature among the Dogra womenfolk in the 19th century A.D. It seems that it was from the undergarment into a garment for outer wear and its features often with round neck of knee-length or even longer with continuing in the middle or at the sides of the neck. So far the *kurti* is concerned, it is almost resembled with *kurta* in nearly all other features except its length which stops short little below the waist. It seems that its technique was extended below the knees or on the knees and took the shape of a *kameez*. It was popular especially among the Punjabi women. B.S. Saini mentions the attire of a Hindu woman comprised a *ghagara* or *lehanga* (skirt) of cotton and a *kurti* or shirt.[440] In the paintings Gujjar women shirt or *kurta* was also fashioned among the Dogra women which hardly touch the knees. Besides the Gujjari women's shirt, Dogra female used shirt long enough to touch the knees, and was called *kameez, kurta, choli*. It was usually worn with *suthan* (a trousers, tight below the ankles) or *salwar*.[441] It shows in the painting the fashion of wearing the *kurta* and *salwar* came from the Punjab in Jammu. *Kurta* or *kameez* has similar and related garments known as *kurti, ghagho, kameez*.[442]

The following types of the *kurta* or shirt which were fashioned among the women of Jammu region are explored in the paintings of the period, elaborated as under:

1. This kind of the shirt or *kurta* we exposed in the picture of a *Ragini Devagiri* of Hindole.[443] She wears it with the *salwar* (draw) or *salvar*. It is a full-sleeves cotton made *kurta*, well-fitted to the body hardly touching to the *knees*, and having *fita* or embroidery type of needle work borders of redish and gold colour. It has U-shape neck and circular shape cut on the breasts as a design which has been covered by wearing a neck-ornament. She has been shown smoking a *hookah*. Colour combination of the shirt demonstrates that she was hesitating to meet her husband, but was interested to meet him in order to dilute issues between themselves. She is shown quite young and healthy. *Kurta* shows Gujjari fashion influence (Fig. 1).

2. In the same plate mentioned above, the maid-servant[444] of the *Ragini* has been displayed wearing a red silken *kurta* of full-sleeves, reaching below the knees and well-fitted to the body. It has gold and black colour needle work on the borders. It has been parted from the sides in the form of a '*suja*' called in the local term of the Dogras. She wears with the *salvar* or *salwar* (draw). Colour scheme of the shirt demonstrates that maid-servant has been displayed happy to reconcile the relation which has been disrupted on some issue between both the husband and wife. She has been fully involved in this matter and feeling happy on their compromise. *Kurta* shows Punjabi fashion influence (Fig. 1).

This female dress has figured in one of the folk song of the Dogra region. As it shows from the study that it was fashioned in the 19th century A.D. from the Punjabi region. It has been described in the following manners:

"सैला सूट, जाली दा दुपट्टा गुड्डो प्यारिये,
दूरा दा तूं मारनी मडाका तेरे सोह।
घाए बड्ढियै कुन्नी लान्नी गुड्डो प्यारिये,
सौहरियें दा चेता निं भलायां तेरे सोह।
सैला सूट, जाली दा दुपट्टा गुड्डो प्यारिये,
दूरा दा तूं मारनी मडाका तेरे सोह।
घाए बड्ढियै कुन्नी लान्नी गुड्डो प्यारिये,
औंदी–जंदी बौहया निं बलावै तेरे सोह।
सैला सूट जाली दा दुपट्टा गुड्डो प्यारिये,
दूरा दा तूं मारनी मडाका तेरे सोह।
घाए बड्ढियै कुन्नी लान्नी गुड्डो प्यारिये,
प्यौकियें दा चेता निं भलायां तेरे सोह।"[445]

Tr. into English:

"A *nayika*, having a green suit and a net type of *dupatta*,
You have a smile from the way, by you.
A *nayika* by cutting the grass put into heap,
Don't forget the in-laws house, by you.
A *nayika* having a green suit and a net type of *dupatta*.
You have a smile from they away, by you.
A *nayika* by cutting the gross put into heap.
By you, do come and go, don't depend on call.
A *nayika* having a green suit and a net type of *dupatta*.
You have a smile from the away, by you.
A *nayika* by cutting the gross put into heap.
Don't forget the parental's house, by you."

3. This example of the *kurta* or a shirt is detected in the picture of a maid-servant of a *nayika*.[448] She wears U-shape neck type of red *kurta* of full-sleeves having gold colour floral design in the main and also has golden borders on the edges. Colour treatment of the *kurta* displays that she was happy while delivering the message of the *nayika's* and interested to make their life rich and enjoyable. *Kurta* made of silken stuff and shows Punjabi fashion influence (Fig. 3).

4. The upper part of the female body was often covered by another type of the garment, i.e., known as *kurta* or *kameez*. It has been worn by the Rani Bandrali,[448] the widow of Maharaja Ranbir Singh. It was also a popular article of clothing in Jammu in the 19th century A.D. *Kameez* has U-shape neck having loose-fitting of full-length, reaching below the knees. It has been made out of mill-made white cotton.[449] It shows that white dress was worn by the widows in the Jammu region. It was the sign of her widowness depicting tolerance, It also shows

Punjabi fashion influence and has been worn by her with the *churidar suthan* (Fig. 3).

There is another Dogri folklore which highlights the attraction of a lady towards her beautiful dress which was fashioned in the early 19th century A.D. showing Muslim fashion influence in the Jammu region. Inspite of the beautiful dress, it was decorate with attractive ornaments. Moreover, the Dogri folksong also reveals the socio-cultural relation of the Dogra people with other states of the Indian country in the following few lines:

"कुर्ता मेरा हरिपुर बनेया वीडा लग्गा मुल्तानी,
कुर्ता फट्टै तां होर स्यागे बीड़ा भज्जै तां मर जान्नी।
चादर मेरी हरिपुर बनऐ फीता लग्गा मुल्तानी,
चादर फट्टै तां भावों होर स्यागे फीता फटटै तां मर जान्नी।
चुड़ा मेरा हरिपुर बनेया ठप्पा लग्गा मुल्तानी,
चुड़ा भज्जै तां भावो होर लआगे, ठप्पा भज्जै तां मर जान्नी।
बालू मेरा हरिपुर बनेया चीडकी बनी मुल्तानी,
बालू भज्जै तां भावो होर बनागे, चीडकी भज्जै तां मर जान्नी।
गजरा मेरा हरिपुर बनेया सीसा लग्गा मुल्तानी,
गजरा भज्जै तां भावो होर मंगागे,
सीसा भज्जै तां मर जान्नी।"[449]

Tr. into English:

"My *kurta* made in Haripur with Multani button.
If *kurta* tears, we shall stitched-up it again,
If its button shatters, than I shall die for it.
My *chadar* made in Haripur and its frill is Multani,
If *chadar* tears, Pabo (sister-in-law) we shall stitch-up again.
If its frill (*fita*) shatters, I shall die for it.
She again says: My *chura* having Haripur made, design having Multani,
If *chura* shatters may *Papo*, we shall brought another,
If its design shatters, than I shall die for it.
My *balu* having Haripur made, bolt or hook made of Multani.
If *balu* breaks Pabo, we shall made another,
If its bolt or hook shatters, than I shall die for it.
Nayika again says : My *gajara* having Haripur made, studded with glass of Multani.
If *gajara* shatters *Pabo*, than I shall die for it."

In the comparative study of the period we also learn that different types of the *kurta or kameez* which was fashioned in Jammu region, was also used in other parts of the Indian territories.[450]

Peswaj (*Peshwaz, Pishwaj, Peswaj*)

In the paintings of the period, the *kurta* or a shirt, the apron or *peswaj* type of outer and upper-garment was popular among the Dogra womenfolk, who named it as, a garment, "*coat, gown, vest, veil, robe, long skirt*, or *frock*, etc." It usually has the breasts part fitting snugly, full-tight-sleeves, over the body with waist seam high of anklet length, and flared into skirt. It was open from the front, stitched round the neck as well as below the cups with the help of some kind of material. It appears that it was made of cotton or transparent type of cloth in different colour. In the *Yaun-Chwang*, it is referred that Indian women used long robe which covers both shoulders and falls down loose.[451] In the Mughal period, during the time of Akbar veil (*parda-arai*)[452] type of garment was fashioned. In the Jahangir time besides the veil or *pard-arai*, the black robes[453] were used at the time of mourning or death, and in the later Mughal period, the women were used to dress themselves with great coats (*barani*) of crimson cloth, like men.[454] A beautiful example of the origin of the Iranian *peswaj* fashioned in Indian via Mughal was used in the Mughal court, and its survived, often as a ceremonial dress, but still worn by the older womenfolk of all classes, in the Punjab hill tracts. It is a chemise or "princess" gown-like frock, reaching from the neck down to the *ankles* with long sleeves, and often with an arrow waist.[455] This dress (the *peswaj*) went out of fashion almost completely, except in remote areas such as Chamba or among the *pardanshin* women of the Muslim community.[456] It has some other similar and related garments known as: *jama*, *ganga*, *angarakhas*, *ghagho*, *tilak*, *kurta*[457] or *kameez*. So far as the word *peswaj* is concerned, it appears that it came from the verb (*pesujana*), "to stitch, to sew with running stitches" so that the word registered and retained, as it was the surprise of the Indian women world when it met for the first time as a stitched garment not only a plain piece of cloth wrapped round the body, but Indian feminine also had been accustomed[458] it.

The following varieties of the *peswaj* which were fashioned among the Dogra womenfolk of the Jammu region are represented in the paintings of the period, explained in detail as under:

1. This variety of the upper-garment is discovered in the picture of the Pahari Regini.[459] In the paintings it appears that it was a popular article of clothing among the Dogra ladies. It has been worn over the *angiya* and the tight-*pyjama*. It is shown well-fitted to the breasts or cups and opened from the front and flared in skirt shape below the bodice reaching on the ankles. It shows that it has been made out of superior cotton cloth. It is lac red colour of an upper and outer garment having V-shape neck and concave type of cut design on the breasts,

which shows that *ragini* wore an inner-garment of indigo (*lapis-lazuli*) colour, known as *angiya*. The colour of the *peswaj* shows that she was ready to face any kind of sacrifice for the sake of her family (nation). *Peswaj* shows Iranian fashion influence which was brought by the Mughal in Indian (Fig. 1).

2. The picture of a women with a *sitar*[460] demonstrated another variety of *peswaj* or an outer garment. It shows that she also wears an ankle-length, red colour of robe having gold pointed strip printing on the surface. It has U-shape neck and full-sleeves well-fitted with arms. On the borders of the arms, *peswaj* has geometrical lining design of gold colour. The colour combination of the *peswaj* depicts that she was a young, healthy and wealthy women. She had to lead a happy and prosperous married life with her husband. *Peswaj* also shows Iranian fashion influence via Mughals (Fig. 1).

3. There is another picture of a *Pahari nayika*[461] showed another different variety of *peswaj*. She wears yellow type of an outer garment, made of superior cotton. It has U-shape neck and concave type of design on the breasts and remains naked for the wearing of an ornament's pendent. The borders of the *peswaj* have needle works of *munga* colour. It is also an *ankle*-length type of outer-garment and full-sleeves, well-fitted to the arms and flared from the lower end of the cups. It has been originated in Iran and came into fashion in India through the Mughals. Colour scheme of the garment shows that winter season of the Jammu region was ending and spring season has been started. The vibration of the *munga* colour shows that in the peripheral areas in Jammu, there was a nice season (Fig. 2).

4. The wall-painting of Radha with *sitar*[462] demonstrated another variety of *peswaj*. It shows that it has been well-fitted to the cups which has the pattern of a bodice having U-shape neck. *Peswaj* has full-sleeves, but loose-fitting from the bodice joint. It has skirt type flared up in skirt shape which from the pleats. It is also a full ankle-length type of *haldi* colour *peswaj* having maroon pleats. The lower edge of the *peswaj* has numerous pleats like frill, decorated with white jewels from its very borders. The colour combination of the *peswaj* depicts that one has to tolerate the past events and should work for the bettermen of the future to make the life happy. It also shows foreign fashion (Persian) influence (Fig. 1).

5. This example of different *peswaj* is detected in the painting of love-lorn lady.[463] She wears transparent type of outer-garment of water colour, well-fitted to the upper part of the body and flared from the waist reaching on the ankles. It is highly transparent that her cups are clearly looking from its stuff. It has white floral pattern of design on its main-field. Colour scheme of the *peswaj* displays that when she

will see her life partner after the long period, she will enjoy her life with her life partner and would be happy. She is awaiting her husband eagerly. It also shows foreign fashion influence i.e., Iranian via Mughals (Fig. 3).

6. There is another painting of Radha giving butter and milk to Krishna[464] of ankles-length. It is also highly transparental apron as mentioned above, and Radha's cups are shown from it. It shows that the borders of the *peswaj* have *munga* (green) colour frill (*gota* or *fita*). It is also a full-sleeves *peswaj* and well-fitted to the upper part of the body. It is looking charming on her body. It shows that such type of transparent garments were worn in the royal families for erotic and romantic life. Colour combination of the *peswaj* depicts that royal lady (young lady has surrendered everything of her life to her life partner either it was physical or material. She was happy to see her husband in her daily life. *Peswaj* also shows foreign fashion influence (Fig. 4).

7. This example of the apron or *peswaj* is detected in the picture of women, love in union[465] in *Rasamanjari*. Here, two women have been painted with a torch and carrying the wine in the trey for *nayika* and *nayaka*. They are feeling hesitation and wearing simple white and light sky blue *peswaj* in the same pattern as already discussed, having full-sleeves, ankle-length, well-fitted to the upper part of the body and flared in skirt shape from the waist. The colour scheme demonstrates that one lady painted feels happy and another displayed feeling hesitation on the meeting of two lovers. The whole picture shows Mughals fashion (Fig. 2).

8. This *peswaz* was not only a fashion among royal family women, but it was prevalent among the maid-servant of the Raja Kirpal Pal.[466] In this picture, two maid-attendants of the Raja Kirpal Pal wore white transparent gown or vest as usually worn by the elite ladies of the period. Their *peswaj* has *mungh* (green) borders either frilled or *gota* or *fita* which embellished the garment elegantly. Its colour treatment shows that in the time of Raja Kirpal Pal, there was a peace and prosperity in his kingdom. It is similar in pattern as elaborated above. But, here difference is visible i.e., in quality the stuffs is of inferior cloth incomparison with the others (Fig. 1).

9. The painting of a marriage scene of Ramnagar Palace[467] demonstrated another kind of the *peswaj* of the same pattern mentioned above. It was a popular feature among the Dogra's womenfolk and is of silken or other kind of cloth. In this picture women have been shown wearing blood red, cream and orange *peshwajs*, decorated with stitched frill or *gota* or *fita* of gold colour on the edges. Some are shown wearing gold pointed printed *peswaj*. They are mostly young ladies. It also have the same pattern, as described above having full-sleeves, well-

fitted with the upper part of the body and flared from the waist in skirt or frock shape, loose down to the anklets and open in the front. Women have also been displayed wearing *dupatta* of different colours with the *peswaj*. The colour scheme of the subject matter shows that this marriage function was attended by the close relative of the bride and the bridegroom. It is the marriage scene of Raja Suchet Singh. All the relative of the bride and bridegroom have been shown happy on this auspicious occasion. Orange and cream *peswajs* with golden pointed colour indicates that bride (young woman) has to be departed from the parental house she is quite young lady and her parents were above to send off her in a grace full manner with a social obligation. *Peswaj* also shows Iranian fashion influence via Mughals (Fig. 3).

The comparative study of *peswaj's* of the period shows that the fashion of the coat or apron or *peswaz* was not limited in Jammu, it was also prevalent in other parts of the Indian territories.[468]

Kamarband

The paintings of the period sheds light that a *dupatta* or scarf type of *kamarband* or *waistband* has been worn by the maid-attendant of the *ragini*. It shows that it was worn round the waist to keep-up the upper and the lower garment at proper position. Sometimes, in place of *patka* or scarf, a girdle, a belt or *mekhala* in ornamental patterns were used to keep-up the lower and upper-garment at proper position round the waist as a fashion trend. Instead of a *dupatta* or a scarf, maid-servant, a high cap and *dupatta* or a scarf as a fashion round the waist which was in the shape of a *waistband* or a *kamarband*. The fashion of tying the *kamarband* in different ways, goes to remote past of Indian, society for example, the Bharhut sculptures of the Sunga period, the women of all classes have been shown wearing a *sari* or a *dhoti*; on the waist with an elaborate girdle and *kamarband* tied in a bow-shaped knot with a loop hanging on a one side and both tassel ends of the *kamarband* hung on the other.[469] Sometimes made of simple cloth and sometimes it made out of needle works. There is a marked development of the small ribbon-like *waistband* that falls over the metal chain girdle, the *mekhala*. It becomes richer, and in the first half of the second century (100-150 A.D.), this *waistband* was worn boldly and in a large variety of famiful knots, usually falling on the left hip. Both men and women make great play with the way this sash was worn and tied; and this was found everywhere, from the donor and donatrix on the façade of the Karle cave temple (Bombay) to Mathura in the North.[470] The fashion of wearing the *kamarband* or *waistband* or *patkas* shows Greco-Roman fashion influence which came into India between the period of 150-100 B.C. In Jammu region, the women of Kishtwar and Bhadhrwa used to wear a long gown with a *kamarband* of a woollen rope usually black, wound many scores of times round[471] that waist called as *kalavuka*.

The main feature of the *kamarband* which was preferred by the female is found in the painting and discussed as under:

1. This variety of the *kamarband* or a scarf is detected in the picture of the *ragini's* maid-servant.[472] She wore it round the waist in two rounds, and knotted at the front and its two ends are shown flunging above the knees. It has been worn over the *kurta*, round the waist and the *salvar*. The main field of the *kamarband* or *waistband* is black and redish coloured pieces of cloth in the pattern of a frill and has been stitched around it and embroidered with gold wire. The *kamarband* is made of silken piece of cloth. The black *kamarband* shows that the life of the couple has been bleak and she (maid-servant) of the *ragini* has tied her waist to reconcile their relation by taking the assignment from the *ragini*. The redish stitched border pieces of cloth and golden embroidery show that they were quite young and it was the time to make life comfortable for future. *Kamabrand* shows Greco-Roman fashion influence (Fig. 1).

The comparative literature of the period sheds light that the fashion of wearing the *kamarband* or a girdle was not only limited Jammu region, but it was also in other parts of the Indian States.[473]

Lower Garment (*Adhovastara*)

In the paintings of the period, lower garment is an important clothing as the upper garment. If we look to the origin of the dresses. It appears that meticulous attention had been paid to the lower garment. A lower garment provides a cover to the most private part of both the male and female body. The lower garment included *ghaghra*, tight-fitting *pyjama* which was used in comparsion with the *choli* or bodice, or with *peshwaj*. Whereas *salwar*, *churidar-pyjama* was used along with the *kurta*'s having different design worn by the Dogra womenfolk. *Sari* or *dhoti* of different colours mostly of cotton was also worn by the Dogra women as a lower garment, and wrapped round the waist over the *ghaghra* than drapped above over the head. Blouse or *choli* was worn as an upper garment with it. It has various names including *ambara*, *smshuka*, *antariya*, *jaghanamshuka*, *nivasana*, *paridhana*, *vasana*, *vastram*, *vasas*, *sanli*.[474] Another typical garment of the Dogra womenfolk at home was a long white sheet of cotton known as '*giddi*'[475] in the local language of the Dogras was a traditional article of clothing.

The main features of the lower garment commonly worn by the Dogra females, are available in the paintings of the period, and elaborated herein:

Sari or Dhoti

It is an unstitched long piece of cloth, drapped over the hip over a *ghaghra*. The upper garment worn with *sari* was a blouse or *choli* or bodice. It developed originally from an indigenous garment used as a breast supporting garment. The period under discussion shows that the fashion of wearing the *sari* or *dhoti* came from Rajputana to Dogra region. It appears that Dogra womenfolk was equal vigilant as the other women of the Indian States in the fashion of wearing the *sari* or *dhoti*. She was conscious to cover the naked part of the body. The *sari* or *dhoti* mostly made of cotton pieces in different colours and in different design was worn. The poignant description of the word '*sari*' is found in the *Mahabharata* of how Draupadi was put into shame by the brutal act by snatching her *sari* from her waist. It appears from the sources of the study, that ancient and today's type of modern *sari* were used round the waist over the *ghaghra* or a *petticoat*. Its one *pallu* (end) thrown over the other was not fashion at all. Neither *choli* or bodice or *kurta* was worn by the lady at that time. The study reveals that Draupadi might have to worn a small piece of cloth called *dhoti* or small *dhoti* or *chhoti dhoti*, wrapped round the hips as no upper garment was fashion at that time. In the period between 150 B.C. to 150 A.D.; women wore a single piece of *cloth*, a *dhoti* or sarong-like cloth drapped round the waist and was held up by a metal girdle (*mekhala*).[476] According to Charles Fabres modern *sari* has developed from the Greco-Roman tradition.[477] By 1100 A.D., a regional difference of the South India and the North India, can be trace out from the *dhoti* or *sarong* which was fashion among the womenfolk (after Muslim invasion). In Northern parts of India, it was wound, wide and voluminous, whereas in Southern India particularly Andhra, Kerala and Madras the *dhoti* was worn tightly round the legs, its end fell between them on the left. The other end was pulled over a waist-cloth which was worn round in many folds[478] and look looked like a tight trousers. The manuscript of the Gujarat dated 1127 A.D., apprises about *choli*, the absence of the skirt or a *ghaghra* which women wore round like a *dhoti* and used with the *choli*. The fashion of wearing the three pieces, i.e., *dhoti*, *choli* and *dupatta* was also in the Mughal period, mostly worn by the Hindu ladies. With the evolution of the skirt or *ghaghra* or a *petticoat* as a sewn garment of the lower part of the body, the development of the *chhoti-dhoti* to *bari-dhoti*, the evolution of head-covering an idea of the women has been diverted into the direction of the *ghaghra's* to tucked the lengthwise piece of the cloth of the *dhoti* round the waist over the *ghaghra* which has taken the shape of the modern *sari*, *dupatta* and *chadar*, were in use in India. In the *Resamanjari* paintings the Dogri *nayikas* are displayed wearing *sari*[479] around the waist over the *ghaghra* and its one end (*pallu*), they put over the shoulders and the head.[480]

The following main-varieties preferred by the Dogra women in the paintings of the period, are as under:

1. The first variety of the *dhoti* or *sari* is detected in the picture of a lady near the spring.[481] She tucked it around the waist like a wide and lenthy *dhoti* and she covers her head with the right end, than it passed over the right shoulder and caught by her with the fingers of the right hand in a very stylistic manner falling above the ankles. The upper garment with *dhoti*, is maroon *choli* or blouse of half-sleeves. She is looking her beauty in the spring water. It is a cotton *dhoti*. The transparent white colour of *dhoti* has been dyed with the indigo (blue) and has rust colour borders. The colour scheme of the *dhoti* shows that she was a young lady and happy with her marriage life. It was the Dogra (Indian) traditional garment (Fig. 2).

2. The variety of the modern *sari* type of garment is explored in the *Rasamanjri* paintings of a *nayika*,[482] who has been displayed waiting her lover, near her an aged lady has laid down for a comfortable sleep on the cot. She wears a *munga* (green) yellow shade *sari* of modern fashion. It shows that it has been wrapped round the waist over the *ghaghra* and its one end covers her head and right shoulders reaching down to the waist. It is a cotton made *sari*. The colour combination of the *sari* shows that an old lady was happy from the core of the heart on the married life of her son and now take rest after the arrival of the newly bride (daughter-in-law). It was also a Dogra (Indian) traditional dress (Fig. 3).

3. There is another variety of the *sari* which was popular among the Dogra womenfolk in during 18th century A.D. It in the pictures of the *Gita Govinda* of Krishna's *Gopias*.[483] It has been worn round the waists over the *ghaghra's*, it covers the head and right shoulder of the *Gopias* falling below the waist. It shows that it was short length type of *sari* and has been worn in multi-colours both in primary and secondary colours. The colour treatment of the *sari* shows that most of the Krishna's *Gopias* used to love with Krishna from the core of the heart and it was difficult for them to separate themselves from him. They were shown feeling happy to play with Krishna. *Sari* demonstrates Rajputana fashion influence. Few women wearing printed design of cotton *sari* while few wore silken-made *sari's* embroidered with gold wire as worn by a royal ladies (Figs. 1, 2, 3).

4. This typical variety of the *sari* is worn by Radha expounded in the picture of Krishna while milking the cow.[484] She drapped it over the red *ghaghra's*. It shows that a maroon *sari* having blackish shade

curvature of cotton cloth, she tucked its one end at the navel than wrapped rond the *ghaghra* as it appears from the surface in loose style terminated in back. There is another pieces of cloth of (*Krsna*) colour has also been tucked at the front of the navel, and its one end covers her head and terminated at back. Besides, two pieces of cloth, there is another *mungh* (green) handkerchief hanged at the right hip in an artistic manners either it was a towel which was utilized by Krishna before milking the cow to wash the nipples of the cow or used by Radha as a fashion trend. An upper-garment with *sari*, Radha wears pinkish *choli* (*piyazi*). Colour scheme of the *sari* shows that in the middle of the 18th century A.D., there was a dark phase in the life of Indians all around, but impresses that they worked hard with strong confidence, to fight alarming problems of the nation i.e., unemployment, and ideology has groomed that only socio-economic development will bring a happy and prospers life. *Sari* shows Gujarat fashion influence (Fig. 1).

5. This variety of the *dhoti* or *sari* is discovered in the *Rasamanjari* painting of threshold youth.[485] She wears round shape *dhoti* or *sari* round the waist line without *ghaghra* and simply wrapped round the waist into two rounds and naked from the upper part of the body. Its one end which covers the upper part of the body has been shown falling on the ground. *Dhoti* or *sari* has been made of superior white cotton having *mungha* colour chain type lining design and striping print. The colour combination of the *dhoti* of Indian tradition shows that she had to wait for the full threshold youth and would enjoy the prime youth youth and after getting married. It will a new music in your life (Fig. 3).

The comparative study of the period sheds light that *dhoti* or *sari* was not worn only in Jammu region, but its similar kinds of garments were also fashion in other parts of the Indian States.[486]

Ghagra (*Ghaghra*, *Ghaghru*)

In the paintings of the period, it appears that *ghagra* usually consisted of densely pleats skirt. A simple *ghaghra* have one vertical seam which turns the cloth or *ghaghra pata* into a tube. It was fashion with a drawing–string passed through a long, narrow slot at the waist and its length would come down to the anklets. Flared skirt type of the *ghaghras* are made of several triangular pieces of clothes stitched together. As a lower garment, study reveals that its was wear was combined with a *choli* or similar type of a bodice over the upper part of the body, with *ordhani* or a *dupatta*, the unstitched pieces of cloth. The wide adoption of the typical Indian "three pieces dress" of the women was the result of the intrusion direct or indirect from the West and North-West. This typical "three-pieces dress" of the Indian woman was the bodice (*choli*), the skirt (*ghaghra*) and the handkerchief (*ordhani*). The first two sewn and tailored garments were unknown in pre-Islamic time.[487] Its popularity as a garment seems to be not much earlier than the medieval period. The earlier word for the garment came to be much more popularity referred to as *ghaghra* is *lehanga*, or *lehnga*, probably a compound of the Sanskrit word *lanks*, standing for the waist and '*anga*' referred to a body (garment).[488] It shows that *ghaghra* or *lehanga* was originated by the Indians with the impact of the foreign invasions in Indian. In the local language of the Dogras it has also been called as *ghaghra*, *ghagrua* or *ghaghri* as generally known in other parts of the Indian states. In the Rajasthani version of the *ghaghra* is sometimes referred to as *chania* or *chanio*, the word probably making a reference to *charana*, meaning feet, and signifying the fact that the *ghaghra* was a garment of the length that would come down to the feet. One knows that *ghaghras* worn a little high, lower than the knew but not markedly so but the standard *chanio* or *ghaghra* is long[489]. Study shows that a *ghaghru* or *ghaghra* by its very nature is an all-purpose clad, it admits high ornamental elements. It to serve as a warm clothing in the winter and in summer keep away heat and dirt and, lastly, it has been so designed as to keep the movement free and gait rhythmic. It has been worn at the waist-line and also leaves an element of appeal to a lady. Mostly, it has been made of cotton cloth in different colours and designing. Some of its pieces have been displayed with *chalar* (frill) at the lower end. It is mentioned that most of the Dogra females used to wear a *orange ghaghra*.[490] It has vertical[491] lining pleats which took the pattern of a skirt after fastening with a string round the waist and reaches on the anklets. It has sky blue and golden floral printed frill stitched to its lower edges. It was a popular article among the women of Jammu along with a bodice of various colours.[492]

The following lower garment i.e., known as *ghaghra* or *ghaghru* preferred by the Dogra women, in the paintings of the period, are described as under:

1. In the *Gita-Govinda* paintings, the most of the *Gopias*[493] of Krishna, wore bell-shape pleated different colours of *ghaghrua* made of cotton pieces i.e., yellow, purple, red, indigo, green, *mungh*, etc. in the same pattern, and tied by the drawing-string (*nara*) round the waist hanging down the anklets. They have been decorated with different colours of frill at the lower edges. Over the *ghaghras* they wore Rajasthani type of *sari* which covers the head and right shoulder, bodice or *choli* as an upper garment. It was fashioned in Jammu region from the 17th century A.D. The colour scheme of the different colour

of *ghaghras* vibrate every sentiments of the life of royal families, i.e., joy, sorrow and playing times of Krishna with *Gopias*. *Ghaghra* shows Indian fashion influence i.e., Rajasthani (Figs. 2, 3).

2. The portrait of *Radha*[494] with *Krishna* demonstrated another variety of the *ghaghra's*. It is a flared type of skirt known as *ghaghra*. It seems that it has been made of two layers of cloth. The upper layer of the *ghaghra's* has been made of transparent of white cloth and its inner layer made of cotton having greyish maroon shade. The lower edge of the upper layer of *ghaghra's* has been decorated with attaching white jewels and curvature in pattern. It has heavy pleats than the above-mentioned *ghaghra*. Here, Radha wears three pieces of dress, i.e., *dupatta, choli* and *ghaghra* purely an Indian dress. The colour combination of the *ghaghra's* shows that Radha is pleasing Krishna with a posture as suggesting Kaishna don't feel worry about the wordly events. World is the home of suffering and sorrow, those will do good, they will get rid from misering or suffering and those will do bad, they will lead sorrowful life, why you are worried about it, let us make our life happy by tolerating the unfortunate events of worldly life. *Ghaghra* shows Indian fashion influence (Rajasthani) (Fig. 1).

A Dogri writer in as folksong, expresses commendably the pattern of various clothes and ornaments which were worn by the Dogra women from 17th to 19th centuries A.D. The cosmetic materials elaborated in the following manners:

"सुन ओ कैंता मेरे टल्लू फट्टी गे,
मिगी लेई दे तूं शैल घघरूआ।
ओ मिगी लेई दे तूं शैल घघरूआ।।
सूही–सूही साटना दी सुत्थन सियाई दे,
मोरा कीना द मिगी झगुआ बनाई दे।
कज्जल पाना, मत्थै बिन्दलू लाना,
ओ मिगी लेई दे फरोजी चदरूआ।
ओ मिगी लेई दे फरोजी चदरूआ।
कशबोई बाला कैतां साबन मगाई दे,
सिर ताई गरिया दा तेल मगाई दे ओ।
तेला बाज सिर इयां होई गेआ जियां,
सुक्केआ सनूं दा रस डुआ,
ओ मिगी लेई दे तूं शैला घघरूआ।
आडंना–गुआडनां झुमके जे लादियां।
सौ–सौ घ्याडी दे मीहने जे लादियां,
इक–दुई बल कोई सारतां जै मारै,
जिसलै चुक्कनी आ गोए दा ढोकरू।

ओ मिगी लेई दे तूं शैला घघरूआ।
ओ मिगी लेई दे तूं शैला घघरूआ।।"[495]

Tr. into English: Lady says her husband:
"Oh! Dear listen, my cloth has torn,
You buy me a beautiful *ghaghrua*,
Oh! You buy me a beautiful *ghaghrua*
You have to stitch me a red-red colour *suthana*, of *sahneel*.
Also stitch me a tight-fitting *kurta* (*choga*)
Having *kajala* (collyrium) for staining the
Eyes and a *bindlu* (*tikka*) for forehead.
Oh! Buy me a bright blue (*Indigo*) colour *chadrua*
Oh! Buy me a bright blue (*Indigo*) colour *chadrua*;
Also buy me a bathing soap of pleasant smell.
Also buy me coconut oil for head sake.
Without oil my hair became as the small strings of *jute*.
Oh! You buy me a beautiful *ghaghrua*
Neighbourer (females) use to wear *jhumakas*.
Hundred-Hundred times in a day and month.
Give gesture to each other.
When, I use to put the *basket* (*tokaruu*) of the manure on my head.
Oh! You buy me a beautiful *ghaghrua*
Oh! You buy me a beautiful *ghaghrua*."

3. This variety of the lower garment i.e., *ghaghra* is detected in the picture of representative of Shiva with two ladies.[496] They wore a skirt type of *ghaghra* of white background, one wears red and other wears black having horizontal lining design. It has been tied by a drawing string passing through a tube (*pata*) round the waist line. In the mean times, they also wears 'three-piece dress' i.e, *dupatta*, *choli* and *ghaghra*. The colour treatment of the *ghaghra* shows that (during the time of Suchet Singh, India was dominated by the Britisher), there was a lawlessness in India. Britishers were committing crimes and Indian were fighting against the unfortunate events, by displaying patience wisdom and courage. It also shows Indian fashion influence (Rajputana) (Fig. 4).

4. The portrait of Raja Suchet Singh's Rani[497] demonstrated another variety of the *ghaghra*. She wears an indigo colour of lower garment i.e., *ghaghra* has white strips in floral design. It is skirt pattern having numerous wrinkels, tied by a drawing cord round the waistline loosly down as usual. It is made of cotton. Colour background of the *ghaghra* demonstrates that the *Rani* of Raja Suchet Singh was interested to share good news but is hesitating to talk with him. *Ghaghra* shows Rajputana fashion influence (Fig. 1).

5. There is another variety of the lower garment explored in the picture of Radha.[498] She has been displayed wearing a red blood colour *ghaghra* of mill-made cotton. It shows that it was plain (without pleat) *ghaghra* in bell-shape. Its lower edge has *fita* type of stitching and short frill of gold colour. It has been tied round the waist with the help of a drawing-string hanging down on the feets. She drapped *sari* over the *ghaghra*. The colour scheme of the *ghaghra* shows that hard work for the sake of nation particularly in the field of agriculture, land will prize us with gold (strengthen our economy). *Ghaghra* shows Gujarati fashion influence (Fig. 1).

6. There is one more example of the different kinds of the *ghaghra*. It discovered in the picture of Sita.[499] She wears dark green *ghaghra* made of cotton in leaf pattern designs. It symbolizes the presence of wildlife in the Jammu region. Besides this colour scheme of the paintings show that Maharaja Ranbir Singh, he had an idea for the agricultural development to develop the economy of the areas. *Ghaghra* shows Rajasthani fashion influence (Fig. 1).

7. The *Rasamanjari* painting of *Parakiya Vasakasajja*[500] *nayika* and the picture of four ladies, depicting them in a who are taking a comfortable sleeping posture on the *cot*. It demonstrates another variety of the lower garment i.e., cotton *ghaghras* of different colours scheme. One wears yellow, another pair of the ladies wear red and blue *ghaghra's* having floral design and golden frills or tape at the lower edges. The pattern of the *ghaghras* is similar like the bell, tied round the waists with drawing-cord and reaches upto the anklets. Colour treatment of the picture and the *ghaghras* show that one lady is feeling hesitation, who has blue *ghaghra*, another lady's colour displays spring season and third one's posture reflects a painted with little bit of doubt in her mind (sentiments). Moreover, they have been shown happy, young and healthy, as it indicates from the golden frills *Ghaghra* shows Rajasthani fashion influence (Fig. 1).

8. In the same picture[501] discussed above, we found that a plain pinkish (*piyazi*) *ghaghra* of the same style mentioned above worn by another lady having gold frill at the lower edge. Colour scheme of the *ghaghra's* shows that she was a young, happy married women (Fig. 1).

9. This example of the superior silken *ghaghra* has golden print on the surface and frill at the lower edge, worn by a royal *nayika*[502] (Gopias of Krishna) is explored in the picture 'on the way to the tryst' of *Rasamanjari*. This beautiful *ghaghra* has numerous pleats round the waist, flared like a heavy skirt, tied round the waistline with the help of a drawing-string. She has been shown taking its lower edge in

the left hand, as it forbids her to walk or run during night to see Krishna (hero). The colour combination of the redish *ghaghra* vibrates the sentiments of the *nayika* that she is young and healthy lady and shown happy to see her *nayaka* (Fig. 1).

10. The portrait of *Prem-Lila* of a *nayika*[503] and *nayaka* shows another variety of the *ghaghra*. Here, we find that *nayika* wore redish *ghaghra* having golden printed design made of silk. It has skirt shape pattern having numerous pleats, tied by the drawing-cord round the waist loosely falling down to the feets. *Nayika* has been displayed feeling hesitation to attend her *nayaka* on the very first day of the marriage in this scene. The colour scheme of the *ghaghra* shows that married life of both the *nayika* and *nayaka* is happy and successful. *Ghaghra* shows Rajputana fashion influence (Fig. 3).

11. There is another similar kind of *ghaghra* mentioned above, has been worn by two ladies,[504] who are shown standing on the door, wear different colour of lower-garment i.e., *ghaghra*. One wears dark green *ghaghra* having golden print and another has been shown wearing black of golden print with golden frills. The colour scheme impresses that *nayika* on the first day of the marriage was hesitating in presence of her husband. The vibrations of the *ghaghras* depict that *nayaka* must to co-operated with *nayika* and he hesitations were not proper at this juncture. Moreover, her hesitant actions can create lasting irretation between the two in the process of life. instead of happiness, there can be misunderstanding between the two. With the *ghaghras*, *nayaki* has been displayed with bodice and *dupatta* as an upper-garments. *Ghaghra* shows Rajputana fashion influence (Fig. 3).

12. There is another different variety of the *ghaghra* detected in the picture of Radha[505] in a love scene with Krishna. She wears a bell-shape *ghaghra* round the waist-line with the help of a tying cord. It is piece of cotton falling on the ground and covers her feets. It shows that on the front surface of the *ghaghra*, indigo colour of *patti* (a piece of cloth) has been stitched on it as a pattern of design. The lower edge of the *ghaghra* has geometrical pattern of design, decorated with pointed strips. Colour combination of the *ghaghra* shows that a couple (Ranbir Singh with his wife) were determined to lead a happy married life inspite of certain zig-zag problems in their way. But sometimes, they got involved in political or social problems. *Ghaghra* shows Rajasthani fashion influence (Fig. 3).

In the comparative study of the period fashion of the *ghaghra* was not limited only to Jammu region, but it was also extended in other parts of the Indian States.[506]

Suthana (*Paijama, Pyjamah, Paejama*)

In the portrays of the period under study a trouser like lower garment was worn on the lower part of the body by the womenfolk of the Jammu region with different kind of tunic in many cuts and shapes, with sight variation in respect of girth, length, fitting, material, etc. tied by the beautiful drawing-string (*nara*)[507] passing through the tube. Sometimes, it becomes wide from the top and comfortably roam around the legs and ankles covering the private part of the body and known as *suthana* made of different kind of cloth and colouring. In the local language of the Dogra it was called as *pyjama, suthana, katana,* etc. The name of type of lower garment possibly come from the Sanskrit work *svasthana* or Hindi word *suthana.*[508] Trousers of a close-fitting kind also were not unknown in early India, as judged from the evidences of the sculptures.[509] *Suthana* has numerous pleats at the ankles, fashioned with foreign influence in India. As already mentioned that *pyjamah* is a Persian term which is composed of two words '*pae*' and '*jama*', '*pae*' means legs or feet and '*jama*' means 'cover'. This signifying cloth for leggings. *Pahari* school of paintings followed the Mughal fashion style under the Sangram Pal and Kirpal Pal. The women clothes included tight *pyjamas,*[510] a loose or tight blouse and along opaque or transparent over garments fastening over the breast and reach down to the ankles.[511] In a village situated in the South-East of Jammu known as Smailpur, the younger one's wear blue trousers, fitted close to the legs below the knee while from the calf to the ankle they fall in numerous folds, over this, they wore an ample *petticoat,* and over it a white cloth hangs down behind, fluttering in the wind.[512] In *Rasamanjari* series of paintings women have been shown in tight-fitting *pyjamas* or *suthan*[513] a peculiar Dogra feature[514] often striped worn by them. In Jammu wall-paintings a *nayika* with green tight *paejama* or *suthan* on her legs peeping out of the opening[515] and also wore in the musicians party by the *nayika*[516] and *nayaka.* People from Udhampur and Jammu districts undertook the journey on foot. Lovely ladies with them clad in *kameez* (long shirts) and bright coloured *chooridar* (trousers) and *chunnis* (scarves).[517] The Gujjar lady of Jammu region dresses with a *suthan* tight (*pyjama*) and a long shirt with colourful designs.[518]

The following varieties of *suthans* or tight fitting *paejamas* which were preferred by the womenfolk of the Jammu region, were represented in the paintings of the period, discussed as under:

1. This variety of the lower-garment i.e., tight-fitting *paejamas* made of superior of black cotton reaching upto anklets without numerous folds, is clearly visible in the picture of a *Pahari Ragini.*[519] It has been tied by an artistic drawing-cord (*nara*) of Dogra tradition.

The stitching joint of the tight-fitting lower-garment i.e., *paejama* has a red vertical lining design and worn by the *Ragini* under the *pesvaj*. It shows Mughal fashion influence. The colour scheme of the *paejama's* shows that at that time there was a lawlessness in the country, no body was in a position to express his opinion on the burning issues of violent suppression launched by the British government (Fig. 2).

2. The another variety of the tight-fitting folders *paejama* detected in the *Rasamanjari* painting of a *nayika*.[520] She wears it under the water colour transparent *peswaj's*. It is well-fitted in the legs made of *pata* type of cotton cloth in vertical lining, design of red and white colour reaches to anklets and tied by a tie-cord round the waist. It shows Mughalian fashion influence. The colour treatment of the trouser depicts that she was a young newly wedded lady awaiting her husband patiently, who has been gone out for some business (Fig. 3).

3. The same kind of the tight-fitting *paejama* of Mughalian fashion mentioned above of different colours i.e., green and bluish shade, is in the picture of two ladies[521] of *Rasamanjari* series. They are feeling glad while meeting two lovers (love in union). This type of *paejama* was a fashion amongst the royal ladies (Rajputs) in the early 18th century A.D. and has been worn by them under the transparent *peswaj*. Colour scheme of the lower garment shows that wife and the husband retished their meeting from the core of the heart. The women was coying on account of her nature (Fig. 2).

4. There is one more example of the Mughalian tight-fitting *paejama* discovered in the picture of Raja Kirpal Pal's maid-servants.[522] The *chouri*-bearer and maid-servant of the Raja's wear dark and sky blue *paejama*, well-fitted to the legs having vertical lining design made of cotton cloth and another maid-servant who has been displayed serving the king by igniting the *hookah*. She wears red and white to tight-fitting *paejama* without pleats made of cotton cloth i.e., *pata* having vertical lining design. They wear it under the *peshwaj*. The colour combination of the *paejamas* demonstrate that grave social problems were erupting at that time i.e., economic, political, etc., and their solution was to be made patiently with efforts (Fig. 1)

5. The picture of a love-lorn lady[523] demonstrated another variety of the tight-fitting *churidar paejama*. She wears it under the transparent *peswaj*. It is well-fitted having numerous wrinkles at the anklets, and tied by a drawing-string round the waist with a beautiful girdle of gold colour tied round the *nayikas* waist to keep up *paejama* at proper position and beautification. It has redish and yellowish shade of lining design in vertical design and made of cotton cloth. The colour scheme of the *suthan* shows that lady was quite young and her life

partner gone out for some business, she was waiting patiently and thinking herself that prime days of the life fleeted in the waiting. It shows Mughalian fashion influence (Fig. 3).

6. There is another different variety of the tight-fitting *paejama's* of Mughalian fashion influence was exposed in the picture of Radha[524] while giving butter-milk to Krishna. She wore it under the transparent *peshwaj* made of red and black cotton well-fitted to the lower part of the body and tied by a tie-cord round the waist reaching to the ankles. It also shows Mughalian fashion influence. Colour vibration of the lower garment depicts that she was a young lady desires to lead a happy life and ready to face the headship of life disorders of the days (Fig. 4).

7. This variety of the *suthan* type of *paejama,* is discovered the picture of *Rani* Bandrali,[525] the widow of Maharaja Ranbir Singh. It has been worn by the *Rani* with the white cotton shirt. It is wide at the top and comfortable roomy around the legs having numerous pleats at the ankles, and tied by a drawing-cord. It was a Dogra traditional lower garment stitched order foreign influences. It has been called as *churidar paejama.* The white *paejama* shows that she was tolerating her miserable days i.e., widowness period. She wears white dress which indicates that Dogra society had a particular dress code for a widow (Fig. 3).

There is a beautiful example pertaining to the dresses and ornaments of a Dogri writer reflects the fashion from 17th century A.D. onwards. He describes it in the following folk song:

"चौत्रिए दा साल सानूं बुरा बिन्देया।
काल जाई पेया जिमींदारें,
हल्ला बिकदियां सनें हालें।
काल जाए पेया लोहारें,
ऐरणी बिकदियां सनें भोडें।
काल जाई पेया कराडें,
सुत्थना बिकादियां सनें नाडें।
काल जाई पेया सुनेयारैं,
चुडियां बिकदियां सनें हारें।
काल जाई पेया शवकारें,
कैंठे बिकदें सने हारें।
चौत्रिए दा साल सानू बुरा बिन्देयां।"[526]

Tr. into English:
We badly passed the month of *chooterya* (chet) of this year.
Caused calamity shortage in the houses of the farmers.
Halana (ploughing instrument) and tools were sold.

Shortage occurred in blacksmith (*Loharen*).
We badly passed the month of *chooterya* (chet) of this year.
We badly passed the month of *chooterya* (chet) of this year.
Calamity caused shortage in the houses of the farmers.
Halana (ploughing instrument) and other tools were sold.
Shortage recurred in blacksmith (*Lohara*) we badly passed in month of *chooterya* (chet) of this year.

The stand of beating the instrument of ploughing are being saled with hammer.

Shortage occurred in clothing merchant (*kararen*).
Suthans are being saled with tie-cord (*naras*).
Shortage occurred in goldsmiths (*sunariyan*)
Churian are being saled along with *hars*.
Shortage occurred in moneylenders,
kanthas are being saled along with *hars*.
The month of *chooterya* (chet) of this year, we badly passed."

In the comparative study of different adjoining states, fashion trends of wearing the tight-fitting *paejama's* or *churidar suthana's* of the Jammu region were also adopted in other states[527] of India.

Salwar (*Shalwar, Izar, Sulwar*)

Besides the tight-fitting *paijama's* or a *suthan*, in the paintings of the period, *salwar* type of drawers as a lower garment was also fashioned among the womenfolk of the Jammu region with the *kurta* and *dupatta* as a dress. It appears that it was also a *paejama* like lower garment which covers the lower part of the body from the cool and hot climate, widen and baggy at the top tied by a drawing-cord passing through a tube tied round the waist and not so tight around the legs and ankles as that of *suthan* or a tight-fitting *paejama*. It was cotton and silken cloth in various colours and designs. But it has been mostly worn by the women and considered a necessary part of the women's dress. In the local language of the Dogras, it has also been called *salwar*, *salwar*, etc. as generally known in other parts of the Indian States. According to Indu Prabha Pandey, women are shown wearing a pair of trousers or a *salwar* of the type worn by male dressed in Greek style.[528] Alberuni in his account describes, as elaborated by Dr. Moti Chandra trousers of *gargantuau* proportions which might have been some prototype of modern *salwar* worn chiefly in Punjabi.[529] A.K. Bhattacharya has rightly remarked that the closer contacts with the immediate western neighbours, e.g., the Afghans, the *salwar* perhaps bears a remote element of similarity to the dress in Central Asia from the second to the nineth century A.D. and carried a definite influence from the Islamic dress of the Mughals. This answers best to the colder climate of the north-western regions and better dispels the dry heat of summer in those region.[530] In the *Tuski-Jahangiri*, it has also been discussed that in Kashmir drawers (*izar*)[531] type of lower garment with tunic was also a fashion amongst the female. The fashion trend of the drawers (*izarband*)[532] type of lower garment with *kurta* or tunic was favourite among the women of the later Mughal period. In Dogra court female used to wear loose *kurta*'s and colourful *churidar salwars* of Mughal styles.[533]

The following types of the *salwar* or *izar* or *sulvar* which were fashioned among the Dogras women, are represented in the portrayals of period, explained as under:

1. The first variety of the lower garment known as *salwar* worn with the *kurta*, detected in the picture of *Devagiri Ragini* (Hindole).[534] She wears a sandal wooden colour of *salwar* of floral design made of superior cotton. It is a baggy type of *salwar* having numerous pleats in upward direction, wide at the top, tied by a drawing-tape passing through a tube around the waist. It appears loose around the legs and ankles. It shows Gujjari fashion influence. The colour treatment of the *salwar* demonstrates that after removing all the misunderstanding with her life partner, she was leading a happy and prosperous life with him (Fig. 1).

2. The portrait discussed above, the maid-servant[535] or messenger of the *Ragini* demonstrated another variety of the *salwar* which has been worn along with a *kurta* or *kameez*. It was a dark green *salwar* in the formation of a loose anklet type like, *paejama*, from the lower edges it has been decorated with a fillet type of design of yellow colour or as a band. It is of silken cotton and shows Punjabi fashion influence. The colour combination of the *salwar* or a trouser depicts that she had taken full initiative to remove the misunderstanding of the *Ragini* with her husband and feels happy on their reconciliation (Fig. 1).

The comparative study of the period also sheds light that the *salwar* of the Jammu region was also fashion in the other parts of the Indian territories[536] among women which shows foreign fashion influence.

Footwear

In the portrayals of the period, slippers, sandals and non-horn shape back heelless shoes made of different leather and materials, coloured and with embroidery were fashion amongst the Dogra womenfolk of the Jammu region. These were known as sandals, *panyianas* or *nukanas*, slippers in the local language of the Dogras. Full-boots and shoes with heavy heels were mostly worn by the men. But the women of the Dogra region used to wear light weight shoes without heavy heels. In the Mauryan period, the shoes that covered the ankles (*moccasins ? putabaddha*, Fig. 64) full-boot (*padigunthima*). The shoes padded with cotton-wool (*tulapunika*), shoes shaped like the wings of a partidge (*tittirapattika*), shoes decorated with the horns of ram and goat, shoes with curved points like a scorpions sting, shoes decorated with peacock fathers etc., were in great use in those days.[537] The wooden sandals made from palm leaves and bamboo was used by layman.[538] The decorated shoes made from gold, silver, jewels, beryle, crystal, bronze, glass, tin and copper were also used by some people.[539] In the Kushana period the Gandhara style of sculptures on a stone slab the woman standing near Kubera, who is drinking wine, have also shoes in her feet. The shoes worn by women is very thick, heavy and long like those worn by men. The description of the sandals of women is also given in the *Soundarananda*.[540] Sandals with foreign fashion[541] influences in India were worn by the elites in the period between 200-300 A.D. The footwear of the Indians in the Gupta period was called as *upanha, paduka*, *padavestanika*, *pula*, and *mandapula* (*mundapula*)[542] as mentioned in the *Mahavyutpati* work. In the Sultanate period the shoes (*svarnopanad*) embroidered with gold (*svarnavalksagumphita*) and jewels are were also in case. The shoe-maker was known as *mocika*.[543] An artistic shoes made of soft skin of animal or woollen fabric in light weight without heels was fashioned among the maid-servant[544] during the Akbar's time. In the Jammu Province, the area known as Rajouri, Gujjar and Bakarwal womenfolk did not use anklets to deck their feet and instead used to wear embroidered leather *mojris* or slipper or shoes embellished with large red woollen pom-pom. They were sturdy and hand made by the *mochia-mocika* or cobblers of the Rajouri. Shoes or slippers were not the essential item of dress in the dowry of the bride but the royal families of the Dogras send and accepted it as a special gift, the same was not a practice among the ordinary families in the Jammu region. The difference is obvious, that rich people used to display superior kind of shoes or slipper made of superior kind of material i.e. leather and needle-works, whereas, the poorer section of the society, used simple and plain kind of shoes made of animals skins. As it has been mentioned by the Fredric Drew, that the royal family of the Dogra used to despatch all, more or less adorned with gold briding or edging, with many of them were gold-worked slipper, these were long and narrow, with the heel pressed down.[545]

The following varieties of the shoes or slippers which were preferred by the Dogra womenfolk, and depicted in the paintings of the period, are discussed as under:

1. The first example of the footwear is in the picture of *Ragini Basant*.[546] She wears an orange slipper made of leather. It is simple kind of slipper having pressed down heel made of single sole. It has hook type of toe turned back from the face. Colour scheme of the slipper shows that she was young lady and leading a comfortable life with her life partner. It was a Dogras traditional footwear (Fig. 1).

2. This variety of shoes or slipper discovered in the picture of Dogra *nayika*.[547] She wears red slipper having sharp toe from the very face, decorated with copper wire in floral design and opened from the spur. It is a single sole type of slipper with out heavy heel. The colour treatment of the slippers demonstrates that she was a young women leading a happy life with her husband. It was also a Dogras traditional footwear (Fig. 2).

3. There is another kind of the *paniyana* or slipper in the wall-painting of the Jammu[548] the style was a popular among the womenfolk of the Jammu region. It is made of leather of animal skin of self colour. It is simple and plain kind of footwear having hook shape toe from the very face and cut off from the spur having single sole without heavy heel. It was also a Dogras traditional footwear and popular among the ladies. Footwear shows normal state of mind of the women (Fig. 3).

4. The wall-painting of the Ramnagar palace demonstrated another variety of the footwear or slippers which was preferred by the Dogri *nayika*.[549] It is made of black and soft leather having needle-works on the upper surface. It is a compressed heel type slipper of Dogra tradition. It was a superior kind of footwear having double sole. The black colour of the footwear shows that on the ground level there was a problem in the time of Raja Suchet Singh and little hope for the survival of it (Fig. 4).

5. This variety of the shoes or slipper or *paniyana*, is expounded in the picture of a love-lorn lady.[550] She wears a superior kind of slipper made of fine piece of leather embroidered with silver wire in an artistic way. The slipper has a sharp shape toe turned in upward direction having a beautiful whisk on the top and pressed down heel, opened from the back (spur) and made of single sole. It was a Dogra's traditional shoes or slipper of silver colour (grey) embroidery shows the sentiments of the love-lorn lady that she had a problem with her lover which was deep rooted in her heart and feeling of loneliness was dominent absence. (Fig. 3).

There is a beautiful example pertaining to the various article of clothing of a female along with footwear given by a Dogri poet. He superbly describes the fashions between the period of 17th century A.D. to onwards in the Duggar region i.e., Jammu:

"खौले–खौले पानिऐ,
गोरी दे पैरें दियां पानियां रूडियां।
थुडै–थुडै पानिऐ,
गोरी दे पैरे दियां छल्लियां रूडियां।
म्हीन–म्हीन बरखै,
गौरी दे गले दा हागियां सिज्जेया।
म्हीन–म्हीन बरखै,
गौरी दे सिरै दा सालू सिज्जया।"[551]

Tr. into English:
"In heavy-heavy water,
The *nayika's* slipper or *paniyana* were drowned.
In little-little water (shallow type of water)
The *chillayan* of a *nayika's* feet were drowned.
In little-little rain (shower type of rain)
The necked *hangia* of the *nayika's* was made wet.
In little-little rain,
Head covered *saloo* of a *nayika's* was made wet."

In the comparative study of the period various kind of shoes or slippers were not only fashioned in Jammu, but also used in other parts of the Indian States[552] which were similar in patern and design.

From the above proceeding pages. It is evident that dresses have played a predominent role for the evolution of the art and culture of the Jammu region, as a fashion trend, besides, the basic need of the human being to cover the naked body. It appears that the development of the art and culture took place in Jammu region with the establishment of the Mughal rule in India and the Sikh empire in this region.

Notes and References

1. Plate III; '*Sawan* is the Month of Lovers', Illustration to the *Baramas*; Basohli, Early 18th century A.D.; D.A.G. Jammu.

2. *Ibid.*, Portrait of "Radha Giving Butter-Milk to Krishna; Illustration to Bihari Sat Saiya; Basohli; (1690 A.D.). Bharat Kala Bhawan, Banaras.

3. Plate X, D.A.G.J. Acc. No. 445 Portrait of Maharaja Gulab Singh in a war procession, 19th century A.D. Jammu.

4. Plate XXXX, Portrait Wall-painting of Ramnagar palace; of Raja Suchet Singh as a soldier.

5. Plate XIV; D.A.G.J.; Acc. No. 21, Portrait of Raja Partap Singh.

6. The *Grihya-Sutras,* Tr. by H. Oldenberg, F. Max Muller; New Delhi (1990); p. 63. Hereafter mentioned as *G.S.*

7. *Ibid.*, p. 64.

8. Dr. Moti Chandra *Costumes, Textiles, Cosmetics and Coiffure in Ancient and Medieval India;* Delhi, 1973, p. 2. Hereafter referred as *C.T.C.C.A.M.I.*

9. *Yuan-Chwang's* Travels in India by Thomas Watters, M.R.A.S.; Delhi-6, First Indian Edition; 1961; p. 148. Hereafter refered as *Y.C.*

10. Dr. Moti Chandra; *C.T.C.C.A.M.I.* p. 2.

11. *Rajatarangini* by Kalhana, Tr. by M.A. Stein Vol. IV, p. 180; Bombay 1900. Quoted from Dr. Moti Chandra C.T.C.C.A.M.I. p. 111. Hereafter cited as *R.T.*

12. *Ibid.*, Vol. VII, pp. 922, 24 (Stein's note). Quoted from K.S. Sexena, *Political History of Kashmir*; Lucknow (U.P.); 1974 p. 204. Hereafter referred as *p.H.K.*

13. *Ibid.*, Vols. I, VII; p. 895.

14. *Ibid.*, Vols. I, VII, pp. 926-31.

15. Charles Fabres; *Indian Dress*, Delhi; 1977, p. 24. Hereafter referred as *I.D.*

16. *William Erskine, History of India under Baber*, Delhi, first reprint, 1989, p. 397. Hereafter cited as *H.I.U.B.*

17. *Khilat's* : It is more than a robe, for its consists of at least three articles of clothing; viz., the turban, the robe and the girdle.

18. *Balaposh*: It means a quilt, but here probably a cloak or upper garment.

19. *Tuman*: Wallaston, mentions the *tuman* is a gold coin worth about 8 shillings. Block man says the Persian turban about equal 33, if so, it might be compared with a gold *Mohar*, but probably it was a silver coin that the soldiers received.

20. The *Akbarnama of Abu-L-Fazl*, Tr. from the Persian by H. Bveridge I.C.S., New Delhi, First Indian Print; 1973, Second print; 1979, p. 425. Hereafter described an *A.N.*

21. *Tusk-I-Jahangiri or Memoirs of Jahangiri*; Tr. by Alexander Rogers; I.C.S Two vols. in one; Delhi 1904-1914; First print, 1989. Second reprint, 1994, p. 322. Hereafter referred as *T.J.*

22. *Ibid.*, Vol. I, p. 384.

23. *Ibid.*, Vol. II, p. 104.

24. *Ibid.*, p. 122.

25. *Ibid.*, p. 148.

26. William Irvine; *Later Mughal*; Vols. I and II Bound in one; New Delhi; 1959; p. 112. Hereafter described as *L.M.*

27. Brown Charles and Hugle; *Travels in Kashmir and the Punjab*; London; 1952, p. 380. Hereafter explained as *T.K.P.*

28. Plate XXXXVII; D.A.G.J. Acc. No. 22/69. Reclining 'A Woman in Yellow Dress; 18th century A.D. Jammu.

29. *Ibid.* D.A.G.J. Acc. No. 23/74; 'A Woman With Sitar'; 18th century A.D Jammu.

30. Plate XIV; Portrait of Raja Ranbir Singh; 19th century A.D. Jammu; D.A.G.J.

31. O.C. Handa; *Textiles, Costumes and Ornaments of the Western Himalaya;* New Delhi; 1988; pp. 182-83. Hereafter referred as *T.C.O.W.H.*

32. Keher Singh 'Madhukar', *Dogri Lok Geet*; Part-8, Jammu; 1971, p. 64. Hereafter referred as *D.L.G.*

33. Plate XI, D.A.G.J. Acc. No. 314, *Panchvakta;* Artist Aziz; 19th century A.D. Jammu.

34. Plate X, D.A.G.J. Acc. No. 445. Maharaja Gulab Singh in a War Procession 19th century.

35. M.S. Randhawa and Krishna Chaitanya; Roopa-Lekha; Vol. 1 and 2; Delhi; 1959; p. 29.

36. *A.N.*; Vol. I; p. 648.

37. India Prabha Pandey; *Dress and Ornaments in Ancient India*; Delhi; 1988; p. 12. Hereafter referred as *D.O.A.I.*

38. B.N. Goswamy; *Indian Costume,* Ahmedabad (U.P.); 1993; p. 7. Hereafter referred as *I.C.*

39. Indu Prabha Pandey; *D.O.A I.* p. 12.

40. Dr. Moti Chandra *C.T.C.C.A.M.I.* p. 17.

41. Afif, Tarikh-Firuz Shah; p. 48. Quoted from Dr. Moti Chandra *C.T.C.C.A.M.I.*; p. 143.

42. *Ibid.*, p. 363.

43. Charles Fabres; *I.D.*; p. 70.

44. *Ibid.*, p. 72.

45. *Ibid.*, p. 82.

46. W.G. Archer; *Paintings of the Sikhs;* London 1966; p. 53. Hereafter referred as *P.S.*

47. *Ibid.*, p. 54.

48. Fredric Drew; *Northern Barrier of India*; Jammu and Kashmir Territories; Jammu 1971; p. 42. Hereafter cited as *N.B.I.*

49. Jamila Brij Bhushan; *The World Miniature Painting*; Delhi, 1989; pp. 178-80. Hereafter explained as *W.M.P.*

50. F.S. Ajjazuddin; *Pahari Paintings and Sikh Portraits*; In Lahore Museum; Karchi and Delhi; 1977; p. 81. Partrait of Raja Hira Singh;

51. Hira Singh : He was the son of Raja Dhian Singh, as soon as Dhian Singh became the Prime Minister of the Sikh empire in 1828 A.D., than Hira Singh was twelve years old, was also created a Raja, and soon afterward (1834), the principality of Jasrota was granted to him as a *jagir*; Jasrota fort had been used as a deposit for all the values of the family, and on the hearing of the death of Hira Singh, Jawahir Singh at once set out for the purpose of transferring everything to Jammu. He died without a male issue or heir.

52. Bingley, A.H. and Cunningham W.B. Revised by S.D.S. Charak; Introduction to the History and Culture of the Dogras; Pathankot; 1979; p. 160. Hereafter explained as *I.H.C.D.*

53. Frederic Drew; *N.B.I.* p. 52.

54. A.K. Coomaraswamy; *Rajput Painting*; Vol. I.Text; London; 1916 revised; 1976; p. 18. Hereafter described as *R.P.*

55. O.C. Handa; *T.C.O.W.H.*; p. 183.

56. Plate XVII; D.A.G.J.; Acc. No. 233/282; *Portrait of Raga Khokhar*; 8th century A.D. Jammu. **Khokhar**: In 1420 A.D. a rebellion broke out in the Punjab and led by Jasrath Shaikha Khokhar one of the local *zamindars* or petty Chiefs, who aimed at the capture of Delhi, on Timur's invasions

towards Delhi he was opposed near the banks of the Bias by one Nasrat Shaikha Khokhar, who was defeated and slain. He was probably a son of Malik Shaikha Khokhar. On his rebellion a force was sent against him from Delhi, and being defeated on the Satluj; he fled northward along the foot of the hills), pursued by the Sultan, seems to have crossed near Jammu. But it is certain that they held way over the west of the Chenab, with their strong holds at Bhimber. Jhakhar lying to the north of Mangla fort. They were thinly scattered upto Akhnur and in the District of Jammu, where they had a small fort near Jammu. One of the eminent chiefs of Khokhar of Jammu was Sarpal. Who wore white compact turban along with a plume in tuft manner. It was an Indian originated turban, worn in the Gujarat. The expression of the turban shows that he had a mastery over turban wearing.

57. *Ibid.*

58. Plate XI., D.A.G.J.; Acc. No. 265/312; Portrait of Babur; 19th century A.D. Jammu. **Babur** was the founder of the Mughal Empire in India. He defeated the Sultan Ibrahim Lodhi, in the first Battle of Panipat in April (1526. A.D.), the ruler of Delhi. He might have come in contact with the Raja's of Jammu earlier; his marked advances upto Sialkot and Lahore on his third and fourth invasion of India during 1522 and 1525 A.D. shows that he had socio-political relation with the Raja of Jammu. He remained in India (1525 A.D. to 1530 A.D.).

59. Plate XIII, D.A.G.J. Acc. No. 118, Portrait of Khwaja Khizer; 19th century A.D. Jammu. **Khwaja Khizer** : Daughter of Babur, named Gulbadan Begum, a sister of Humayun, who married Khwaja Khizer, a Sultan or Khan of the race of the Mughul Sultans. He was the son of Muhammed Khwaja Khan.

60. Plate XVII., D.A.G.J.; Acc. No. 144/166; Portrait of Sultan Abu Said; 19th century A.D. Jammu. **Sultan Abu Said** : He was the grandfather of Babur son of Mirza Sultan. Muhammad does not appear to have taken any active part in public life. When visited on his death-bed by his cousin Ulugh Beg, he took his son Abu Said's hand, and placing it that Ulugh Beg, recommended the youngman's protection. The trust, thus committed to him, Ulugh Beg faithfully fulfilled; and Abu Said, for some years, served him with diligence affection.

61. *Ibid*: D.A.G.J.; Acc. No. 313; Portrait of Umar Sheikh Mirza; 19th century A.D. **Umar Sheikh-Mirza**. He was the father of Babur, the ruler of Farghama, with Andijans as its capital. It was a fertile track of land 40,000sq miles in area and contained Khokand, now in Russia Turkishtan. Immediately, on the death of Yunas Khan Baburs maternal grandfather (1486-1487), his paternal uncle, Amhed Khan and his maternal uncle Muhammad Mirza planned to joint attack on Farghana. Umar Sheikh Mirza proceeded and met them in the battlefield. But during the course of quarrels, Umar Sheikh Mirza died of an accidental fall (8th June, 1494). Thus his father's sudden death called Babur to the throne of Farghana when he was only seven years of age.

62. Plate XX; D.A.G.J.; Acc. No. 247/294; Portrait of Rai Raodeh (Dharmsalwala); 19th century A.D. Jammu. **Rai Raodeh** : He was the Raja

of (Dharmswala). In the 35 year of the Akbar, reign in 1588-1589 A.D.; the revolt broke out throughout the Hill states, from Satluj to Chenab river. All the hilly Chiefs united led by Raja Bidhi-Chand of Kangra to fight against the Akbar. It appears that Rai Raodeh was dispatched in the Rajputana states for the assistance.

Camel: According to William Moorcroft, there are said to be about 2,00 camels in Kashmir, all of which belong to the Highness the Maharaja, but this number probably exaggerated. Gulab Singh is said to have introduced them into the valley for the first time (A Gazetteer of Kashmir, Bates; 1980; p. 21). In Jammu Camels were also available in the 17th and 19th centuries.

63. Plate XIII; D.A.G.J.; Acc. No. 240/287; Portrait of Raja Jagat Singh; 17th century A.D. **Jagat Singh**: Jagat Singh of Nurpary was a contemporary of the Bhupat Pal of Basohli through his influence at the Mughal court, He gained paramount power over the surrounding states. He was waiting for a favourable opportunity. When Bhupat Pal was absent from the court Emperor Jahangir, who without an inquiry, had decided to put him into prison. In about 1627 A.D., possibly on the death of Janangir, he recovered liberty and disguised himself. Jagat Singh by 1629 A.D., become the ruler of his territory. When he was out to conquer the Bhadrawah a force form Babour (Basohli) under Bhupat Pal and an officer named Kantak of the Balawaria family advanced upon Kishtwar, captured him and killed.

64. Plate I; Portrait of Raja Kirpal Pal of Basohli circa (1663-1695 A.D.). **Raja Kirpal Pal**. He (1678-1693 A.D.) married two *ranis*, the first being a princess of Bandralta (Ramnagar) and second of Mankot (Ramkot). He ruled for fifteen years and died in 1693 A.D.

Medini Pal : Plate II, Fig. 1. He wears same style of turban as worn by Raja Kirpal Pal. Here we see, he has placed (*sir-panch*) on it. His two attendances have been shown wearing same style of turban but their colour and stuff is shown inferior incomparison with Medini Pal (1707 A.D.). He founded the present town of Bhadhrawah, and made it capital.

65. Plate I; Portrait of Raja Dhiraj Pal of Basohli (1693-1708 A.D.). **Raja Dhiraj Pal** : He was the contemporary ruler with Raja Udai Singh of Chamba.

66. Plate X; D.A.G.J.; Acc. No. 241/287; Portrait of Rafi-Ud-Darjat; 18th century A.D. Jammu. **Rafi-Ud-Darjat**: He was born in 1700 A.D. and expired on 11th June 1719 A.D. He was addicted of opium and from the day that he ascended the throne, he became weaker and weaker. He only ruled for a period of three months and nine days. At his death, he was about 20 years of age. His style and title as emperor was Abulbarakat, Sultan Shams-ud-din, Muhammed Rafi-ud-Darjat, Badshah Ghazi. At the first audience on the prayer of Maharaja Ajit Singh, Raja Bhim of Kota, and Raja Rattan Chand, *Jaziya* tax which was imposed on Hindu was again abolished by him.

67. Plate XI; D.A.G.J. Acc. No. 263/310; Portrait of Raja Kishan Singh; 18th century A.D. **Kishan Singh:** He was the younger brother of ruler, Ranjit Sen (1762-91 A.D.) from Suket. Sansar Chand of Kangra married a princess from Suket daughter of Raja Kishan Singh. Suket had soon cause to regret the alliance with the aggressive and ambitious Lord of Kangra for he assisted

Kishan Singh in a revolt and burnt the capital, Kartarpur. Later, however, he came to an understanding with Ranjit Sen and his son, Bikram Sen.

68. Plate XI; D.A.G.J.; Acc. No. 243/289; Portrait of Raja Jai-Singh; 19th century A.D.; **Raja Jai Singh:** The Amrit Pal of Basohli and Jai Singh, they were of the same age. Prithvi Pal probably had a long reign and was succeeded by his son, Jai Singh, who seems to have ruled sometimes late than 1820 A.D. In his reign the Jammu state came entirely under the possession of Maharaja Ranjit-Singh of Punjab; probably about (1808-09 A.D.), but the Raja continued to rule under the burden of a year tribute. He was, however, the last Chief of Bhadu State to exercise any real power.

69. Plate XXI; Portrait of Hataf Bandral; Collection made from the A.K. Coomaraswamy; *R.P.* Vol.1 pp. 18, 20, 74 and Vol.11, Plates. **Raja Hataf Bandral**. It appears from the study that before the Raja Suchet Singh, Bandralta (Ramnagar) was ruled by Hataf Bandral. His rising popularity of the *Mian* with the ruler of Lahore excited jealous by the *rani* Bandral and Prince Kharaq Singh's managers which led to the *Mians* assassination.

Note : Muslim and Sikh. It is important to note from the study that the Dogra artists or painters encouraged paintings without any religions bias; for instance, the portraits of Sultan Abu Said, Umar Sheikh-Mirza, Babur, Rafi-Ud-Darjat, Ranjit Singh, Kharaq Singh, Nao Nihal Singh, etc. thus shows that regional ties were important with the law community.

70. Keher Singh Madhukar; *D.L.G.*, Part 8; p. 75.

71. **Kikkar:** It is a wild plant mostly having black colour. It means that Dogras were used to wear black colour *pagri*.

72. Plate XII; D.A.G.J.; Acc. No. 10/57; Portrait of Raja Kharaq Singh 19th century A.D. Jammu. **Raja Kharaq Singh**: He was the son of great Maharaja Ranjit Singh. In 1812, Jammu was assigned to him as *jagir* by his father. He was desposed after a reign of only a few month, and died a year later, Nov. 1840 A.D.

73. *Ibid.*, D.A.G.J. Acc. No. 11/58; Portrait of Raja Sher Singh; 19th century A.D. Jammu. **Raja Sher Singh**. He was a reputed son of Maharaja Ranjit-Singh; when he was raised to the throne, he was assassinated on 15th Sept. 1843 A.D.

74. *Ibid*; D.AG.J.; Acc. No. 12/59; Picture of Raja Naunihal Singh; 19th century A.D. Jammu. **Raja Nau-Nihal Singh**. He was the only son of Raja Kharaq Singh, who had not good terms with his father, was killed along with Udham Singh, eldest son of Raja Gulab Singh, on his way back from his funeral, by the mass of masonry falling on him as he passed under one of the arched gate ways of the Lahore fort. He was born in Feb. 1821 A.D.; married at 17th to a daughter of Sardar Sham Singh Attariwala.

75. Plate VI; Why the Hesitation My Love; Illustration to the *Rasamanjari*; Basohli; circa 1690 as A.D.D.A.G., Jammu.

76. Plate XXI; Portrait of Rajput Prince, Early 18th century A.D. Collection made form A.K. Coomarswamy *R.P.*, Vol. II; Plate XXIV. **Note**: No name of the prince has been described in the booklet.

77. Plate VI; Portrait of *Parakiy Vasakasajja Nayika Rasamanjari*; Basohli; (1760-1770 A.D.); D.A.G., Jammu.

78. Plate VII; Love in Union; Basohli; Early 18th century A.D.; *Rasamanjari*; National Museum, Delhi.

79. Plate XV; D.A.G.J.; Acc. No. 548; Portrait of a Male and Two Female; 19th century A.D. Jammu.

80. **Readymade Turbans**: It is said during the time of Dogra rule (1846-1947); *lungis* (turbans) and *salwars* were manufactured in Muzaffarabad Tehsils from raw material imported of machine made goods, was generally the market and the industry has showing the sign of decay (Census report of Indian; 1931, Vol. XXIV; printed 1933, p. 229).

81. Gujarat: Raja Ranjit Dev also held many *jagirs* in the Punjab; especially in the district of Gujarat. During the reign of Sikh, it appears that there were socio-cultural relation between the ruler of Jammu and the Gujarati Daya Kour was the widow of Sardar Sahib Singh Bangi of Gujarat and was taken into Maharaja Ranjit Singh harem in 1811, soon after the death of her husband, she died in 1843. A Dogra army under colonel Stein Bach also took part on the side of British in the battle of Gujarat, which proved a disaster to Sikh army (*Gulabnama*; Tr. by S.S. Charak; Jammu 1977; p. 376.)

82. Plate IV; Portrait of Birth of Lord Krishna, Illustration *Bhagwat Purana,* Mankot; Early 18th century A.D. Pb. M. Patiala.

83. Plate X; D.A.G.J.; Acc. No. 445; Portrait of Maharaja Gulab-Singh in a war procession; 19th century A.D. Jammu. **Raja Gulab Singh**: He was a Dogra ruler, founder of the Jammu and Kashmir State. He ruled form (1846 to 1857 A.D.). Battle: In August 1842 Gulab Singh faced a bold contest with Chinese invading forces in Ladakh and Balti rebels, Gulab Singh reached in Leh where he "build a fort of the place of the weak redoubt form which the insurgents at the instigation of the Chinese expelled his small party of troops" (ORPS; VII; 154/36, letter No.349 of 16-8-1842; G.R. Clerk to Moddock); *Gulabnama* p. 225.

84. Plate XIII; D.A.G.J.; Acc. No. 13/60; Portrait of Raja Gulab-Singh On Horse Back, 19th century A.D. Jammu.

85. Plate XXVII; Portrait of Maharaja Gulab Singh as a soldier; Wall-Painting; Miran Shib Temple.

86. Plate XIX; A *Darbar* scene of Maharaja Singh. Door panel of the Dogra Art. Gallery, Jammu.

87. *Ibid*.

88. *Ibid*.

89. Keher Singh; *D.L.G.*; Part 8; p. 135.

90. Plate X; D.A.G.J; Acc. No. 445; Portrait of Maharaja Gulab Singh, in other procession 19th century A.D. Jammu

91. Plate X; D.A.G.J.; Acc. No. 242 Raja Suchet-Singh; 19th century A.D. Jammu. Raja Suchet Singh: He was the brother of Maharaja Gulab Singh, general of the Sikh forces, in 1822, he was made a Raja, as a chief of Ramnagar (Bandralta) was given to him.

92. Plate XXVIII; Portrait Raja Suchet Singh on horseback, a hunting scene; wall-painting of Ramnagar Palace.

93. Plate XIV; D.A.G.J; Acc. No. 21, Portrait of Maharaja Ranbir Singh; 19th century A.D.

94. Champa Sharma and Veena Gupta; *Pullsariyan;* 1980 p. 56.

95. Plate XVIII; D.A.G.J.; Acc. No. 236/283; Portrait of Raja and Rani; 19th century A.D. Jammu.

96. Plate XI; D.A.G.J. Acc. No. 314; Portrait of *Panchvakta;* Artist; Aziz, 19th century A.D. Jammu. *Panchvakta*: It was the Hindu god, which used to provide power to confront the event. Raja Ranbir Singh: He was the son of Maharaja Gulab Singh, occupied the throne of Jammu and Kashmir state from (1857-1885 A.D.)

97. Plate XVII; Portrait of Maharaja Partap Singh on Horse Back; 19th century A.D. Jammu.

98. Plate XIV; D.A.G.J.; Acc. No. 21; Portrait of Maharaja Partap Singh, 19th century A.D. Jammu. *Maharaja Partap Singh*: He was the son of Maharaja Ranbir Singh, occupied the throne of Jammu and Kashmir in 1885, after the death of his father.

99. Plate IV; D.A.G.J.; Acc. No. 21; Portrait of Raja Ram Singh 19th century A.D. Jammu. *Raja Ram Singh*: He was the second son of the Raja Ranbir Singh. After the death of Raja Suchet Singh, Ramnagar was granted as a *jagir* to Ram Singh.

100. *Ibid.*, Portrait of Raja Amar-Singh; 19th century A.D. Jammu. *Raja Amar Singh*: He was the son of Maharaja Ranbir Singh, the brother of Maharaja Partap Singh. Bhadarwah *jagir* was given to him by Maharaja Ranbir Singh, later on submitted to Jammu.

101. Plate XXXII; Portrait of Toy-seller and two children; Wall-Painting of Purmandal Temple of Radha Krishan.

102. According to Baron Charles Hugel, the Sikh's of Punjab *pagri* consists of a long piece of linen in which the hair is wrapped up, and it is so fastened either in the front or a little on one side, that one cannot see either end or knot. It lies upon down smooth, on the head, one end half way down the back Ranjit Singh hinder this end under his upper garment (Baron Charles; Hugel *Travels in Kashmir and the Punjab*; London; 1952; p. 380. Hereafter referred as *T.K.P.*). It is said that fine *lungis* or turbans of cotton with silk borders were made at Ludhiana, Multan, Peshwar and elsewhere in India (Jumic Donie; *The Punjab North-Western Frontier*; New Delhi; 1997; p. 153. Hereafter explained as *P.N.W.F.*). In Kanet, between the area of Satluj and Jamuna men wear *pagri* a seven meter white coarse cotton piece, which is tied round the head in a cursory manner. It use was confined to the older people, and the younger generation use *Kishti-numa-topi* or go bare-headed (O.C. Honda *T.C.O.W.H.;* p. 198). The nomadic Gujjar male of the Western Himalayan region wear a *safa*, a white or coloured cloth turban and its one end called *lar*, keeping hanging over the shoulder (*Ibid.*, p. 261)

103. Dr. Moti Chandra *C.T.C.C.A.M.I.*; p. 40.

104. B.N. Goswamy; *I.C.*; p. 251.

105. Indu Prabha Pandey; *D.O.A.I.*; p. 4.

106. Charles Fabers; *I.D.*; p. 4O.

107. Dr. Moti Chandra *C.T.C.C.A.M.I.* p. 46.

108. *Ibid.*, p. 85.

109. *Ibid.*

110. *Ibid.*

111. *Ibid.*, p. 106

112. *Ibid.*, p. 107.

113. *A.N.*; Vol.1; p. 345.

114. Bingley, A.H. and Cunningham, W.B. Revised by S.S. Charak; *I.H.A.D.;* p. 160

115. Fredric Drew; *N.B.I.*; p. 77.

116. O.C. Handa; *T.C.O.W.H.*; p. 77

117. Plate XVIII; D.A.G.J.; Acc. No. 235/282; Portrait of *Raga Khokhar*; 18th century A.D. Jammu.

118. Plate XVII; DA.G.J. Acc. No. 268/307; Portrait of Mirza Rustam Qandahari, Early 17th century A.D. Jammu.

Mirza Rustam Qandahari: He was the commander of the Mughal force under the Akbar and for the first time to operate against the Eastern States especially Nurpur, then ruled by Raja Basu in 1594-95 A.D.; who had been implicated in the previous rebellion. He was besiezed in the fort of Mankot for three months, and on his surrender was sent in Lahore, Akbar handed over the *jagir* of Basu to Mirza Rustam Khan Qandahari between the Ravi and Chakki, rivers, of which Paithan (Pathankot) was the capital.

119. Plate XII; D.A.G.J. Acc. No. 9/56; Portrait of Maharaja Ranjit Singh 19th century A.D. Jammu.

Ranjit Singh: He was a Sikh ruler of Punjab, who dominated the Jammu from1809 A.D. to 1846 A.D.

120. Plate IV; The Diversion of the Jamuna. Illustration to *Bhagwata Purana*; Basohli; 1730 A.D. Also see Plate IX; Fig. 3 and Plate V, Fig. 2.

121. *Sudama*: He was the fast friend of Lord Krishna. Here he has been shown wearing a golden and pinkish floral type of head-ornament known as diadem *Rani* colour scarf having golden embroidery and blue (*krsna*) colour of *dhoti* of golden print of Dogra tradition shows that the economic condition of the Dogra people was not normal and they were unhappy. The sign of the golden colour shows that there was a great need of the economic reform to cultivate the dry areas (*Kandi area*) through irrigation. As it makes clear from the flame colour of the background of the picture.

122. Plate XXIV; D.A.G.J. Acc. No. 99; Portrait of Krishna and Radha in a love scene, 19th century A.D. Jammu.

123. Plate XXIV; D.A.G.J. Acc. No. 105/152; Portrait of *Sati Parikashan*; 18th century A.D. Jammu.

Sati: It is said, "Thirteen *Rani's* and slave-girls of Raja Suchet Singh and three widows of Rai Kesari Singh burnt themselves as *satis* at Sambha, a large town in the Jammu hills by order of Raja Hira Singh". (Ganesh Lal *Siyahat-I-Kashmir*. F.9a). Quoted from *Gulabnama*; p. 250.

124. Plate XIX; Door Panel of Dogra Art Gallery Jammu; Portrait of a *Darbar* scene of Maharaja Gulab Singh. *Note*: Jammu painter has painted this head-dress mentioned above in the *Ramayana* and *Mahabharata* war scenes worn by the army Chief for the protection of head.

125. Plate XXXXVI; Painting of Rama and Lakshmanaa setting out to do battle with Ravana; Wall Painting of Mansar Temple.

126. In Kashmir, there was another change during the time of Dogra rule visible in the form of dress the use of hat and the for caps which generally supported the turban (*dastar*). (Census Report of India; 1931 Vol.1, p. 102). Whereas the Ladakhi on their heads, wear either quilt skull-cap, as filthy as their cloaks, or cap of sheep-skin with the wool inside and with a large flap behind, which covers the back of the neck as well as the ears. Those in better circumstances have fur caps of the same shape (Alexander Cunningham; *Ladakh*; Srinagar (Kashmir); 1997, p. 301. Hereafter explained as *L*. While woollen caps which are circular in shape with a velvet band of **shaneel** around it, have been very popular in Himachal Pradesh and outside have assumed names like *Bushahari-topi* or *Kulu-topi* (K.L. Vaidya; *the Cultural Heritage of The Himalayan*; New Delhi, 1977, p. 73. Hereafter cited as *C.H.H.*). The pointed skull-cap or *kulah* (*kulla*) of which there are many varities was strong by associated with the Muslims in Indian even though certain sections of the Hindu and Sikh especially in the provinces, it was widely worn (B.N. Goswamy *I.C.*; p. 252). Whereas the head-dress of the Nepali people is a small skull-cap of black or white clothe thinly wadded with cotton and generally turned up on inch or so at the border (E.T. Atkinson *G.H.*; p. 27). In the Punjab, the Gaddis were "fond of high peaked caps with flaps reaching down the ears, and flowers and a plume adorning the front (B.S. Saini; *The Social and Economic History of Punjab* (1901-1939); New Delhi; 1975; p. 121. Hereafter referred as *S.E.H.P.*). The Galcha statesmen wear a close fitting cap lined with fur and turned up at the bottom (E.T. Atkinson; G,H.: p. 37). Other *topis* equally simple made were in use in other parts of India, but more elaborately made caps were also known the four-cornered **changoshia**; the **Kisati-nums**; the **mandil**; being some of the style known according to the statement of B.N. (B.N. Goswamy; *I.C*,: p. 252).

127. Interview conducted with the old person of the Jammu interiors. He is said unfortunately, garment making, as a regular factory, has not developed entirely in this state (Smt, Amrita Devi, tailor) Goswamy.

128. *G.S.*; pp. 57-58.

129. Dr. Moti Chandra *C.T.C.C.A.M.I.*; p. 8.

130. *Y.C.;* pp. 149-50.

131. *A.N.* Vol.1 p. 421.

132. Mira Seth; *Dogra Wall Painting in Jammu and Kashmir*; Bombay; 1987 p. 37. Hereafter narrated as *D.W. J.K.*

133. Dr. Moti Chandra *C.T.C.C.A.M.I.* p. 65.

134. *Ibid.*, p. 19.

135. *Cotton*: Under the Dogra rule 1846-1947 A.D. Jammu province had at one time a fairly prosperous cotton weaving cottage industry. Sambha being the best known centre. *Dariyas*, plain silk goods, also used to woven in Sambha. With competition from mill-made cloth the industry gravely declined. Due to the immigration of a number of Muslim weavers (*Julahas*) to Pakistan after the partition of India.

136. O.C. Handa; *T.C.O.W.H.*; p. 183.

137. Ganeshdas Badehras; *Rajadarshani*, p. 101.

138. Plate XXVII; Portrait of Maharaja Gulab Singh as a Soldier, Miran Sahib Temple, Wall Paintings.

139. Plate XVIII; D.A.G.J.; Acc. No. 235/282, *Raga Khokhar*; Jammu.

140. Plate XX; D.A.G.J.; Acc. No. 247/294. *Dharmsawala* on camel back 19th century A.D. Jammu.

141. Plate XI; D.A.G.J.; Acc. No. 314, *Panchvakta*, Artist Aziz; 19th century A.D. Jammu.

142. Plate X; D.A.G.J.; Acc. No. 445, 10/57,11/58,12/59, Maharaja Gulab Singh in war Procession; Portrait of Kharaq Singh, Sher Singh; Nau-Nihal singh, etc. *Note*: *Kurta* was popular among the royal class of the Jammu region and the Punjabis in 19th century A.D.

143. Plate XXX; Portrait of Suchet Singh; Purmandal Temple; Wall Painting.

144. Plate XXXVIII; Portrait of Suchet Singh in a war Procession; Ramnagar Palace Wall Painting.

145. Om Goswami; *Dogri Lok Geet*, Jammu; Part 15 1981; pp. 78-79. Hereafter referred as *D.L.G*.

146. Plate XXXVII; Portrait of Suchet Singh, a hunting scene, Ramnagar Palace, Wall Painting.

147. The ordinary dress of a man in Kangra consisted of a cap, a *kurti* or a *cholu*. The *cholu* was a longer garment reaching to the knees (K.L. Vaidya; *C.H.H.*; p. 72). In the area of Punjab the upper part of the body was clothed by various types of *kurta*, a loose and wide shirt reaching upto knees (B.S. Saini. *S.E.H.P.*; p. 120). In Kanet, the area between Satluj and Jamuna, male *kameez* or *kurta*, with or without sleeves and lollar is a common wear, for the body. Ordinary people did not used any underwear, it was generally home-made under shirt with pockets (O.C. Handa; *T.C.O.W.H.*; p. 190). The traditional upper-garment of the Western Himalayan region Gujjar male wears a loose, collarless shirt; *kurta* or *kameez* is a knee-long dark shirt, with a pocket on the left side of the chest made of cotton (*Ibid.*, p. 261).

148. Charles Fabres; *I.D.*; p. 24.

149. *Ibid.*, p. 76.

150. Jamila Brij Bhushan; *The World Miniatures Paintings*; London 1979; p. 179. Hereafter mentioned as *W.M.P.*

151. Plate XVII; D.A.G.J. Acc. No. 244/291. Portrait of Sultan Abu Said. Jammu. D.A.G.J; Acc. No. 3/3; Portrait of Umar Sheikh Mirza, 19th century A.D. Jammu. *Note*: He wears same kind of *jama* as worn by Sultan Abu-Said.

152. Plate XI; D.A.G.J.; Acc. No. 265/312; Portrait of Babur; 19th century A.D. Jammu.

153. Plate X; D.A.G.J.; Acc. No. 241/288, Portrait of Hazrat Raffh-Ud-Darjat Jammu.

154. Plate XIII; D.A.G.J.; Acc. No. 240/287; Portrait of Raja Jagat Singh; Artist Aziz; 19th century A.D. Jammu.

155. Plate XI; D.A.G.J.; Acc. No. 263/310; Portrait of Raja Kishan Singh; 19th century A.D. Jammu.

156. *Ibid.*, D.A.G.J, Acc. No. 243/289; Portrait of Raja Jai Singh; 19th century A.D. Jammu.

157. Plate 1; Portrait of Raja Kirpal Pal Basohli, circa (1690-1693 A.D.). Pb. Mm. Patiala.

158. Plate I; Portrait of Raja Medini Pal; Basohli circa (1725-36 A.D.); D.G. Jammu. Also see plate VI, Figs. 1 & 2, *Nayakas* wore same kind of *jama*.

159. Plate1; Portrait of Raja Dhiraj Pal; Basohli; circa (1720-25 A.D.); Pb. Mm. Patiala. *Note*: Plate IV; The Birth of Krishna; Illustration to the *Bhagawat Purana* Mankot, Early 18th century A.D. Pb. Mu. Patiala. ***Jama*** Here, we see the security personals and attendance have worn a printed red and pinkish colour of upper-garment of the same pattern as worn by Raja Dhiraj Pal.

160. Plate XXV, D.A.G.J. Acc. No. 85/132; Portrait of Sanjay a character of *Mahabharata*; 19th century A.D. Jammu. Mahabharata : The *Mahabharata* and the *Ramayana* are the two great epics of India. The core theme of *Mahabharata* is the great battle fought in the field of Kurukshetra between two camps of cousins, the five Pandavas and the one hundred Kuravas, symbolizing evil against good. It has always fired the imagination of painters and poet and its many of the incidents have been reproduced in a myriad ways. In short, on Pandu's death, his brother Dhritrashtra took charge of the body and brought them up with his own one hundred sons, who were known as Kauravas from Kuru, their ancestor. The Kauravas especially Duryodhana, become jealous of their cousins, and the rivalry became more pronounced after Dhritrashtra formally nominated Yudhisthira as his heir. The Pandavas themselves escaped and returned to Hastinapur, the capital and were reconciled with their uncle Dhritarashtra, who later retired to the forest and died in a fire. The epic ends will all those who had upheld their *dharma* being united in heaven irrespective of which side they had fought for.

161. Plate III; Fig. 2; Portrait 'Sawan is the month of lovers' Illustrations to the *Baramasa*; Basohli; Early 18th century D.A.G. Jammu.

162. Plate XXVI; Fig. 3. A Scene of Mahabharata Hero's i.e Rama and Lakshmana. Here they wear orange colour of *jama*, Bhurja Temple; Wall Painting also. See Plate XVI; Fig. 2; D.A.G.J. Acc. No. 532; Portrait of Rama and Panchayat Artist Hari Chand; 19th century A.D. Jammu. Here, Rama wears a pinkish colour of *jama*.

163. Plate XX; D.A.G.J. Acc. No. 183/231; Portrait of a Brahmin Returning from a Muslim Court 19th century A.D. Poonch. *Note*: To the West of Chenab, the state of Poonch was ruled by a Raja Bhimber, including Naoshara, named Sultan Khan, made a brave resistance against Sikh, Raja Dhian Singh who was the Prime Minister at that time in the Sikh Court. It appears from the picture that he had determined to crush the Sultan Khan and had to laid down his own power. In the mean while he dispatched a Brahmin to surrender his power to Maharaja Ranjit Singh. But he did not agree. Ultimately, Sultan Khan had been over thrown by Maharaja Ranjit Singh. The overpowered Sikh's imprisoned him for seven years in Lahore and Poonch was granted in fief to Raja Dhian Singh about 1822 A.D. Sultan Khan was set at liberty and assisted Ranjit Singh in the invasion of Kashmir in 1819 and was after ward killed in Jammu.

164. Plate XXXII, Fig. 3; Portrait of a (*Kilonai-Wala*) Toyseller; Purmandal, Temple, Wall Painting. *Note*: He wears same kind of side-

fastened frock type of *jama* as mentioned above, but he has been shown wearing an inferior kind of dress. It shows his economic status was not high during the time of Dogra rule. He wears blue (sky) *jama* as it reflects he is hesitating to proceed in the house of superior.

165. Plate XXI; Collection made from A.K. Coomarswamy's *R.P.* Vol. II, London, Plates 1916 and 1976. Plate XXI; Fig. A *Darbar* of a Dogra Rajput Prince. The Prince seated with one attendant facing his courtiers retainers *Pahari* (Jammu); 18th century A.D. He made the collection from William Rothenstein Vol. 1, pp. 17 and 18.

166. Plate 11; Portrait of Raja Medini Pal; Basohli; circa (1725-36 A.D.); D.A.G. Jammu.

167. In the Western Himalayan region, the inner garment of the Gaddis male body is a cotton shirt, called *kurta* (O.C. Handa; *T.C.O.W.H.*; p. 271). Over the *kurta* is the Gaddis all pervasive *chola*. The *chola* has broad collar, which hang like lappets. The *chola* is long enough to reach below the knees. In the lappets are stowed needles, threads, flint-cotton etc. Numerous ornamentations are tucked over the lappets of which *chhatta* (a beaded adornment attached with *gharat*) and *gharat* (or round looking mirror, adorned with wild beads, and attached with a leather string to the *chola* or *dora* are significant. The *chola* is kept loose above the waist. So that the space so created (called *khuku* from Hindi *kokh* i.e., the womb) may be used for keeping essential items and white on the move, serves as an incubator for the new born lambs, and still feel at ease. Gaddis *chola* is a costly affair. It needs 20 to 30 metres of woollen *patta* to make one piece. It is securely gathered round the waist by innumerable folds and round of a 60 metres long back woollen rope, called *dora* (*Ibid.*, pp. 271-72).

168. Dr. Moti Chandra *C.T.C.C.A.M.I.*; p. 36.

169. *Y.C.*; p. 150.

170. Dr. Moti Chandra; *C.T.C.C.A.M.I.*; p. 142.

171. *A.N.*, Vol. 1, p. 58.

172. *T.J.*, Vol. 2 in one; p. 290.

173. B.N. Goswamy; *I.C.*; p. 87.

174. Plate XVII; D.A.G.J. Acc. No. 244/291; Portrait of Sultan Abu Said; 1914 century A.D. Jammu.

175. Plate XVII, D.AG.J. Acc. No. 313; Portrait of Umar Sheikh-Mirza; 19th century A.D. Jammu.

176. *Ibid.*, D.AG.J. Acc. No. 268/307; Portrait of Mirza Rustam Quandahari; 19th century A.D. Jammu.

177. Plate XXI; D.A.G.J. Acc. No. 9/56; Portrait of Maharaja Ranjit Singh 19th century A.D. Jammu.

178. *Ibid.*, D.A.G.J. Acc. No. 10/57; Portrait of Raja Kharaq Singh; 19th century A.D. Jammu.

179. *Ibid.*, D.A.G.J. Acc. No. 1/58; Portrait of Raja Sher Singh; 19th century A.D. Jammu.

180. Plate X; D.A.G.J.; Acc. No. 445; Maharaja Gulab Singh in was procession; 19th century A.D. Jammu.

181. Plate XI; D.A.G.J. Acc. No. 314; Portrait of *Panchvakta*; Artist Aziz.; 19th century A.D. Jammu.

182. Plate XXI; Portrait of Ranbir Singh. Collection made form B.N. Goswamy *I.C.*; Plate 27, p. 87. The picture of Maharaja Ranbir Singh of Jammu; c. 1880. *Note*: Author narrates that many of the *choghas* that have survived are made of shawl cloth wool, and when we see portraits of the Chiefs at the Sikh court in Lahore or the Maharaja of Jammu and Kashmir, wearing these *choghas*, we get conformation of the fact that much work in embroidery of this kind was at Lahore and Amritsar *chogha* made of brocade material of velvet embroidered with silver and gold thread and wire etc. from other parts of the country were also known.

183. Plate XIV; D.A.G.J. Acc. No. 21; Portrait of Ranbir Singh; 19th century A.D. Jammu.

184. Plate XVII; D.A.G.J. Acc. No. 21; Portrait of Maharaja Partap Singh on Horseback; 19th century A.D. Jammu.

185. Plate XXI; Portrait of Ranbir Singh on Royal Throne along with chouri-bearer. Collection made from the B.N. Goswamy; *I.C.* Fig. 27; p. 87.

186. Plate XX; D.A.G.J Acc. No. 256/303; Portrait of Shishu Pala and Jarasand; 19th century A.D. Jammu. *Shishu Pala*: In the *Mahabharata*, it has been described that Shishu Pala was a criminal emperor of his time. The people of his kingdom, they used to fear from his criminal activities. People complained to Lord Krishna about his criminal acts. Lord Krishna announced at that juncture, after the hundred crime, he will be killed. When Shishu Pala exceeded the limit of the hundred crimes and also insulted the Bimsen. A grand *Rajshurya* function was organized all the Brahmin kings were also participated in it. Shishu Pala was killed at that time by Lord Krishna. It is mentioned in the *Mahabharata* at that time whole world was shakened. (Reference made from the Hindi Translation of *Mahabharata* written by Pt. Ramnarayan Datta Pandey; Lucknow (U.P.) India, 2045. Reprinted 2059. See pages 840-845), *Jarasand*: In the *Mahabharata*, it has been elaborated that Jarasand used to belong from Magadhian empire. He was a powerful ruler of his time. He defeated the Yudirisatar. Yudirisatar was discouraged by this terrible defeat and inspired by Arjun, Shri Krishna did enquire about the history of Jarasand and also killed him (*Ibid*., See pages 713714).

187. The costume of the Buddhist in Ladakh is very different to that of the inhabitants of their parts of the frontier districts, usually they fasten band round their waist above the *chogha* (Census Report of India, 1901,Vol. XXIII; p. 81). In Giligit and Astove, during the time of Dogra rule (1846-1947 A.D.), the men also used to wear a long *chogha* with a cap is in the form of a sark folded at the ends, they not unoften make use of cap as their pocket. (Barown Charles Hugel; *K.A.P.* ; p. 380). In Kirata males on their body; here used to wear a loose long woollen frock or long; coat called *gonchas*, made of white wool. The higher-class people wear the *gonchas* made of scartered woollen fabric. The long-coat is sometimes made of sheep of goatskin. It is called *lhakpa*. The same garment, when made of cotton, lined with fur of goat or sheep, is known as *charlak*. The cap and the long-coat are generally

of maroon, red or black colours. The well-to-do ones also wear a cotton or silk under-coat called *tochay* (O.C. Handa; *T.C.O.W.H.*; p. 222).

188. *Y.C.*; Vol. 1; p. 148. Also quoted by Dr. Moti Chandra *C.T.C.A.M.I.*; p. 62.

189. *T.J.*; Vol. II; p. 102.

190. Jama Brij Bhushan; *W.I.M.*; p. 179.

191. O.C. Handa; *T.C.O.W.H.*; p. 183.

192. *Ibid.*

193. S.S. Charak; A Short History of Jammu. Raj: From Earliest Times to 1846 A.D.; Pathankot; 1985; p. 6. Hereafter explained as *S.H.J.R.*

194. B.N. Goswamy; *I.C.*; p. 119.

195. Plate XIV; D.A.G.J. Acc. No. 21; Portrait of Maharaja Ranbir Singh; 19th century A.D. Jammu.

196. Plate XXXV; Portrait of Raja Suchet Singh; Wall Painting of Ramnagar Palace.

197. A *sadari* known as jacket like waist-coat was used by both ladies and gents in Kotgarh and Kumargain and a dress known as *chuba* which men put on in Chini Tehsils of Simla district. Other dresses known as *gachi*; trousers, coat, shirt, waistcoat and *chadaru* i.e. blanket. For head, the people here used round cap which was generally black in colour (K.L. Vaidya; *C.H.H.*; p. 74). In Himalayan region, a tribe Monpas resemble the inhabitants of Bhutan on the West, they mostly keep cattle's, sheeps and pigs wore a small skull cap of woollen clothe of felt. Instead of a long gown of Tibet, a short coat was worn which reaches to the knees, and was fastened by a woollen girdle that invariably holds a straight knife (E.T. Atkinson; *G.H.*; p. 23). In various parts of India, over the shirt or *kurti*, a Gujjar normally wears a *basket*, a sleeveless collars half-coat of velvet or *shanil*. The *basket* is adorned with closely-fitted buttons all-over. (O.C. Handa; *T.C.O.W.H.*; p. 261).

198. Dr. Moti Chandra; *C.T.C.C.A.M.I.*; p. 14.

199. *G.S.*; p. 147.

200. Dr. Moti Chandra; *C.T.C.C.A.M.I.*; p. 14.

201. *Ibid.*

202. Charles Fabres; *I.D.*; p. 74.

203. *Ibid.*, p. 25.

204. Fredric Drew, N.B.I.; p. 76; Also quoted by S.D.S. Charak; *H.C.H.S.*; Vol. IV; p. 57.

205. Jamila Brij Bhushan; *W.M.P.*;p. 179.

206. Plate X; D.A.G.J.; Acc. No. 445; Maharaja, Gulab Singh in a war Procession; 19th century A.D. Jammu.

207. Plate XVIII; D.A.G.J.; Acc. No. 235/282; Portrait of Raga Khokhar; 19th century A.D. Jammu.

208. Plate X; D.A.G.J.; Acc. No. 241/288; Portrait of Rafi-Ud-Darjat; 19th century A.D. Jammu.

209. Plate XVII; D.A.GJ. Acc. No.268/307; Portrait of Mirza Rustam Quandahari; 19th century A.D. (Mughal Copy) Jammu.

210. Plate XVII; D.A.G.J.; Portrait of Raja Partap Singh on Horseback; 19th century A.D. Jammu.

211. In the Western parts of the Himalayan region, the *chola* of the Gaddis was securely gathered round the waist by innumerable folds and rounds of a 60 meter long black woollen rope, called *dora*. This *dora* normally acts as a waist-belt, but at the time of need, it was used for the rescue operation. In the innumerable folds of the *dora* was tucked a *kulhari* (axe), a *bansari* (a flute), a *runka* (a flint-iron), a *mandua* (a leather pouch), his favourite *chilam* (a small *hukah*); a *darat* (an iron sickle with a long handle) and host of other items of use. During a marriage ceremony, the bridegroom feigns to be a recluse by carrying a lack on his shoulders, and wearing a *dora*, which having been gifted by Shiva, symbolizes asceticism, as the tradition has it (O.C. Handa; *T.C.O.W.H.*; p. 272).

212. Dr. Moti Chandra; *C.T.C.C.A.M.I.*; p. 11.

213. *Ibid.*, p. 59.

214. Charles Fabres; *I.D.*; p. 42.

215. Dr. Moti Chandra; *C.T.C.C.A.M.I.*; p. 89.

216. Charles Fabres; *I.D.*; p. 58. It is the picture of 10th century A.D.

217. Dr. Moti Chandra; *C.T.C.C.A.M.I.*; p. 108.

218. R.C.KAK; *A.R.B.*; p. 9.

219. *Ibid.*, p. 11.

220. Plate X; D.A.G.J.; Acc. No. Portrait of Maharaja Gulab Singh in a war Procession; 19th century A.D. Jammu.

221. *Ibid.*,

222. Plate XVII; D.A.G.J.; Acc. No. 35/82; Portrait of Khokhar; 19th century A.D. Jammu.

223. Plate XIII; D.A.G.J.; Acc. No. 118; Portrait of Khwaja Khizar; 19th century A.D. Jammu.

224. Plate XIX; D.A.G.J.; Acc. No. 219/166; Gulab Singh on Horseback; 19th century A.D. Jammu.

225. Plate XXIX; Natraga; Basohli circa; (1700-1720 A.D.) Bharat Kala Bhawan Banaras.

226. Plate XXII; D.A.G.J.; Acc. No. 176/23; Portrait of Daksh Yajan (Birbha-Delra-Usinatting) in the Hawan-kund; 19th century A.D. Jammu. *Note*: Daksha had two daughters i.e., Diti and Aditi. Diti bore gods and Aditi bore *rakashas*. It is said that the origin of the man took place from Daksh. In the *Bhagawat Geeta*, it has been mentioned that Daksh organized a *sati* function of daughter or Durga. Therefore, it has been called as Daksh-Yajan (Birbh Ddra-Uninatting) in a Hawan-kund.

227. Plate XXIV; D.A.G.J.; Acc. No. 105/ 152; Portrait of *Sati-Parikashan*; 18th century A.D. Jammu.

228. Plate XXV; D.A.G.J; Acc. No.85/732; Portrait Sanjaya relating to *Mahabharata* to Dhritrashtra; 19th century A.D. Jammu.

229. Plate XX; D.A.G.J.; Acc. No.184/231, A Brahmin returning from the Muslim Court; 19th century A.D. Poonch.

230. In the area of Kanet, men as a matter of habit, carry a piece of white cotton cloth or *parana* on their shoulders, which was used as a hand-towel or a handy sheet to wrap something (O.C. Handa; *T.C.O.W.H.*; p. 190).

231. Dr. Moti Chandra; *C.T.C.C.A.M.I.*; p. 9.

232. Plate XXXVII; A marriage scene of Raja Suchet Singh; Wall-Painting, Ramnagar Palace.

233. Champa Sharma and Veena Gupta; "————" or 'Long Standing Desire; Jammu; p. 62, line Nos. 12 and 13.

234. In Punjab, a man's dress was marked by a *pagri* (turban) invariably in one colour, shaped in a peculiar mode so as to cover the tuft on head. The lower garment was an *achkan* with a *pyjama churidar* tight (A.K. Bhattacharya). *A Pageant of Indian Culture, Art and Archaeology*; Vol. 1; New Delhi; 1995; p. 111. Hereafter cited as *P.I.C.A.A.*

235. Dr. Moti Chandra; *C.T.C.C.A.M.I.*; pp. 90-91.

236. *Ibid.*, p. 143.

237. *T.J.*, Vol. 1; p. 384.

238. Plate XIV; D.A.G.J; Acc. No. 21; Portrait of Maharaja Partap Singh; Jammu.

239. In Ladakh, the men used to wear warm clothes even in Summer a thick, shapeless and long-sleeved gown or cloak or *chogha* girdled in the middle with a clothe band. The gown was usually made of dark red cloth and it reaches well below the knees. Loose trouser was also worn. The Buddhist nuns of Ladakh had their clean shaved head wore caps. They were also put on sheep-silken on their back and long gown like men (Alexander Cunningham; *L.*; p. 302). *Loia*, a woollen or *pashmina* blanket or sheet used by menfolk of Sirmur District, was a woollen gown which was supported on the shoulders and hang down over the back. The sleeves of the *loia* were seldom wore, though no *loia* was ever without them. The *loia*, put on the body appears like gown in reverse but that was the way goes with it (L.K. Vaidya; *C.H.H.*; p. 74). The area known as Kulu, Lahul and Spiti; the men dress resembles that of Pangi men with the exception that many of them wore long woollen gowns belted round the waist with a coarse scarf and their *pyjama's* were also loose (B.S. Saini; *S.E.H.P.*; p. 121).

240. Dr. Moti Chandra; *C.T.C.C.A.M.I.*; p. 62.

241. Charles Fabres; *I.D.*; p. 70.

242. *Ibid.*,

243. *Ibid.*, p. 82.

244. *Ibid.*, p. 84.

245. *Ibid.*, p. 92.

246. *Ibid.*,

247. Mira Seth; *D.W.J.K.*; p. 21.

248. *Ibid.*, p. 37.

249. W.G. Archer; *P.S.*; p. 53.

250. Fredric Drew; *N.B.I.*; p 76. Also quoted by S.D.S. Charak; *H.C.H.S.*; Vol. IV; p. 57.

251. O.C. Handa; *T.C.O.W.H.*, p. 183

252. Plate XIV; D.A.G.J. Acc. No. 21; Portrait of Ram Singh, Amar Singh and Pratap Singh (Figs. 2 & 3 of the same Plate).

253. In Pangi, in Himachal Pradesh, men wore a long woollen coat tightened round the waist by means of string made of wool. The lower garment consisted of *pyjama* of *pattoo*, loose above and tight below. The use of gaiters was also common (Gazetter of Chamba State; 1909; p. 206; quoted from B.S. Saini; *S.E.H.P.* ; pp. 120-21). The 'Aka' by caste a tribe known in Assam rearing cattle, sheep and pigs, they wear instead of the long gown of Tibet, a short-coat is worn which reaches to the knee, and is fastened by a woollen girdle that invariably holds a long straight knife (E.T. Atkinson; *G.H.*; p. 23).

254. Dr. Moti Chandra; *C.T.C.C.A.M.I.*; p. 56.

255. *Ibid.*, p. 71.

256. *Ibid.*, p. 122.

257. Plate XIV; D.A.G.J.; Acc. No. 21; Portrait of Maharaja Ranbir Singh; 19th century A.D. Jammu.

258. *G.S.*; p. 64.

259. Dr. Moti Chandra; *C.T.C.C.A.M.I.*; p. 6.

260. *Ibid.*, p. 32.

261. Fredric Drew; N.B1; p. 76. Also quoted by S.D.S. Charak; *H.C.H.S.* Vol. IV; p. 57.

262. Plate XXVI; Portrait of a Sadhu Standing on one leg. Wall Painting of Sui-Simble Temple.

263. Plate XXV, D.A.G.J.; Acc. No.85/256; Portrait of Sanjaya-narrating the *Mahabharata* to Daritrashtra; 19th century A.D. Jammu. Chapter IV.

264. *Ibid.*, D.A.G.J.; Door panel; Portrait Representative of Lord Shiva.

Note: The same kind of theme has also been reflected by the painter from the Wall-Painting of Ramnagar Palace Plate XXXIV (Fig. 1).

265. Interview conducted with old persons more than 85 year of age in the interior villages of Jammu in Jan. 2001.

266. Dr. Moti Chandra; *C.T.C.C.A.M.I.*; p. 5.

267. *Y.C.*; p. 148.

268. Mohd. Isaq Khan; *H.S.*; p. 55.

269. *T.J.* Vol. II; p. 122.

270. Bates; A. Gazetter of Kashmir; New Delhi, 1980; p. 61.

271. Mohd. Isaq Khan; *H.S.*; p. 58.

272. Bates; A Gazetter of Kashmir; 1980; p. 59.

273. Census Report of India, 1931; 1933 Vol. XXIV, Jammu and Kashmir part report by Rai Bahadur; p. 225.

274. *Ibid.*, p. 226.

275. *Ibid.*

276. Plate XXVI; Portrait of *Nayaka*; Shiva Math; Wall-Painting of Mansar.

277. In Himachal Pradesh, plain shawls of *pashmina* were termed as *loai* in Kulu valley. *Pashmina* shawl was a costly thing but wool shawl was a thing of the common use (K.L. Vaidya; *C.H.H.*; p. 75).

278. DR. Moti Chandra; *C.T.C.C.A.M.I.*; p. 6.

279. *Y.C.*; p. 149.

280. *A.N.*; Vol. II; p. 457.

281. *T.J.;* Vol. II; p. 148.

282. A.H. Bingley and W.B. Cunningham revised by S.D.S. Charak; *I.C.H.D.*; p. 60.

283. Desh Bahdu; Jammu, Kashmir and Ladakh; Delhi; 1989; p. 85. Hereafter referred as *J.K.L.*

284. *Ibid.*, p. 86.

285. S.D.S. Charak; *H.C.H.S.*, Vol. IV; p. 14.

286. S.D.S. Charak; Jammu Kingdom; Part 1 (Ancient and Medieval upto 1800 A.D.) Delhi; 1980, p. 57. Hereafter explained as *J.K.*

287. Censeus Report of India; 1931, printed; 1933; p. 226.

288. Census Report of India; 1921, printed; 1923; p. 178.

289. Plate XX; D.A.G.J.; Acc. No. 247/294; Portrait of Rai Raodeh Dhamerwal; 19th century A.D. Jammu.

290. Plate XVII; D.A.G.J; Acc. No. 98; Portrait of Krishna Playing on Flute; Artist Channu; 19th century A.D. Jammu.

291. Plate XXII; Picture of Sadhu; Wall-Painting of Purmandal Temple.

292. Plate XXV; Picture of Sadhus Likely to be Guru of Gulab Singh, instructing to him and his troops; Wall-Painting of Su-Simbli Temple.

293. In Himachal Pradesh, *pattoo* bearing flowers, was called *phool-dar-pattoo*. The *phool*-work was also called as *Bushari dhari* and it seems that it was Rampur Bushari which first was introduced with the designs and flowers of the plains blanket sheets (K.L. Vaidya; *C.H.H.*; p. 75). Under the Dogra rule (1846-1947 A.D.), in Srinagar, there was only one *pattoo* factory employing 11 persons all old, but the weaving of *pattoo* and *loia* (coarse woollen blanket) was a well-known industry of Kashmir and was largely used to practice as a subsidiary occupation in the village. The Srinagar factory which had been newly started, used to turn out home-spuns and tweeds of improved qualities and patterns. Another fabric which had been growing in popularity owing to its cheapness was 'Raffle'. It was woven from German and local wool and was fast replacing the plain and double *pattoo*. The aggregate value of *loia* and *pattoos*, etc., exported annually from Kashmir was estimated at about 3 lacs of rupees. (Census Report of India; 1921, Vol. XXII, 1923; p. 181).

294. B.N. Goswamy; *I.C.*; p. 8.

295. *Tambi*: It is parallel kind of *pyjama* locally called as tambi as also in the Dogri language.

296. *Khuli-Mohari-bala-pyjama*: It has no pleats or tapering. It is known as *rebb-dar*-kind of *pyjama*.

297. Dr. Moti Chandra; *C.T.C.C.A.M.I.*; p. 81.

298. Charles Fabres; *I.D.*; p. 72. It was also popular and worn by Akbar.

299. *T.J.*; Vol. II; p. 148.

300. B.N. Goswamy; *I.C.*; p. 9.

301. W.G. Acher; *P.S.*; p. 53.

302. O.C. Handa; *T.C.O.W.H.*; p. 183.

303. P.N.K. Bamzai; Social, *Economic History of Kashmir* (1846-1925); Delhi; p. 342. Hereafter referred as *S.E.H.K.*

304. Plate XIII; D.A.G.J.; Acc. No. 118; Portrait of Khwaja Khizer; 19th century A.D. Jammu.

305. Plate XVIII; D.A.G.J.; Acc. No. 235/282; Portrait of Raga Khokhar; 19th century A.D. Jammu.

306. Plate I; Portrait of Raja Kripal Pal; Basohli; circa 1690-93 A.D. (Pb. Mm. Patiala).

307. Plate II; Picture of Raja Mecini Pal, Basohli; circa (1725-30 A.D.); D.A.G.J.; Jammu.

308. Plate XI; D.A.G.J.; Acc.No. 263/310; Pportrait of Raja Kishan Singh; 19th century A.D. Jammu.

309. *Ibid.*, D.A.G.J; Acc. No. 243/289; Portrait of Raja Jai Singh; 19th century A.D. Jammu.

310. Plate XIII; D.A.G.J.; Acc. No. 240/287; Portrait of Raja Jagat Singh. Artist Aziz; 18th century A.D. Jammu.

311. *Ibid.*, D.A.G.J.; Acc. No. 13/60; Portrait of Maharaja Gulab Singh; 19th century A.D. Jammu.

312. Plate XXVIII; Portrait of Maharaja Gulab Singh; Wall-Painting; Miran Sahib Temple.

313. Plate XI; D.A.G.J.; Acc. No. 314; Portrait of *Panchvakta*; Artist Aziz; 19th century A.D. Jammu.

314. Plate XIV; D.A.G.J.; Acc. No. 21; Portrait of Maharaja Partap Singh, 19th century A.D. Jammu.

315. Om Goswami; *D.L.G.*; Part 15; p. 74.

316. In Kashmir, the old type of Brahmin *pagrie* continued with a tight-*pyjama* of Dogra style during the Dogra rule (1846-1947). (*P.N.K.* Bamzai; *S.E.H.K.*; p. 342). In Ladakh, men coat is tied round the waist with a broad shash, known as *kira*. For legs, the people wear a tight woollen trousers, the *suthan*. (O.C. Hands; *T.C.O.W.H.*; p. 222). A Gujjar male of the Western Himalayan region, normally, for legs, a *teehmad* of checked and dark coloured cotton sheet, wrapped round the waist, is a common wear. But sometimes *tamba* or *salwar* a pair of loose *pyjama* (*Ibid.*, p. 261), made of cotton which usually reaches upto the knees only was worn. While the Gaddis, normally, prefer to remain bare-legged. But when required, the wear *pattoo-pyjama* a woollen trouser in the severe cold or ordinarily, a cotton one *Gaddis pyjama* is loose upto knees and tight below, but without puckers (*Ibid.*, p. 271). In

Kanet, between the area of Satluj and Jamuna, ordinarily a tight coarse cotton *pyjama* was worn. Stripped cotton cloth was also used for *pyjamas* (O.C. Handa; *T.C.O.W.H.*; p. 190).

317. Dr. Moti Chandra; *C.T.C.C.A.M.I.*; p. 4.

318. *Ibid.*, p. 18.

319. *Ibid.*, p. 76.

320. *Amarakosa*; 11,6,117. Quoted from Dr. Moti Chandra *C.T.C.C.A.M.I.*; p. 59.

321. Charles Fabres; *I.D.* See pages 62, 66.

322. Dr. Moti Chandra; *C.T.C.C.A.M.I.*; Chapter 5, Fig. 36.

323. Plate XXVIII; Portrait of Lord Krishna Fluting (playing) under a tree; Wall-Painting of Miran Sahib Temple.

324. Plate XXV; Portrait of Sadhus, instructing to Gulab Singh and his troops pertaining the war; Wall-Painting of Sui-Simbli Temple.

325. Plate XXVIII; Portrait of Krishna, Radha and a Gopa's listening the voice of flute; Wall-Painting of Miran Sahib Temple.

326. Plate XXV; D.A.G.J.; Door panel; Portrait of Representative of Lord Shiva.

327. Om Goswami; *D.L.G.*; Part 16; p. 55.

328. In Kanet, the people living between the area of Satluj and Jamuna including the Dun valley (Paonta area) used *dhoti*. *Dhoti* was ordinarily made of cheap unbleached cotton. (O.C. Handa; *T.C.O.W.H.*; p. 190). According to A.K. Bhattacharya, a piece of cloth five yards long in varied width from 106 cms. (42") to 122 cms. (48"), worn in different modes, was marked by a simplicity in texture and colour. Worn with pleats and tucked into the waist was also used by the Hindus in Southern parts of the Punjab. In southern part of the India wear was cloth wrapped around the body at the waist level with a knot in front, as in the former case and at the sides as in the latter (A.K. Bhattacharya; *P.I.C.* Vol. I, p. 110).

329. Dr. Moti Chandra; *C.T.C.CA.M.I.*; p. 39.

330. *A.N.*; Vol. II; p. 271.

331. Plate XX; D.A.G.J.; Acc. No. 247/294. Rai Raodeh Dhamerwal on Camel back; 19th century A.D. Jammu.

332. Plate XVII, D.A.G.J.; Portrait of Maharaja Partap Singh as a Prince; 19th century A.D. Jammu.

333. In the adjoining area of Jammu i.e., Punjab the wardrobe of men in the ruler areas comprised the *pyjama* or a loin-cloth, *tehmat* or *majhla* as the lower-garment and the shirt as upper garment (B.S. Saini; *S.E.H.P.*; p. 120). It is said that *tehmat* or *majhla* usually worn by Muslims, was a sheet of cotton cloth of three yard long and one yard and half wide and was wrapped round the loin's reaching the ankles. In many cases, especially among those who had any connection with official life. This gave place to the *pyjama's* which was fairly loose upto the knee, but fitted rather tightly below up to the ankles and rested in large number of horizontal folds. (*Ibid.*, p. 120).

334. Plate XXI; D.A.G.J.; Acc. No. 176/223; Portrait of Daksh Yajan (Birbha-ddra-Usinatting) in Hawan-Kund; 19th century A.D. Jammu. Same kind of an antelope black spotted skin has also been worn by Kali. See Plate XIX; Fig. 2; D.A.G.J.; Acc. No. 96/143; Portrait of Kali and Shiva; 19th century A.D. Jammu.

335. Dr. Moti Chandra; *C.T.C.C.A.M.I.*; p. 37.

336. *Ibid.*

337. *Ibid.*, p. 71

338. *Ibid.*, Chapter V, Fig. 32.

339. Fredric Drew; *N.B.I.*; p. 76. Also quoted by S.D.S. Charak; *H.C.H.S.*; Vol. IV; p. 57.

340. O.C. Handa; *T.C.O.W.H.*; p. 183.

341. W.B. Cunningham and A.H. Bingley, revised by S.D.S. Charak *I.H.D.C.*; p. 159.

342. Plate XVI; D.A.G.J.; Acc. No. 532, Portrait of Rama's Panchayat; 19th century A.D. Jammu.

343. Plate XXVI; Portrait of a Sadhu, Who has been shown standing on one leg; Wall-Painting of Sui-Simble Temple.

344. *Ibid.*, Portrait of soldiers, Wall-Painting of Sui-Simbli Temple.

345. Plate IX; Portrait of Repentance of Krishna; Illustration to the *Gita Govinda*; Basohli; 1730 A.D. Pb. Mm. Patiala. *Note*: The comparative study of Tira-Sujanpur, Early 18th century, Portrait mountain Govardhana, Illustration to *Bhagavata Purana* reveals that wearing of different prints of short breech i.e., vertical lining design of different colours was worn by Gopas and Lord Krishna himself. It shows that this fashion was not limited upto Jammu but it was also prevent in other parts of the Indian territories. See Plate V, Figs. 2 and 4.

346. Plate XIV; D.A.G.J.; Acc. No. 21; Paintings of Maharaja Partap Singh, Amar Singh; Ram Singh. Early 20th century A.D. Jammu.

347. Plate XXXV; Portrait of Raja Suchet Singh as a soldier; Wall-Painting of Ramnagar Palace.

348. In the Jammu region, under the Dogra rule (1846-1947 A.D.), a special variety of shoes was made in the Tehsil and found favour with this late Highness whose sad demise led to the cessation of demand and decline industry (Census Report; 1931; Vol. XVIV; Part 1, 1933; p. 226).

349. Hutchison, J. and Vogel, J.P. ; *H.P.H.S.*; p. 601.

350. *Jora:* In English, it means pair of shoes and designated in the shape of boat with a horn back on the toe was manufactured by locals.

351. *Paniyanas:* It has slipper formation having long turned toe and sometimes embroidered.

352. *Nukayanas:* It was the general term of the shoes in the local language of the Dogras.

353. *G.S.*; p. 16.

354. *Ibid.*, p. 71.

355. Charles Fabres; *I.D.*; p. 36.

356. *Y.C.*; p. 151.

357. Dr. Moti Chandra; *C.T.C.C.A.M.I.*; p. 128.

358. Charles Fabres; *I.D.*; p. 70.

359. *Ibid.*, p. 72.

360. *Ibid.*, p. 78.

361. *Ibid.*, p. 84.

362. William Irvine; *L.M.*; Vol. I; p. 254.

363. S.D.S. Charak; *H.C.H.S.*; Vol. IV; p. 14.

364. F.M. Hassnain; A Cultural History of Kashmir and Kishtwar; Delhi; 1992, p. 98. Hereafter explained as *C.H.K.K.*

365. *Ibid.*, p. 99

366. Mohd Isaq Khan; *H.S.*; p. 89.

367. R.C. Kak; *A.B.R.*; p. 19.

368. Plate XXXXIX; D.A.G.J.; Acc. No. 445; Portrait of Gulab Singh in a war Procession; 19th century A.D. Jammu.

369. *Ibid.*

370. Plate XXXXIX; D.A.G.J.; Acc. No. 21; Portrait of Maharaja Partap Singh 19th century A..D. Jammu.

371. *Ibid.*, D.A.G.J.; Acc. No. 166/213; Portrait of a Dogra *Nayaka*, 19th century A.D. Jammu.

372. *Ibid.*, D.A.G.J.; Acc. No. 243/289; Portrait of Jai Singh, 19th century A.D. Jammu.

373. *Ibid.*, D.A.G.J.; Acc. Nos. 69/136, 82.129,85/132 to 88/135, 92/139, 95/142, 97/144 to 99/146 and 101/148. *Note*: These accession nos. mostly display *Mahabharata* scenes of warfare, and boots mostly worn by the Lord Krishna.

374. *Ibid.*, Portrait of an Ordinary Man; Wall-Painting of Mansar Temple of Radha Krishna.

375. *Ibid.*, Wall-Painting of Mansar Temple, Portrait of an Ordinary man.

376. Shiv Ram Deep; *D.L.G.*; p. 140.

377. *Ibid.*, Wall-Painting of Mansar Temple; Portrait of Dogra soldier.

378. *Ibid.*, Wall-Painting of Sui-Simbli Temple; Portrait of the Army Chief.

379. *Ibid.*, *Ibid.*

380. *Ibid.*, D.A.G.J; Acc. No. 264/311; Portrait of Raja Man Singh; 19th century A.D. Jammu.

Raja Man-Singh : Raja Man Singh of Guler was also in Mughal camp, and in the record of the campaign in the *Badshahnamah*, he is called "the mortal enemy of Jagat Singh". On returning with the allied force, Prithvi Singh was directed to seize and hold, in conjunction with Raja Man Singh; near a hill at the back of Taragarh, the possession or ambushing of it was necessary in order to capture the fort. This having been done, Jagat Singh supplies were cut off and he was compelled to surrender after a three months.

381. *Ibid.*, Wall-Painting of Ramnagar Palace; Portrait of Raja Suchet Singh.

382. It is known to us that ordinary footwear of the Kashmiri were made of leather, wood or straw. The straw sandal is called *trapli* or *pulahru* and every Kashmiri made his own *pulahru* out of the rice straw. In the first quarter of the 20th century the Kashmiri Pandits dislike the use of leather owing to religious prejudices. That is why they wore wooden clogs (*kharavas*) instead of leather shoes. (Mohd. Isaq Khan, *H.S.* p. 89.). While the Muslim of Kashmir used the leather shoes in addition to the wooden clogs. On marriage days, with other finery, they put on shoes of horse or mule skin, which, for such occasions were ornamented with silk-work. (*Ibid.*). But the use of *kharavas* gradually began to be discarded by the literate Pandits and grass shoes have been commonly worn for hundreds of years by the poor coolies or porters of Kashmir, Kishtwar and Bhaderwah, while a sophisticated and ornamental version was worn by the elite classes (*Ibid.*). Similar Kind of opinions have been given by B.S. Saini, that in the foot hill of the Punjab people not only used to wear leather made shoes, but also grass sandals. The shoes were of various shapes. The communist shape was the pothowari which had a sharp pointed toe. The shoes worn by the richer classes with embroidery work was also a feature among on them. The poorer classes contented themselves with plain shoes. In Hindu homes, wooden sandals known as *kharawan* were used by men and women alike (B.S. Saini; *S.E.H.P.*; p. 123). The boots or footwear of the Ladakh were flat, with soles of sheep or goat-skin, which are turned up all round and sewn. The upper part of the flat boot was open in the front, and was allowed to fall over, something in the manner of boots worn in England during Charles II's time. The *lamas* have red boots, and the others mostly have their ornamented with bits of coloured cloth in the front. (Alexander Cunningham; *L.*; p. 301.

383. Charles Fabres; *I.D.*; p. 34.

384. Dr. Moti Chandra; *C.T.C.C.A.M.I.*; p. 21.

385. Charles Fabres; *I.D.*; p. 64

386. *Amarakosa* 11, 6, 117-18; Quoted from Moti Chandra; *C.T.C.C.A.M.I.*; p. 59

387. *A.N.*; Vol. 1; p. 426.

388. O.C. Handa; *T.C.O.W.H.*;P. 184.

389. *Chund* : It is sort of a draw of *dupatta*.

390. Interview conducted with my mother Smt. Amrita Kumari tailor by profession aged; 80 years January 2001.

391. O.C. Handa; *T.C.O.W.H.*; p. 184.

392. Plate XXXVII; Picture of a marriage scene; Wall-Painting Ramnagar Palace.

393. Plate III; Portrait of Love-Lorn lady; Basohli; circa 1690-93 A.D. Bharat Kala Bhavan; Banares. *Note*: In the work of Jamila Brij Bhushan; *The World of Indian Miniature*, it has been mentioned that such type of scarf

or *ordhani* was fashion in Jammu during the period of Raja Sangram Pal and Raja Kirpal Pal of Basohli; (p. 172).

394. Dr. Om Parkash Gupta; D.L.G., Delhi; 1979; p. 23.

395. *Oodhanu*: It was also a kind of *dupatta* which was usually worn at home.

396. Plate XXIV; Portrait of a *Ragini*; Wall-Painting Suchet-Singh; Bedroom Ramnagar Palace.

397. Om Goswami; *D.I.G.*; Part-16; p. 33.

398. In the above folk song, author describes that the people of Chananni; they were uncivilized and not used to pay respect to women. It is 96 km away from Jammu.

399. Plate XXVII; Portrait of Rani Bandrali; Purani Mandi Temple, Jammu.

400. Plate XXXVII; Portrait of a Marig Priya *Nayika*; Shiva Math; Mansar.

401. Om Goswami; *D.L.G.*; Part 15; p. 75.

402. Plate VII; Portrait of love in Union, *Rasamanjari*; Basohli; Early 18th century A.D. National Museum, Delhi.

403. *Ibid*.

404. *Ibid*

405. Plate VI; Portrait Waiting for the Lover; Illustration to the *Rasamajari* Basohli; Early 18th century; Pb. Mm. Patiala.

406. Plate I; Portrait of Raja Kirpal Pal Basohli, 1690-93 A.D.; Pb. Mm. Patiala.

407. *Ibid*.

408. Plate VII; Portrait 'The Dilemma of the Heroine'; Illustration to the *Rasamanjari* Basohli; 1695 A.D.; D.A.G. Jammu.

409. Plate XXIII; D.A.G.J.; Acc. No. 22/53; Portrait of *Ragini Devagiri* (Hindol); 19th century A.D. Jammu.

410. *Ibid*., D.A.G.J; Acc. No. 154; Portrait of Pater Lakhni *Nayika*; 19th century A.D. Jammu.

411. Shiv Ram Deep: *D.L.G.* Jammu; Part-17 1990' pp. 140-41.

412. Plate XXIII; D.A.G.J.; Acc. No. 32/79; Portrait of a *Ragini* Dowhri of Hindole; 18th century A.D. Jammu.

413. Plate XXVII; Portrait of Radha and Krishna; Wall-Painting of Radha-Krishna Temple; Miran Sahib.

414. In the Hill States of Punjab and plains between the period of 17th and 19th centuries A.D., a basic element of clothing i.e, *ordani* or *orhani* was a longish scarf made usually of fine silk or cotton, plain or decorative, and was used as a veil to cover the head from the back leaving the face visible as little as possible in certain cases, e.g., a newly wedded bride in her husband's house used it both for a sign of modestly and of bashfulness. It, however, was started as soon as a girl attained puberty. In a slightly variant use of the *ordhni*, it was flung over the shoulders, with the mid-portion resting on, end covering the bosom (A.K. Bhattacharya; *P.I.C.*; p. 110). For it, there

were various named as *chuni, chuneriya, dupatta* or *ordhani* was the only head-gear of the women. Though in the hills, they covered their heads with handkerchiefs and in certain tracts they wore caps (B.S. Saini; *S.E.H.P.*; p. 122). While the head-geat of a Gaddan in the Himalayan region, was a *chadaru*. It was generally decorated with interesting appliqué workdone along the edges and in the main-field with *zari* or *gota* made of silver or gold thread (O.C. Handa; *T.C.O.W.H.*; p. 273). Besides this, a *chadar* thrown loosely over the body and sometimes fastened in the shape of a turban by them (B.S. Saini; *S.E.H.P.*; p. 122). According to A.K. Bhattacharyya the modern version of the *ordani* or *dupattas* is very fine cloth, usually 140 cm long with a deliberate transparence, that hangs over the shoulders with ends flung towards the back and the middle portion gathered up in folds (A.K. Bhattacharya; *P.I.C.*; p. 111).

415. Dr. Moti Chandra; *T.C.C.A.M.I.*; p. 47.

416. *Ibid.*, p. 96.

417. B.N. Goswamy; *I.C.*; p. 252.

418. Plate XXVII; Portrait of Rama, Laxamana and Sita with *Rakasins* Wall-Painting Purani Mandi Temple, Jammu.

419. Plate XXIII; D.A.G.J.; Acc. No. 22/ 53; Portrait of a *Ragini Devagiri* Hindole; 19th century A.D. Jammu.

420. *Ibid.*, D.A.G.J.; Acc. No. 154; Portrait of a *Pater Lekhni Nayika*; 19th century A..D. Jammu.

421. Plate XXXXIV; Female Angel with a Peacock; Wall-Painting of Saiva Matha, Mansar.

422. In the area of Kashmir, most of the Gujjars nomadic women wore a tailored cap called a *lachka* which was stitched and embroidered by the women. It is close-fitting with a flap extending down to the neck at the back, the *lachka* was a distinctive feature of the nomads. Similar caps were worn by children in communities of the same origin in the desert areas of Gujarat and Rajasthan. Same *lackas* were embroidered in cotton thread and imitate the fine criss-cross Sindhi stitch of Gujarat and Pakistan or the chain stitch of Kashmir. During the Dogra rule the usual head-dress of little Muslim girls of Kashmir was skull-cap. After the marriage, however, she would have as her head-gear a thickish turban like red cap (*qasaba*), studded with innumerable pins and over it a spare of country cloth (*pooch*) to act, in the case of necessity, as a veil which also usually covered the whole back. (Mohd. Isaq Khan *H.S.*; p. 88). Whereas the head-gear of a Pandit women in Kashmir was called as *taranga* (*Ibid.*). Sometimes a white round turban was skilfully set (*Ibid.*). Besides these, they were also used to covered their heads, with apron quite similar to the *dhatto* used in the interiors of Himachal Pradesh. A spherical skull-cap has also been used by the women but their traditional wear have now fallen out of vogue, and jean-culture is the fastion of the day among the youngster (O.C. Handa; *T.C.O.W.H.*; pp. 223-23). Whereas the Kirata women normally go about bare-head, displaying their intricate hair-do, which involves a number of thin plaits interwoven with Yak's hair their

plaits hang down over their backs well below the waist where these are gathered together and tried with turquoise beads strings. But, during the cold weather conditions, the women used to wear a graceful round high-cylindrical cap with flat top, lined with fur. This cap is known as *shame*. The Drokmos wear, on the festive occasions is typical hat made of felt or wool, adorned with silver ornaments and a colourfully arranged banquet of five fresh flowers over it, tied with multi-coloured ribbons, which flutter in the festive air (*Ibid.*, p. 199). The Gujjar women of the Western Himalayan region wear traditional head-gear, called *joji*—a type of the skull-cap. It is a small saucers like cap with a 'tail' hanging behind down the knees. It is made of black cotton and embellished with needle-work of coloured threads or the appliqué work. They also use head-gear made out of cotton sheet knotted at the one end in a typical manner on the head, with its other end falling on the back as a protective flap against the sun and showers. It may be interesting to find this type of head-gear depicted in the *Pahari* miniatures on the *Krishna-Lila* themes, in which the cow-herds are shown wearing it (*Ibid.*, pp. 261-62). In Ladakh, the dancing women used to cover their head, either with a coloured and quilted skull-cap, or with a circular, flat-topped, stiff woollen hat, something like a short *shako* without a peak. There were ornamented with carnelians and turquoises (Alexander Cunningham; *L.*; p. 302).

423. Dr. Moti Chandra; *C.T.C.C.A.M.I.*; p. 8.

424. B.N. Goswamy; *I.C.*; p. 5.

425. Dr. Moti Chandra; *C.T.C.C.A.M.I.*; pp. 8-9.

426. Charles Fabres; *I.D.*; p. 6.

427. *Ibid.*, p. 64.

428. B.N. Goswamy; *I.C.*; p. 185.

429. Jamila Brij Bhushan; *W.I.M.;* p. 172. *Note* : Author takes the example of the bodice description in the Basohli paintings and narrates that pictures have been painted in the Mughal court. He also motions that Devi Das, painter of the Dogra region had to the training as a painter under the Aurangzeb.

430. A.K. Billwaria; *Jammu Wall-Paintings*; Jammu 1990; p. 30; A scene of Gopies of Radha. Hereafter referred as *J.W.P.*

431. M.S. Radhawa and S.D. Bambari; *Basohli Painting of Rasamanjari*; Delhi; 1981; p. 96. Hereafter cited as *B.P.R.*

432. S.D.S. Charak; *M.R.D.R.F.J.K.*; p. 95.

433. Plate XXVII; Portrait of Radhas and Krishna fluting; Wall-Painting of Miran Sahib; Temple.

434. Plate VIII; Portrait on the way to the Tryst; Illustration to the *Rasamanjari* Basohli; 1690-95 A.D.; D.A.G. Jammu.

435. *Ibid.*, Sports of Krishna in Spring Time; Illustration to the *Gita-Govinda* Basohli; 1730 A.D. Nm. Delhi.

436. *Ibid.*, How Krishna wantoned in the wood; Illustration to the Gita-Govinda; Basohli 1730 A.D. National Mm., Delhi.

437. Plate XIII; D.A.G.J.; Acc. No. 232/279; Portrait of *Prem Lila*; 19th century A.D. Jammu.

438. Keher-Singh Mandukar; *D.L.G*; Jammu; 1971; Part. 8; p. 5. *Note*: Folk song narrates the poor economic condition of the common people.

439. In the South-East of the Punjab Province, married women usually wore a bodice called *angiya* or *choli* which supported the breasts and left the lower portion of the trunk naked. (B.S. Saini; S.E.H.P.; p. 121). It has been known to that *cholis* still is in use in remote Southern and Eastern part of India as a older custom and use. The *choli* in the blouse style, full-sleeved, or cut at the armpit, as in Naga trivial girls dress (PL, 11) also acquired a distinctive form being combined and continued with the *ghaghra* or the *sarong* at the seventeenth and eighteenth centuries A.D.; as is reflected in contemporary *Pahari* miniature Paintings (A.K. Bhattacharyya; *P.I.C.*; pp. 109-10). In the Western Himalayan region, a Gaddan wears *launchari*. It is made up two parts. The upper part is called *choli*, i.e., a blouse. Mostly it is made of the same fabric as of the lower part, but is many cases, the *choli* is made of velvet or *shanil*, with graceful appliqué work around its deep V-shaped neck. The *choli* is stitched to the *palle*, i.e., the skirt, to make one *lanuchari*. It takes well over twelve meters of black-printed cloth to make one *launchari*. of late, mill-made and machine-printed chintz or mixed fabric is also being used for making the garment (O.C. Handa; *T.C.O.W.H.*; p. 274).

440. B.S. Saini; *S.E.H.P.* ; p. 121.

441. O.C. Handa; *T.C.O.W.H.*; p. 184.

442. B.N. Goswamy; *I.C.*; p. 136.

443. Plate XXIII; D.A.G.J.; Acc. No. 22/53; Portrait of *Ragini Devagari*; 19th century A.D. Jammu.

444. *Ibid.*

445. Shiva Ram Deep; *D.L.G.*; Part-17, Jammu, 1990; p. 141.

446. Plate XXIII; D.A.G.J.; Acc. No.154; Portrait of Pater Lakhni *Nayika*; 19th century A.D. Jammu.

447. Plate XXVII; Portrait of Rani Bandrali Miniature-Painting; in Purani Mandi Temple Jammu.

448. *Cotton Textile and Dress Industry*: In Jammu province perior to Gulab Singh rule had a fairly prosperous cotton weaving cottage industry, Samba being the best known centre. It is said that Maharaja Ranjit Singh intended to start a textile hand-printing industry in Amritsar. Slowly and gradually with competition from mill-made cloth the industry it declined during Dogra rule. Further, it was an industry moved from the Jammu to Kashmir Province.

449. Keher Singh Mandukar; D.L.G.; Jammu; Part-8; p. 11.

450. In Kanet, female *kameez* was a shirt with collar and sleeves, touching the knees. Mostly women prefer simple cotton *kameez*, but printed cotton cloth was also used by the young girls (O.C. Handa; *T.C.O.W.H.*; p. 184). Whereas the Kirata female used *hoojuk*. It was a collarless full-sleeved cotton shirt without buttons. They also wore a long frock-like cotton or

cordurory garment, called *tochay*. The garment, was made of the woollen fabric, and known as *rigoya*. It is adorned with colourful and golden piping and border, the women used a waist-band, called *kira* to keep their garments tightly in position,. The *lingchary* was a woollen shawl, that the women put on. Sometimes they put on a fur-lined woollen shawl, known as *lukpa*. The longer the hair on the *lukpa*, which in variably was white, and more valuable. On the occasion of fertility festival, the Brokpas of Ladakh dress themselves in attractive costumes. On the occasion, they wear Yak-skin stoles to cross their shoulders over the woollen *kurta* and the woollen *churidar pyjama*. (O.C. Handa; *T.C.O.W.H.*; p. 223).

451. *Y.C.*; p. 148.

452. *A.N.*; Vol. 1; p. 181.

453. *T.J.*; Vol.1; p. 141.

454. William Irvin; *L.M.*; Vol. II; p. 338.

455. Charles Fabres; *I.D.*; p. 23.

456. *Ibid.*, p. 88.

457. B.N. Goswamy; *I.C.*; p. 156.

458. Charles Fabres; *I.D.;* p. 23.

459. Plate XXXIV; Portrait of *Pahari Ragini*; Wall-Painting of Ramnagar Palace.

460. Plate XXXXVIII; D.A.G.J.; Acc. No. 23/70; Portrait of a Women with Sitar; 18th century A.D. Jammu.

461. *Ibid.*, D.A.G.J.; Acc. No. 22/69; Portrait of a Women in Yellow Dress; Artist; Channu; 18th century A.D. Jammu.

462. Plate XXIX; Portrait of Radha and her friend with Sitar, Wall-Painting of Miran Sahib Temple.

463. Plate III; Portrait of love-lorn lady; Basohli; circa (1690-93 A.D.) Bharat Kala Bhavan, Banaras.

464. *Ibid.*, Portrait of Radha Giving Butter-Milk to Krishna; Illustration to Bihari's Sat Saiya Basohli, circa 1690 A.D. Bharat Kala Bhavan, Banaras.

465. Plate VII; Portrait of Women love in union; Basohli; Early 18th century A.D. Illustration to *Rasamanjari*. National. Mm. Delhi.

466. Plate 1; Portrait of Raja Kirpal Pal; Basohli; circa 1690-93 A.D. Pb. Mm. Patiala.

467. Plate XXXVII; Painting of a Marriage Scene of Raja Suchet Singh; Wall-Painting of Ramnagar Palace.

468. In the Punjab Hill States, the women's costume did not differ much their sister's in the plains, but in winter they usually wore a gown called *doru* which covered their whole body, fitting close round the neck. In Kulu, they used a blanket fastening it skilfully on each shoulder with a large silver or brass pin. They also wore long trousers greater in length than the leg and gathered it in folds round the leg. (B.S. Saini; *S.E.H.P.*; pp. 121/22). Sometimes on ceremonial occasions such as marriage, *mundan* or any festival, *ghaghra* gives way to *pishwaz* a type of coloured gown made of very

fine muslin, waist coat and *dupatta* for breasts and head respectively are other components which go along with *pishwaz*. *Pishwaz* or *pashwaj* was a dress common in both Mandi and Chamba. It was another name for *ghaghra* or *cholu* having a short bodice reaching to the waist and below it the skirt fall away in numerous folds and would measure from 25 to 90 meters in circumference. (K.L. Vaidy; *C.H.H.*; pp. 71-72). Besides the *peswaj*, *reshta* or *rechta* is a long gown touching the anklets with a tight fitting for the breasts and back, it is a loose garment with plaits downwards. Somewhat similar is another gown, known as *pagti* which is worn by womenfolk in Rohru Tehsil of Shimla district (*Ibid.*, p. 74). In the Western Himalayan region, the dress of a Gaddan comprised along frock reaching the ankles and secured with a woollen cord at the waist. (B.S. Saini; *S.E.H.P.*; p. 122). While in Lahul and Spiti the women attire comprised a long woollen robe or coat with sleeves, trousers and thick gaiters (*Ibid.*).

469. Dr. Moti Chandra; *C.T.C.C.M.I.*; p. 19.

470. Charles Fabres; *I.D.*; p. 38.

471. S.S. Charak; *H.H.S.*; Vol. IV; p. 57.

472. Plate XXIII; D.A.G.J.; ACC. NO. 22/53; Portrait of a Ragini Devagiri (Hindole); 19th century A.D. Jammu.

473. In Lahul and Spiti the women's robe is secured at the waist with sash or girdle, from the back of which descend two strings of brass bells attached to the ends of them (B.S. Saini; *S.E.H.P.*; p. 122). The Gaddan of Western Himalayan region, wears *dora*, the length is reduced to about 50 meters, against 60 meters for the Gaddis. Wearing of *dora* for one after the death of her husband, is a taboo for the widowed women. During that period, she must wear a waist-belt made of natural colour *gota-hari* (O.C. Handa; *C.T.O.W.H.*; p. 274).475. 474. B.N. Goswamy; *I.C.*; p. 6.

475. *Giddi*: Inspite of the motioned fact, it was also used to wear against the hot climate of the areas. At that time, there were no modern facilities as today like fan, coolers, etc.

476. Charles Fabres; *I.D.*; p. 34.

477. *Ibid.*, p. 44.

478. *Ibid.*, p. 62

479. M.S. Randhawa and S.D. Bhambri; *B.P.R.*; p. 25.

480. *Ibid.*, p. 82.

481. Plate XXIII; D.A.G.J.; Ac. No. 288/275; Portrait of a Lady near the Spring ; 20th century A.D.; Early; Jammu.

482. Plate VII; Portrait of Waiting for the Lover; Illustration to the *Rasamanjari*; Basohli; Early 18th century A.D.; Pb. Mm. Patiala.

483. Plate VIII; Portraits, On the Way to the Tryst; How Krishna wantoned in the wood; Sports of Krishna in spring time. Illustration to the *Gita Govinda*. Basohli; 1730 A.D. National Mm. New Delhi. Also see Plate II; (Fig. 2).

484. Plate V; Portrait Krishna Milking the Cow; Illustration to the *Bhagawat Purana*; Basohli; circa (1750-55 A.D.); D.A.G. Jammu.

485. Plate VI; Portrait of the Threshold Youth; Illustration to the *Rasamanjari*; Basohli; circa 1695 A.D.; D.A..G. Jammu.

486. In Kashmir, the *saree* was coming into vogue amongst females of the upper class Pandits. In fact, Kashap Bahdhu did a lot to popularize the *saree* (Mohd. Isaq Khan; *H.S.*; p. 88). In Rajasthan, the sari forms the usual lower garment, especially of the more well-to-do households, contacts with other parts of India have drawn the Rajasthani women more towards the *sari* these days (A.K. Bhattacharya; *P.I.C.*; pp. 111-12). While for *sari*, the Gujarati styles was marked by the dominating pleats at front tucked into the petticoat (*Ibid.*, p. 112).

487. Charles Fabres; *I.D.*; p. 14.

488. B.N. Goswamy; *I.C.*; p. 219.

489. *Ibid.*, p. 221.

490. M.S. Randhawa; *B.P.;* p. 30.

491. Mira Seth; *D.W.P.J.K.*; pp. 29, 31 and 37.

492. S.S. Charak; *M.R.D.R.F.T.K.*; p. 95.

493. Plate VIII; (a) How Krishna Wantoned in the Wood; Illustration to the *Gita Govinda*; Basohli 1730 A.D. National Mm. Delhi. (b) Sports of Krishna in Spring Time; Illustration to the *Gita-Govinda*; Basohli; 1730 A.D. National Mm. Delhi. Also see Plate II Fig. 2. Hail; Keshava *Gita Govinda*; Basohli; 1730 A.D. National Mm.; Delhi. Also compares with Plate VIII; Fig. 1. On the way to the Tryst. Illustration to the *Rasamangari*,; Basohli; circa (1690 A.D.) Jammu.

494. Plate XXVII; Portrait of Radha with Krishna; Wall-Painting of Mira Sahib Temple. Radha-Krishna.

495. Om Goswami; *D.L.G.*; 1981 Part-15, p. 76.

496. Plate XXXIV; Portrait of Representative of Shiva with two ladies a bull and Gaurd; Wall-Painting of Ramnagar Palace. Also see Plate XXV; Fig. 3; door panel of D.A.G. Jammu.

497. Plate XXXI; Portrait of Raja Suchet Singh with his Rani. Raja is shown drinking the water to Sadhu; Wall-Painting of Purmandal Temple.

498. Plate III; Krishna Milking the Cow; Illustration to the *Bhagawat Purana*. Basohli circa; 1750-55 A.D.; D.A.G. Jammu.

499. Plate XXVII; Portrait of Ram, Lakshman and Sita in the forest exile; Wall-Painting of Purani Mandi Temple Jammu.

500. Plate VI; Portrait of *Parakiya Vasakasajja Nayika*; Basohli; circa 1760-67 A.D. Illustration *Rasamanjari* D.A.G. Jammu.

501. *Ibid.*

502. Plate VIII; On the Way to the Tryst. Illustration to the *Rasamanjari*; Basohli; circa; (1690-95 A.D.); D.A.G.; Jammu.

503. Plate XII; D.A.G.J.; Acc. NO. 232/279. Portrait of Prem Lila; 19th century A.D. Jammu.

504. *Ibid.*

505. Plate XXIV, D.A.G.J.; Acc. No. 99. Portrait of Radha and Krishna in a love scene; 19th century A.D. Jammu.

506. In the Hill States of the Punjab between the period of 17th to 18th centuries A.D. most of the miniature paintings around the valley of Chamba have a more common wearing style with the adoption of the loose flowing *ghaghra* with a thin quarter-sleeve *choli* type of the upper garment. (A.K. Bhattacharya; *P.I.C.*; p. 110). Whereas the *sari* or *ghaghras* of Rajasthan have distinctive designs, mostly floral, either in embroidery or in prints. The tie-and-dye print of Jaipur and other areas constitutes a special contribution of Rajasthan in cloth printing. The *ghaghra* generally goes with a tight-fitting bodice wherein the upper valley of the breasts is given separate patch with a distinctive colour with sometimes the midriff left bare, especially with working women. Both together appear to be a practical dress for women whose daily life was quite hard. In cut and fashion, the bodice is short-sleeved and open at the back, tied by strings drawn from the corners (*Ibid.*, p. 112). West and South-West of Rajasthan, in Gujarat, the *ghaghra* is in use though mostly confined to the peasant and the working class. The rest of the people wear *sari*, where, in most cases, retains its use as an undergarment in a less pleated variety, as is proved by the fact that even as a petticoat the under wear *ghaghra* is embellished, being reminiscent of the original practice of having the latter as the principal wear (*Ibid.*, p. 112). In the South-East provinces of India the attire of a Hindu women comprised a *ghaghra* or *lengha* (*skirt*) of cotton and *kurti* or shirt (B.S. Saini; *S.E.H.P.* ; p. 121).

507. *Nara* : *Nara* wearing was an age old industry of the village around Jammu. Sumail Pur, Kot Balwal, Bishnah and Sarbah villages were particularly known for the job. Jammu excels in the art of *nara* weaving. Most of the tourists and visiting of progressively increasing demand of this article the dealer supply yarn to ladies in villages and get *naras* woven to order. Besides white *naras* the trouser typing tapes in many colours and designs are now available in the market of Jammu *nara* is prized for its softness (Sukhdev Singh Chib; *The Beautiful India, Jammu and Kashmir*; New Delhi, 1977, p. 84). Hereafter explained as *B.I.J.K.*). The witness of the *nara*, we can see this example in Plate XXXIV Fig. 1; Portrait of *Ragini* Ramnagar Palace.

508. Indu Prabha Pandey; *D.O.A.I.*; p. 87.

509. B.N. Goswamy; *I.C.*; p. 9.

510. Jamila Brij Bushan; *W.M.P.*; p. 172.

511. *Ibid.*, p. 170.

512. Baron Charles and Hugel; *Travels in Kashmir and Punjab*, Jammu. 1972; p. 68. Hereafter referred as *T.J.K.*

513. S.D.S. Charak; *M.R.D.R.F.J.K.*; p. 95.

514. M.S. Randhawa; *B.P.;* p. 30.

515. A.K. Billarwaia; *J.W.P.*; p. 29.

516. *Ibid.*, p. 34.

517. J.N. Ganhar; *J.S.P.* ; p. 7.

518. S.D.S. Charak; *H.C.H.S.*; Vol. IV; p. 58.

519. Plate XXXIV; Wall-Paintings of Ramnagar Palace; portrait of a *Ragini*.

520. Plate VII, Waiting for the lover. Illustration to the *Rasamnjari* Basohli, Early 18th century A.D. Jammu. Pb. Mm. Patiala.

521. *Ibid*; Love in union., *Ibid*.

522. Plate 1; Portrait of Raja Kirpal Pal; Basohli circa 1690-93 A.D. Pb. Mm. Patiala.

523. Plate III; Portrait of a lore-lorn lady; Basohli; circa 1690-93 A.D. Bharat Kala Bhawan Banaras.

524. *Ibid*., Portrait of Radha Giving Butter-Milk to Krishna. Illustration to Bihari's Sat Saiya Basohli; circa 1690 A.D. Bharat Kala Bhawan Banaras.

525. Plate XXVII; Portrait of Rani Bhandrali; Purani Mandi Jammu. *Note*: Possible the *Sanakrit* word *svasthana* mentioned in the *Harshacharita* for *suthana*.

526. Keher Singh Mandukar; *D.L.G.*; Part 7; p. 70.

527. In Kanet areas, old women used to wear tight-*paejama* called *rebdar* or *churidar pyjama*, made of thick cotton cloth of dark colour. (Handa; *T.C.O.W.H.*; p. 191). Whereas on the occasion of fertility festival, the Brokpas of Ladakh dress themselves in attractive costumes. On the occasion, they wore Yak-skin stoles across their shoulders over the *kurta* and the woollen *churidar paejama* (*Ibid*., p. 223). The Western Himalayan Gujjar women, wear *suthan* a type of tight trouser below knees, with numerous puckers between knees and ankles, and very loose above (*Ibid*., 262). A Gaddan of Chamba, under the Punjabi or Muslim influence after the 19th century, some women took to wearing *kurti-suthan* under the *launchari* it was considered a bad influence. A women, thus attired was not taken kindly, and was referred to as "that woman". Now, however, *kurti-suthan*, worn under the *launchari* is an accepted part of the Gaddan's dress (*Ibid*., 274). Under the Dogra rule (1847 to 1947) close contact with the Punjabi Hindu and Muslim women, however, brought about many changes in the mode of dress of the Kashmiri women. Not only *qaraba* and *taranga* disappeared with the advent of *dupatta*, but also *shalwar*, *churidar pyjama* and frock type shirt were preferred because they permitted greater activity. (Mohd. Isaq Khan; *H.S.*; p. 88). In Himachal Pradesh, *ghaghra* stands for petticoat and *suthan* for long trouser. The dress has been popular with women of Mandi town but is now. Only a relic of the past *dupatta* and shawl is thrown on the head and body to make this dress complete. While gay and bright colour was favourite of the married women, the widows must remain satisfied only with white dress (K.L.Vaidya; *C.H.H.*; p. 71).

528. Indu Prabha Pandey; *D.O.A.I.*; p. 89.

529. Dr. Moti Chandra; *C.T.C.C.A.M.I.*; p. 132.

530. A.K. Bhattachyra; *p. I.C.*; p. 109.

531. *T.J.*, Vol.11.; p. 148.

532. William. Irvine, *L.M.*, Vol.1; p. 188.

533. Hugel and Brown Charles; *T.K.P.*; p. 68.

534. Plate XXIII; D.A.G..J.; Acc. No. 22/53; Portrait of *Ragini* Devagiri (Hindole); 19th century A.D. Jammu.

535. *Ibid.*

536. In Kanet areas, *salwar* was a common wearer for legs, usually, it was made of black, grey or any other dark colour which may not look dirty even after longer use (O.C. Handa, *T.C.O.W.H.*; p. 191). In Western Himalayan, Gujjar women are also seen wearing Punjabi *salwar* (*Ibid*, p. 262). In the South-East Provinces of India, the favourite apparel of the Muslim ladies was *salwar* and a loose shirt. This dress was also common among the Hindu and Sikh women. In the districts of Gujarat, Shahpur, Gujranwala and Muzaffargarh women of all communities preferred to wear *tahmat* like men (B.S. Saini; *S.E.H.P.*; p. 121). In Punjab in case of the newly weds or those in the presence of elders in the father-in-laws place the veil is drawn further down coming upto the tip of the nose. The bride's *salwar*, as already noted else where, is also a bit longer and almost covers the feet (A K. Bhattacharya; *P.I.C.*; p. 111). The variation in the *salwar* worn by a [illegible]d the one by a women lies in the shorter length of the former, and the absence of the colour or decoration (*Ibid.*).

537. Dr. Moti Chandra; *C.T.C.C.A.M.I.*; p. 15.

538. *Ibid.*

539. *Ibid.*

540. Indu Prabha Pandey; *D.O.A.I.*; p. 89.

541. Charles Fabres; *I.D.*; p. 42.

542. Dr. Moti Chandra; *C.T.C.C.A.M.I.*; p. 57.

543. *Ibid.*, p. 147.

544. Charles Fabres; *I.D.*; p. 74. See the picture of a maid-servant of Akbar's time.

545. Fredric Drew; *N.B.I.*, p. 63.

546. Plate XXXXX; D.A.G.J.; Acc. No. 251/298; Portrait of Ragini Basant; 19th century Jammu. (See Chapter 1).

547. *Ibid.*, D.A.G.J.; Acc. No. 214/261; Portrait of a Dogri *Nayika*; 19th century A.D. Jammu.

548. *Ibid.*, Wall-Painting of Mansar Temple; Portrait of a Dogri *Nayika* (Radha).

549. *Ibid.*, Wall-Painting of Ramnagar Palace, Portrait of a Dogri *Nayika*.

550. Plate III; Portrait of a love-lorn lady; Basohli; circa (1690-93 A.D.) Bharat Kala Bhawan Banaras.

551. Keher Singh Mandukar; *D.L.G.*; Part 8, 1971, p. 39.

552. A Ladakhi women, on her feet, she wore boots made of thick cloth and with turn up toes. The boot came half way up to her legs. The footwears of the Gilgit and Baltistan people were called as *taoolis* or *thawits* or *pabboos* made of goat or ibex skin. In Dards to the North-West of Kashmir, was an Aryan tribe known as Brokpa. Tibetans, in their feet, they have scraps of

leather put under, over and around the foot and keep in their place by straps of the same material around them (E.T. Atkinson; *G.H.*; p. 32). They had to protect themselves against cold and heat. While in Kirghiz (now Kirghizistan) the footwear of the people were of embroidered leather with high heels (*Ibid.*, 37). The area known as Kara-Karchins to the north of the Altyn-Tagh, their feet were uncovered in Summer and in winter shoes of untended hide were worn (*Ibid.*). In Himachal Pradesh term '*pullas*' are footwear's used both for indoor and outdoor purposes. When indoors they used slippers and when outdoors, they use shoes. *Pullas* are current in all the upper region of the Himachal Pradesh such as Saraj are of Kulu, Mandi and Rampur Bushahr. The bottom i.e., the sole of the *pulla* was made of *bhang* fiber and was quite tough for wear and tear. The upper part, when made of the same fiber, is rough but it made a stout wear. The upper part is also made of goat-hair called *sheli*. Marina or wool fiber in multi-colours was also used in place of goat-hair and footwear, slippers every where inside the house except the latrines and bathrooms as these are saved from getting wet and spoiled (K.L. Vaiidya; C.H.H., p. 73). According to the Census Report of 1961 in Himachal Pradesh, there was a village known as Devi-Kothi as *chamar* stayed here for a small duration. He prepared *tille-dar-paini*, *gole jutti* and *chappals*. The upper part of a *tille-dar-paini* is embroidered. This footwear was used variablly by the bride, *gole jutti* was an ordinary footwear. A chappal has got strips in the lower portion, so that it may not slip on snow while walking. ((Census Report of India Vol. XX Part VI-Note Himachal Pardesh; 1961, p. 60). In Bushahr State, the usual kind of shoes had the uppers made of clothes and the shoes of leather (B.S. Saini, S.E.H.P.; p. 123). On the Tibetan border only long cloth-boots were worn (*Ibid*). In Kulu, Saraj, Lahul and Pangi soles made of hemp and nettle fiber were commonly used (*Ibid.*). However, as the means of communications improved leather shoes were found their way into the remotest parts of the hills in ever-increasing numbers (*Ibid.*).

Plate I.

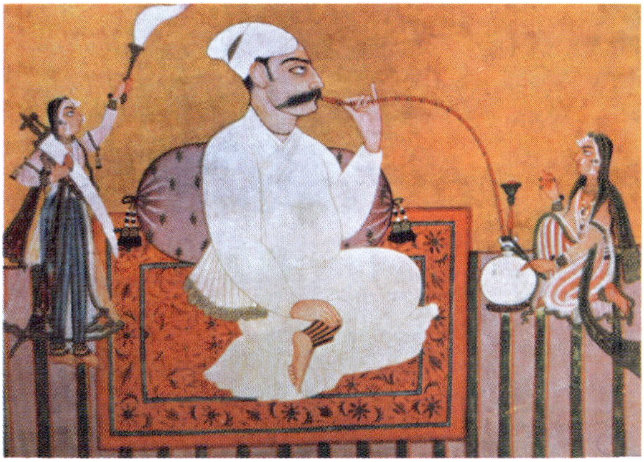

Fig.1.Portrait of Raja Kirpal-Pal; Basohli; Circa (1690-93 A.D.) Punjab Museum Patiala.

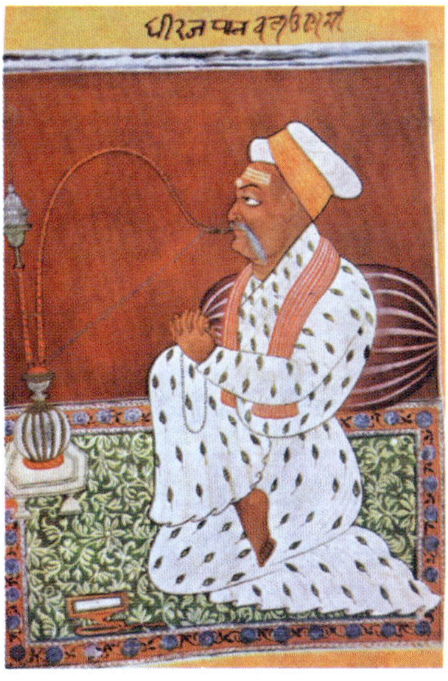

Fig.2.Portrait of Raja Dhiraj-Pal; Basohli; Circa (1720-25 A.D.); Punjab Museum Patiala

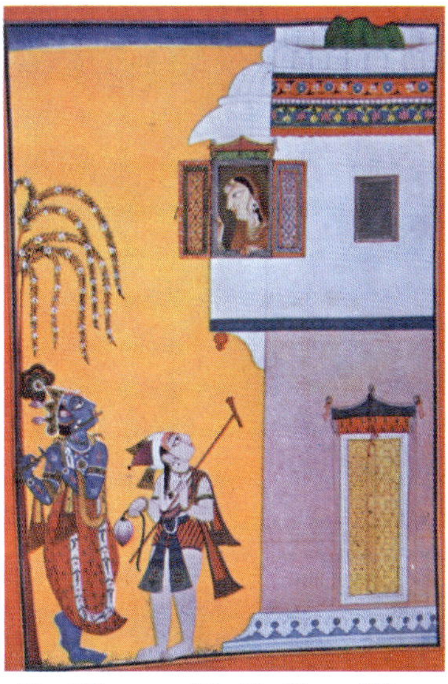

Fig.3.Rapture fills My Heart When I hear 'The Sound of the Flute' Illustration to the Bhagawata Purana; Tira-Sujanpur; Circa (1730-50 A.D.).

Plate II

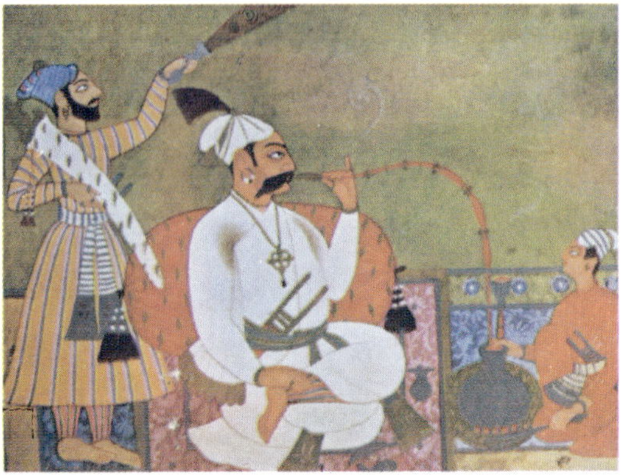

Fig.1.Portrait of Raja Medini-Pal, Basohli; Circa (1725-35 A.D.) D.A.G. Jammu.

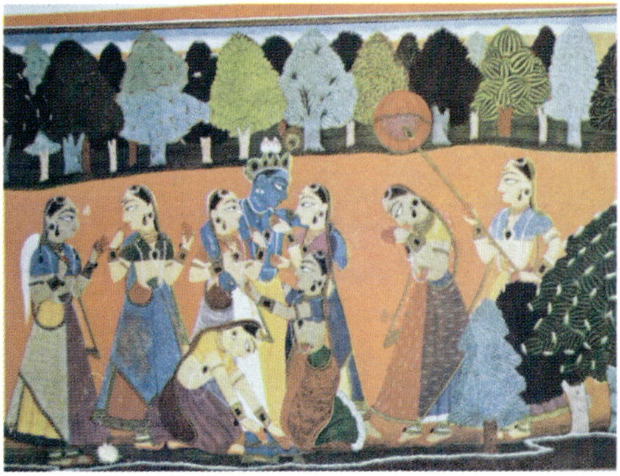

Fig.2.'Hail Keshava, Hail' Rulers of wave and wood; Illustration to the Gita-Govinda; Basohli 1730 A.D. National Museum Delhi.

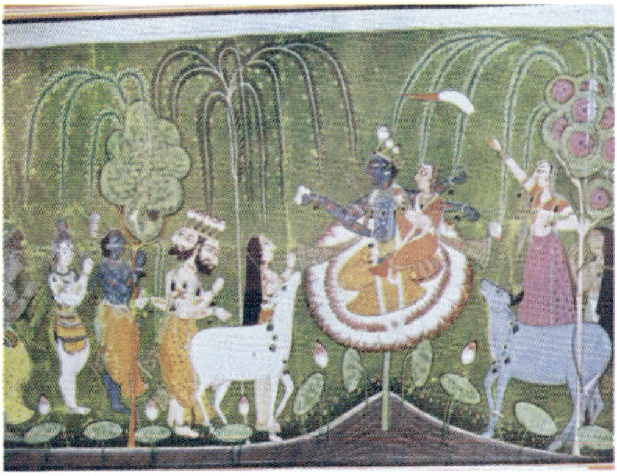

Fig.3.The Adoration of Vishnu; Illustration to the Bhagawata Purana; Basohli; Early 18th century: Punjab Museum Patiala.

Plate III

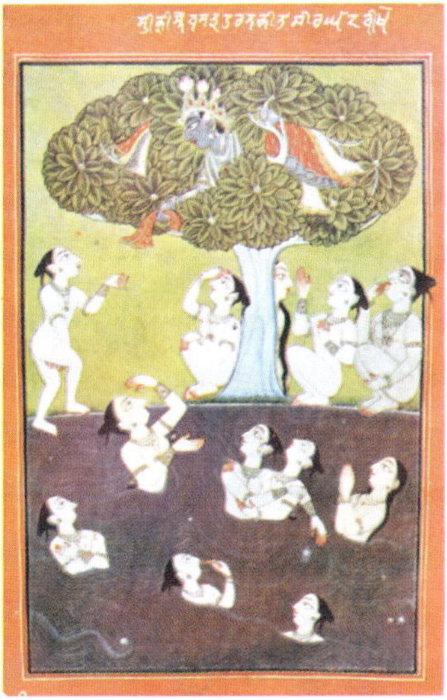

Fig.1.Krishna Stealing the Cloth of Gopies; Basohli.

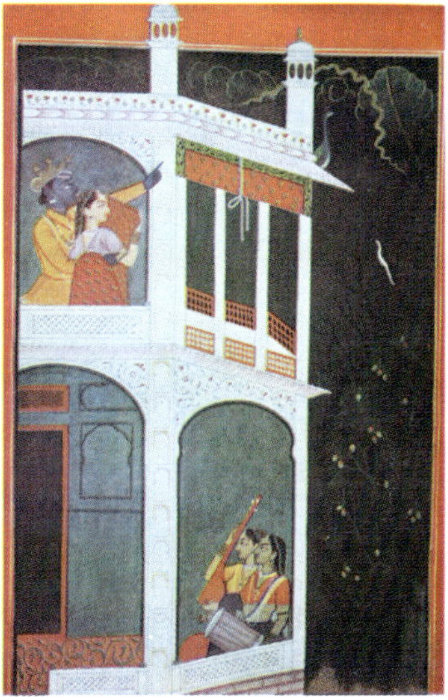

Fig.2.'Sawan is the month of lovers' Illustration to the Baramasa; Early 18th century; A.D.D.A.G. Jammu.

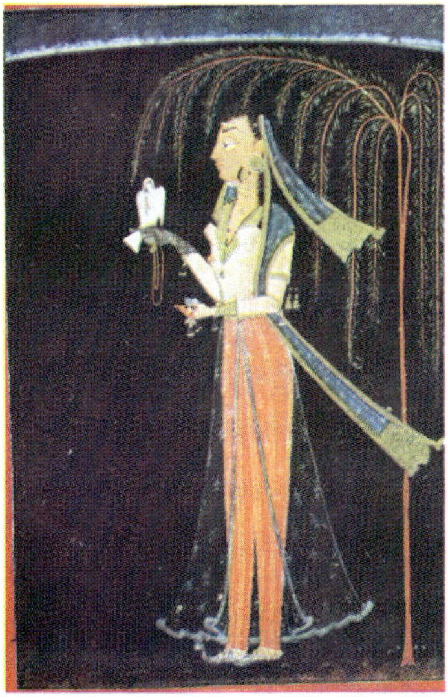

Fig.3.The love lorn Lady; Basohli; 1690-93 A.D. Bharat Kala Bhawan Banaras.

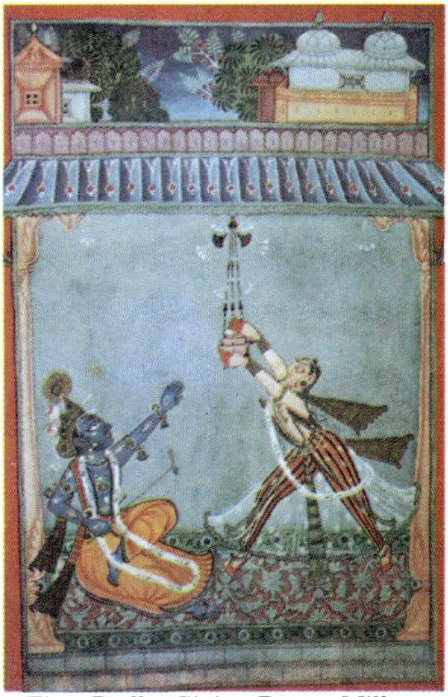

Fig.4.Radha Giving Butter-Milk to Krishna; Illustration to Bihari's Sat Saiya, Basohli Circa 1690 A.D. Bharat Kala Bhawan Banaras.

Plate IV

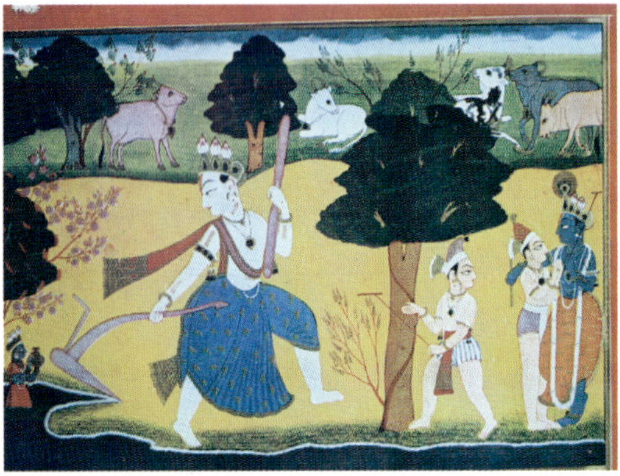

Fig.1.The Diversion of the Jamuna; Illustration to the Bhagawata Purana; Basohli; Circa 1730 A.D. Punjab Museum Patiala.

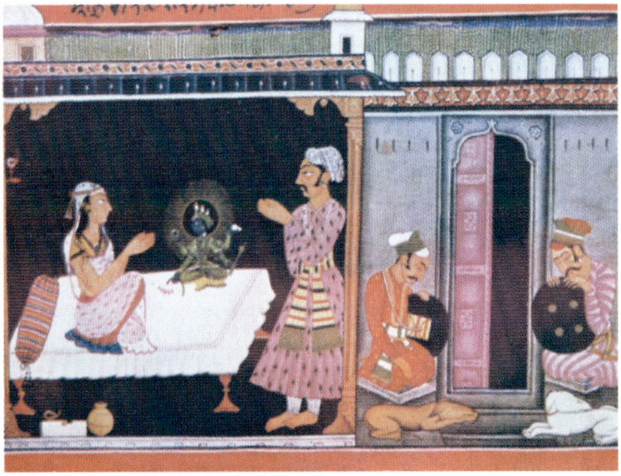

Fig.2.The Birth of Lord Krishan; Illustration to the Bhagawat Purana; Mankot; Early 18th Century, Punjab Museum Patiala

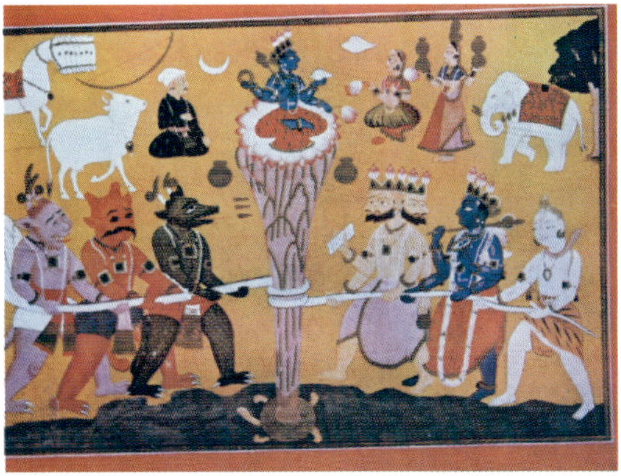

Fig.3.The Churning of theocean of Milk; Basohli; Circa; 1730 A.D. Bhagawata-Purana. Punjab Museum Patiala.

Plate V

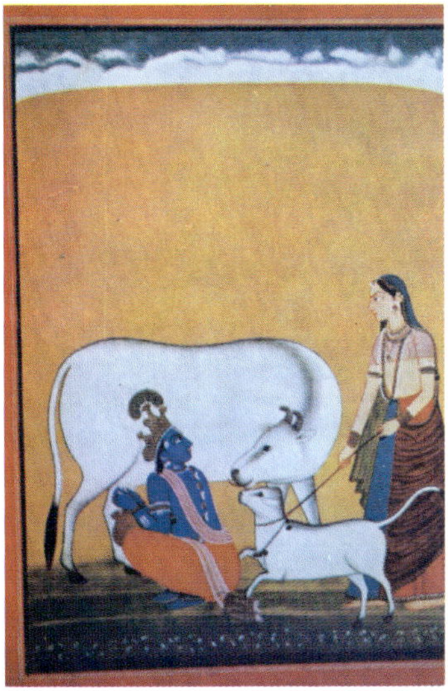

Fig.1.Krishna Milking the Cow; Illustration to the Bhagawat Purana; Basohli Circa 1750-55 A.D.; D.A.G. Jammu.

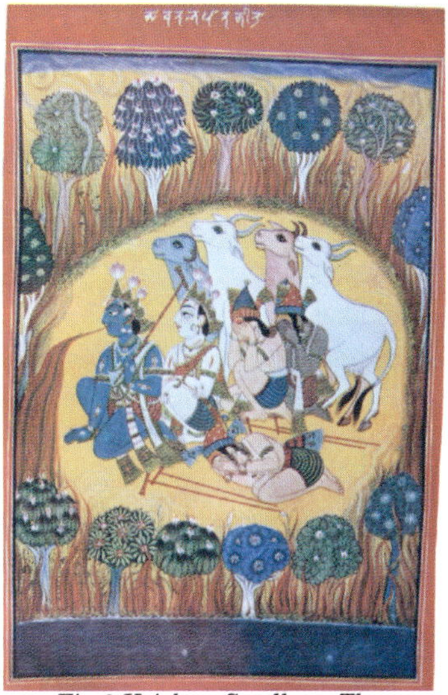

Fig.2.Krishna Swallows The forest Fire; Illustration to the Bhagawat-Purana; Tira-Sujanpur, Early 18th Century. Century A.D.D.A.G. Jammu

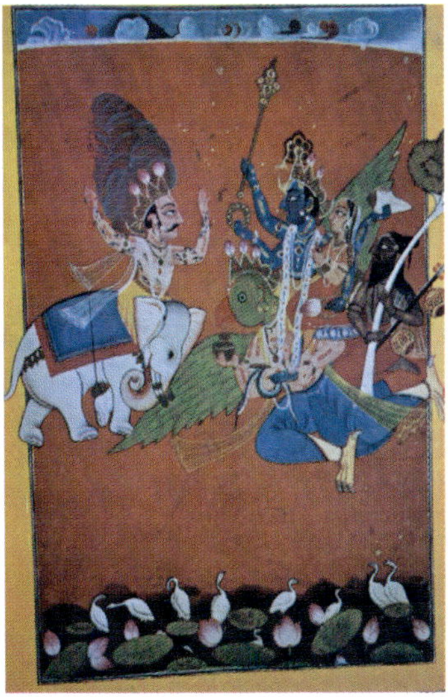

Fig.3.Krishan Bringing The Parijata From Indra's Heaven. Illustration to the Bhagawata-Purana;

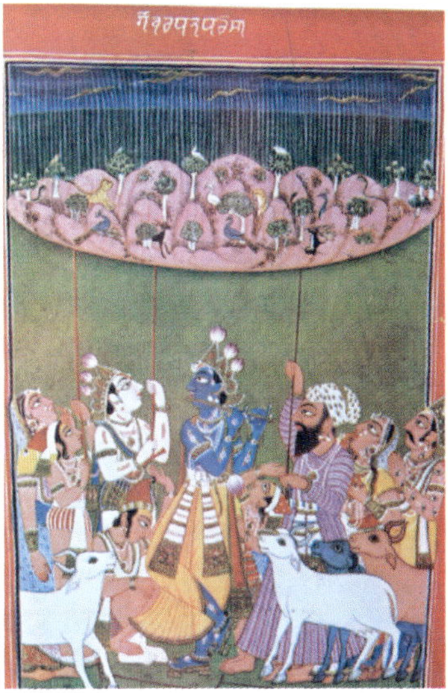

Fig.4.Krishna Lifting the Mountain Govardhan; Illustration to the Bhagawata-Purana; Tira-Sujanpur; Early 18th Century A.D.D.A.G. Jammu.

Plate VI

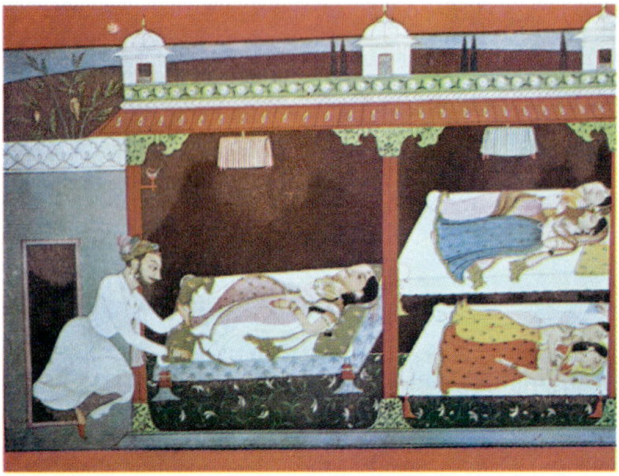

Fig.1.Payarakiya Vasakasjja Nayika; Basohli; Circa 1760-70 A.D. Rasamanjari. D.A.G. Jammu.

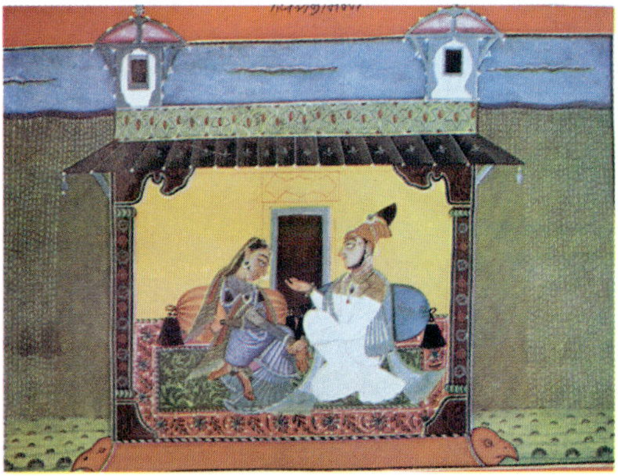

Fig.2.'Why this Hesitation, My Love? ' Illustration to the Rasamanjari; circa 1690-95 A.D.; D.A.G. Jammu.

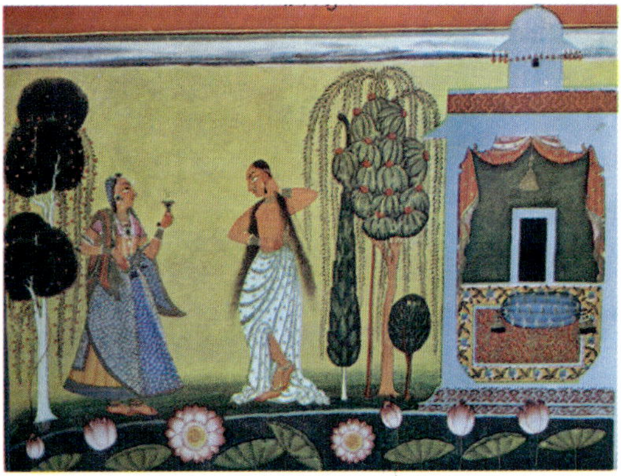

Fig.3.On the Threshold of Youth; Illustration to the Rasamanjari Basohli; Circa 1695 A.D., D.A.G. Jammu.

Plate VII

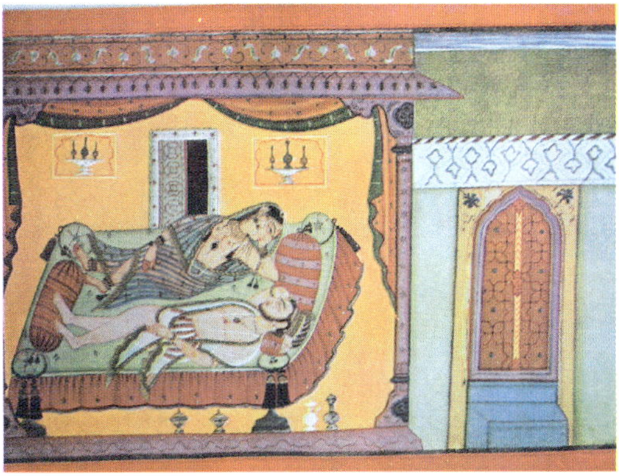

Fig.1.The Dilemma of The Heroine; Illustration to the Rasamanjari; Basohli, Circa 1695 A.D., D.A.G. Jammu.

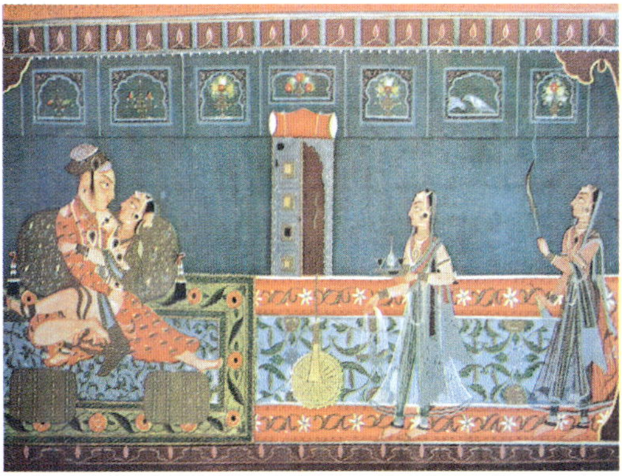

Fig.2.Love in Union; Basohli; Early 18th Century; Rasamanjari. National Museum Delhi.

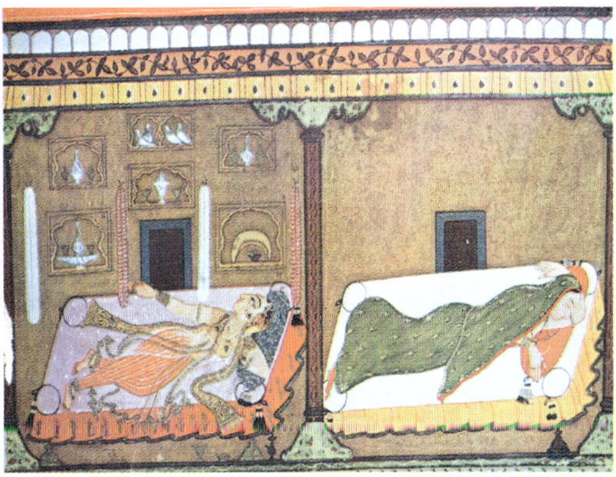

Fig.3.Waiting for the Lover. Illustration to the Rasamanjari; Basohli; Early 18th Century; Circa 1690-95 A.D.; D.A.G. Jammu.

Plate VIII

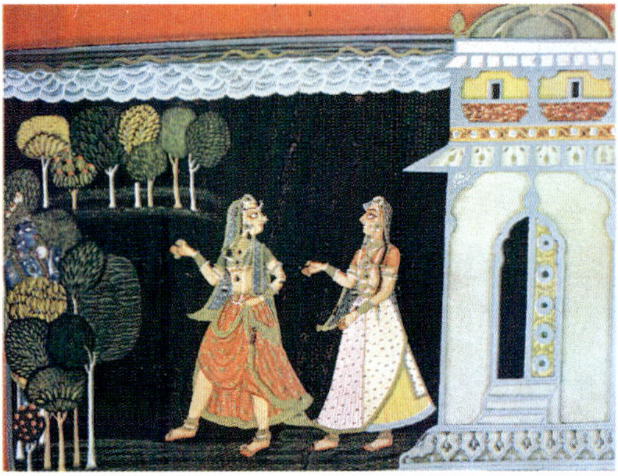

Fig.1.On the Way to the Tryst. Illustration to the Rasamanjari, Basohli; Circa 1690-95 A.D., D.A.G. Jammu.

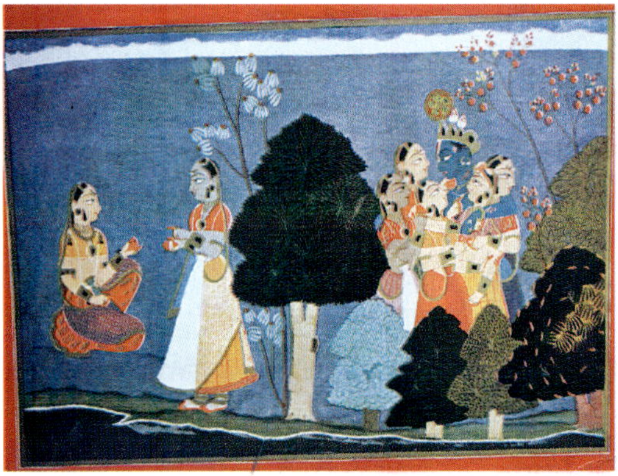

Fig. 2.How Krishna Wanton in the Wood. Illustration to the Gita Govinda; Basohli; 1730 A.D. National Museum Delhil.

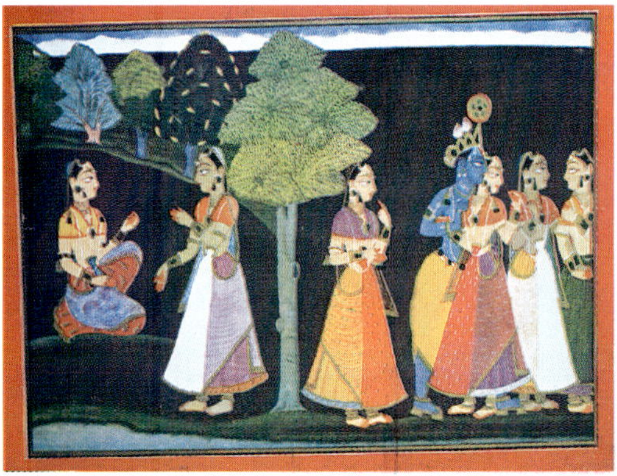

Fig. 3.Sports of Krishna in Spring time. Illustration to the Gita Govinda; Basohli; 1730 A.D. National Museum Delhi.

Plate IX

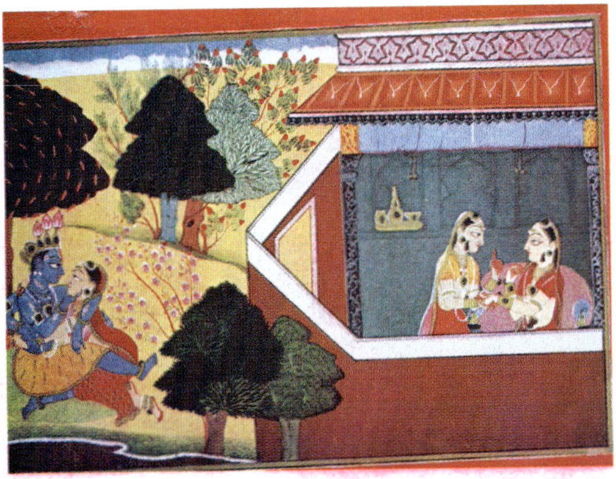

Fig.1.The Ecstary of Love. Illustration to the Gita Govinda; Basohli; 1730 A.D. Punjab Museum Patiala.

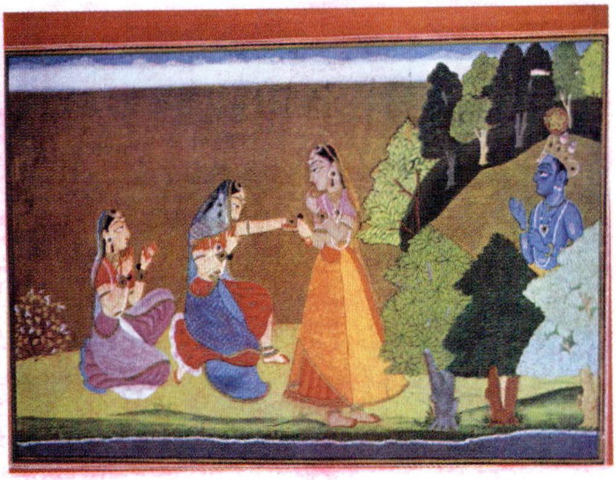

Fig.2.Enter the power of love, O Beautiful; Illustration to the Gita Govinda; Basohli; 1730 A.D. National Museum Delhi.

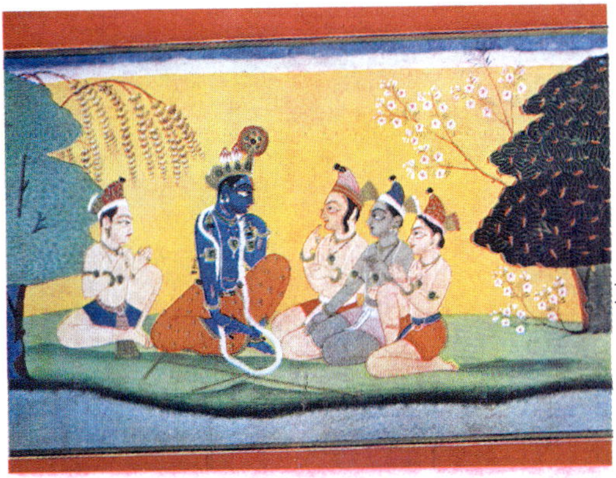

Fig.3. Repentance of Krishna; Illustration to the Gita Govinda; Basohli; 1730 A.D. Punjab Museum Patiala.

Plate X

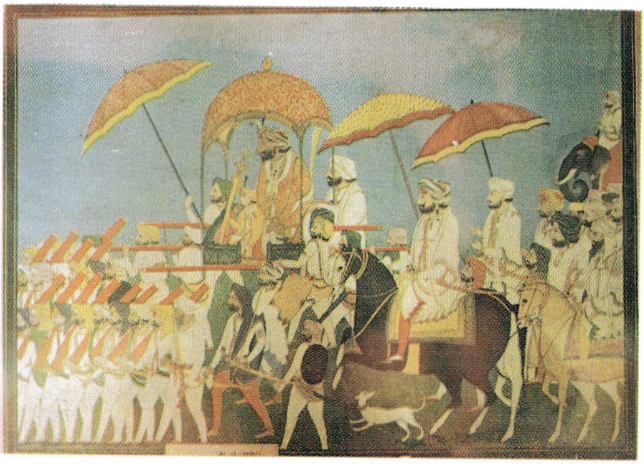

Fig.1.D.A.G. Jammu. Acc. No. 445; Maharaja Gulab Singh in a War Procession; 19th Century A.D. Jammu.

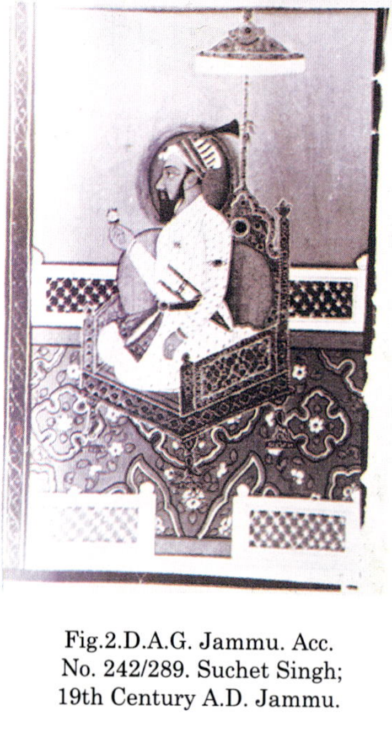

Fig.2.D.A.G. Jammu. Acc. No. 242/289. Suchet Singh; 19th Century A.D. Jammu.

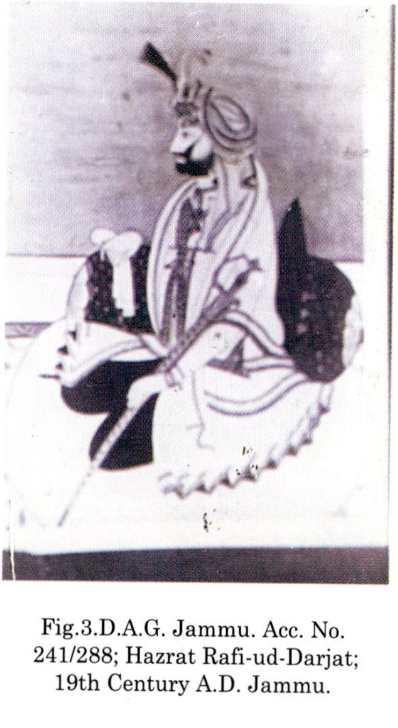

Fig.3.D.A.G. Jammu. Acc. No. 241/288; Hazrat Rafi-ud-Darjat; 19th Century A.D. Jammu.

Plate XI

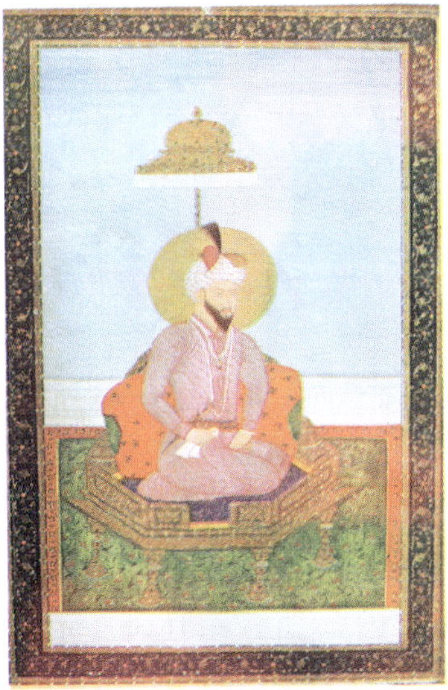

Fig.1.D.A.G. Jammu. Acc. No. 265/312; Babur, 19th century A.D. Jammu.

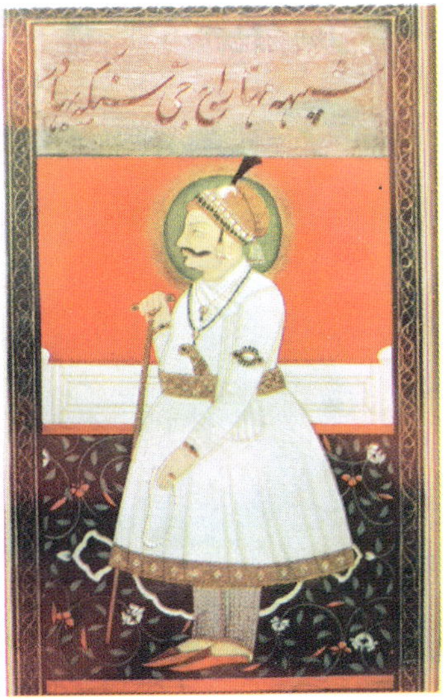

Fig.2.D.A.G. Jammu. Acc. No. 243/290, Raja Jai Singh; 19th Century A.D. Jammu.

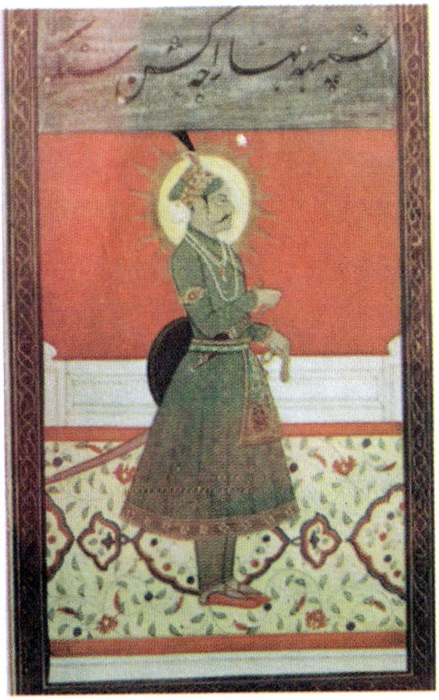

Fig.3.D.A.G. Jammu. Acc. No. 263/310, Kishan Singh; 19th Century A.D. Jammu.

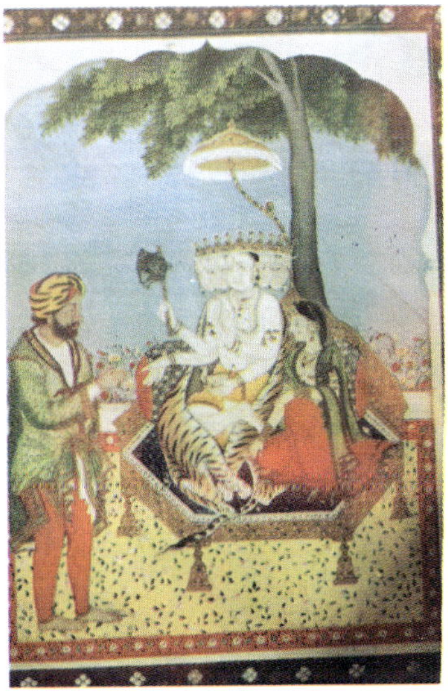

Fig.4.D.A.G. Jammu. Acc. No. 314, Panchvakta; Artist; Aziz. 19th Century A.D. Jammu.

Plate XII

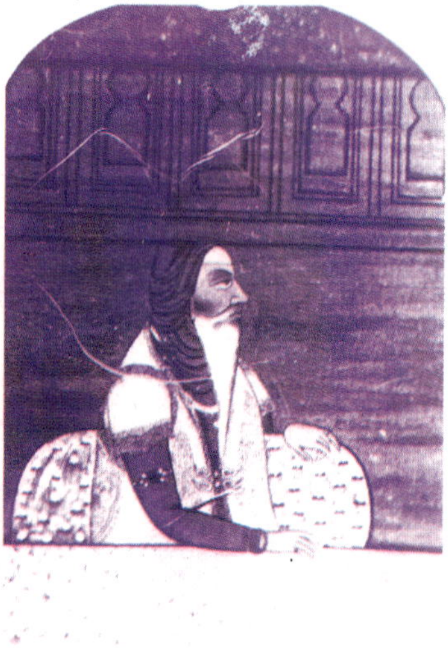

Fig 1.D.A.G. Jammu. Acc. No. 9/56, Ranjit Singh; 19th Century A.D. Jammu.

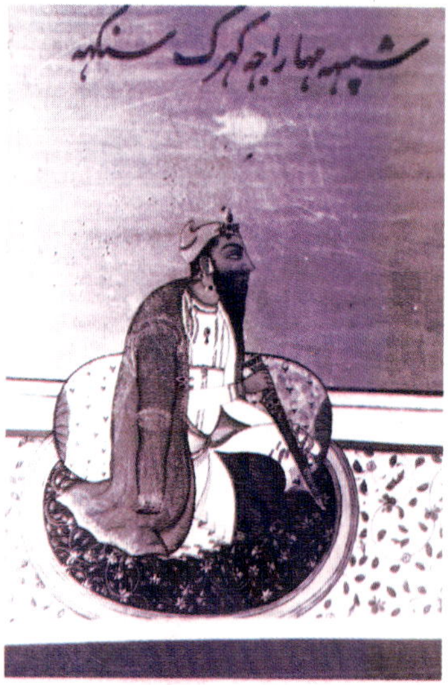

Fig.2 .D.A.G. Jammu. Acc. No. 10/57, Kharaq Singh; 19th Century A.D. Jammu

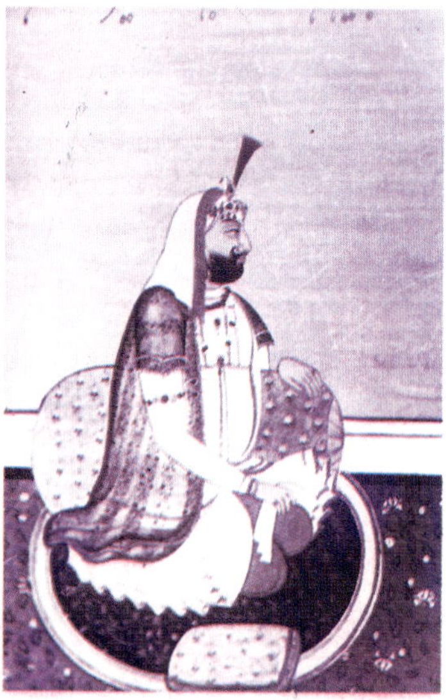

Fig. 3 .D.A.G. Jammu. Acc. No. 11/58, Sher Singh; 19th Century A.D. Jammu.

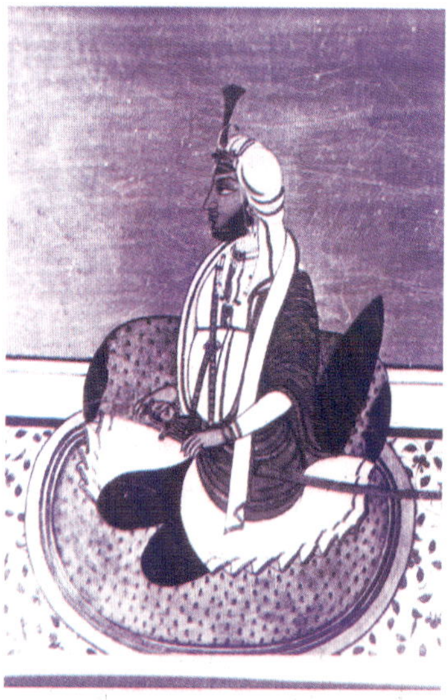

Fig. 4 .D.A.G. Jammu. Acc. No. 12/59, Noo Nihal Singh; 19th Century A.D. Jammu.

Plate XIII

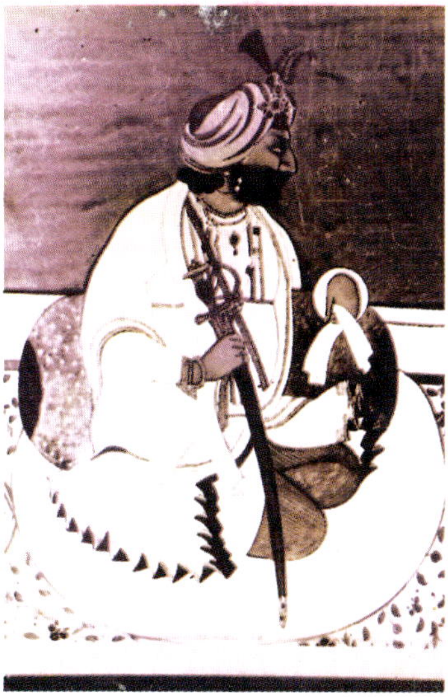

Fig 1. D.A.G. Jammu. Acc. No. 13/60, Maharaja Gulab Singh; 19th Century A.D. Jammu.

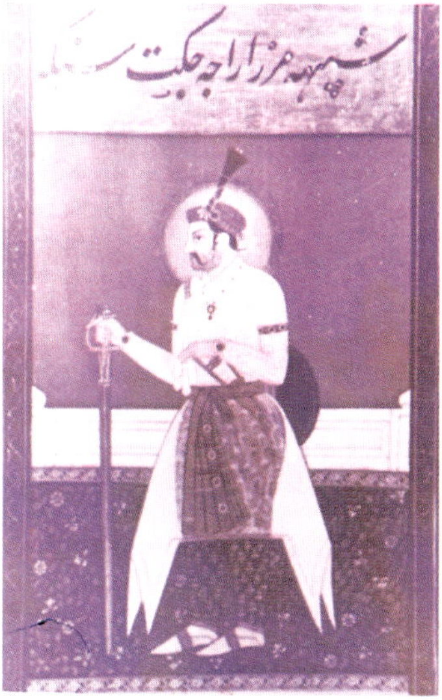

Fig.2.D.A.G. Jammu. Acc. No. 240/6287, Raja Jagat Singh; 19th Century A.D. Jammu.

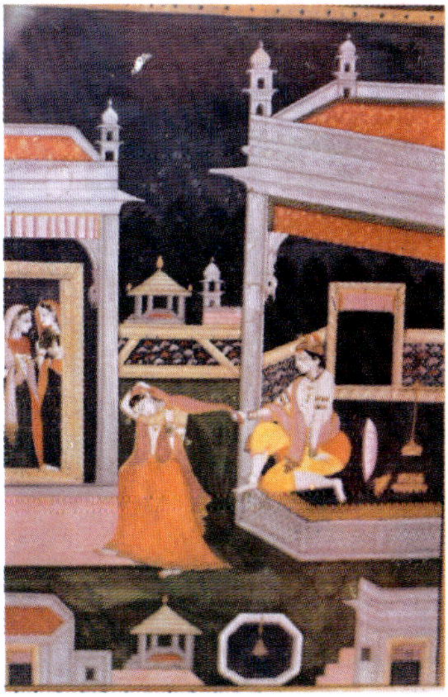

Fig.3.D.A.G. Jammu. Acc. No. 232/279, Prem Lila; 19th Century A.D. Jammu.

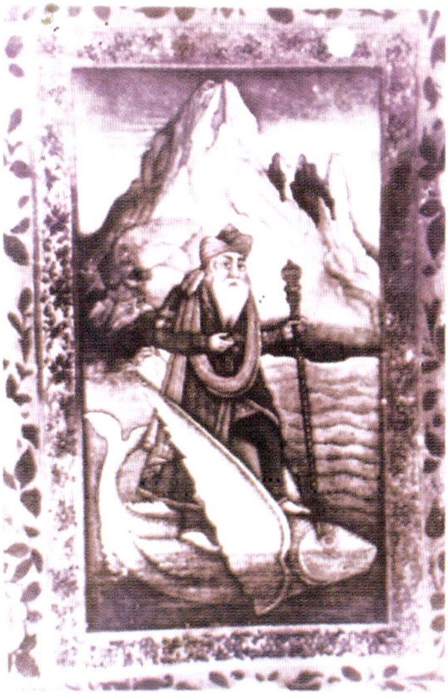

Fig.4.D.A.G. Jammu. Acc. No. 118, Khwaja Khizar; 19th Century A.D. Jammu.

Plate XIV

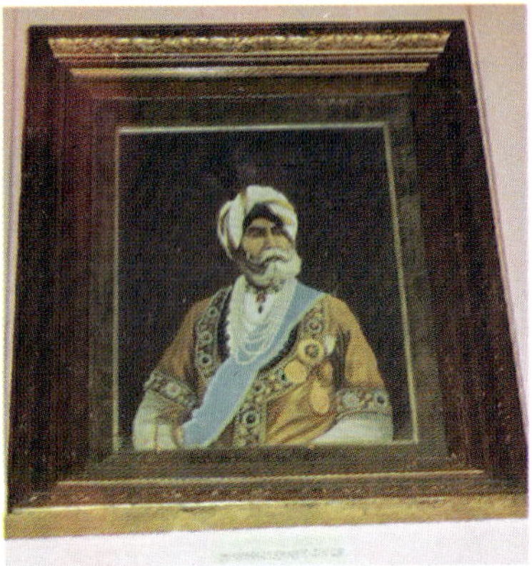

Fig.1.D.A.G. Jammu. Acc. No. 21, Ranbir Singh; 19th Century A.D. Jammu.

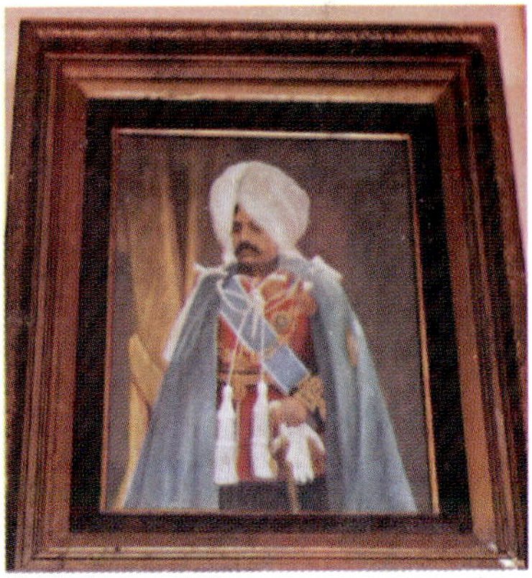

Fig.2.D.A.G. Jammu. Acc. No. 21, Pratap Singh; 19th Century A.D. Jammu.

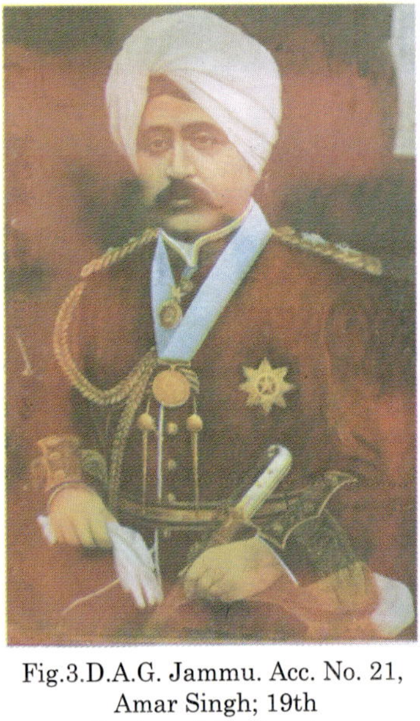

Fig.3.D.A.G. Jammu. Acc. No. 21, Amar Singh; 19th Century A.D. Jammu.

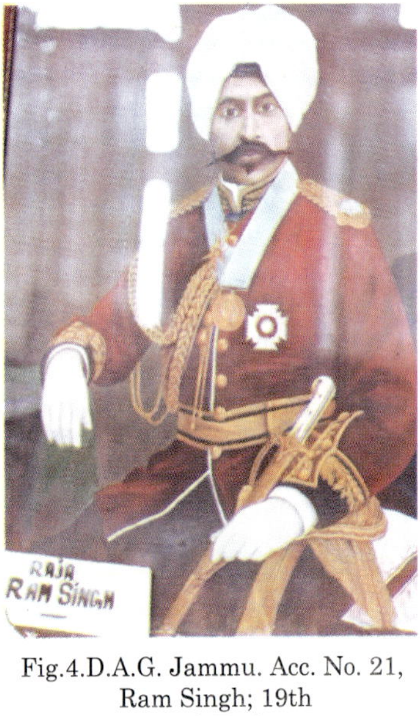

Fig.4.D.A.G. Jammu. Acc. No. 21, Ram Singh; 19th Century A.D. Jammu.

Plate XV

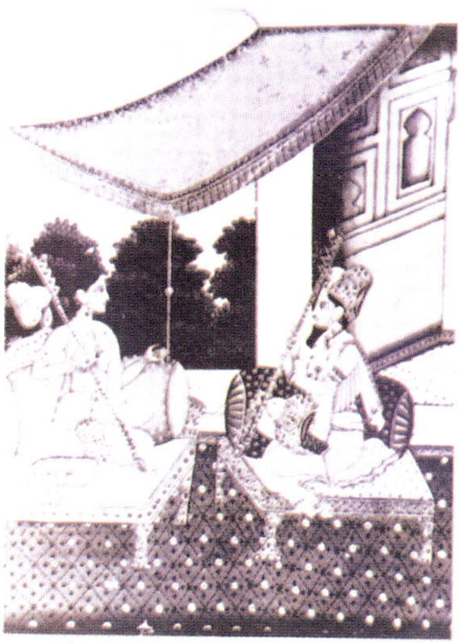

Fig.1.D.A.G. Jammu. Acc. No. 211/258, Raga Madhur; 19th Century A.D. Jammu.

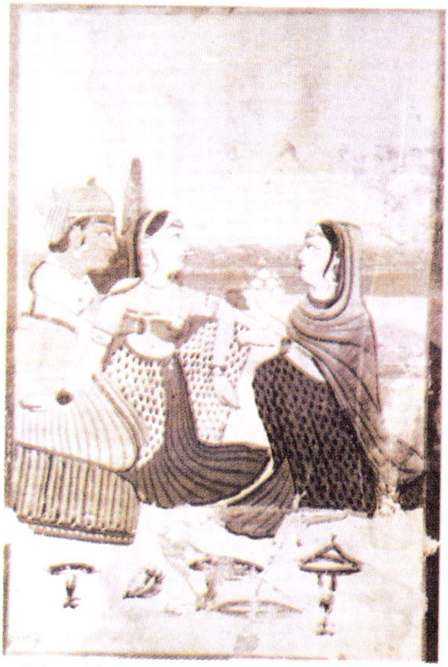

Fig.2.D.A.G. Jammu. Acc. No. 548, Male and two Female; 19th Century A.D. Jammu.

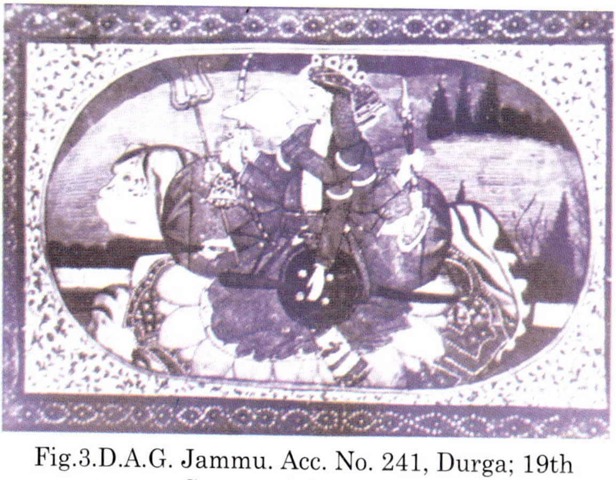

Fig.3.D.A.G. Jammu. Acc. No. 241, Durga; 19th Century A.D. Jammu.

Plate XVI

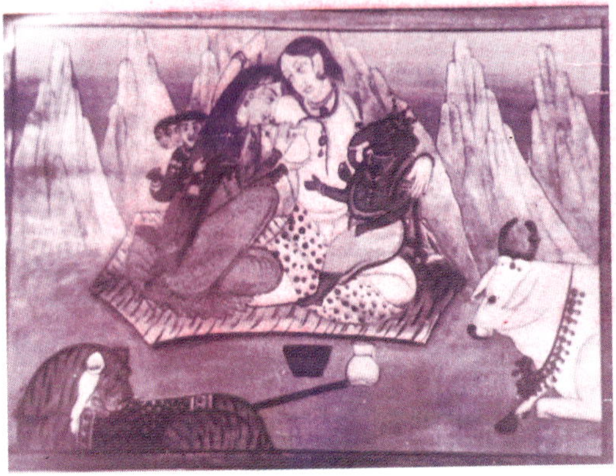

Fig. 1.D.A.G. Jammu. Acc. No. 138, Shiva Parvati; Early 20th Century A.D. Jammu.

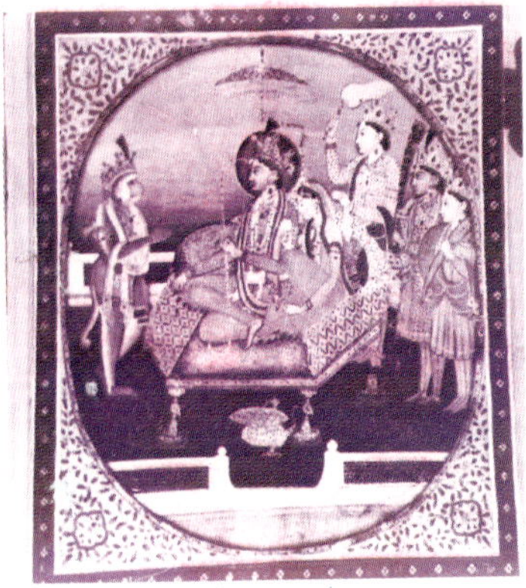

Fig.2.D.A.G. Jammu. Acc. No. 532, Rama and Panchyat; Artist Hari Chand; 19th Century A.D. Jammu.

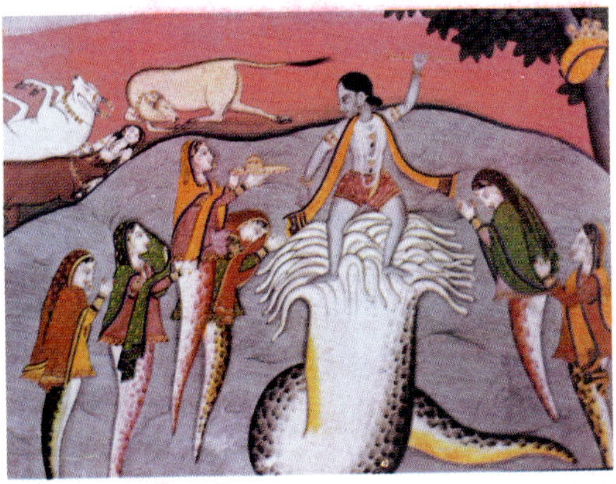

Fig.3.D.A.G. Jammu. Acc. No. 115/162, Kaliya Damon; 19th Century A.D. Jammu.

Plate XVII

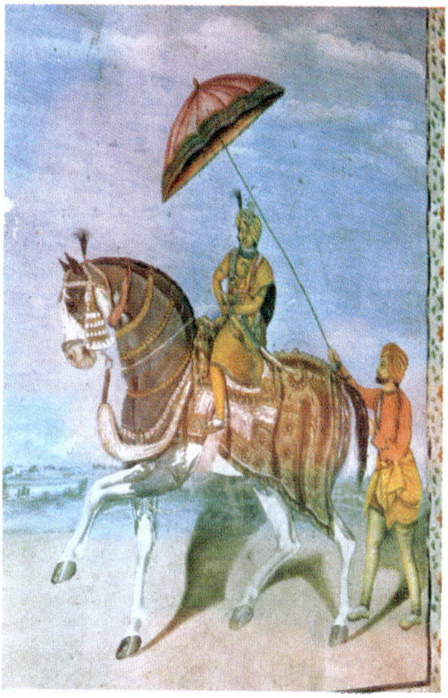

Fig.1.D.A.G. Jammu. Prince Partap Singh on horse back; 19th Century A.D. Jammu.

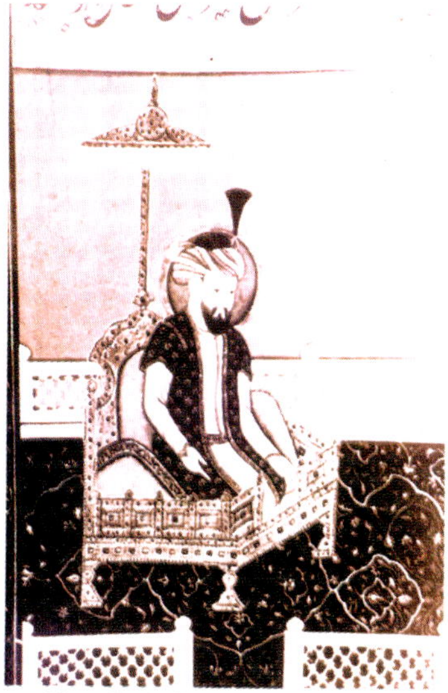

Fig.2.D.A.G. Jammu. Acc. No. 263/313, Umar Sheikh Mirza; 19th Century A.D. Jammu.

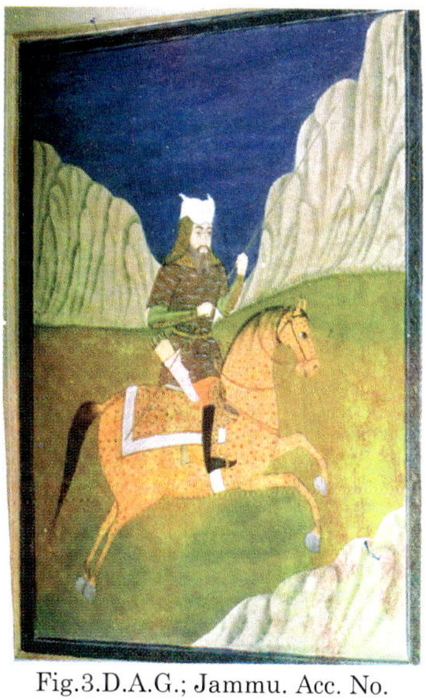

Fig.3.D.A.G.; Jammu. Acc. No. 268/307; Mirza Rustam Qandahari (Mughal Copy) 19th Century A.D. Jammu.

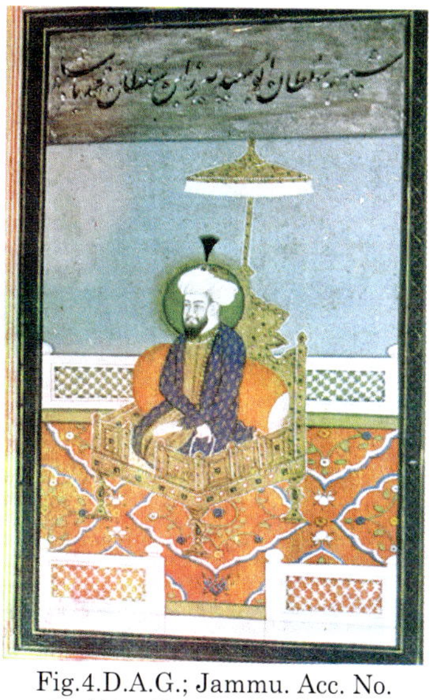

Fig.4.D.A.G.; Jammu. Acc. No. 244/291; Sultan-Abu-Said S/o Sultan Mohd-Badshah; 19th Century A.D. Jammu.

Plate XVIII

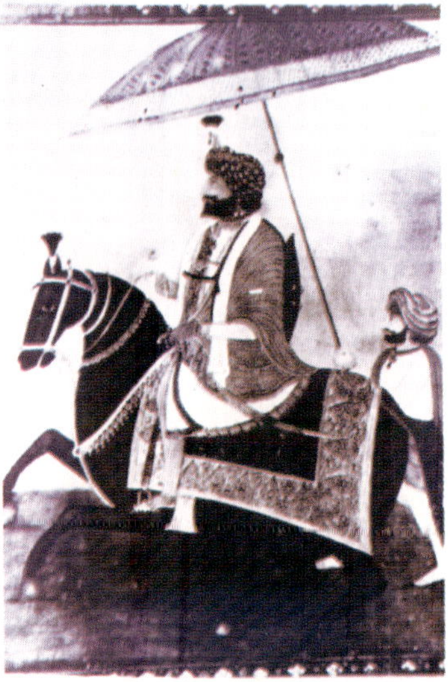

Fig.1.D.A.G. Jammu Acc. No. 219/266; Gulab Singh on Horse back; 19th Century A.D. Jammu.

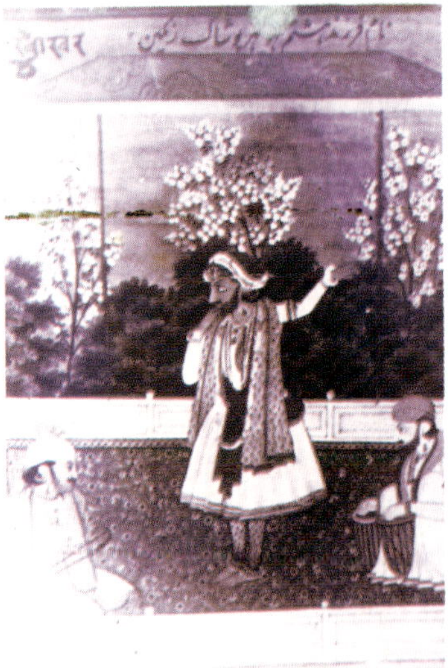

Fig.2.D.A.G. Jammu. Acc. No 235/282, Raga Khokhar; 19th Century A.D. Jammu.

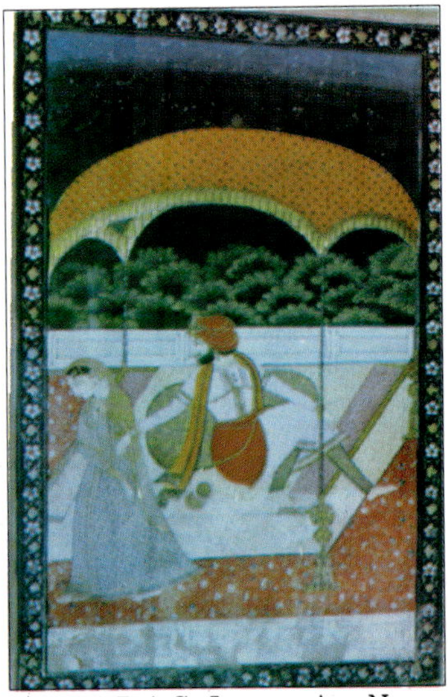

Fig.3.D.A.G. Jammu. Acc. No. 236/283, Raja and Rani; 19th Century A.D. Jammu.

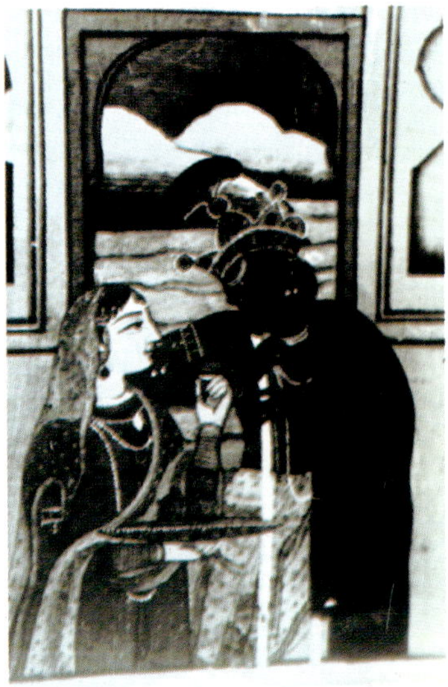

Fig.4.D.A.G. Jammu. Acc. No. 98, Krishna Play on Flute; Artist; Channu; 19th Century A.D. Jammu.

Plate XIX

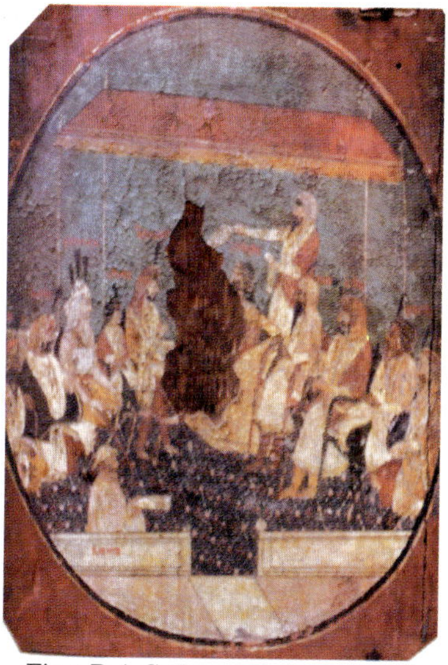

Fig.1.D.A.G. Jammu's Door Panel Darbar Scene of Maharaja Gulab Singh among his generals. Jammu.

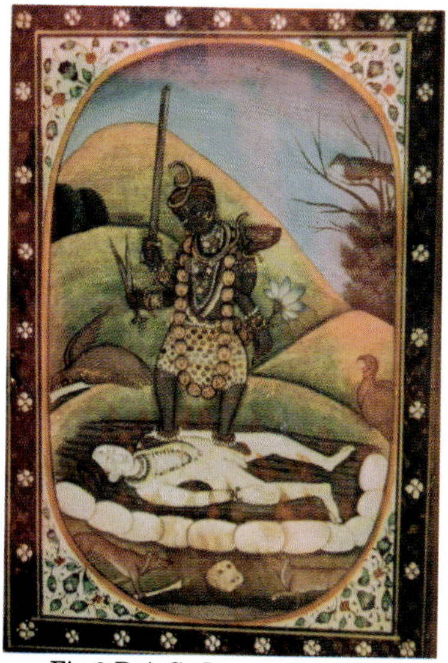

Fig.2.D.A.G. Jammu. Acc. No. 96/143; Kali and Siva. 19th Century A.D. Jammu.

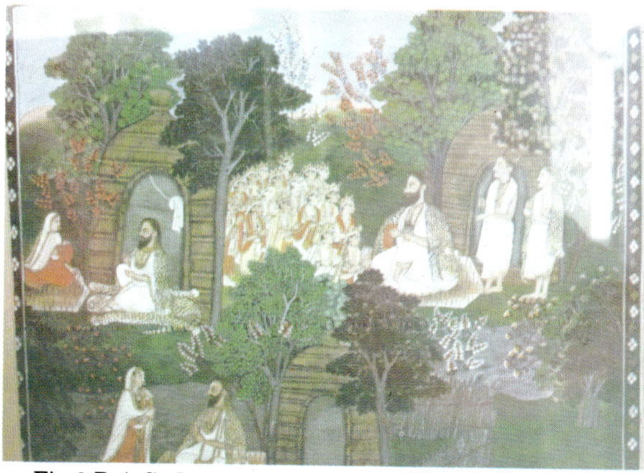

Fig.3.D.A.G. Jammu. Acc. No. 122; Bhardwaj Asharm; 19th Century A.D. Jammu.

Plate XX

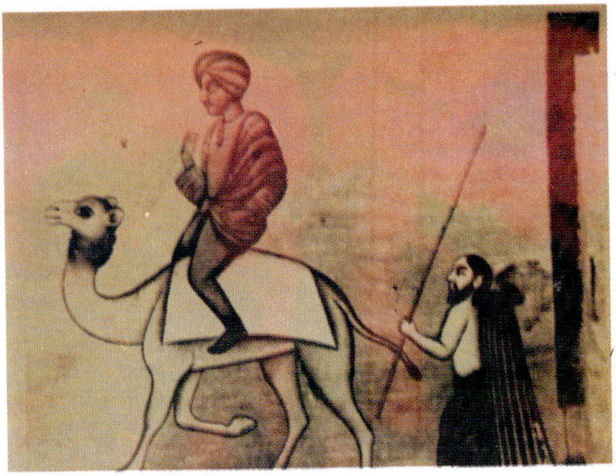

Fig.1.D.A.G. Jammu. Acc. No. 247/294; Rai Raodeh Dharmer-wali; 19th Century A.D. Jammu.

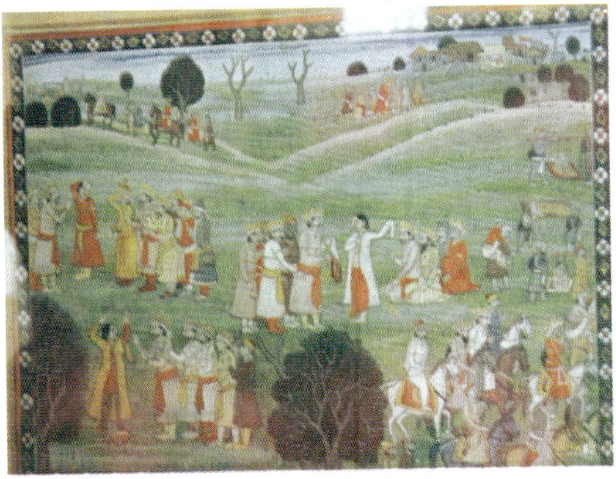

Fig.2.D.A.G. Jammu. Acc. No. 256/303; Shishu Pala and Jarasand; 19th Century A.D. Jammu.

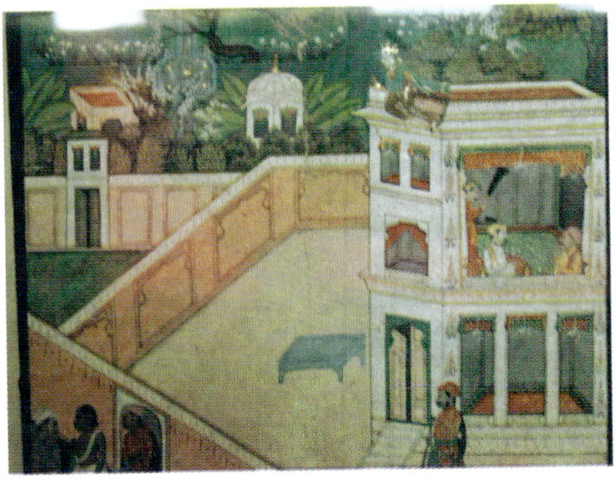

Fig.3.D.A.G. Jammu. Acc. No. 184/231 Brahmin Return From a Muslim Court; 19th Century A.D. Poonch.

Plate XXI

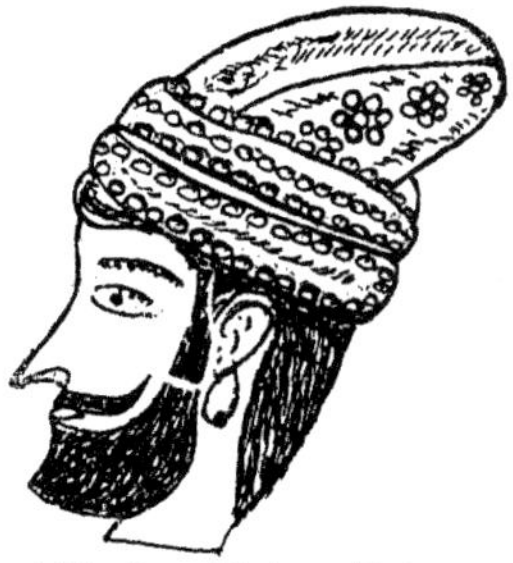

Fig.1.Turban-Rajput Prince.

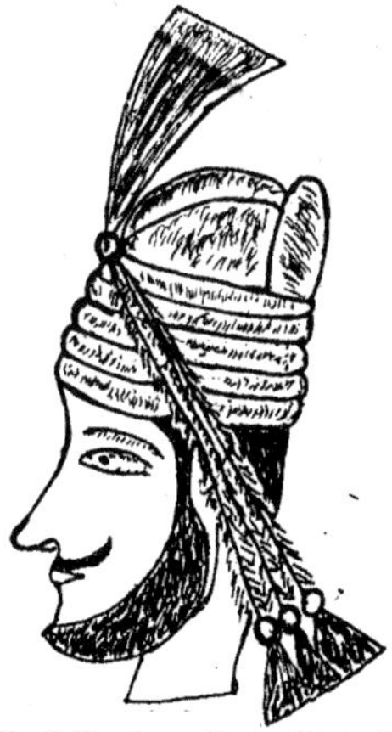

Fig.2.Turban-Raja Hataf Bandral.

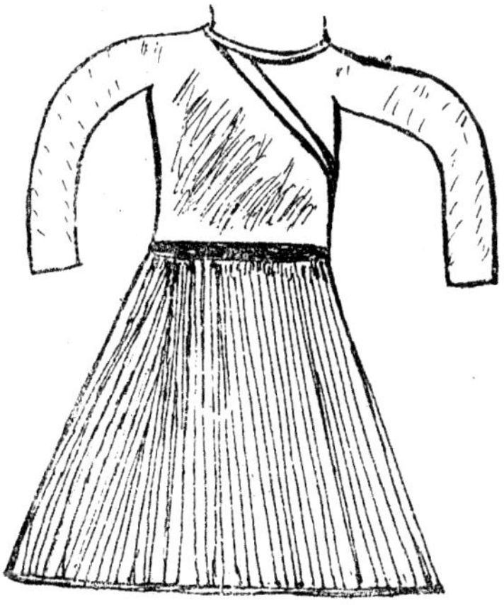

Fig.3.A shirt of an attendant.

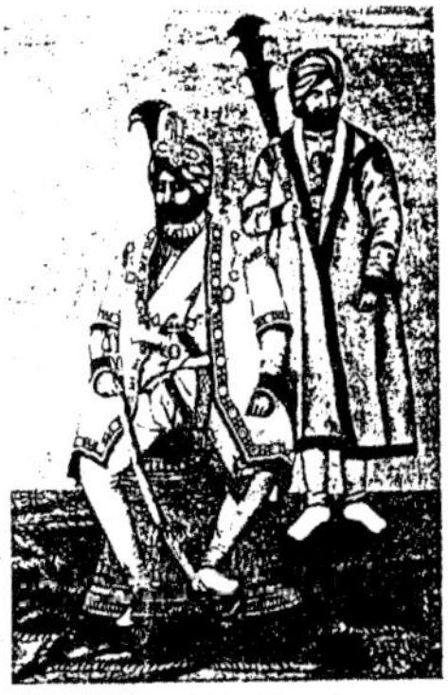

Fig.4.Ranbir Singh on a Royal Throne with an attendant.

Plate XXII

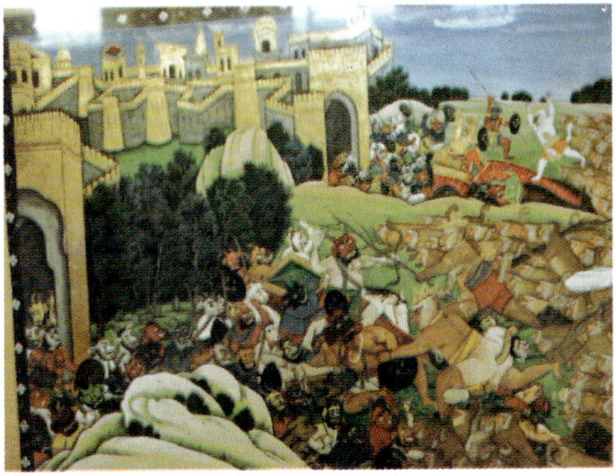

Fig.1.D.A.G. Jammu. Acc. No. 144/223; Invasion of the Monkey; 19th Century A.D. Jammu.

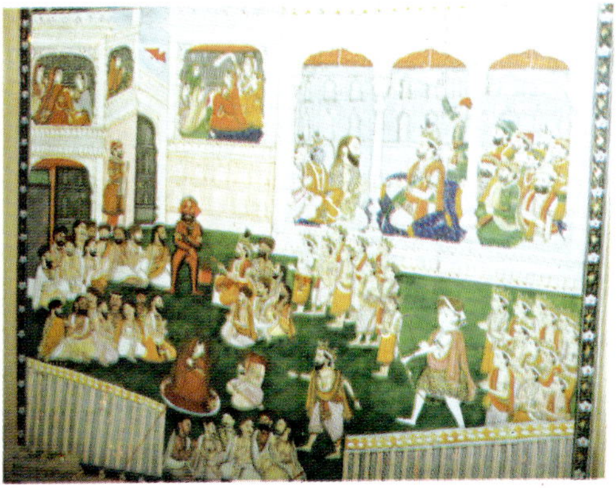

Fig.2.D.A.G. Jammu. Acc. No. 176/223; *Daksh-Yajan* (Birbh-ddra-usinatting) in; Hwan Kund; 19th Century A.D. Jammu.

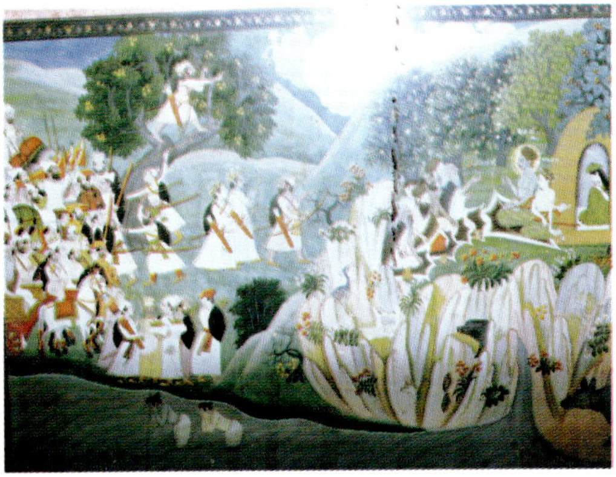

Fig.3.D.A.G. Jammu. Acc. No. 254/301; *Bharat Milap*; 19th Century A.D. Jammu.

Plate XXIII

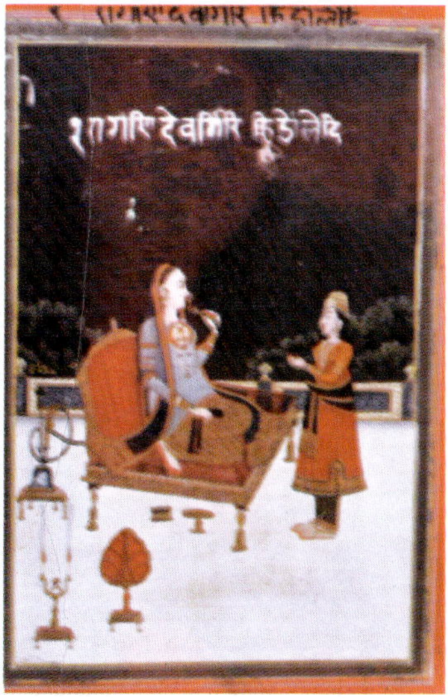

Fig.1.D.A.G. Jammu. Acc. No. 22/53 *Ragini Devagiri Hindol*; 19th Century A.D. Jammu.

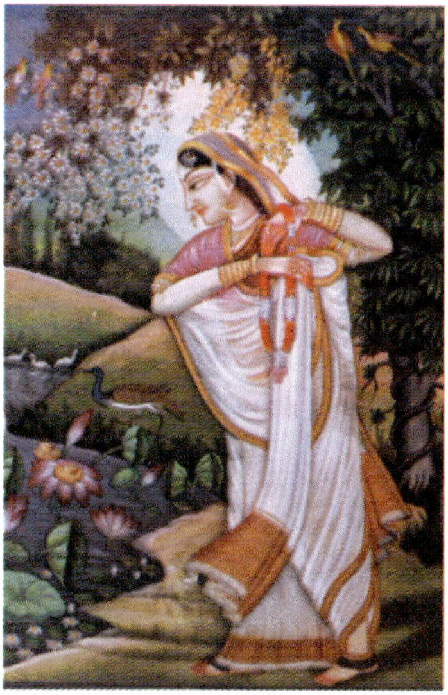

Fig.2.D.A.G. Jammu. Acc. No. 288/275; A Lady Near the Spring, Early 20th Century A.D. Jammu.

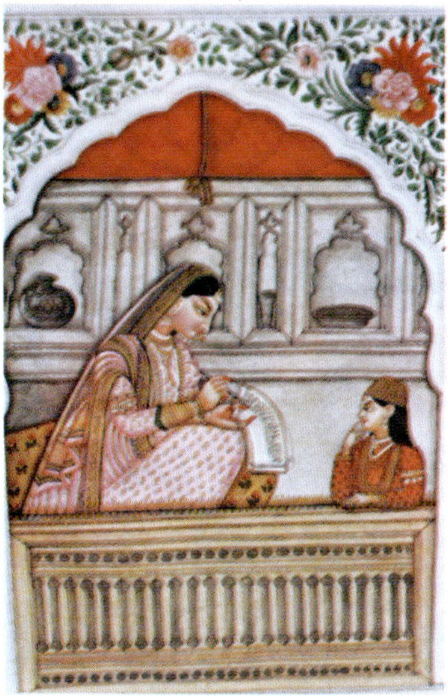

Fig.3.D.A.G. Jammu. Acc. No. 154; Peter Lakhni Nayika; 19th Century A.D. Jammu.

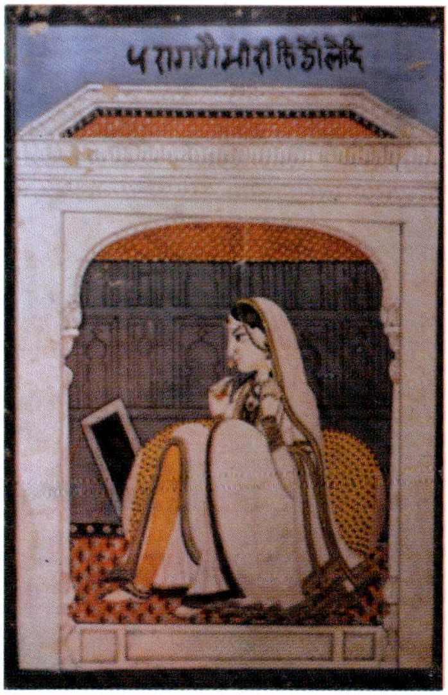

Fig.4.D.A.G. Jammu. Acc. No. 32/79; *Ragini Dowhari of Hindola*, 18th Century A.D. Jammu.

Plate XXIV

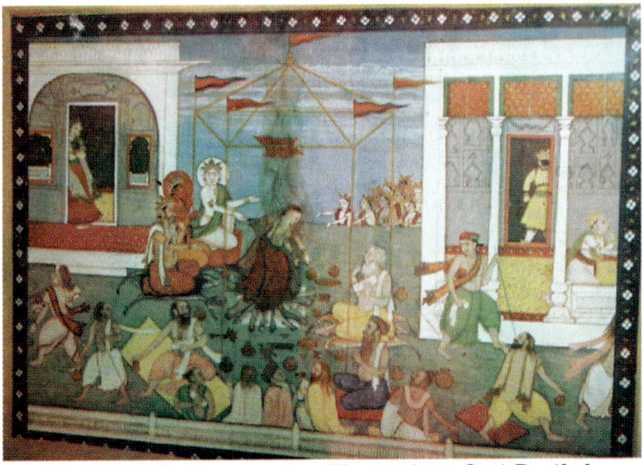

Fig.1.D.A.G. Jammu. Acc. No. 105/152 *Sati-Parikshan*; 18th Century A.D. Jammu.

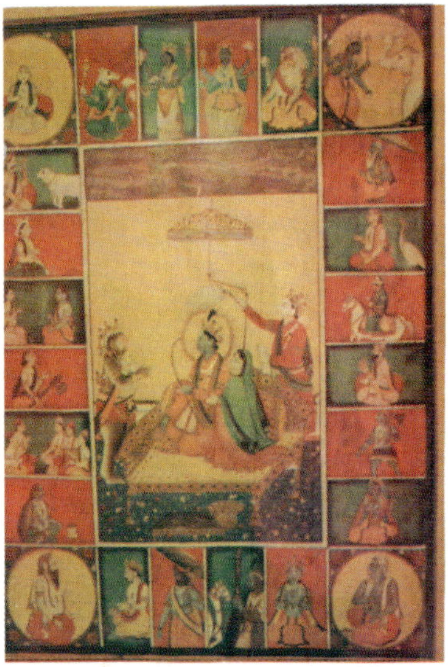

Fig.2.D.A.G. Jammu. Acc. No. 209/256; Rama and other Avatars; 19th Century A.D. Jammu.

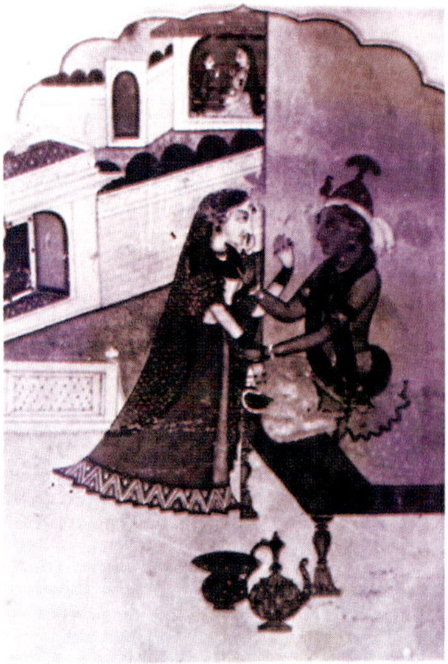

Fig.3.D.A.G. Jammu. Acc. No. 99; Krishna and Radha in a love scene; 19th Century A.D. Jammu.

Plate XXV

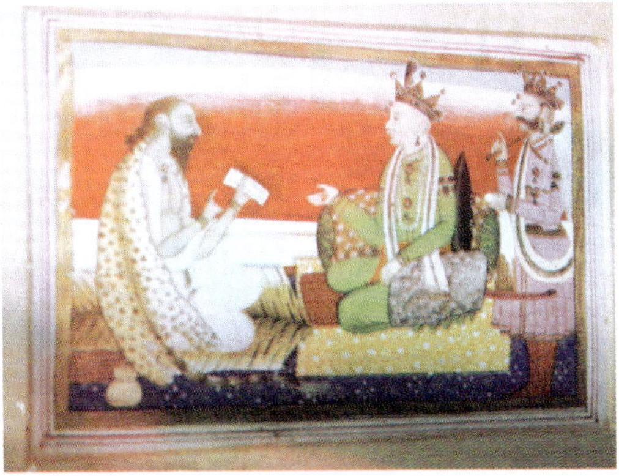

Fig.1.D.A.G. Jammu. Acc. No. 85/256; Sanjay-Relating the Mahabharata to Daritrashtra; 19th Century A.D. Jammu.

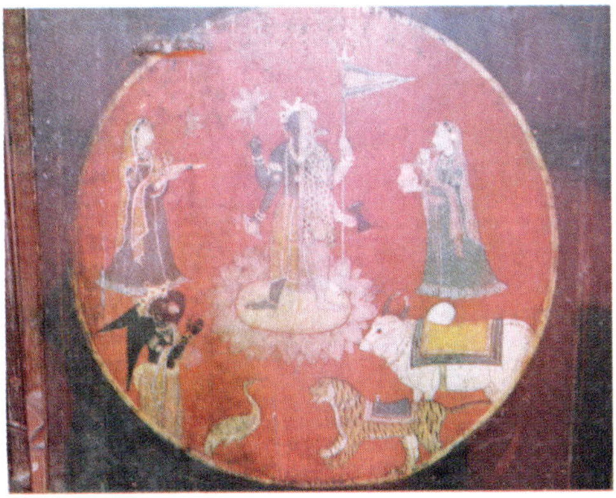

Fig.2.D.A.G. Jammu. Door Panel; Representa-tive of Lord Shiva.

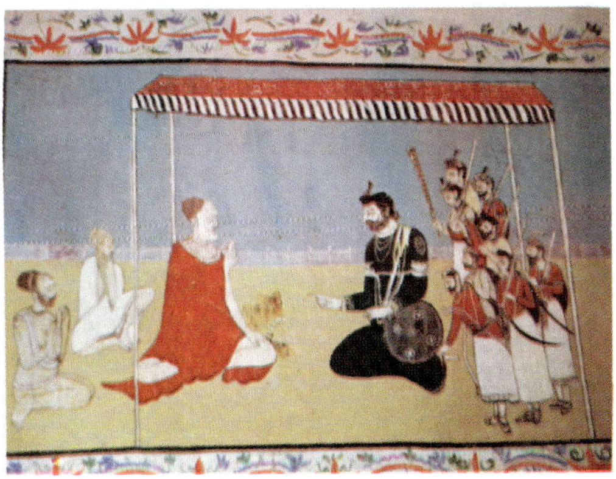

Fig.3.Sadhu Blessing to Gulab Singh and his Troops; Wall-Painting; Sui-Simbli Temple.

Plate XXVI

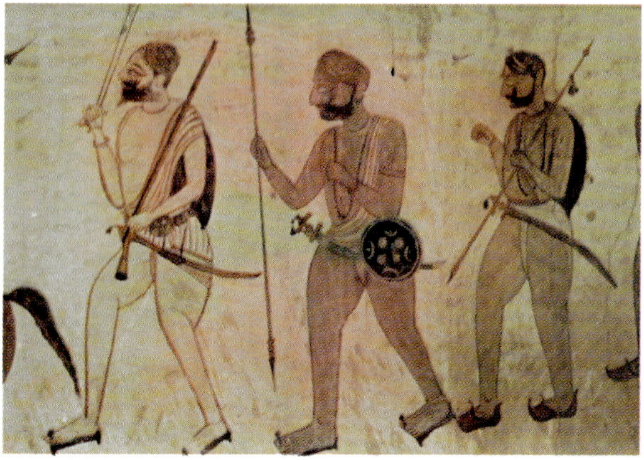

Fig.1.Pictures of Soldiers. Wall-Painting;
Sui-Simbli Temple.

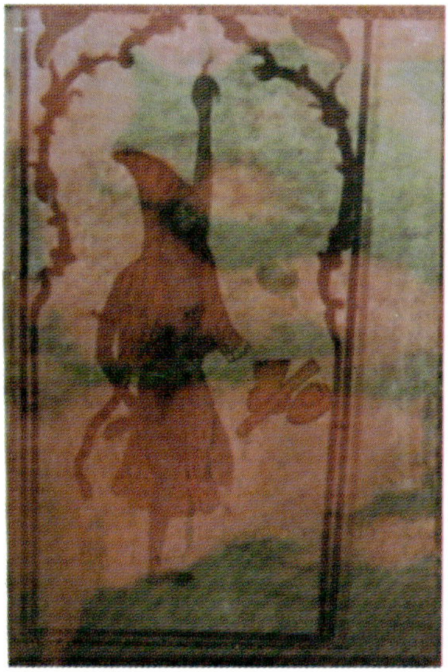

Fig.2.A Sadhu Standing on one leg.
Wall-Painting Sui-Samble. Tample.

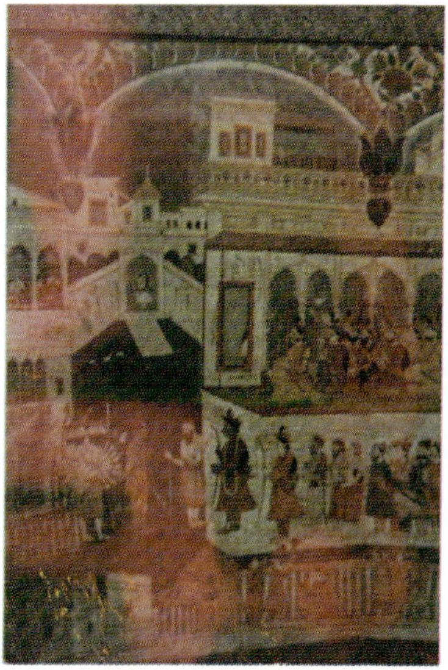

Fig.3.Rama and Lakshman
Returning to Aoudhy;
Wall-Painting Bhurja Temple.

Plate XXVII

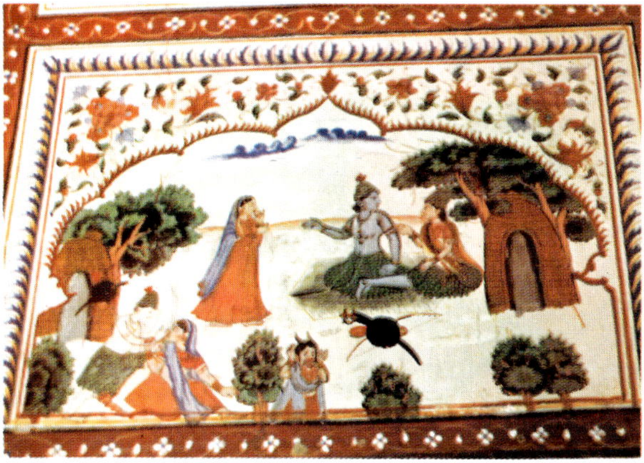

Fig.1.Ram, Sita and Lakshman; In the Ashram of a Jungle, Punishing the Rakashes, Wall-Painting; Purani Mandi Temple.

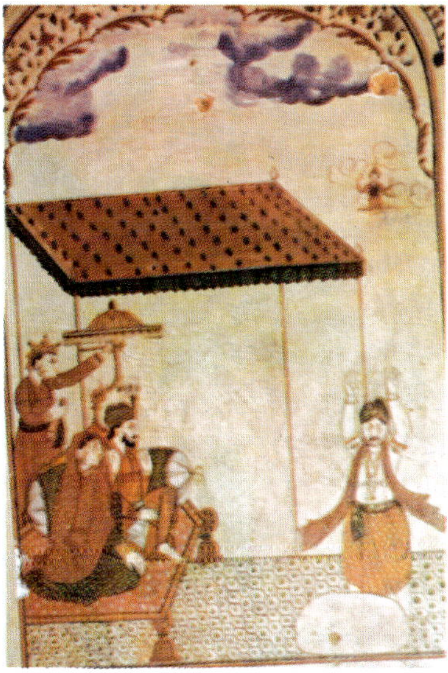

Fig.2.A Raja Punishing to a man; Wall-Painting; Purani Mandi; Temple Jammu.

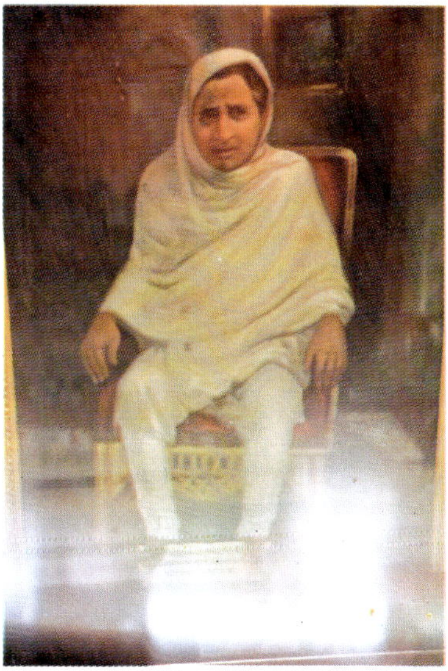

Fig.3.Rani Bhandrali; Purani Mandi; Jammu

Plate XXVIII

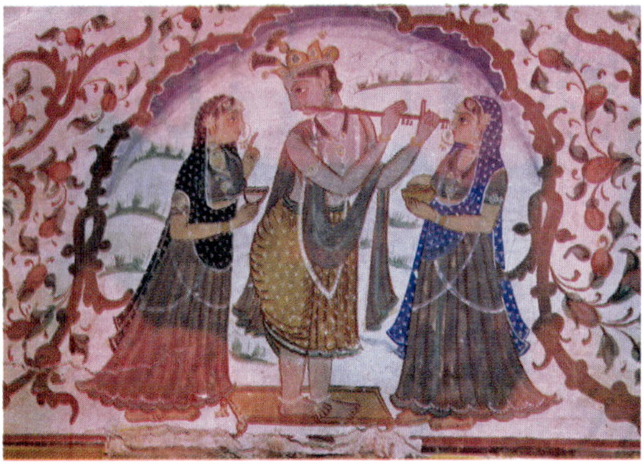

Fig.1.Krishna playing with Gopies, Wall-Painting of Miran Sahib Temple.

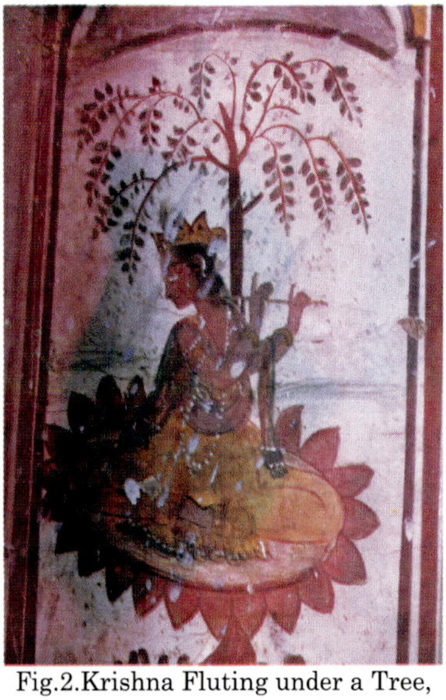

Fig.2.Krishna Fluting under a Tree, Wall-Painting of Miran Sahib Temple.

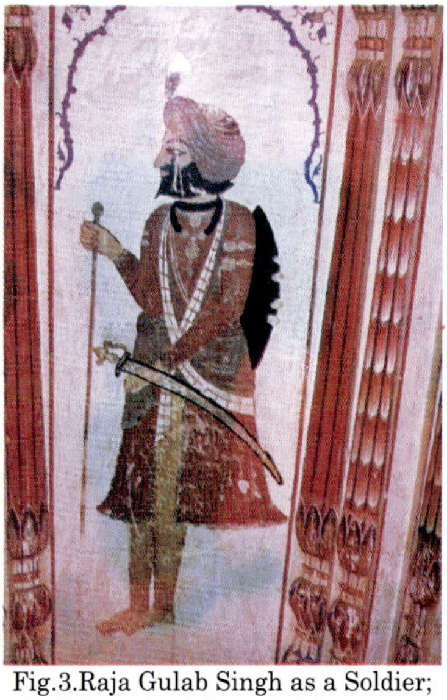

Fig.3.Raja Gulab Singh as a Soldier; Wall-Painting Miran Sahib Temple.

Plate XXIX

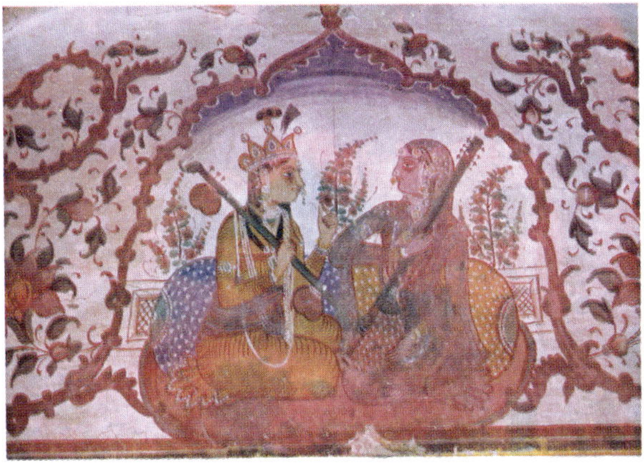

Fig.1.Radha and a Gopies with sita, Wall-Painting of Miran Sahib Temple.

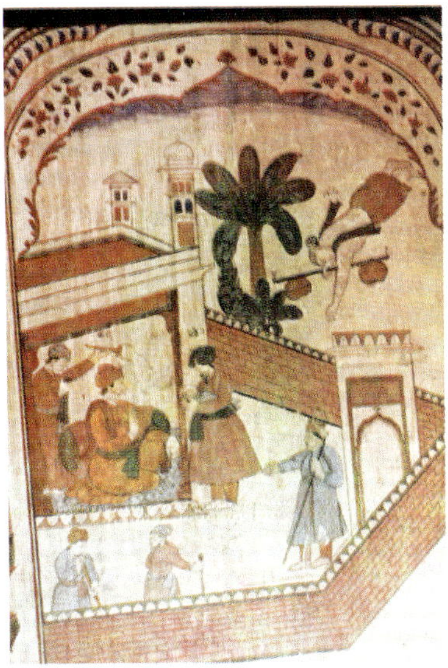

Fig.2.A man appearing with a child; Purani Mandi Temple Wall-Painting.

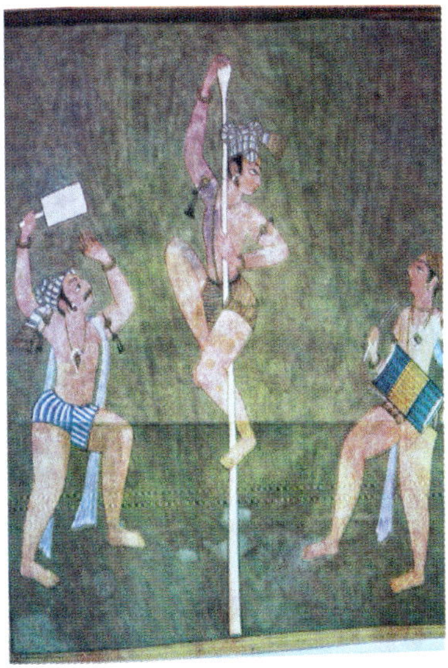

Fig.3.Nat-Raga, Basohli; circa 1700-20 A.D. Bharat Kala Bhawan, Banaras.

Plate XXX

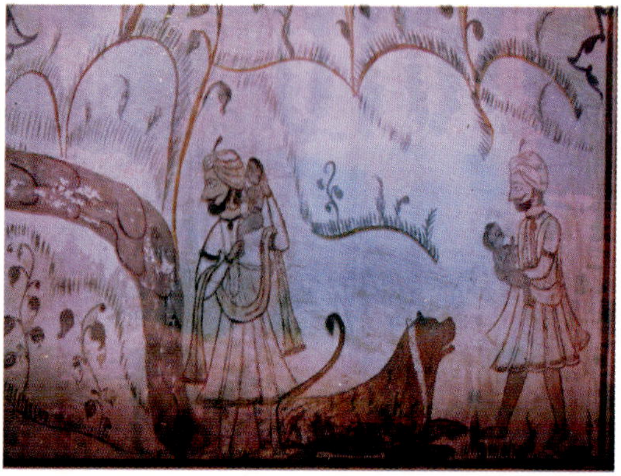

Fig.1.Vasudeva Carrying the Newly born Krishna across the Jamuna. Wall-Painting of Purmandal Temple.

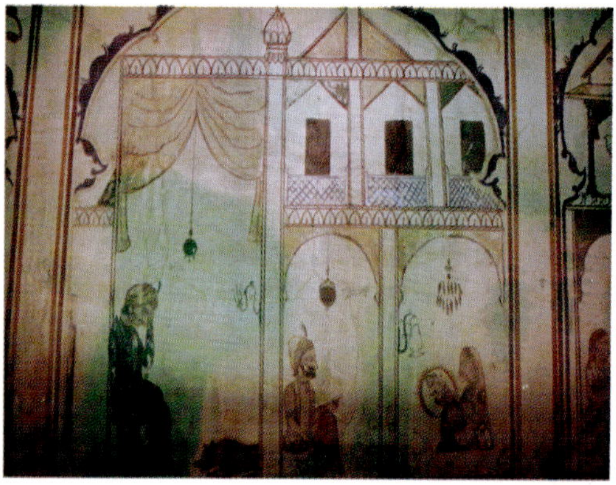

Fig.2.Two men and a Lady in a sad mood; Wall-Painting of Puramandal Temple.

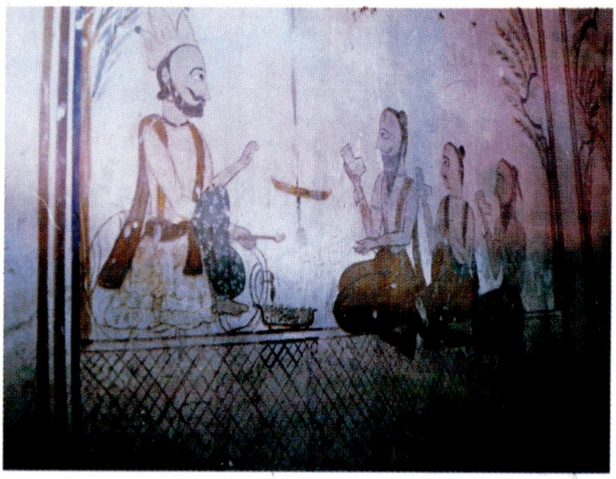

Fig.3.A King, listening the three Sadhu, Wall-Painting Puramandal Temple.

Plate XXXI

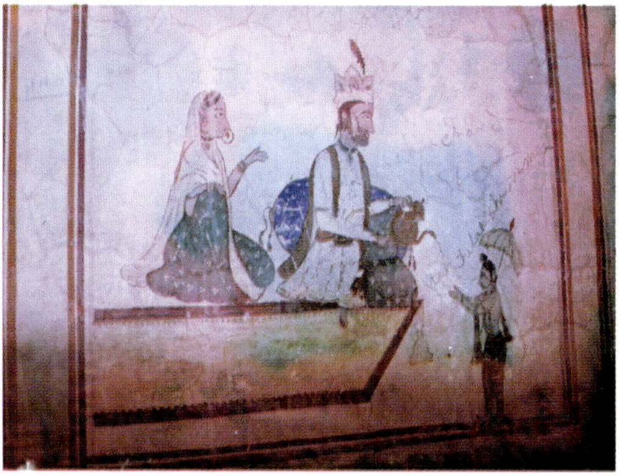

Fig.1.A Nayaka, Watering to a Sadhu, Wall-Painting of Puramandal Temple.

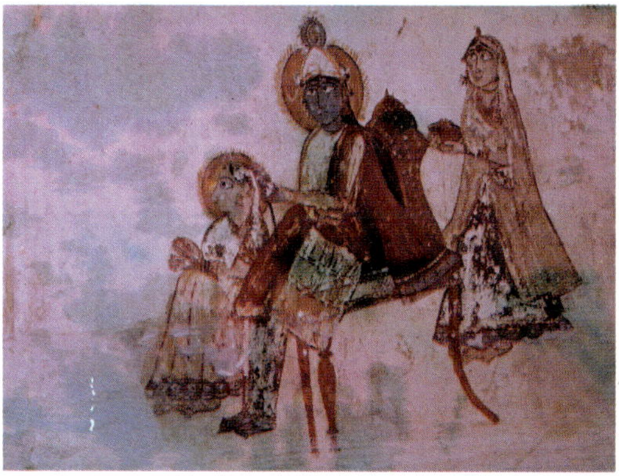

Fig.2.Krishna Combing Radha; Wall-Painting of Purmandal.

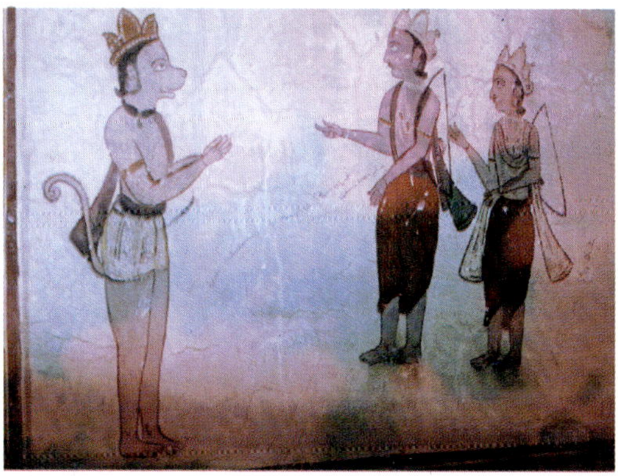

Fig.3.Rama and Lakshman Return to Aoudhy received by Hanuman; Wall-Painting of Purmandal Temple.

Plate XXXII

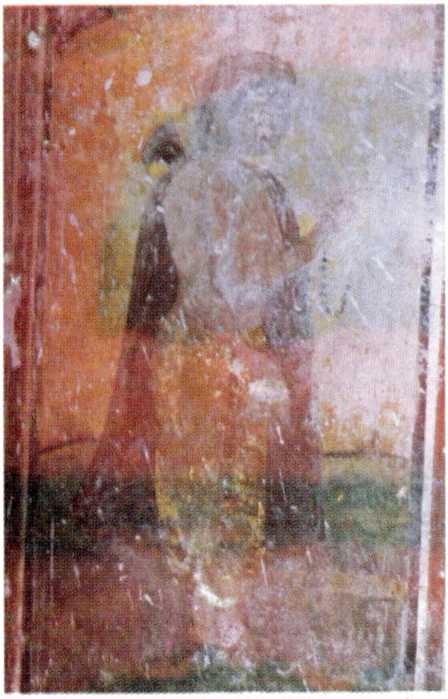

Fig.1.A Sadhu, Mediating, carrying a Kambala on the left shoulder; Wall-Painting of Purmandal Temple.

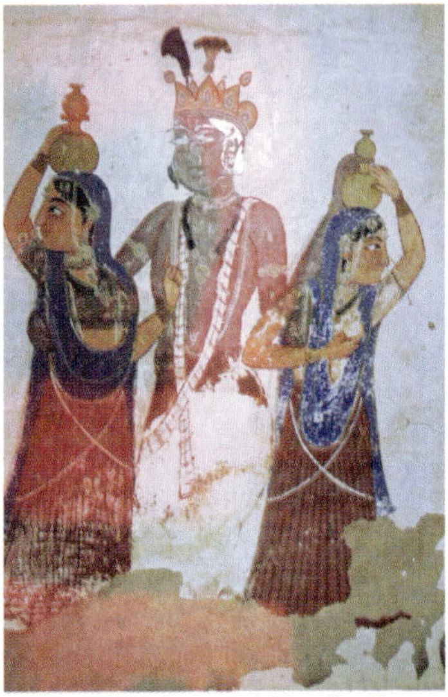

Fig.2.Krishna and Two Ladies Carrying Vessels on Head. Wall-Painting of Purmandal Temple.

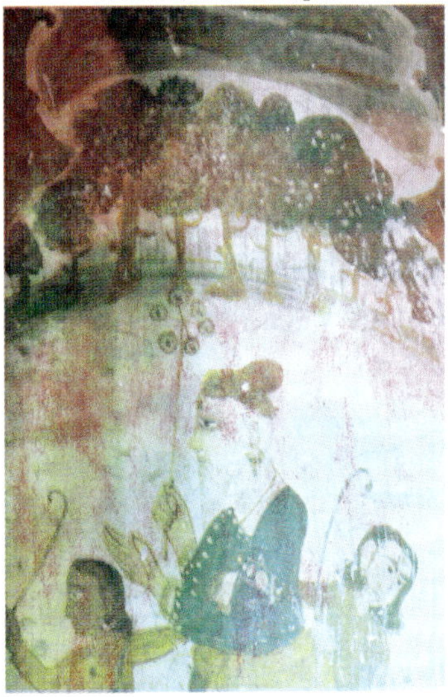

Fig.3.A Toy-seller with two children. Wall-Painting of Purmandal Temple.

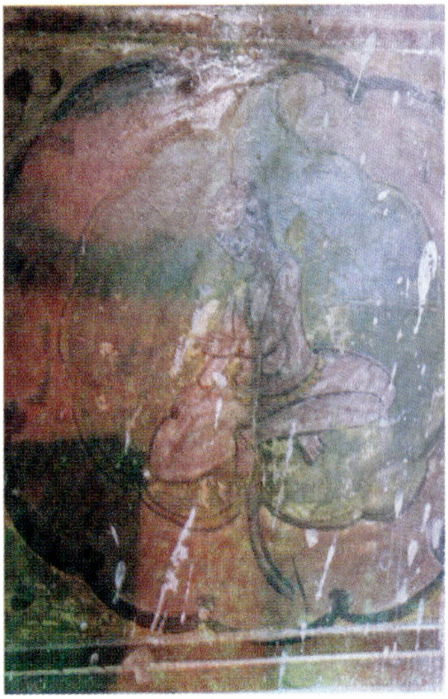

Fig.4.a Shiva; Wall-painting Of Purmandal Tempel

Plate XXXIII

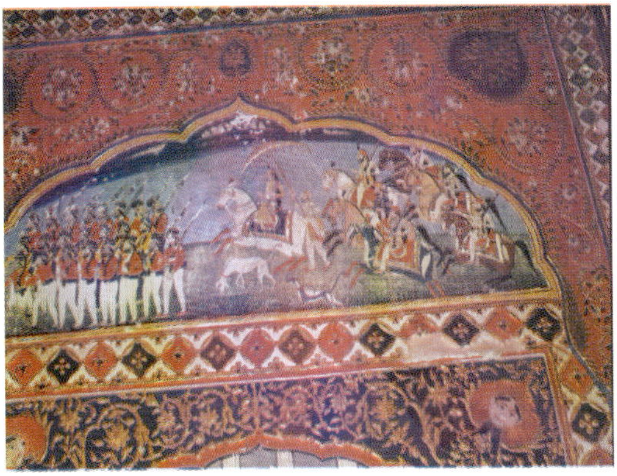

Fig.1.Suchet Singh proceeding in a War Procession, Wall-Painting of Ramnagar Palace.

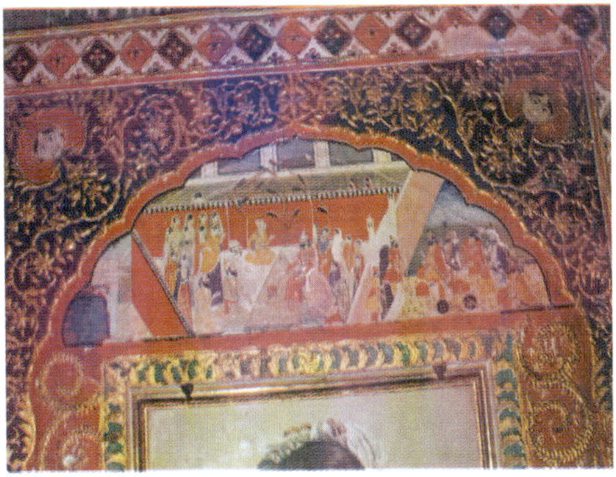

Fig.2.Darbar scene of Maharaja Suchet Singh; Wall-Painting of Ramnagar Palace.

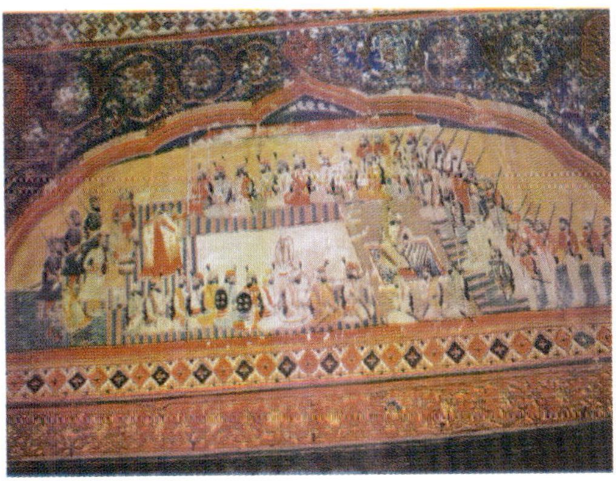

Fig.3.Suchet Singh celebrating his victory; Wall-Painting of Ramnagar Palace.

Plate XXXIV

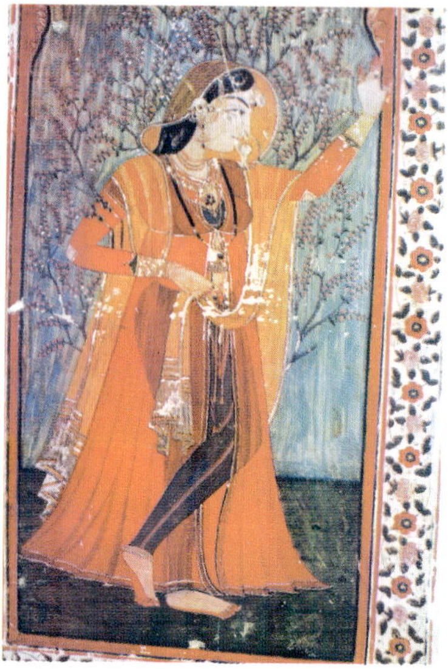

Fig.1.Ragini; Wall-Painting of Ramnagar Palace.

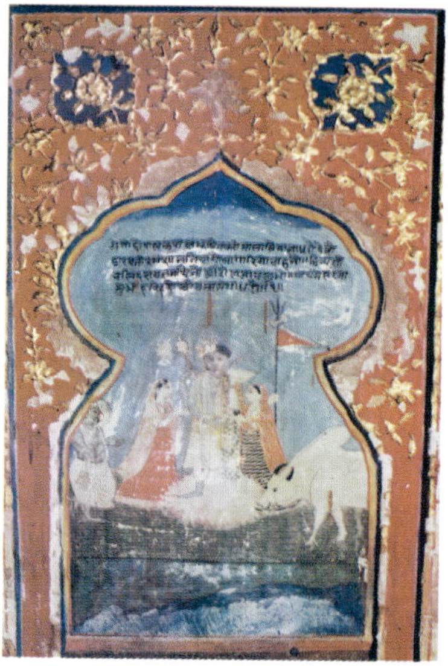

Fig.2.Representative of Lord Shiva; Wall-Painting; Ramnagar Palace.

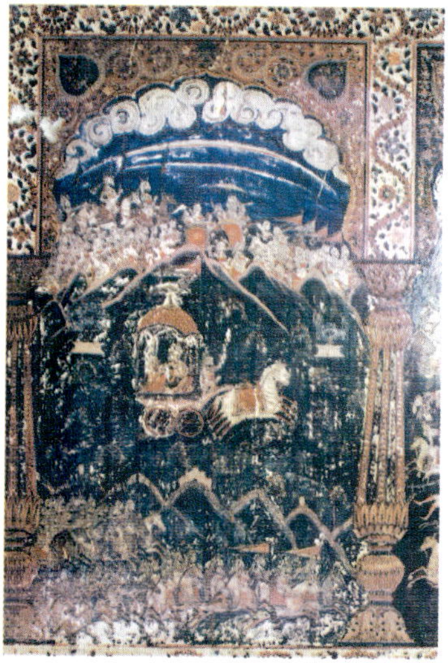

Fig.3.Battle scene of Mahabharata; Wall-Painting; Ramnagar Palace.

Plate XXXV

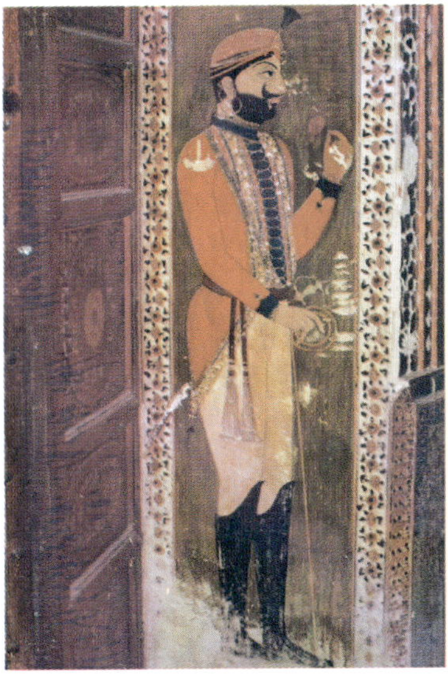

Fig.1.Raja Suchet Singh as a soldier's in a uniform; Wall-Painting Ramnagar Palace.

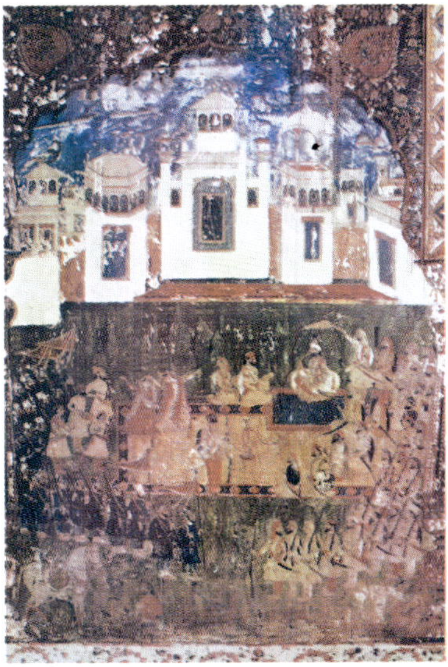

Fig.2.A culture scene in the Darbar Hall of Raja Suchet Singh. Wall-Painting; Ramnagar Palace.

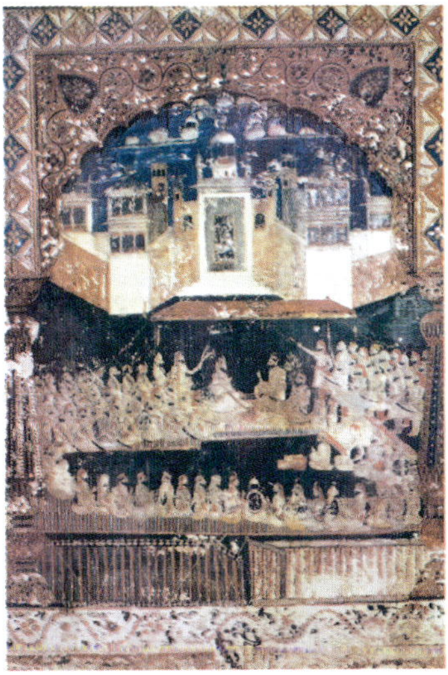

Fig.3.A war preparatory scene of Raja Suchet Singh; Wall-Painting; Ramnagar

Plate XXXVI

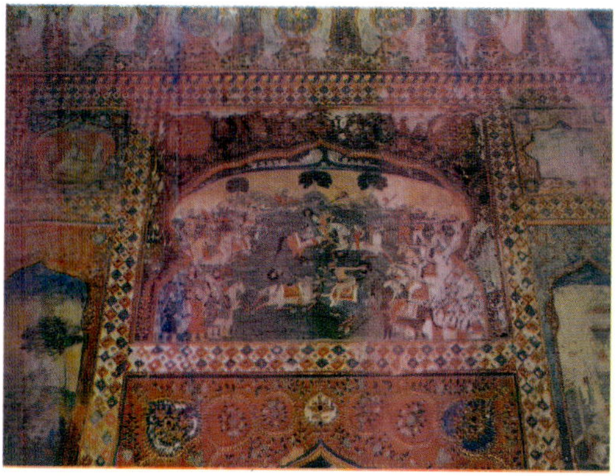

Fig.1.Fighting scene of Mahabharata Epic, Wall-Painting; Ramnagar Palace.

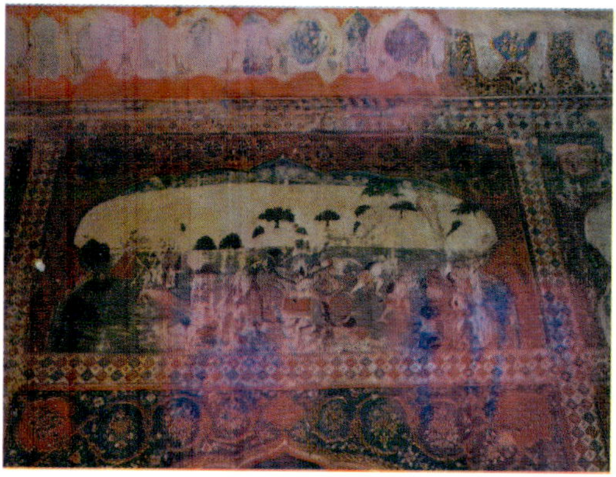

Fig.2.A war Scene of Mahabharata; Wall-Painting of Ramnagar Palace.

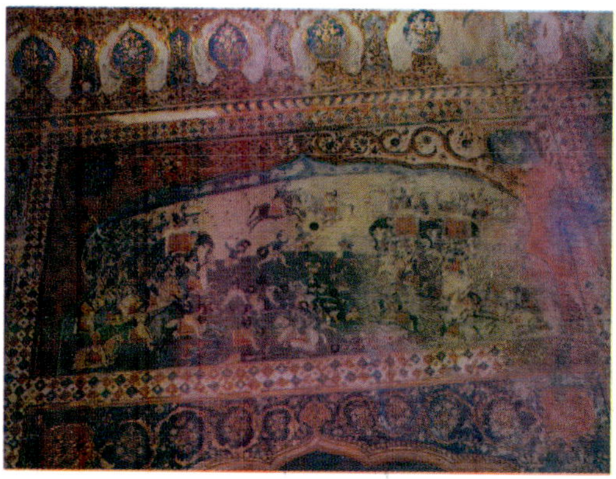

Fig.3.'The Battle Scene of Krishna and Rukamni' Wall-Painting of Ramnagar Palce.

Plate XXXVII

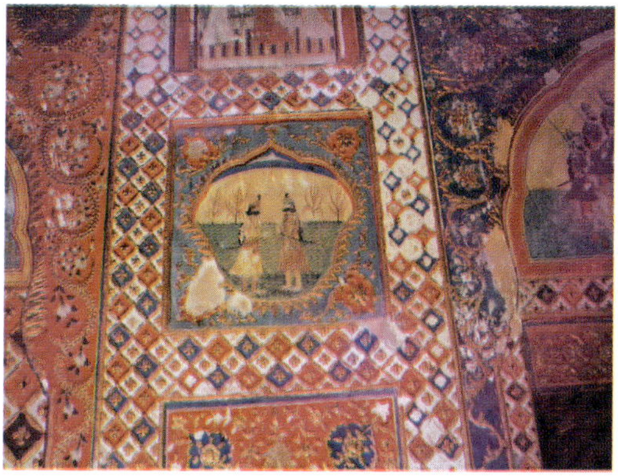

Fig.1.Suchet Singh appearing as a soldier in lawn; Wall-Painting of Ramnagar Palace.

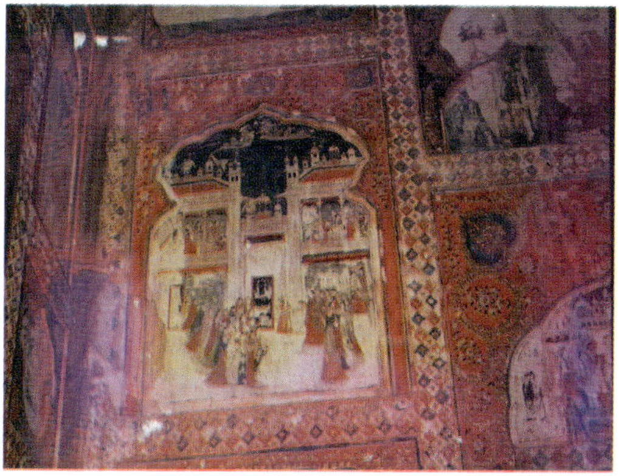

Fig.2.A Festive scene of Suchet Singh's Palace; (Gori Puja) Wall-Painting of Ramnagar Palace.

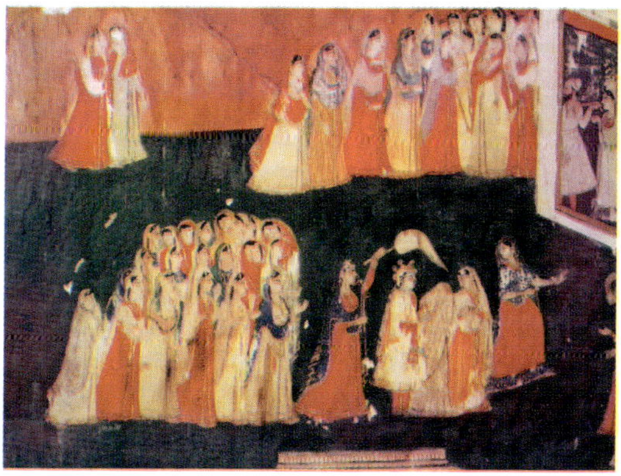

Fig.3.A Marriage scene; Wall-Painting of Ramnagar Palace.

Plate XXXVIII

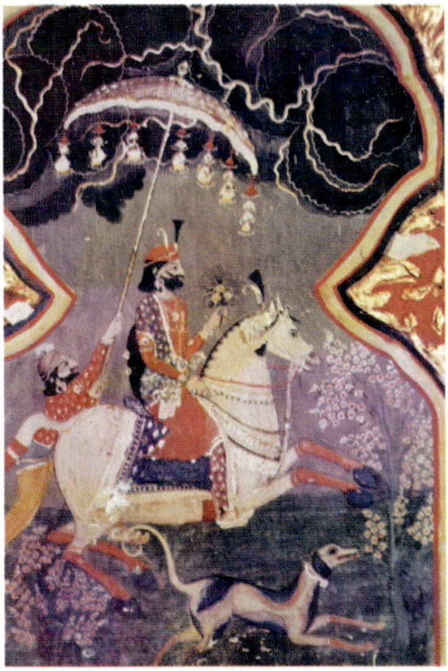

Fig.1.Suchet Singh on horse back, A hunting scene; Wall-Painting of Ramnagar Palace.

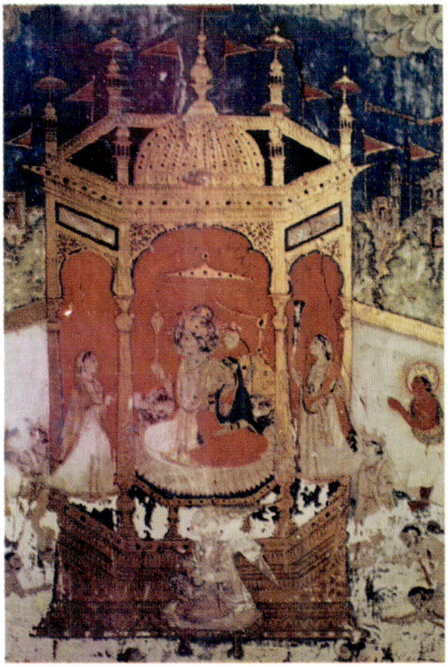

Fig.2.A scene of Radha-Krishna in a Temple; Wall-Painting of Ramnagar Palace.

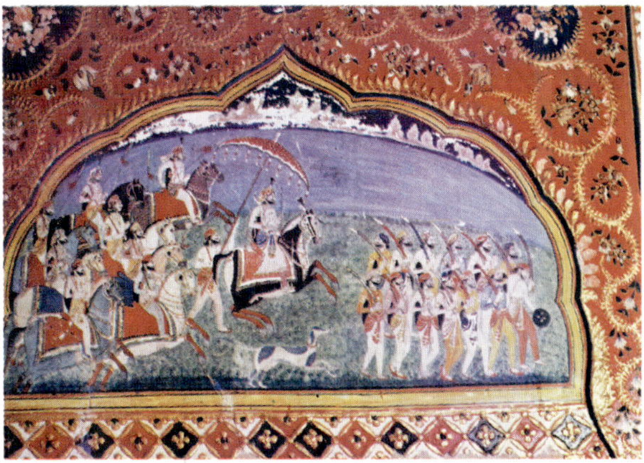

Fig.3.Suchet Singh with his troops proceeding on war; Wall-Painting of Ramnagar Palace.

Plate XXXIX

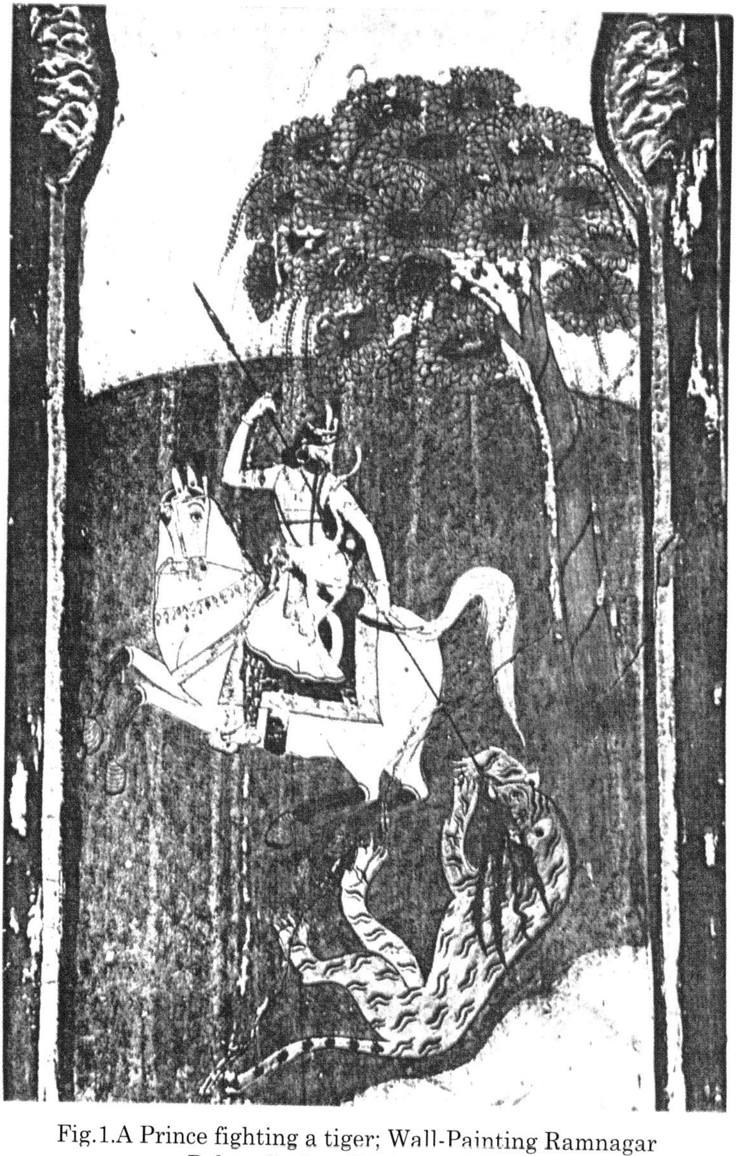

Fig.1.A Prince fighting a tiger; Wall-Painting Ramnagar Palace Suchet Singh's Bedroom.

Plate XXXX

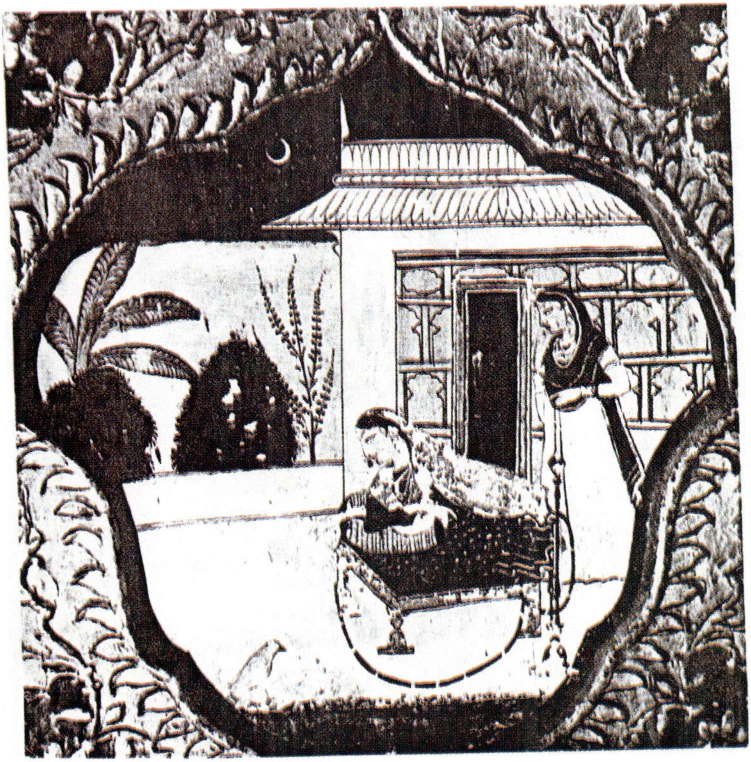

Fig.1.A Rani smoking a hookah, Ramnagar Palace
Suchet Singh's Bedroom.

Plate XXXXI

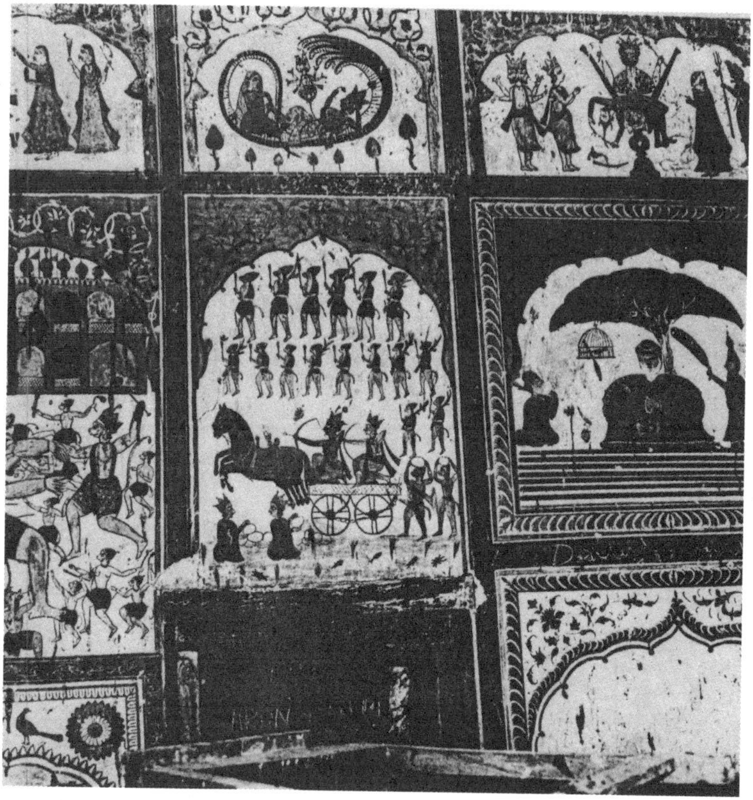

Fig. 1Painted walls of the Mahanta's baithak, Saiva Math Mansar.

Plate XXXXII

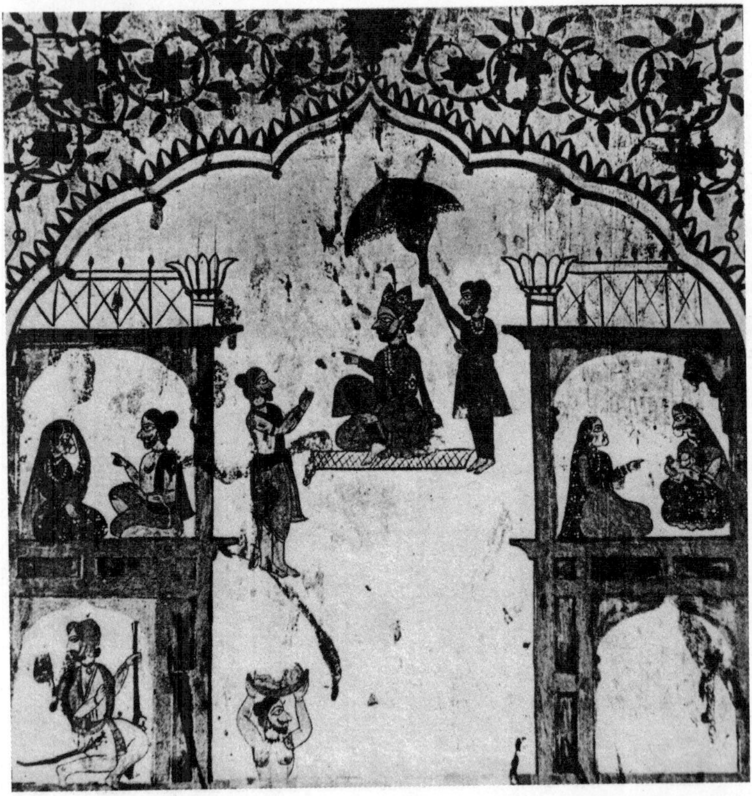

Fig. 1Woman in a Palace, Siva Math, Mansar Wall-Painting.

Plate XXXXIII

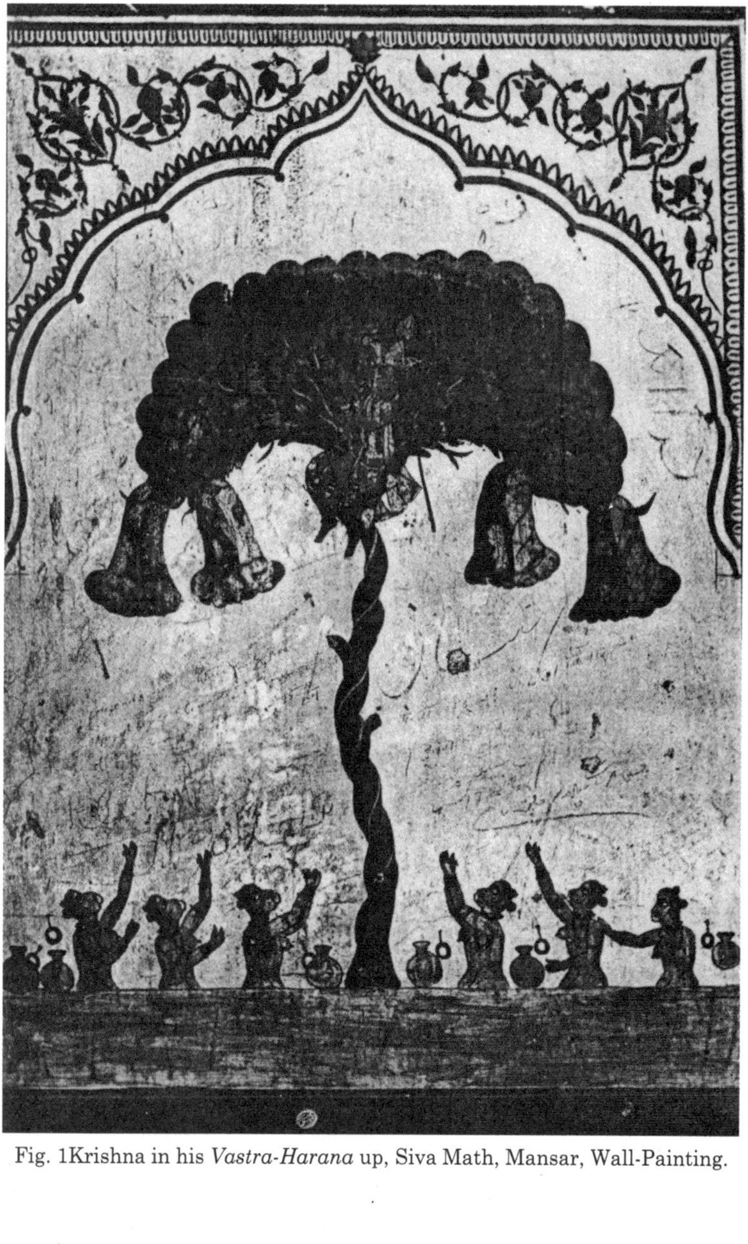

Fig. 1Krishna in his *Vastra-Harana* up, Siva Math, Mansar, Wall-Painting.

Plate XXXXIV

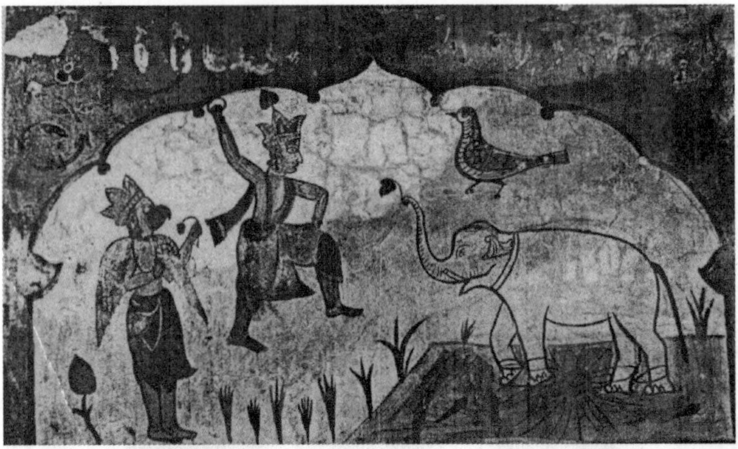

Fig. 1Gajamoksa, Siva Math, Mansar Wall-Painting.

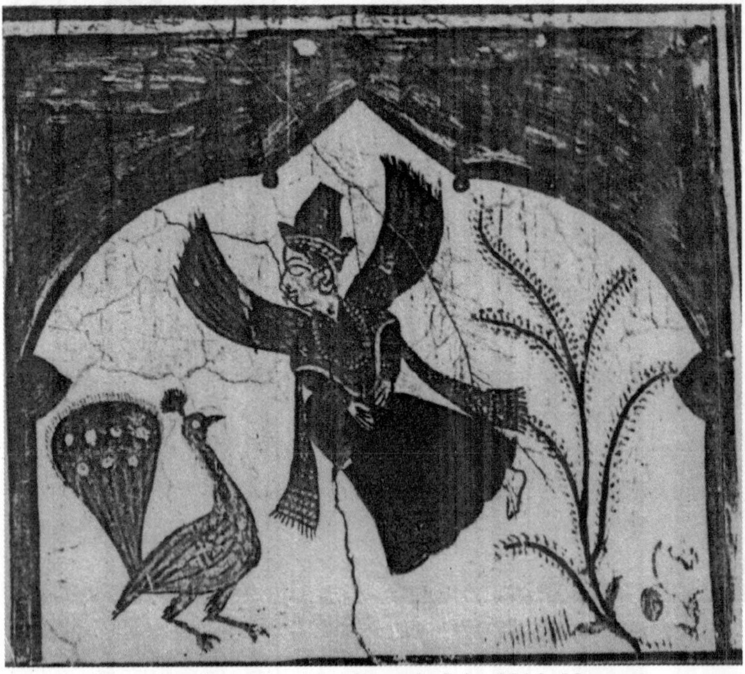

Fig. 2Female Angle with a Peacock, Saiva Math. Mansar.

Plate XXXXV

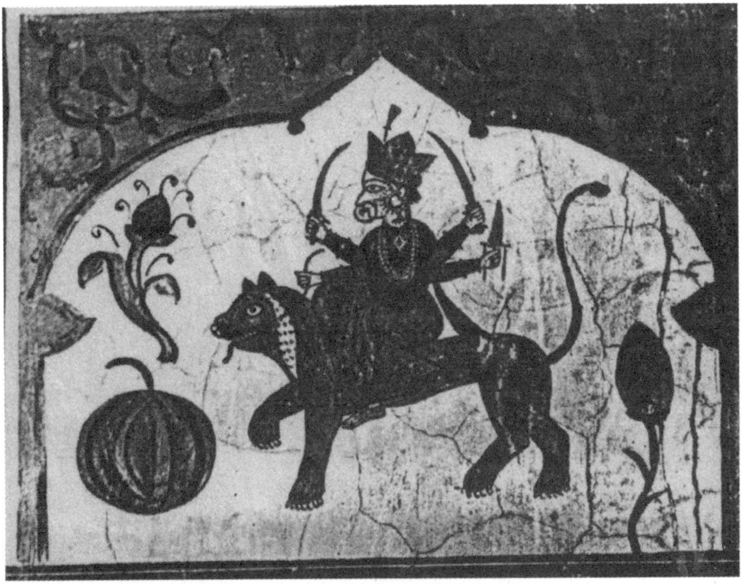

Fig. 1Mahisamardini Devi, Saiva Math. Mansar. Wall-Painting.

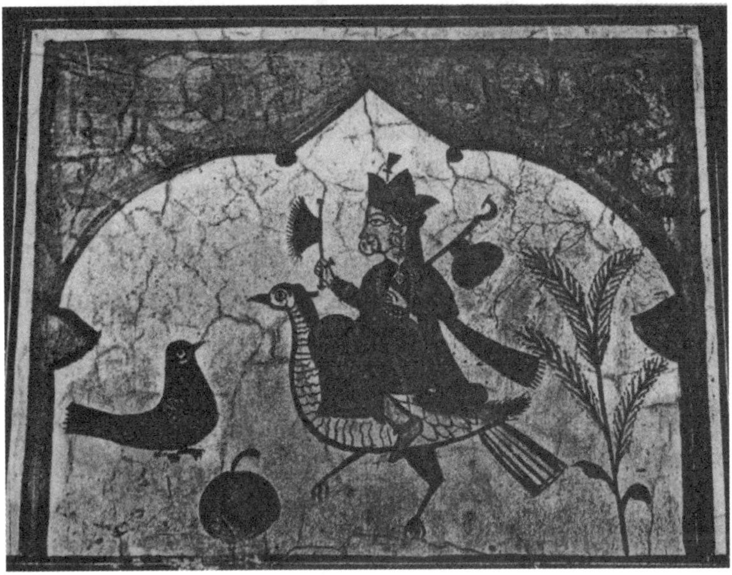

Fig. 2Sarsvati; Saiva Math Mansar; Wall-Painting.

Plate XXXXVI

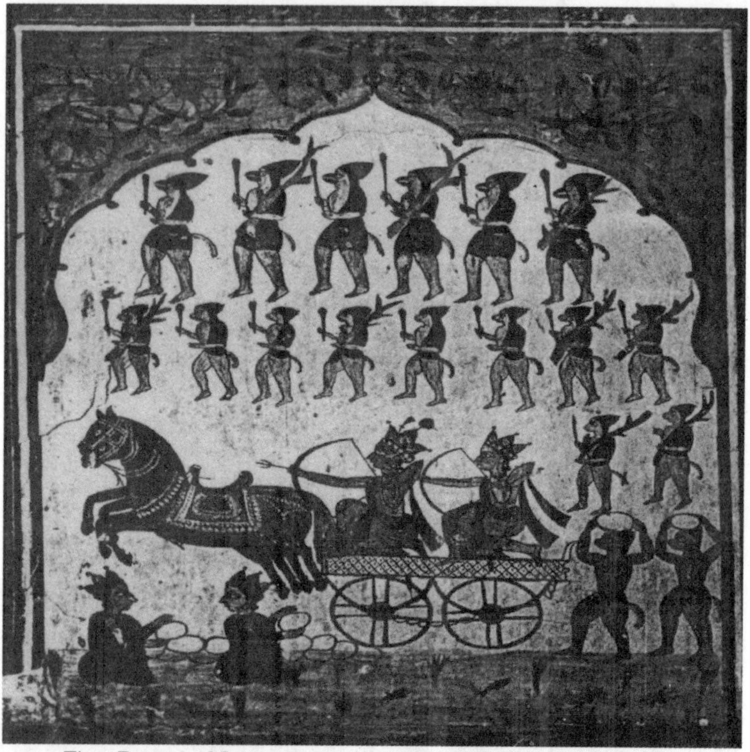

Fig. 1Rama and Laxsmana setting out to do battle with Ravana's Armies Saiva Math, Mansar; Wall-Painting.

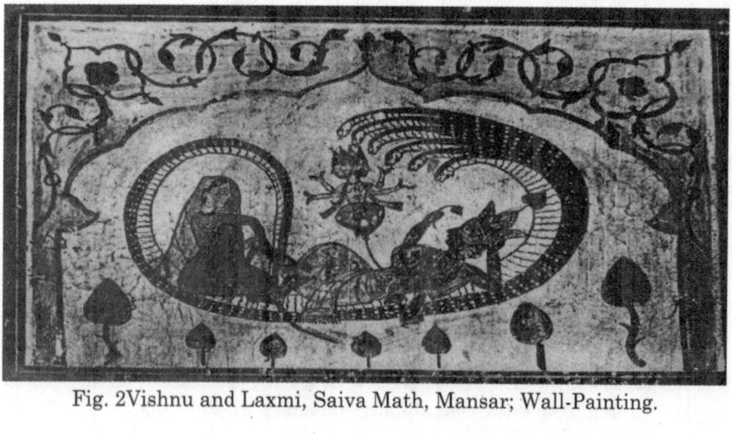

Fig. 2Vishnu and Laxmi, Saiva Math, Mansar; Wall-Painting.

Plate XXXXVII

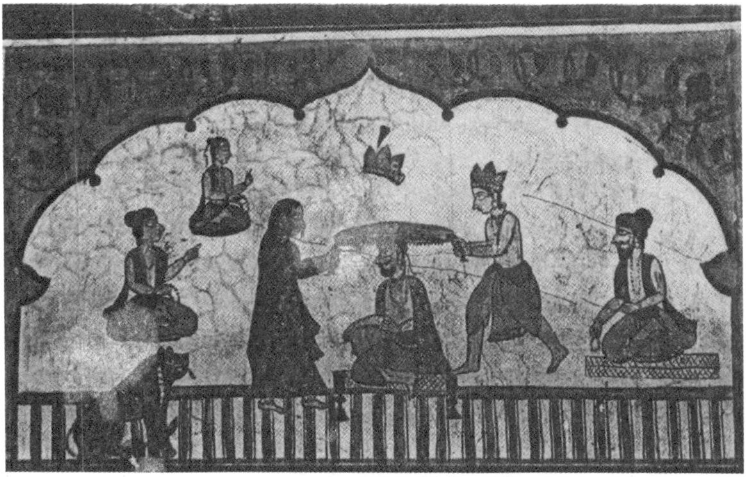

Fig. 1Rama bathing prior to his anointment,
Saiva Math. Mansar, Wall-Painting.

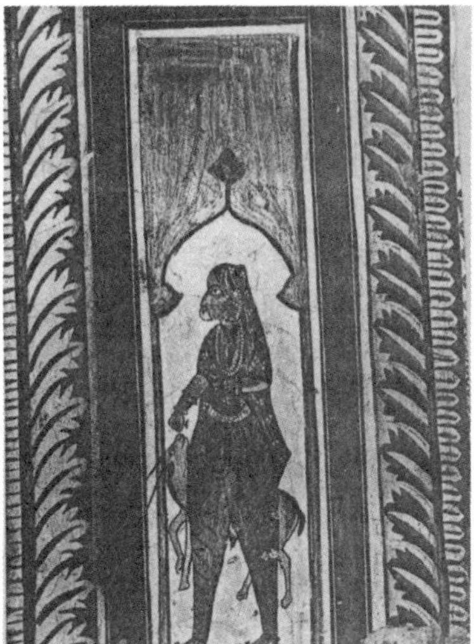

Fig. 2A Nayika, Saiva Math.
Mansar Wall-Painting.

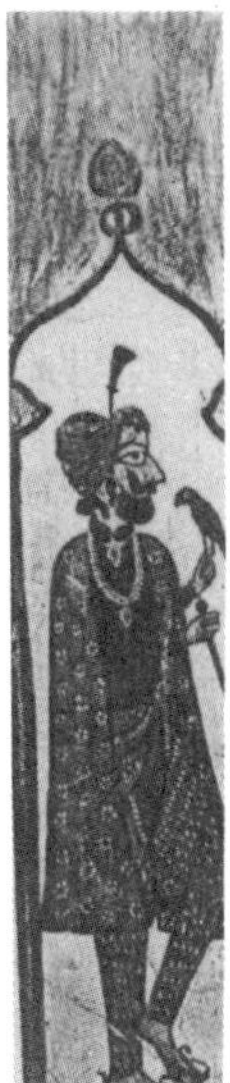

Fig. 3A Nayak, Saiva
Math. Mansar,
Wall-Painting.

Plate XXXXVIII

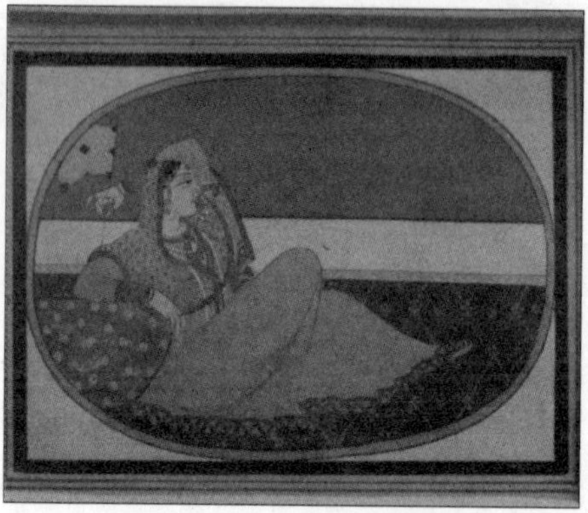

Fig. 1D.A.G. Jammu. Acc. No. 22/69. Reclining, A woman in Yellow Dress; 18th century A.D. Jammu; Artist Channu.

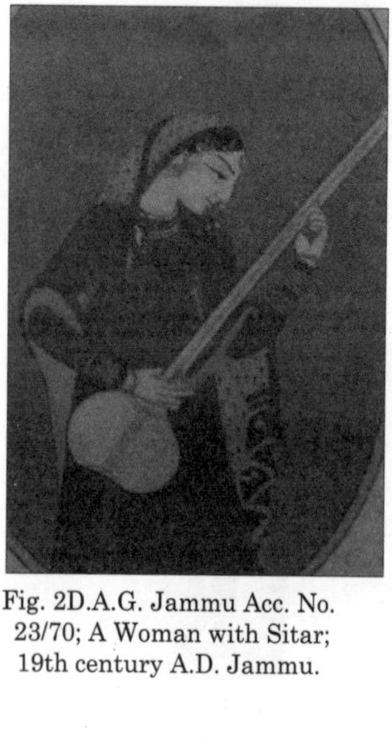

Fig. 2D.A.G. Jammu Acc. No. 23/70; A Woman with Sitar; 19th century A.D. Jammu.

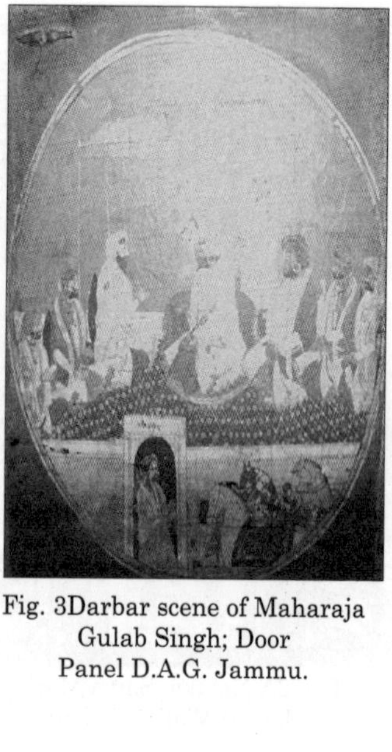

Fig. 3Darbar scene of Maharaja Gulab Singh; Door Panel D.A.G. Jammu.

Plate XX XXIX.

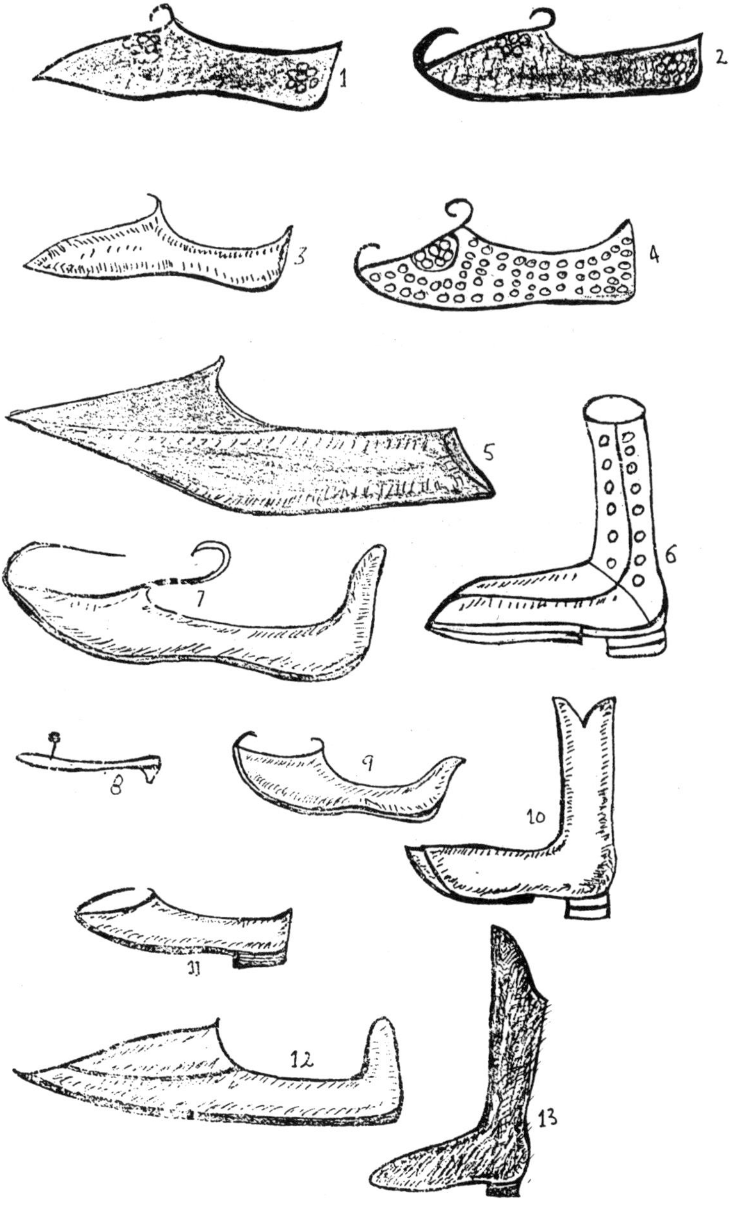

Plate XXXXX

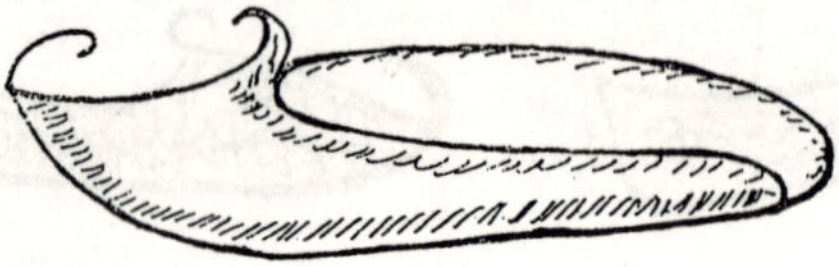

1

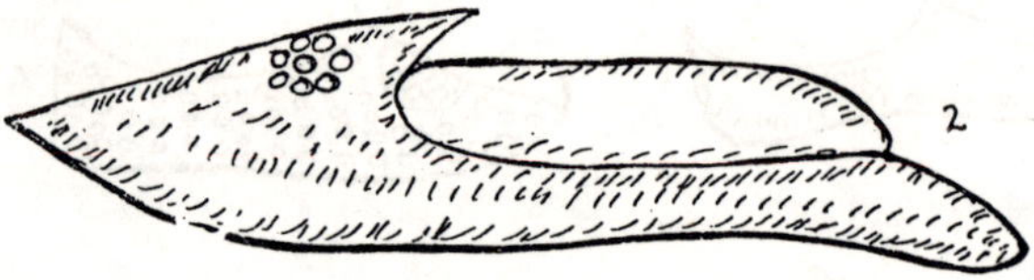

2

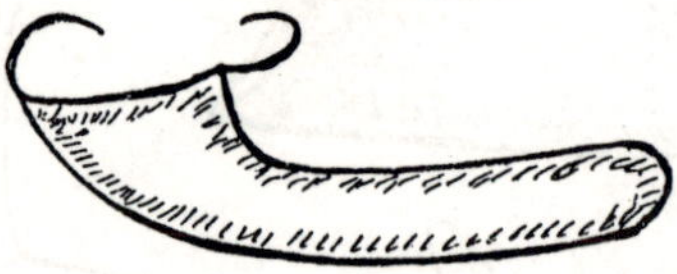

3

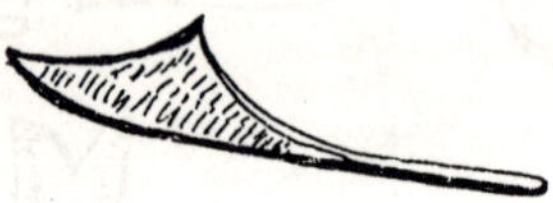

4

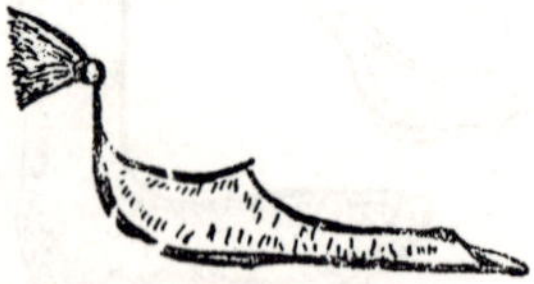

5